the ACCELERAT RS

VOLUME 1

TIME GAMES

creator & writer
R.F.I. PORTO

pencils & inks
GAVIN P. SMITH

colors
TIM YATES

letters
CRANK!

original series covers
WALT FLANAGAN

Created by R.F.I. Porto

Writer - R.F.I. Porto
Pencils & Inks - Gavin P. Smith
Colors - Tim Yates
Letters - Crank!

Cover Pencils & Inks - Gavin P. Smith
Cover Colors - Tim Yates

Original Series Cover Pencils - Issues #1-5 - Walt Flanagan, Issue #6 - Gavin P. Smith
Original Series Cover Inks - Issues #1, 5, & 6 - Gavin P. Smith
Original Series Cover Colors - Issues #2-5 - Wayne Jansen, Issues #1 & 6 - Tim Yates

Editor - Thomas Mumme
Layout & Design Editor - Adam Miller

Lead Copy Editor - Megan Miller
Copy Editors - Ealish Waddell, Bethany Murray, Chris Richcreek

Pinups - Niko Walter, Charles Wilson III, Will Castellucci, Chris Campana, Carly Frank,
         Will Robson, Sean Douglas, Craig Cermak, Mark Morales, Gavin P. Smith

Blue Juice Comics / Accelerators Pinup - Gavin P. Smith

Publishers -
Thomas Mumme
Adam Miller
Michael Misconi
Jeremy Schneider

THE ACCELERATORS VOLUME 1: TIME GAMES. FIRST PRINTING. NOVEMBER 2014.
Published by Blue Juice Comics, a division of Blue Juice Films, Inc. Originally published
in single issue form as THE ACCELERATORS #1-6. Copyright 2013, 2014 by Blue Juice
Comics and R.F.I. Porto. All rights reserved.

Library of Congress Control Number: 2014950253

Blue Juice Comics, 730 Campina Avenue, Palm Bay, FL 32909
For more information go to www.bluejuicecomics.com
PRINTED IN USA
ISBN: 978-1-940967-51-6

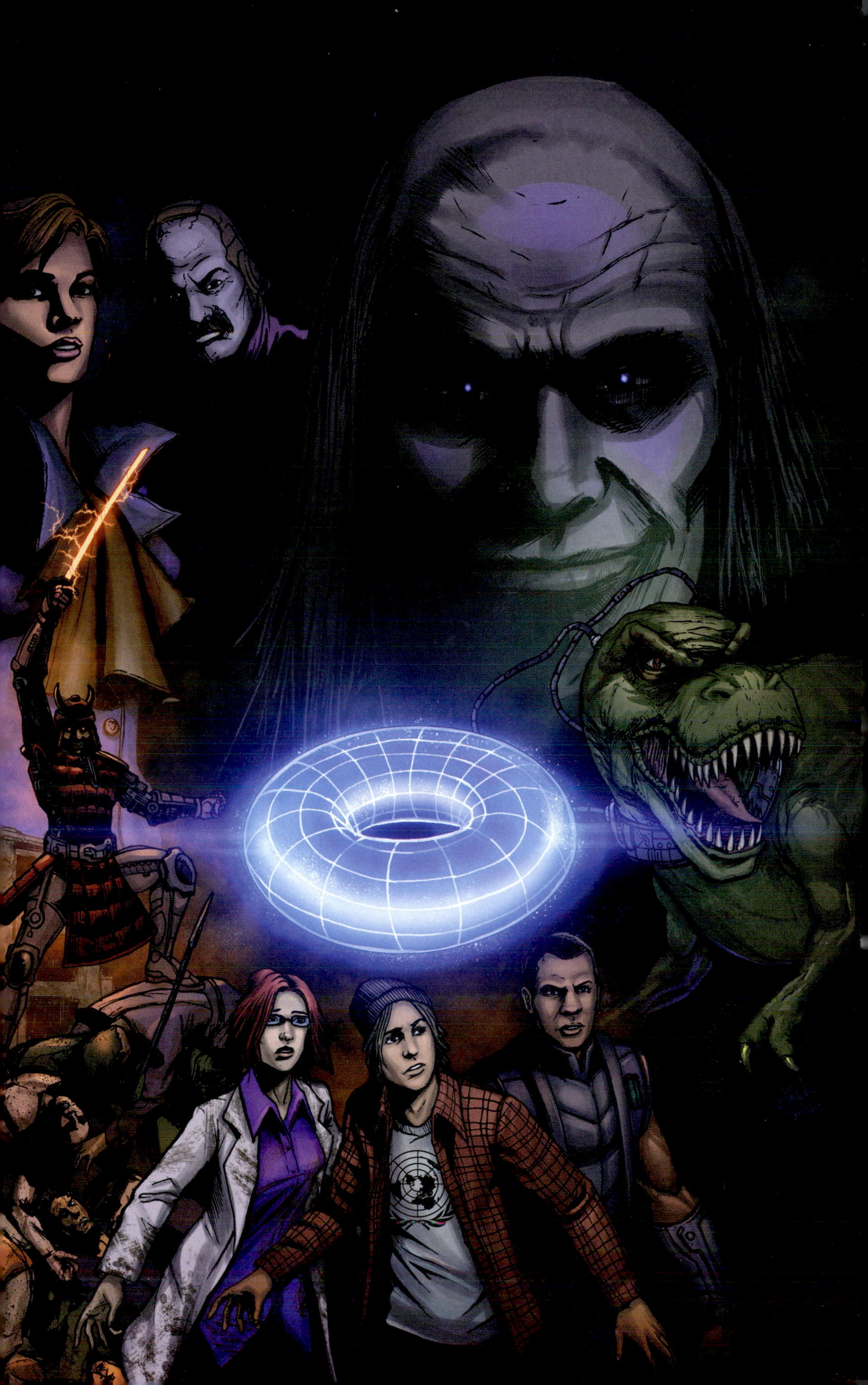

INTRODUCTION

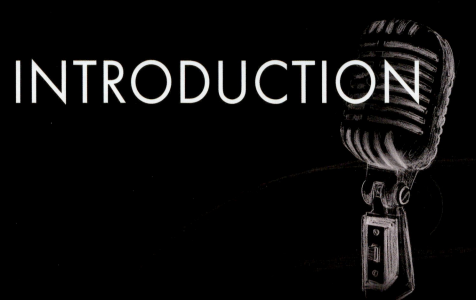

"Hello, everybody, and welcome to the Introduction to 'The Accelerators'! My name is Ming Chen, and across from me is ..."

"Umm, Ming, you DO realize this isn't a podcast, don't you?"

"Ladies and gentlemen, give it up for Mike Zapcic!!!"

"Thanks, Ming, and trust me, NOBODY appreciates your enthusiasm more than I do, but this intro's a big thing for us. I consider it a HUGE honor for the guys at Blue Juice Comics to ask us to do it, so let's not screw it up, shall we?"

"Mike, that's the problem ... none of you guys look at the world like I do. EVERYTHING is a podcasting opportunity! And what IS podcasting, you ask? It's a couple of guys and/or gals sitting around TALKING. And let's be frank, the guys at Blue Juice came up with the idea to do a comic book BECAUSE of podcasting. More specifically, because they podcasted with US!!! They were regular guests of ours on our podcast 'I SELL COMICS' more than a few times, and through that, we literally watched a comic book and new publisher take off in real time right in front of our eyes." (Go to smodcast.com, 'I Sell Comics' Episodes 40-51, to hear the chronicles of the process of making "The Accelerators.")

"Holy crap, Ming ... that may just be THE MOST COGENT THING you've ever said!"

"Thanks, Mike! What does 'cogent' mean?"

"That's not important right now, Ming. What is important is giving the readers (all three of you, because nobody EVER reads an introduction) a little background on what this story means and has meant to us. For me, it was a way to see how a comic book is truly made, from the initial idea, to a script, ably drafted by Ronnie Porto (a comic fan from way back), to being penciled AND inked by Gavin Smith, an artist who will remain an undiscovered gem for a very limited time, and (as I'm sure you will all agree) to the amazing colors of Tim Yates, who gives this story a down-to-earth, human touch. Add to that the phenomenal covers by our friend, the ever-brilliant Walt Flanagan, and you've got a blueprint for a truly fantastic comic series.

Now, time-travel stories are almost as familiar to comic book readers as capes and long johns. Having read comics for 40+ years, I've come across a metric ton of time-travel stories. Although each of them has their charms, 'The Accelerators' kicks it up a notch in its simple narrative hook that the time-travel device can only move forward. Even when Ronnie originally pitched us that concept, we were blown away with how original that idea was, and mad that we didn't think of it ourselves."

"That's right, Mike. For me, I just plain-out LOVE time travel! Anyone who has ever listened to me talk knows of my love for 'The Terminator' and 'Back To The Future.' So it was only natural for me to gravitate toward a story that includes characters who bounce across the decades."

"That's another great point, Ming. What also makes 'The Accelerators' stand out is the well-crafted characters, and this first arc is not only a great introduction to our main three heroes (through a fantastic cat-and-mouse chase), but also opens up the world around them and the secondary characters that shape this brave new world."

"And, how cool is the Time Games?"

"Yeah, we've all had the age-old banter about who would win in a fight between historical figures, like a Nazi fighting a Samurai, and the Time Games gets to explore that as a reality. And who DOESN'T want to see THAT?!?"

"That's great and all, Mike, but could you just say the line so everyone can crack open this book and get absorbed in a story that you and I ALREADY know and love, please????"

"All right, then ... on behalf of Ming Chen, Blue Juice Comics and myself, Mike Zapcic, I have no doubt you'll love what follows!

And here ya go!"

Mike Zapcic and Ming Chen host a popular podcast called "I Sell Comics" on Kevin Smith's SMODCAST Network. They can also be seen on AMC's "Comic Book Men," and are both considered pop-culture experts.

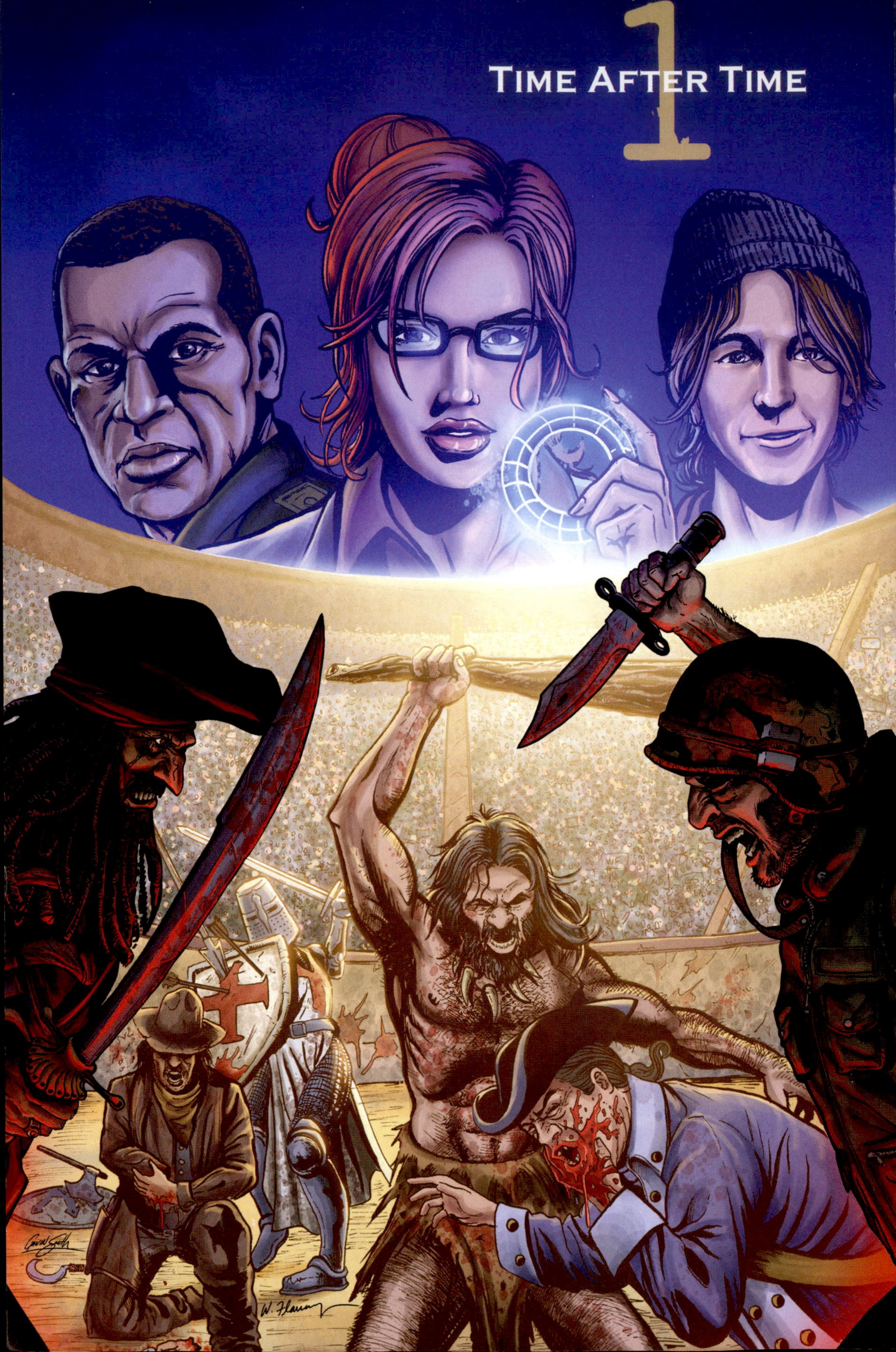
1
TIME AFTER TIME

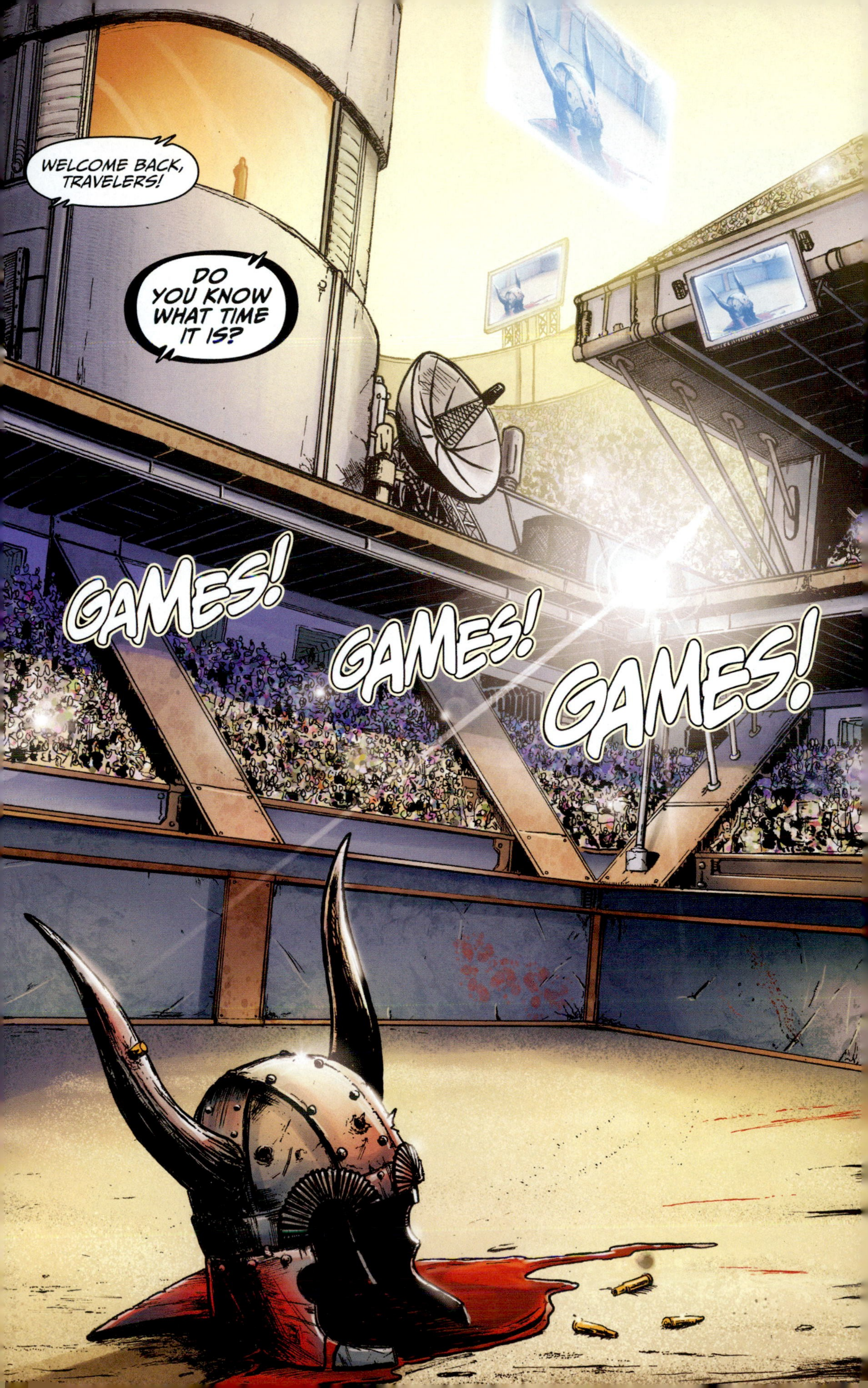
WELCOME BACK, TRAVELERS!
DO YOU KNOW WHAT TIME IT IS?
GAMES!
GAMES!
GAMES!

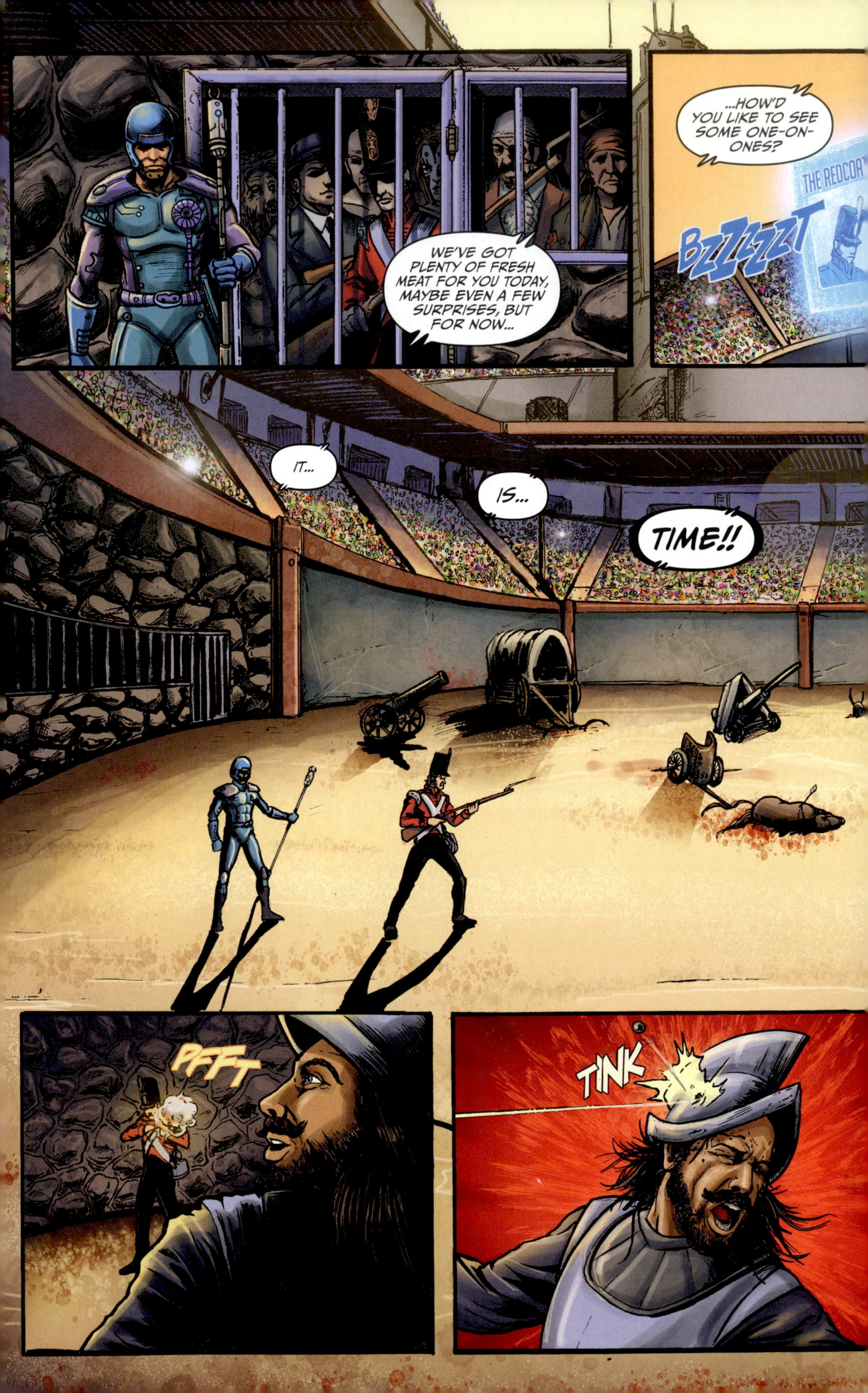
WE'VE GOT PLENTY OF FRESH MEAT FOR YOU TODAY, MAYBE EVEN A FEW SURPRISES, BUT FOR NOW...
...HOW'D YOU LIKE TO SEE SOME ONE-ON-ONES?
THE REDCOAT
BZZZZZZT
IT...
IS...
TIME!!
PFFT
TINK

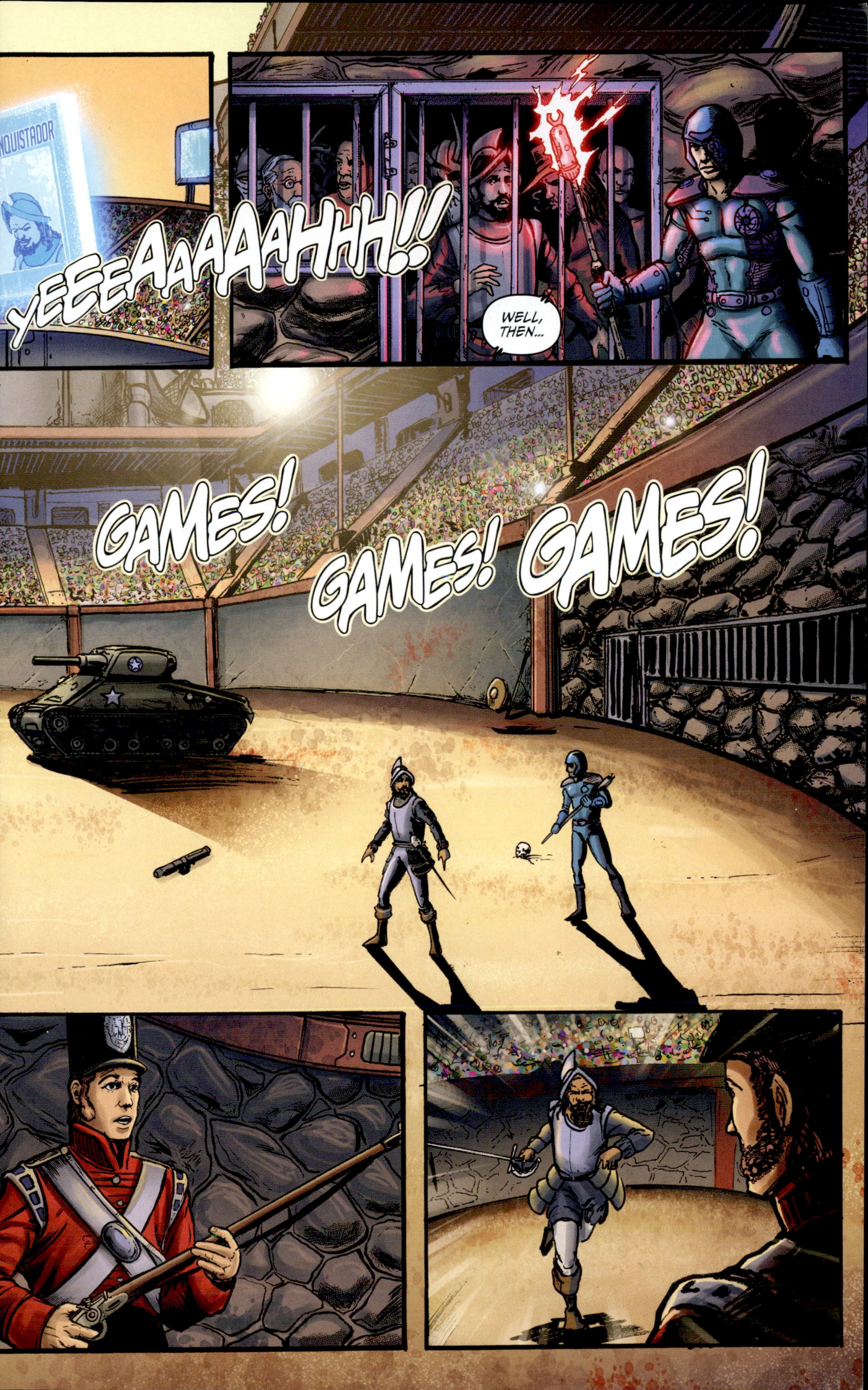
NQUISTADOR
YEEEAAAAHHH!!
WELL, THEN...
GAMES!
GAMES! GAMES!

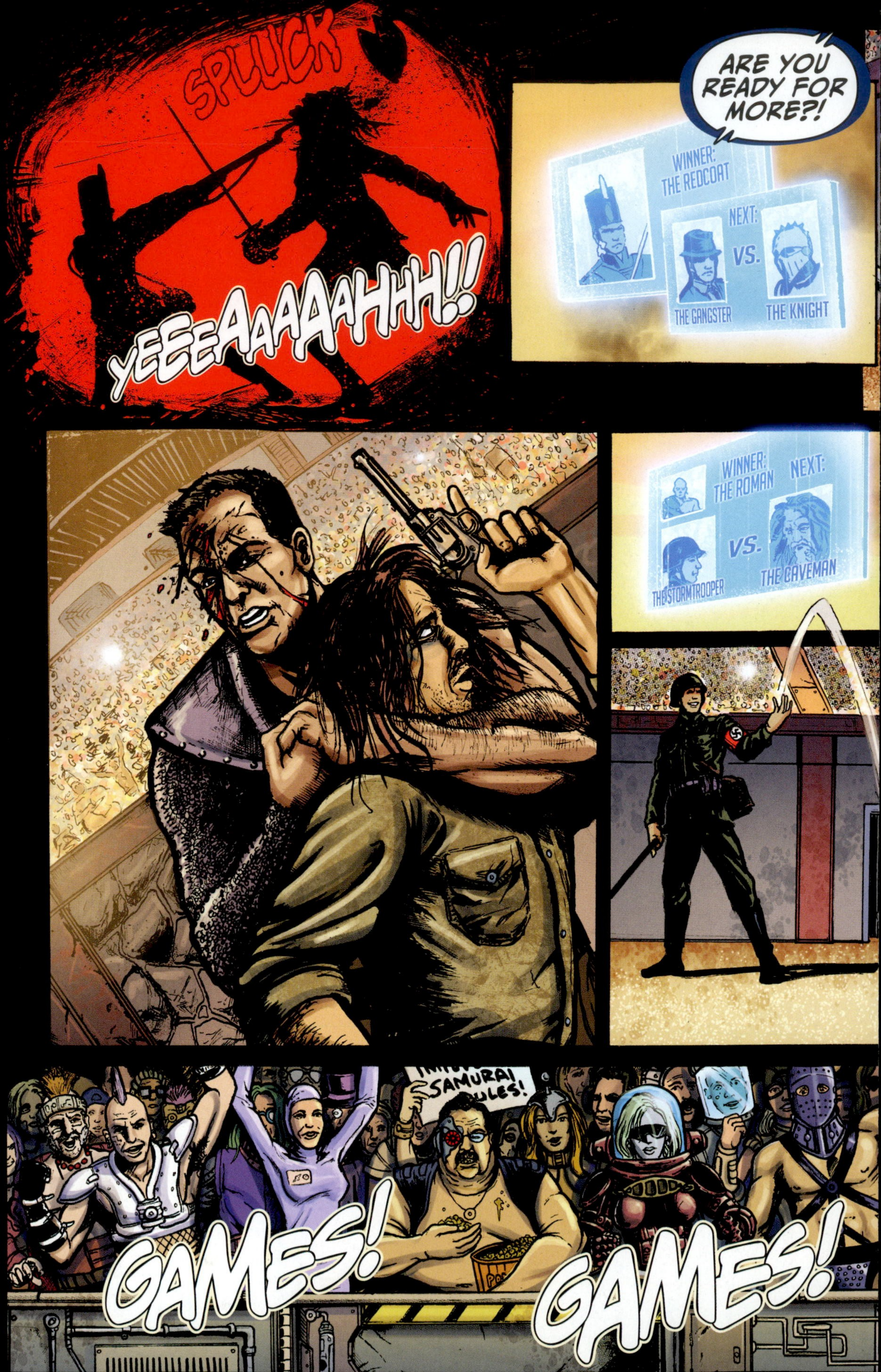
SPLUCK
YEEEAAAAAHHH!!
ARE YOU READY FOR MORE?!
WINNER: THE REDCOAT
NEXT:
THE GANGSTER
VS.
THE KNIGHT
WINNER: THE ROMAN
NEXT:
THE STORMTROOPER
VS.
THE CAVEMAN
SAMURAI RULES!
GAMES!
GAMES!

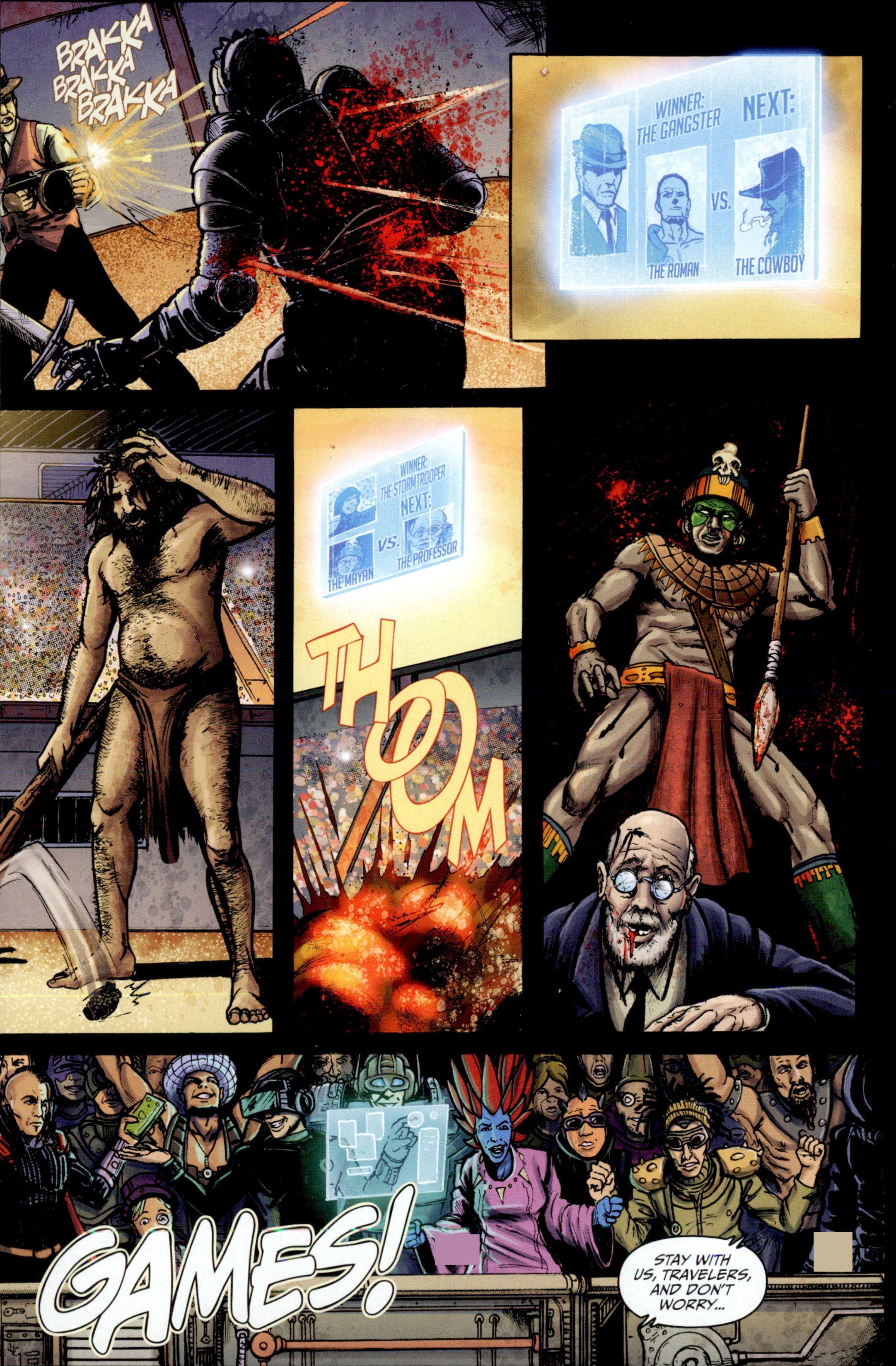
BRAKKA BRAKKA BRAKKA
WINNER: THE GANGSTER
NEXT:
VS.
THE ROMAN
THE COWBOY
WINNER: THE STORMTROOPER
NEXT:
VS.
THE MAYAN
THE PROFESSOR
THOOM
GAMES!
STAY WITH US, TRAVELERS, AND DON'T WORRY...

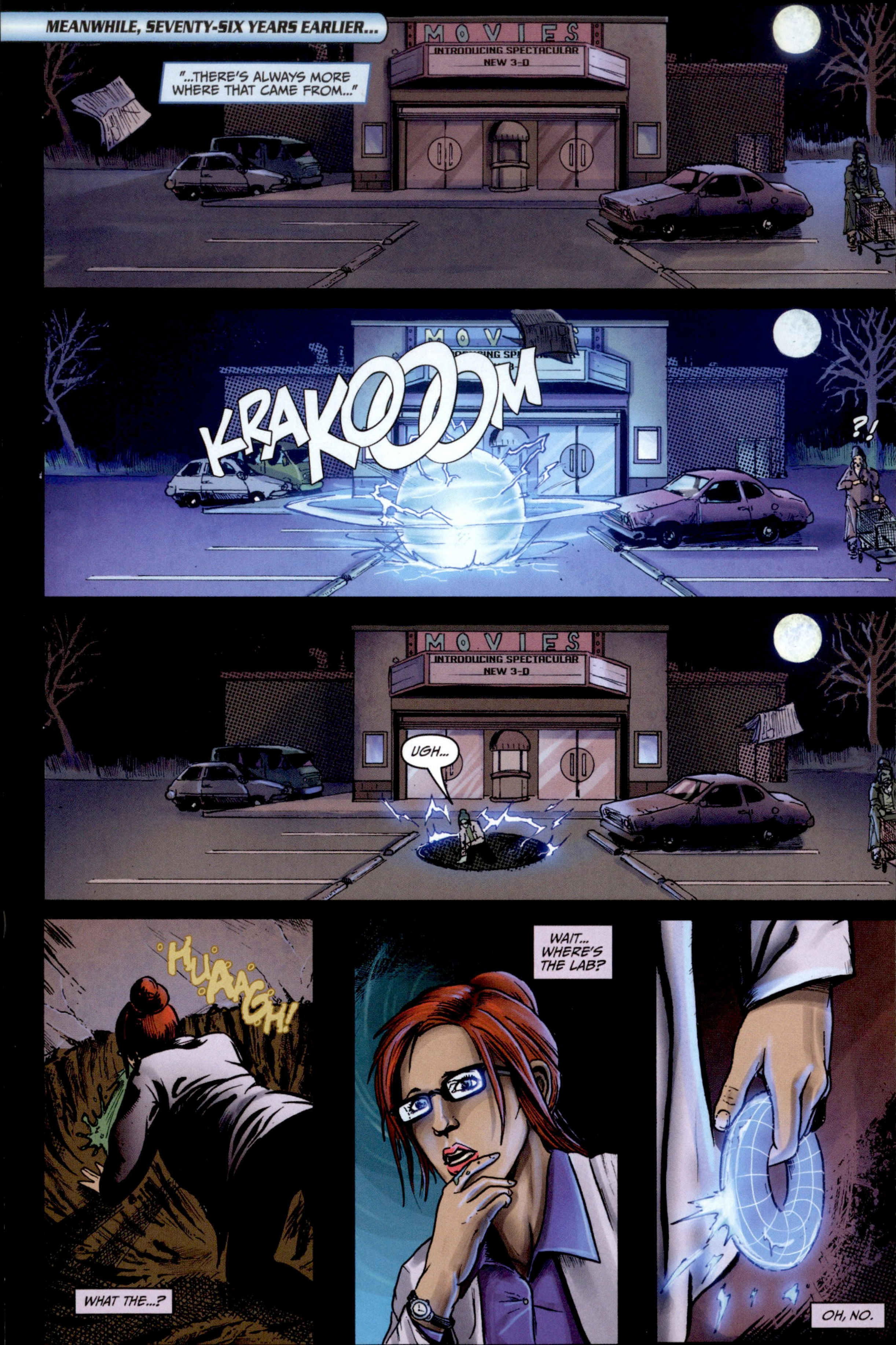
MEANWHILE, SEVENTY-SIX YEARS EARLIER...
MOVIES
INTRODUCING SPECTACULAR
NEW 3-D
"...THERE'S ALWAYS MORE WHERE THAT CAME FROM..."
KRAKOOOM
?!
MOVIES
INTRODUCING SPECTACULAR
NEW 3-D
UGH...
HUAAGH!
WHAT THE...?
WAIT... WHERE'S THE LAB?
OH, NO.

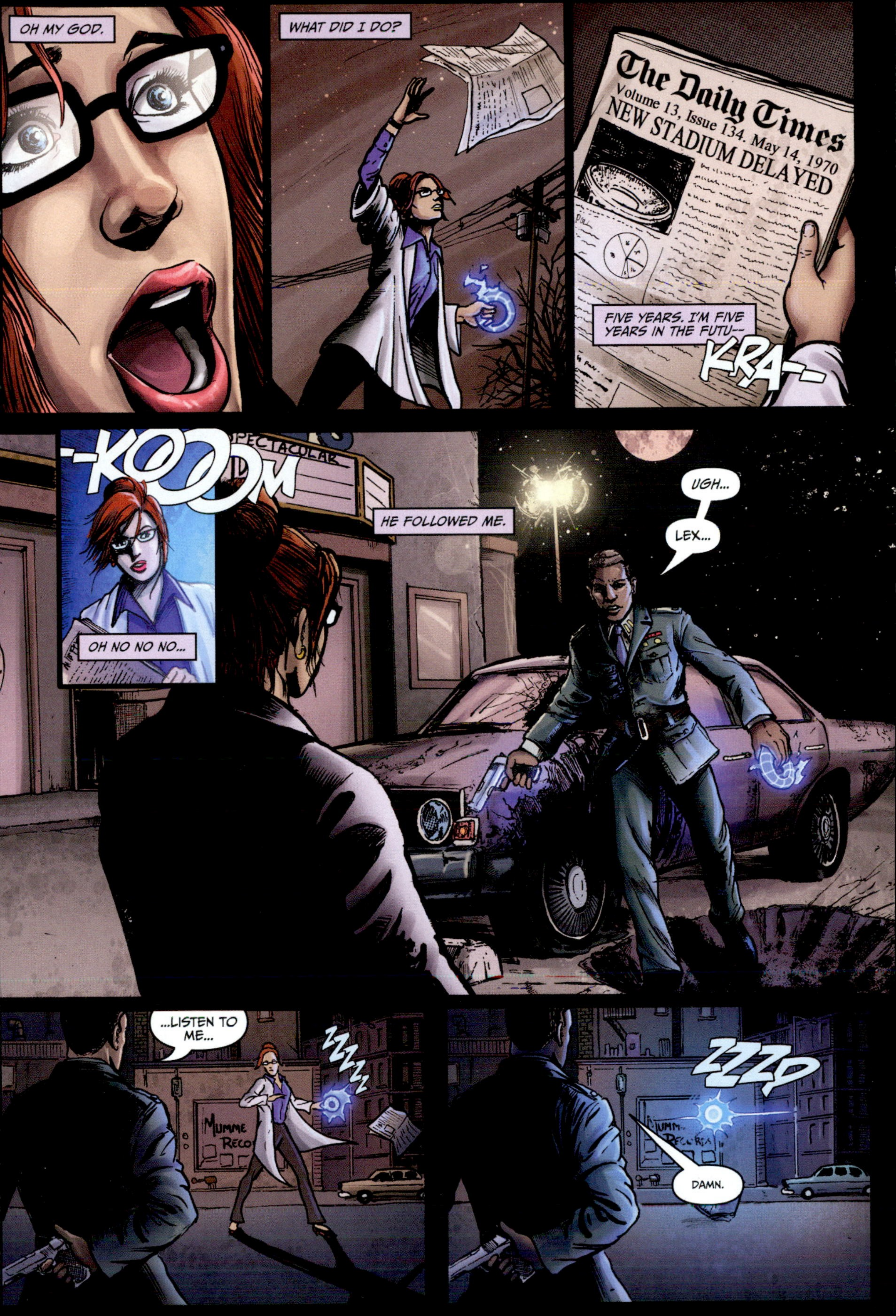
OH MY GOD.
WHAT DID I DO?
The Daily Times
Volume 13, Issue 134. May 14, 1970
NEW STADIUM DELAYED
FIVE YEARS. I'M FIVE YEARS IN THE FUTU--
KRA--
--KOOOOM
OH NO NO NO...
HE FOLLOWED ME.
UGH...
LEX...
...LISTEN TO ME...
ZZZZZ
ZZZZD
DAMN.

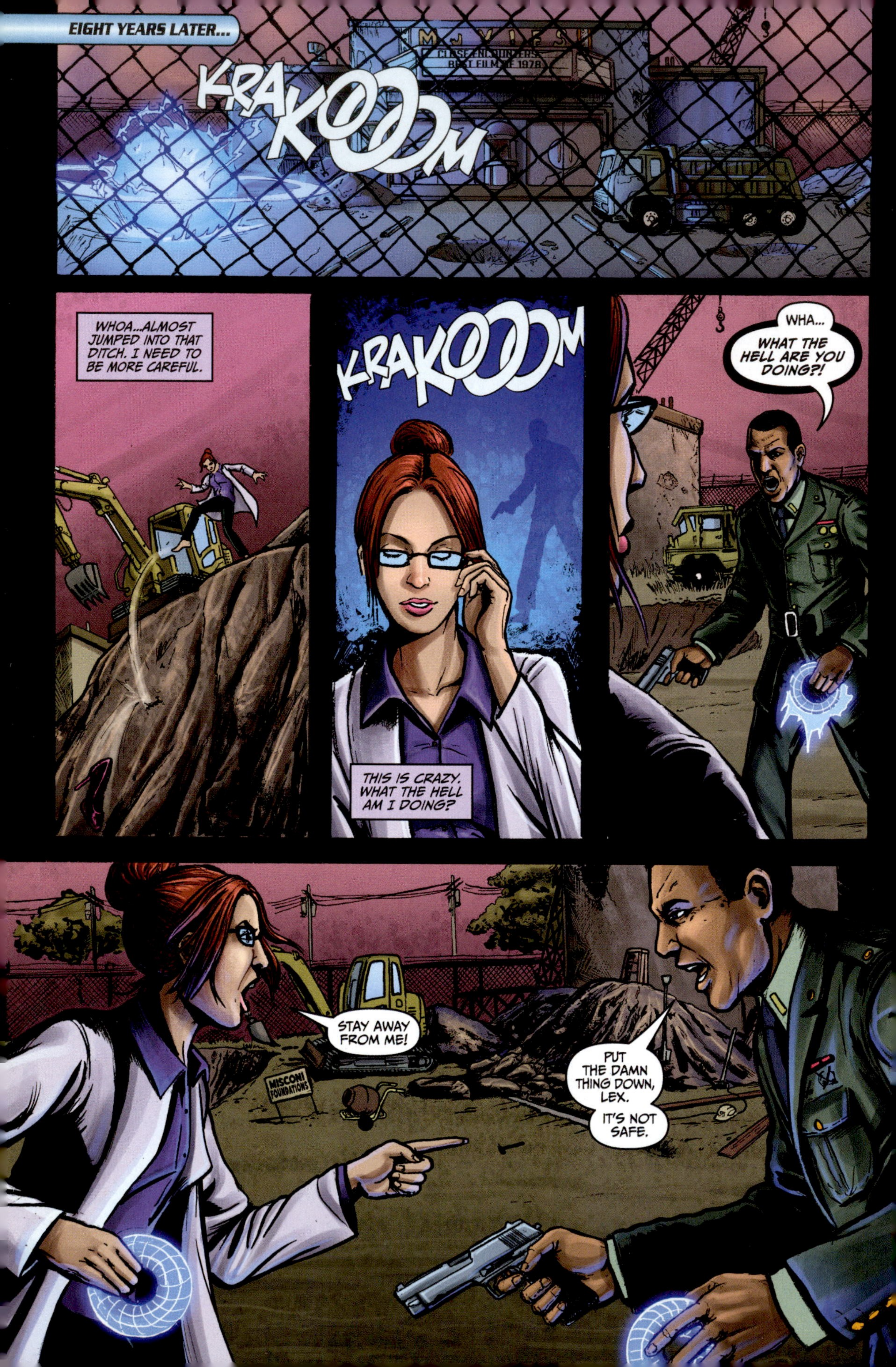
EIGHT YEARS LATER...
KRAKOOOM
WHOA...ALMOST JUMPED INTO THAT DITCH. I NEED TO BE MORE CAREFUL.
KRAKOOOM
THIS IS CRAZY. WHAT THE HELL AM I DOING?
WHA...
WHAT THE HELL ARE YOU DOING?!
STAY AWAY FROM ME!
MISCONI FOUNDATIONS
PUT THE DAMN THING DOWN, LEX.
IT'S NOT SAFE.

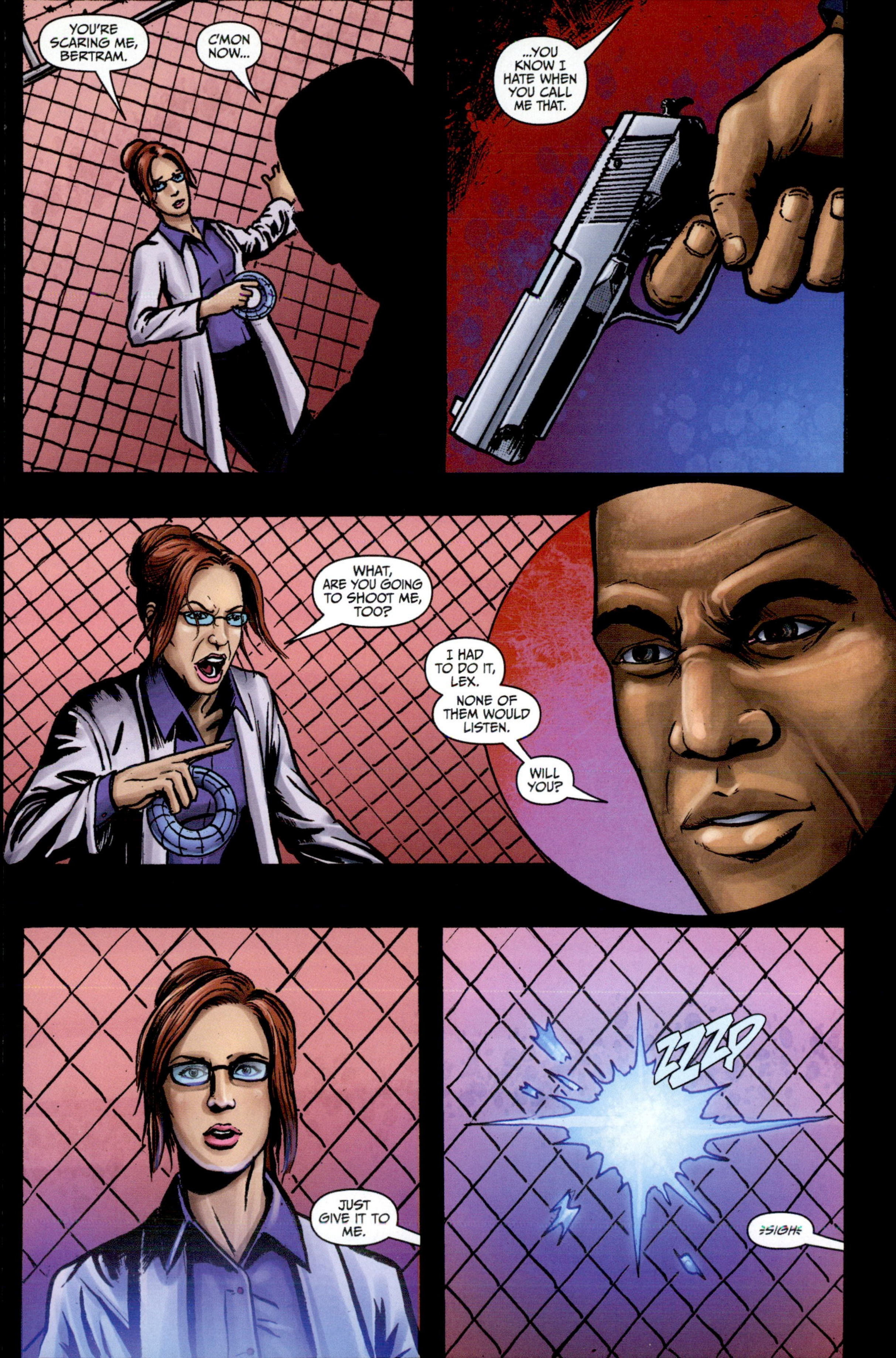
YOU'RE SCARING ME, BERTRAM.
C'MON NOW...
...YOU KNOW I HATE WHEN YOU CALL ME THAT.
WHAT, ARE YOU GOING TO SHOOT ME, TOO?
I HAD TO DO IT, LEX.
NONE OF THEM WOULD LISTEN.
WILL YOU?
JUST GIVE IT TO ME.
ZZZP
=SIGH=

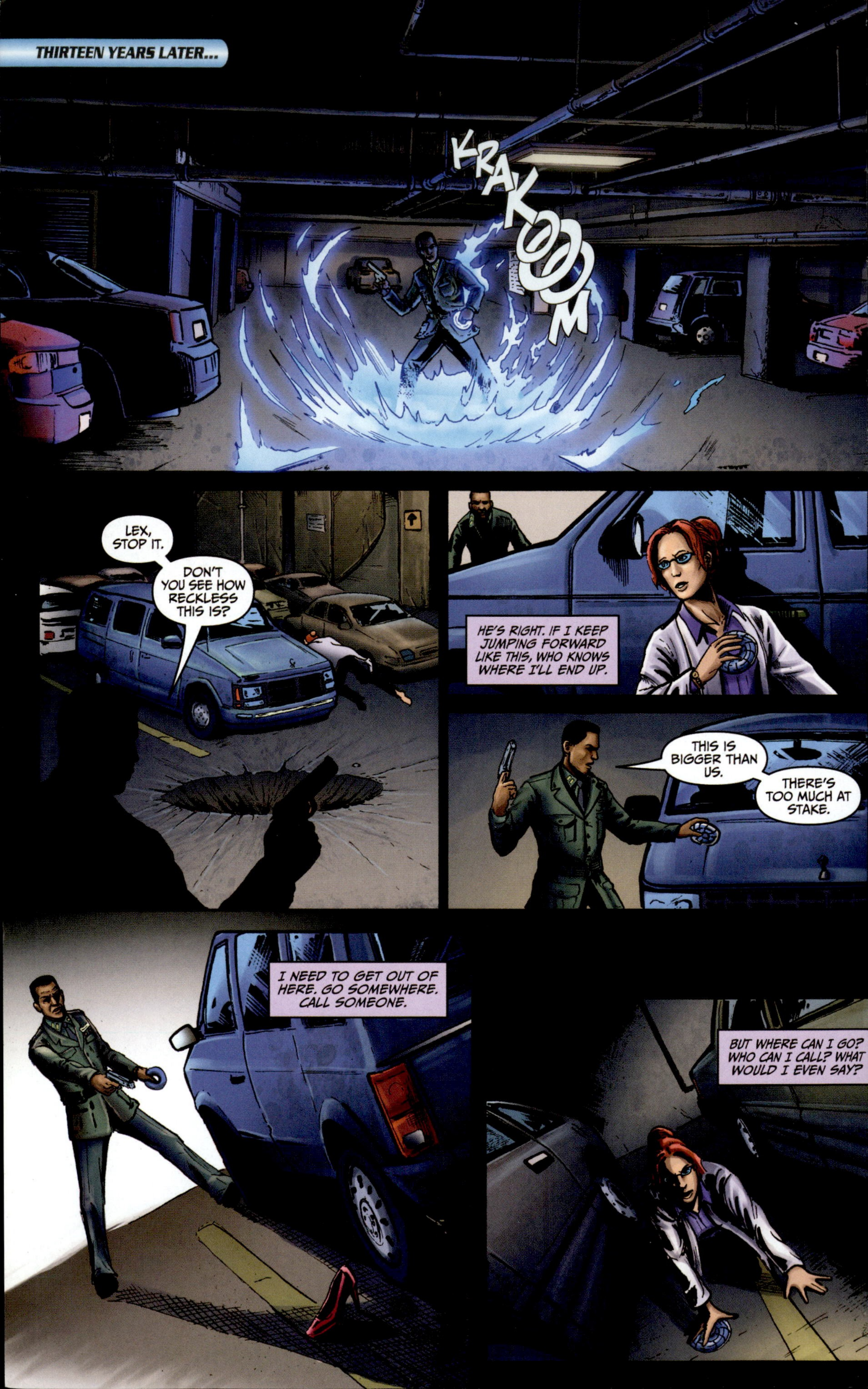
THIRTEEN YEARS LATER...
KRAKOOOM
LEX, STOP IT.
DON'T YOU SEE HOW RECKLESS THIS IS?
HE'S RIGHT. IF I KEEP JUMPING FORWARD LIKE THIS, WHO KNOWS WHERE I'LL END UP.
THIS IS BIGGER THAN US.
THERE'S TOO MUCH AT STAKE.
I NEED TO GET OUT OF HERE. GO SOMEWHERE. CALL SOMEONE.
BUT WHERE CAN I GO? WHO CAN I CALL? WHAT WOULD I EVEN SAY?

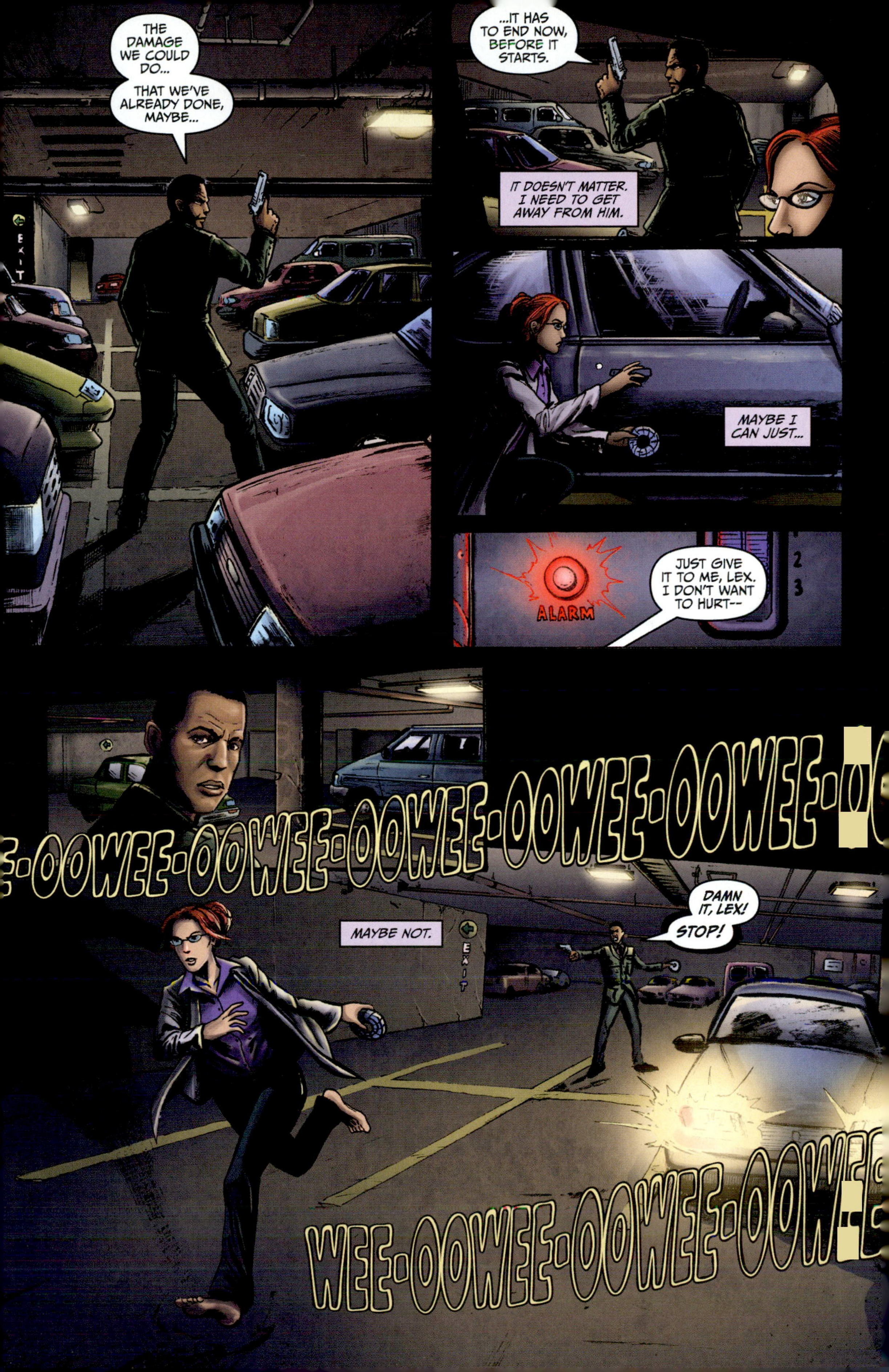
THE DAMAGE WE COULD DO...
THAT WE'VE ALREADY DONE, MAYBE...
EXIT
...IT HAS TO END NOW, BEFORE IT STARTS.
IT DOESN'T MATTER. I NEED TO GET AWAY FROM HIM.
MAYBE I CAN JUST...
ALARM
JUST GIVE IT TO ME, LEX. I DON'T WANT TO HURT--
2
3
E-OOWEE-OOWEE-OOWEE-OOWEE-OOWEE-O
MAYBE NOT.
EXIT
DAMN IT, LEX! STOP!
WEE-OOWEE-OOWEE-OOWEE-OOWEE

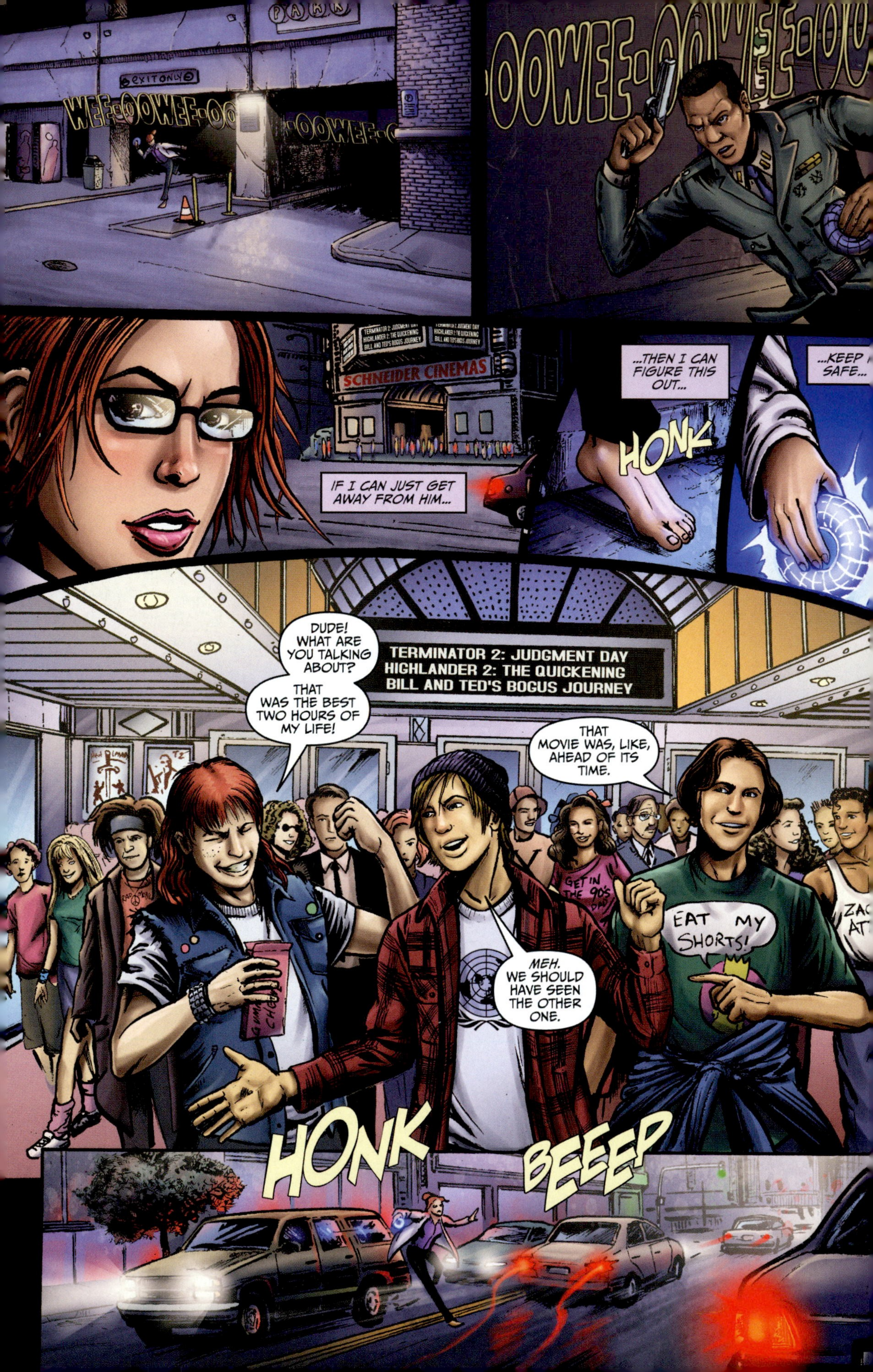
PARK
EXIT ONLY
WEE-OOWEE-OO
OOWEE-O
OOWEE-OOWEE-OO
TERMINATOR 2: JUDGMENT DAY
HIGHLANDER 2: THE QUICKENING
BILL AND TED'S BOGUS JOURNEY
SCHNEIDER CINEMAS
IF I CAN JUST GET AWAY FROM HIM...
...THEN I CAN FIGURE THIS OUT...
HONK
...KEEP SAFE...
TERMINATOR 2: JUDGMENT DAY
HIGHLANDER 2: THE QUICKENING
BILL AND TED'S BOGUS JOURNEY
DUDE! WHAT ARE YOU TALKING ABOUT?
THAT WAS THE BEST TWO HOURS OF MY LIFE!
THAT MOVIE WAS, LIKE, AHEAD OF ITS TIME.
MEH. WE SHOULD HAVE SEEN THE OTHER ONE.
GET IN THE 90's
EAT MY SHORTS!
HONK
BEEEP

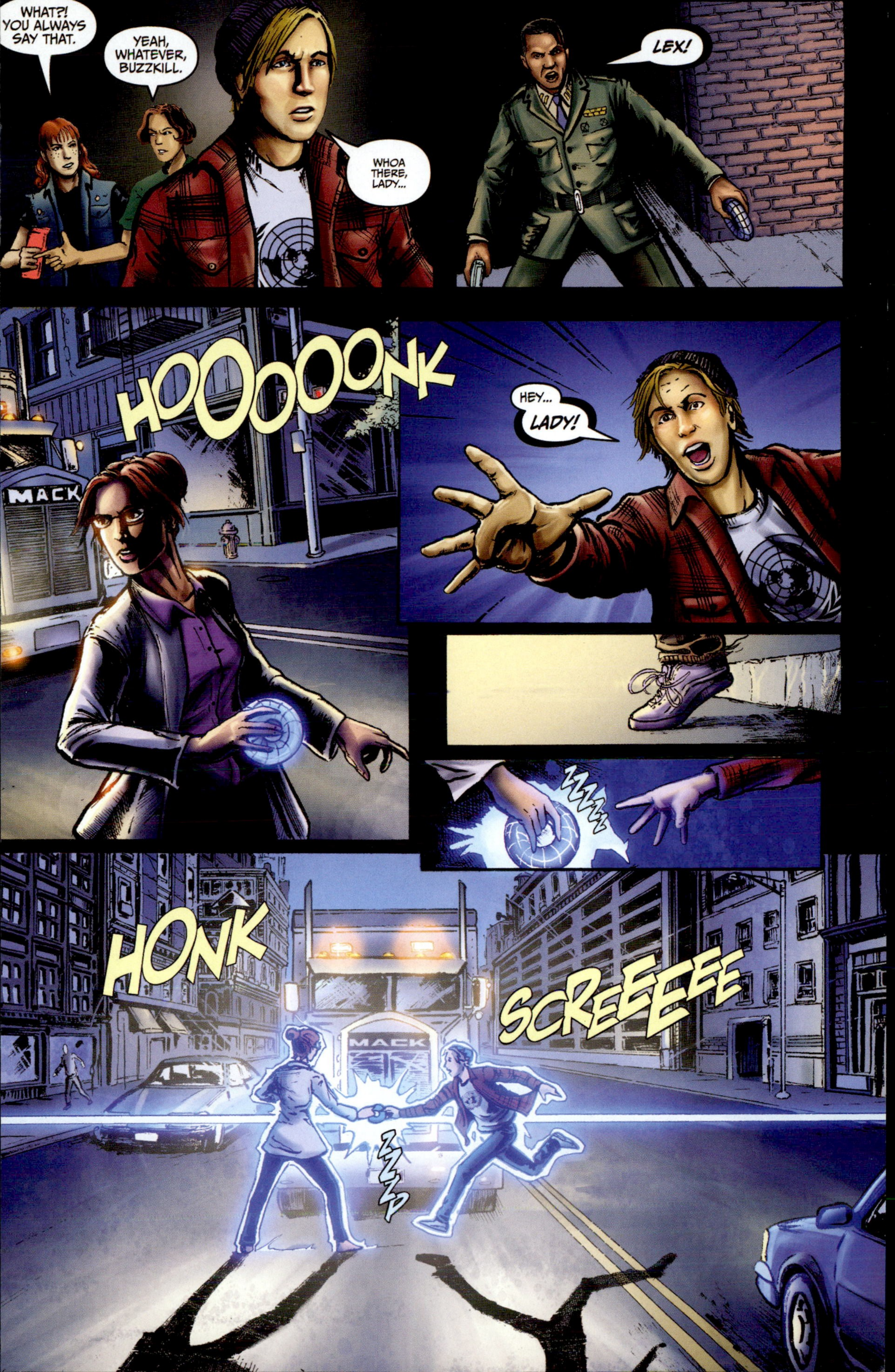
WHAT?! YOU ALWAYS SAY THAT.
YEAH, WHATEVER, BUZZKILL.
WHOA THERE, LADY...
LEX!
HOOOOONK
HEY... LADY!
MACK
HONK
SCREEEEEE
MACK

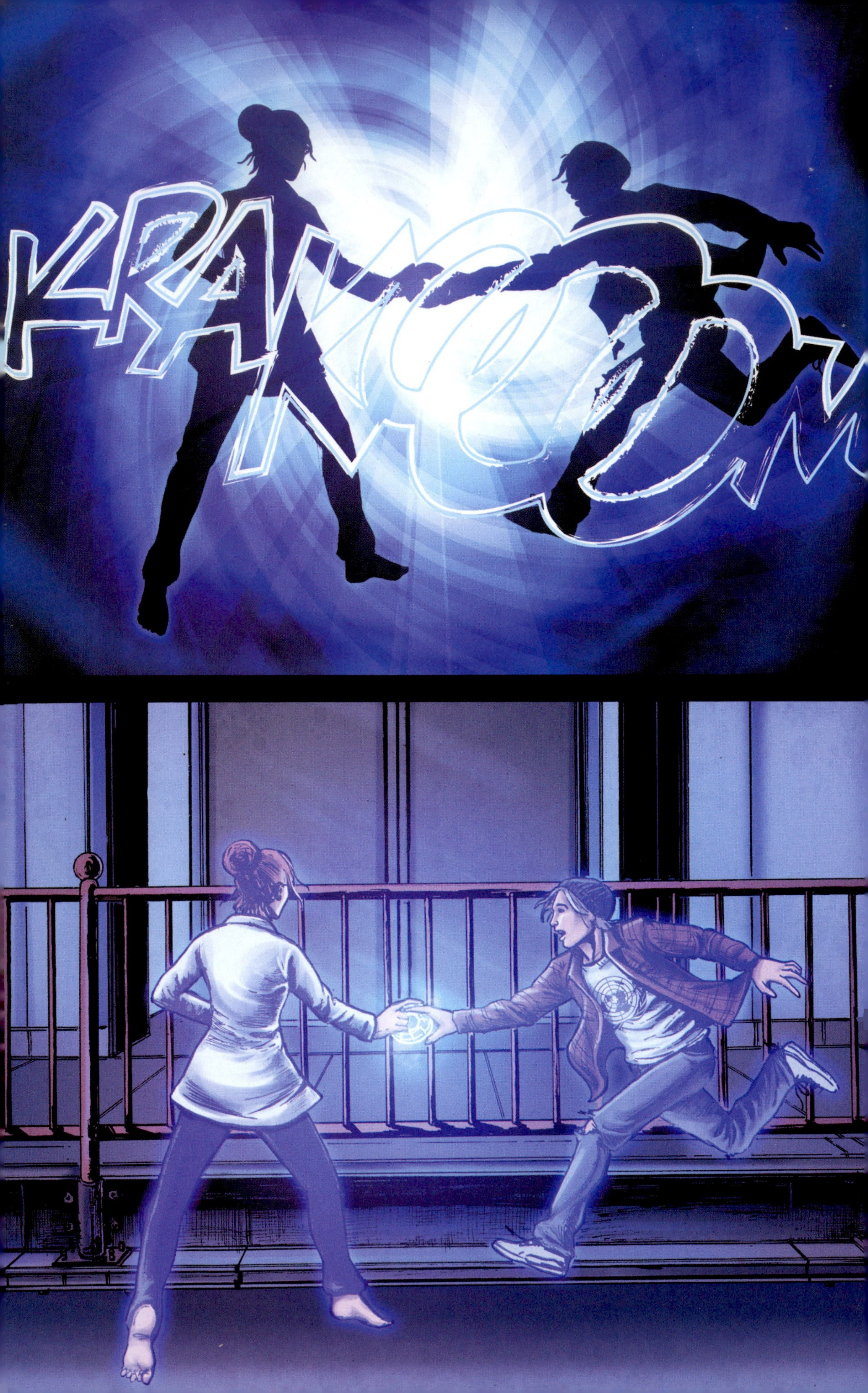
KRAKOOM

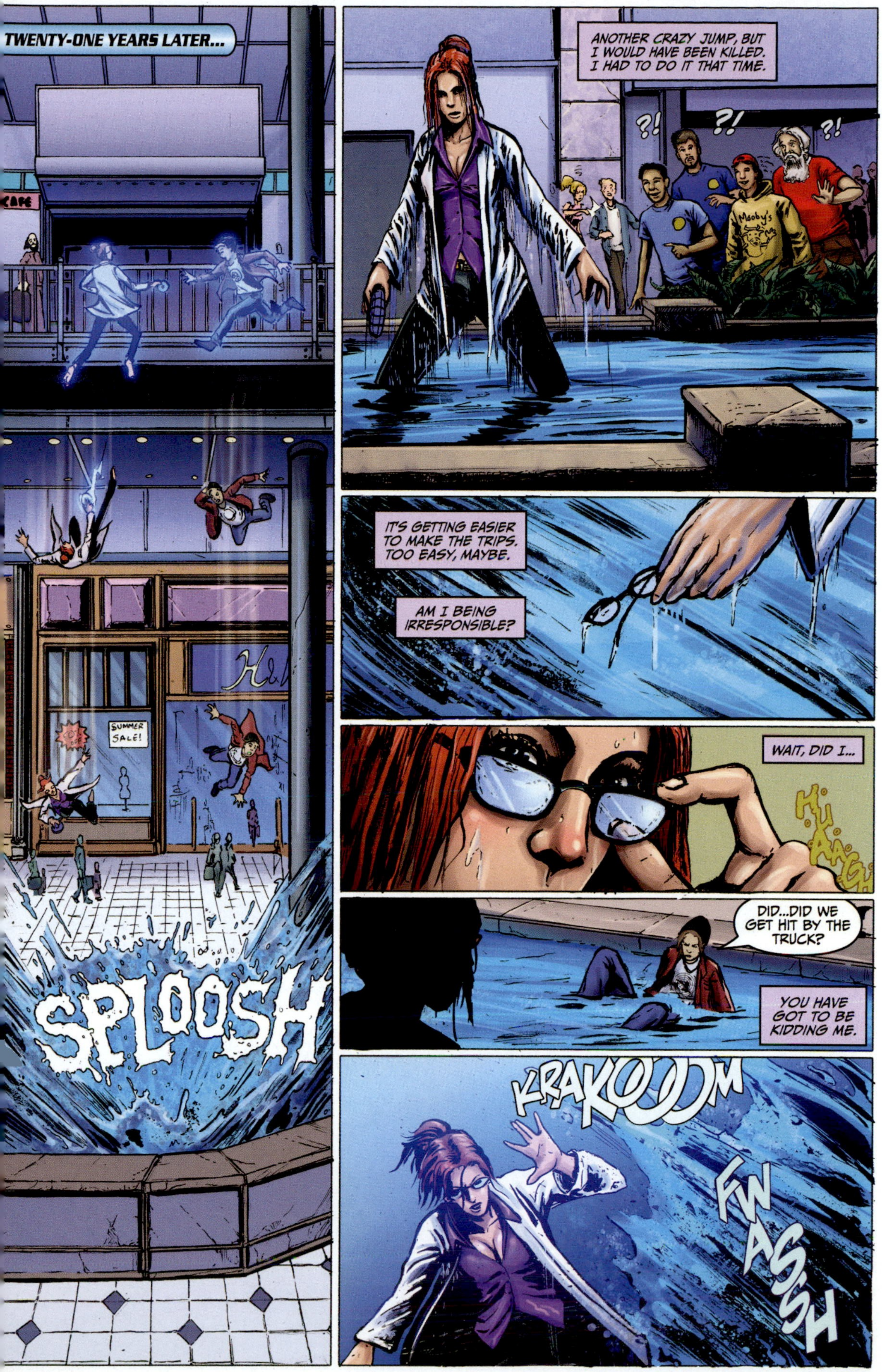
TWENTY-ONE YEARS LATER...
CAFE
SUMMER SALE!
SPLOOSH
ANOTHER CRAZY JUMP, BUT I WOULD HAVE BEEN KILLED. I HAD TO DO IT THAT TIME.
?!
?!
?!
Mooby's
IT'S GETTING EASIER TO MAKE THE TRIPS. TOO EASY, MAYBE.
AM I BEING IRRESPONSIBLE?
WAIT, DID I...
HUAAGH
DID...DID WE GET HIT BY THE TRUCK?
YOU HAVE GOT TO BE KIDDING ME.
KRAKOOOM
FWASSH

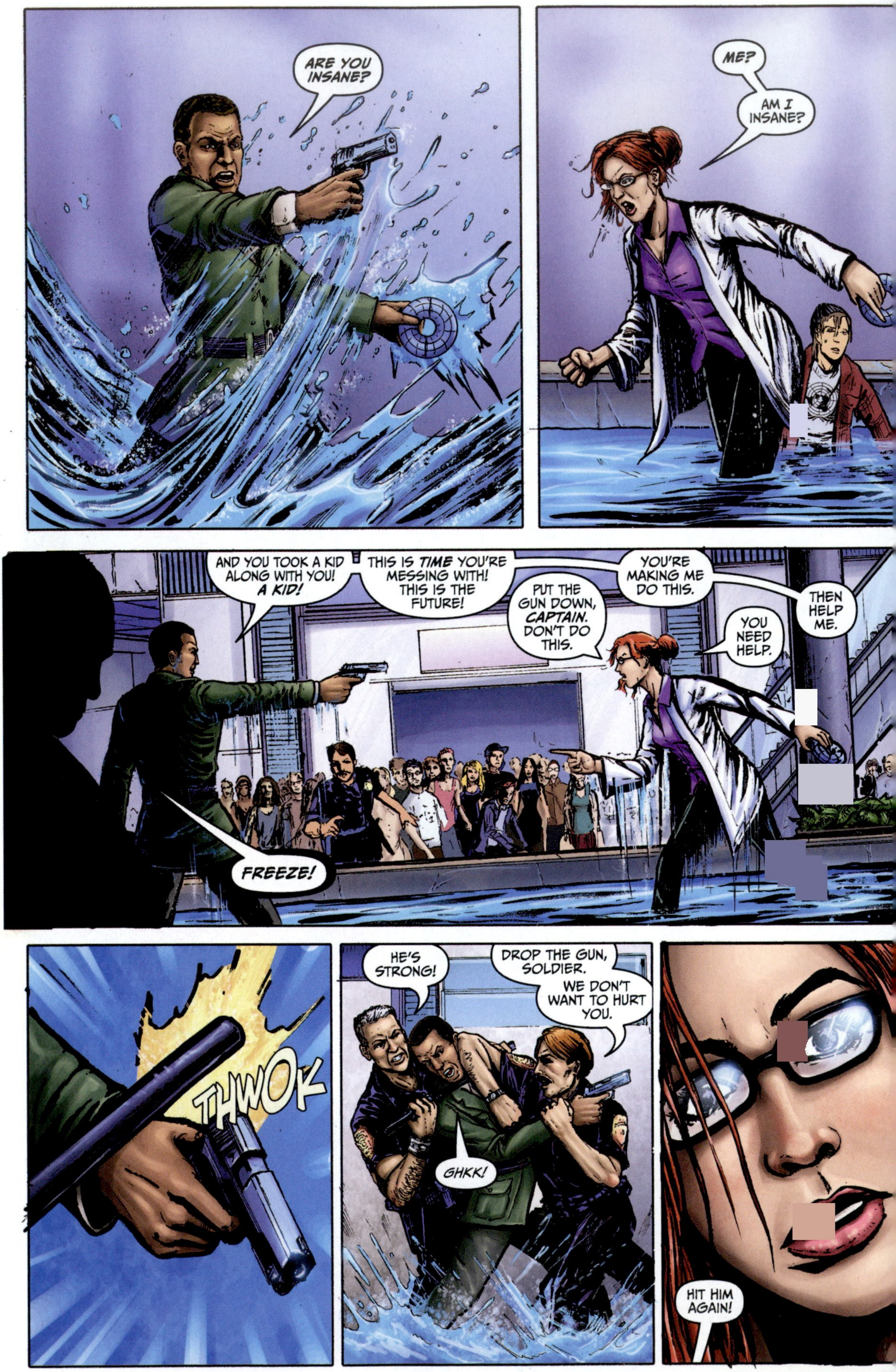
ARE YOU INSANE?
ME?
AM I INSANE?
AND YOU TOOK A KID ALONG WITH YOU! A KID!
THIS IS TIME YOU'RE MESSING WITH! THIS IS THE FUTURE!
PUT THE GUN DOWN, CAPTAIN. DON'T DO THIS.
YOU'RE MAKING ME DO THIS.
YOU NEED HELP.
THEN HELP ME.
FREEZE!
THWOK
HE'S STRONG!
DROP THE GUN, SOLDIER.
WE DON'T WANT TO HURT YOU.
GHKK!
HIT HIM AGAIN!

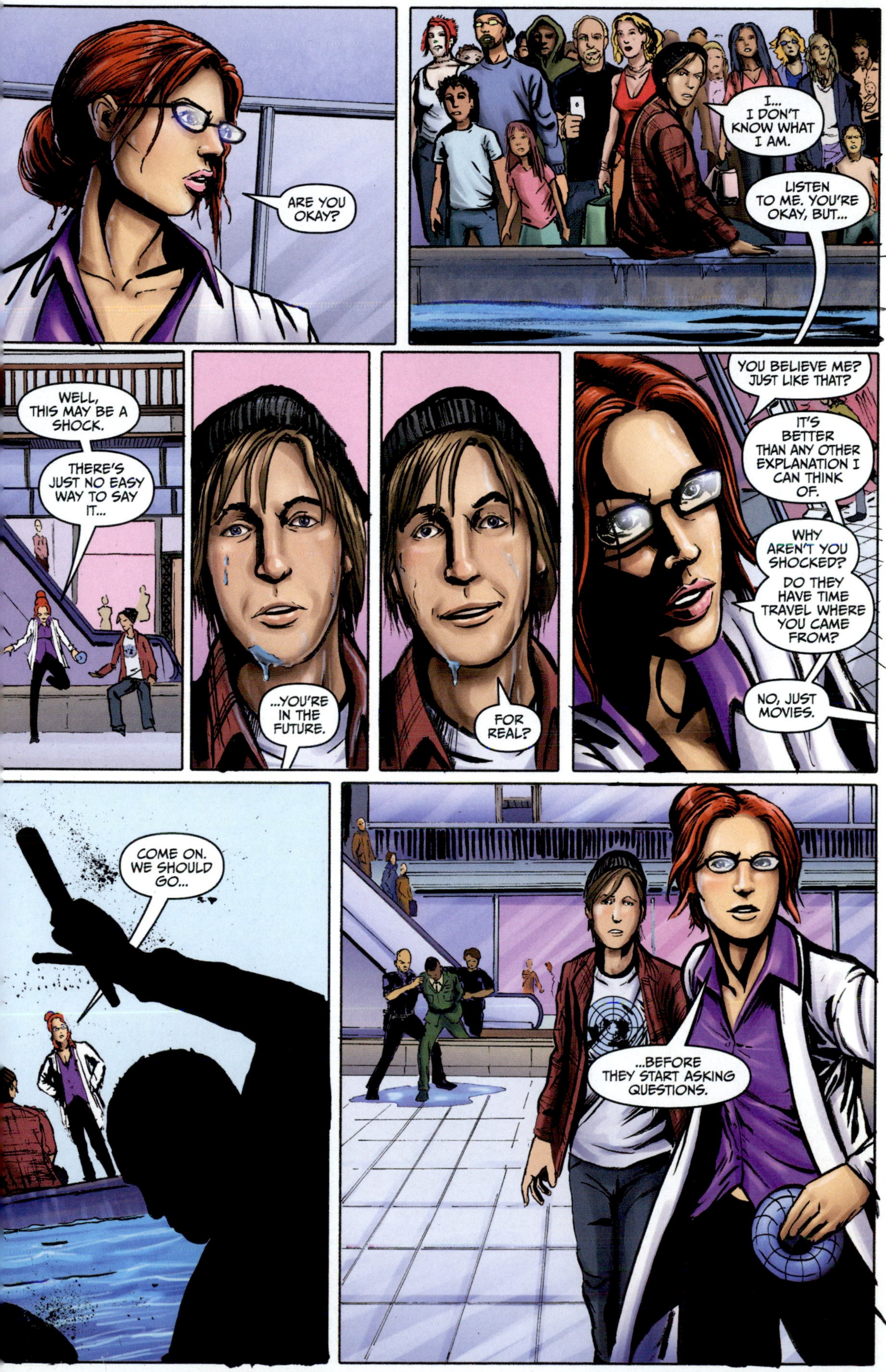
ARE YOU OKAY?
I... I DON'T KNOW WHAT I AM.
LISTEN TO ME. YOU'RE OKAY, BUT...
WELL, THIS MAY BE A SHOCK.
THERE'S JUST NO EASY WAY TO SAY IT...
...YOU'RE IN THE FUTURE.
FOR REAL?
YOU BELIEVE ME? JUST LIKE THAT?
IT'S BETTER THAN ANY OTHER EXPLANATION I CAN THINK OF.
WHY AREN'T YOU SHOCKED?
DO THEY HAVE TIME TRAVEL WHERE YOU CAME FROM?
NO, JUST MOVIES.
COME ON. WE SHOULD GO...
...BEFORE THEY START ASKING QUESTIONS.

SO...WHAT YEAR IS THIS?

I'M NOT SURE. LET'S ASK SOMEONE.

NAH, THAT NEVER WORKS. THEY'LL JUST THINK WE'RE NUTS.

HEY, ARE YOU GUYS OKAY?

DID YOU FALL OVER THE RAILING?

YEAH! THAT WAS CRAZY!

WE'RE FINE. WHAT YEAR IS IT?

UH... TWO-THOUSAND TWELVE.

HEY, MAYBE YOU HAVE A CONCUSSION OR SOMETHING...

NO, WE'RE COOL. LATER, MAN.

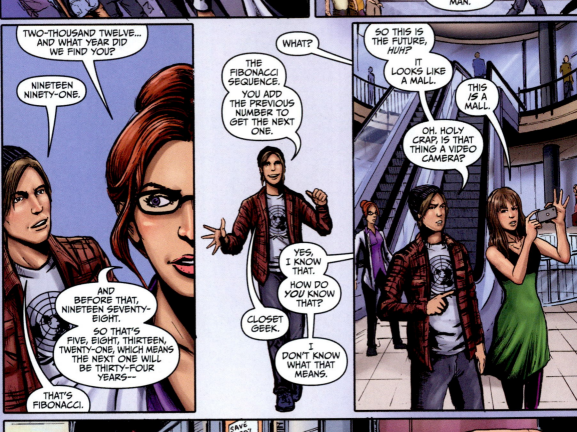

TWO-THOUSAND TWELVE... AND WHAT YEAR DID WE FIND YOU?

NINETEEN NINETY-ONE.

AND BEFORE THAT, NINETEEN SEVENTY-EIGHT.

SO THAT'S FIVE, EIGHT, THIRTEEN, TWENTY-ONE, WHICH MEANS THE NEXT ONE WILL BE THIRTY-FOUR YEARS--

THAT'S FIBONACCI.

WHAT?

THE FIBONACCI SEQUENCE. YOU ADD THE PREVIOUS NUMBER TO GET THE NEXT ONE.

YES, I KNOW THAT. HOW DO YOU KNOW THAT?

CLOSET GEEK.

I DON'T KNOW WHAT THAT MEANS.

SO THIS IS THE FUTURE, HUH?

IT LOOKS LIKE A MALL.

THIS IS A MALL.

OH. HOLY CRAP, IS THAT THING A VIDEO CAMERA?

SAVE 50% ON ALL '08

NO, IT'S JUST MY CELL PHONE.

WOW. TWO-THOUSAND TWELVE, HUH...

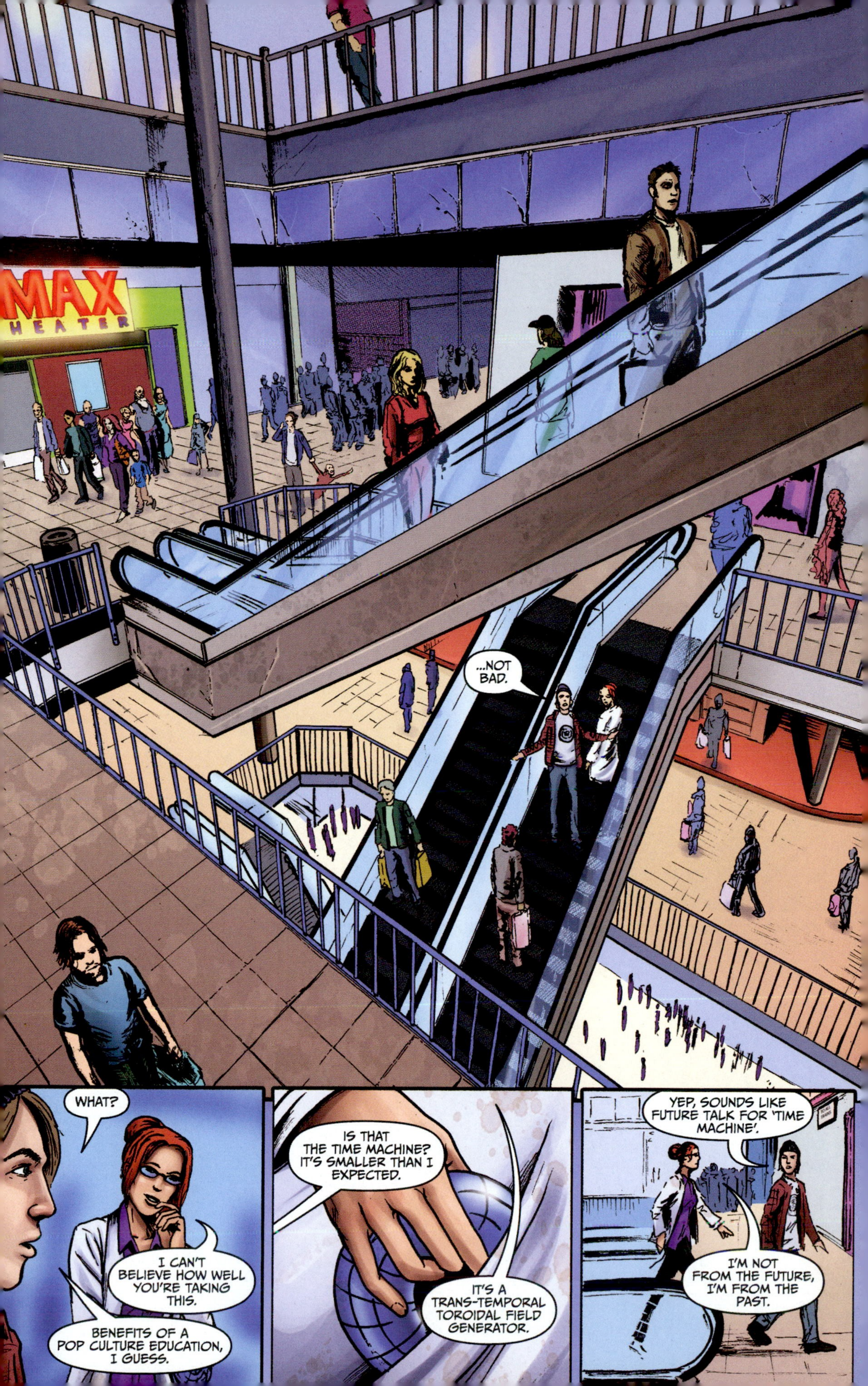
MAX
HEATER
...NOT BAD.
WHAT?
I CAN'T BELIEVE HOW WELL YOU'RE TAKING THIS.
BENEFITS OF A POP CULTURE EDUCATION, I GUESS.
IS THAT THE TIME MACHINE? IT'S SMALLER THAN I EXPECTED.
IT'S A TRANS-TEMPORAL TOROIDAL FIELD GENERATOR.
YEP, SOUNDS LIKE FUTURE TALK FOR 'TIME MACHINE'.
I'M NOT FROM THE FUTURE, I'M FROM THE PAST.

I'M A PHYSICIST FROM NINETEEN SIXTY-FIVE.

REALLY? THEN HOW DO YOU HAVE A TIME MACHINE?

IT'S A LONG STORY.

TRANS...

TRANS-TEMPORAL TOROIDAL FIELD GENERATORS. BUT WE ALWAYS JUST CALLED THEM 'DONUTS' FOR SHORT.

TIME DONUTS. FUNNY.

SO, WHEN CAN YOU SEND ME BACK?

WELL, ACTUALLY... I CAN'T.

WAIT, WHAT? WHY NOT?

THEY JUST DON'T WORK THAT WAY. WE DON'T COMPLETELY UNDERSTAND THEM OURSELVES.

I'M SORRY, BUT WE CAN'T GO BACK.

OKAY, WELL THAT SCARES ME A LITTLE.

ME TOO.

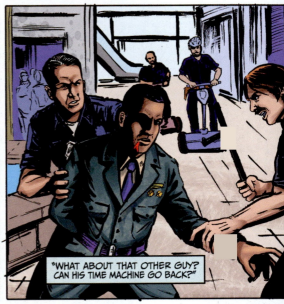

"WHAT ABOUT THAT OTHER GUY? CAN HIS TIME MACHINE GO BACK?"

KRAK

"THEY ONLY GO FORWARD. THERE IS NO BACK."

TWUNK

GEEZ. WHAT AM I GONNA DO, THEN?

WHAT ARE YOU GONNA DO?

I DON'T KNOW.

MAYBE I CAN FIND SOMEONE WHO REMEMBERS OUR EXPERI...

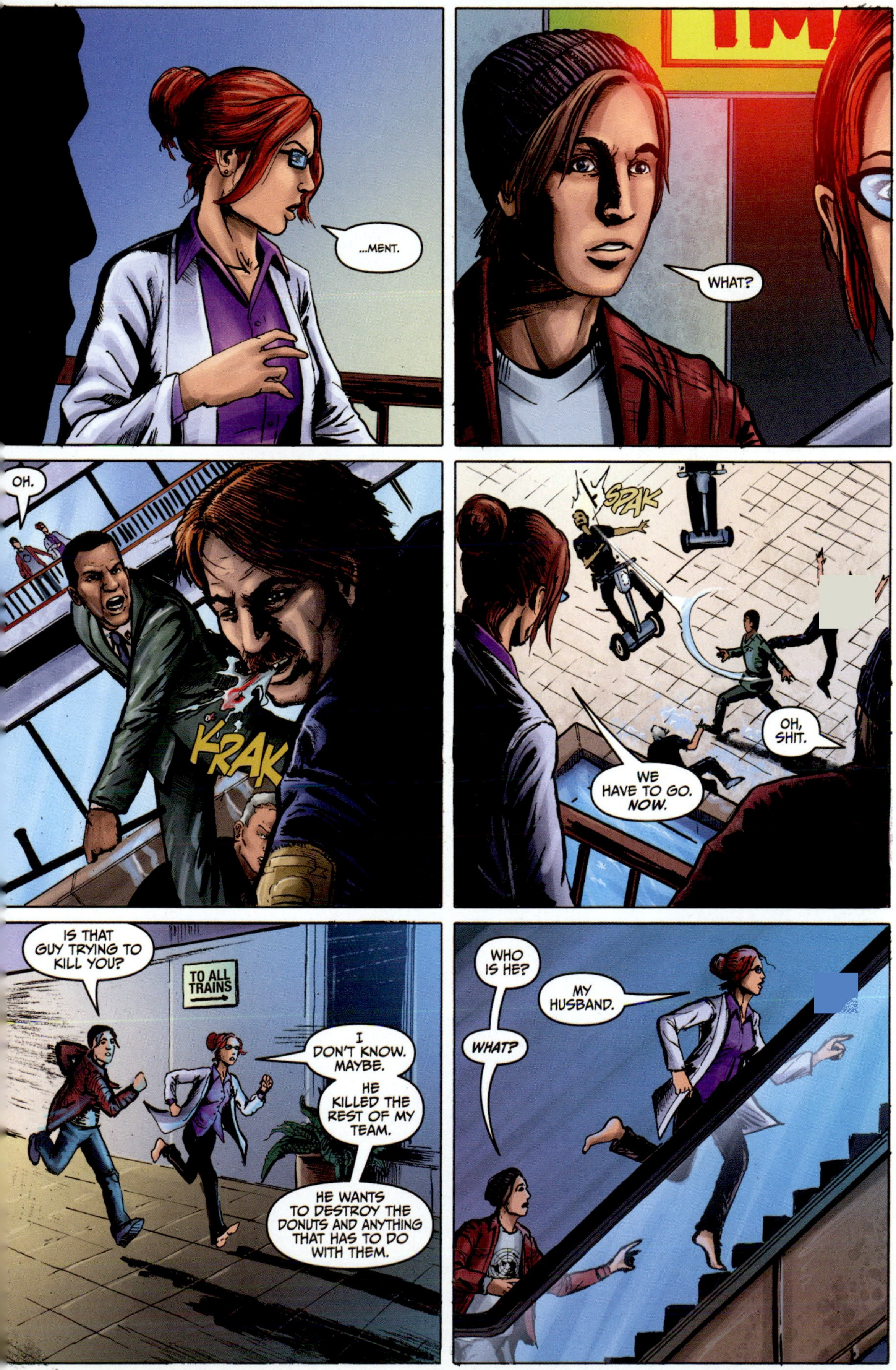

...MENT.
WHAT?
OH.
KRAK
SPAK
OH, SHIT.
WE HAVE TO GO. NOW.
IS THAT GUY TRYING TO KILL YOU?
TO ALL TRAINS
I DON'T KNOW. MAYBE.
HE KILLED THE REST OF MY TEAM.
HE WANTS TO DESTROY THE DONUTS AND ANYTHING THAT HAS TO DO WITH THEM.
WHO IS HE?
MY HUSBAND.
WHAT?

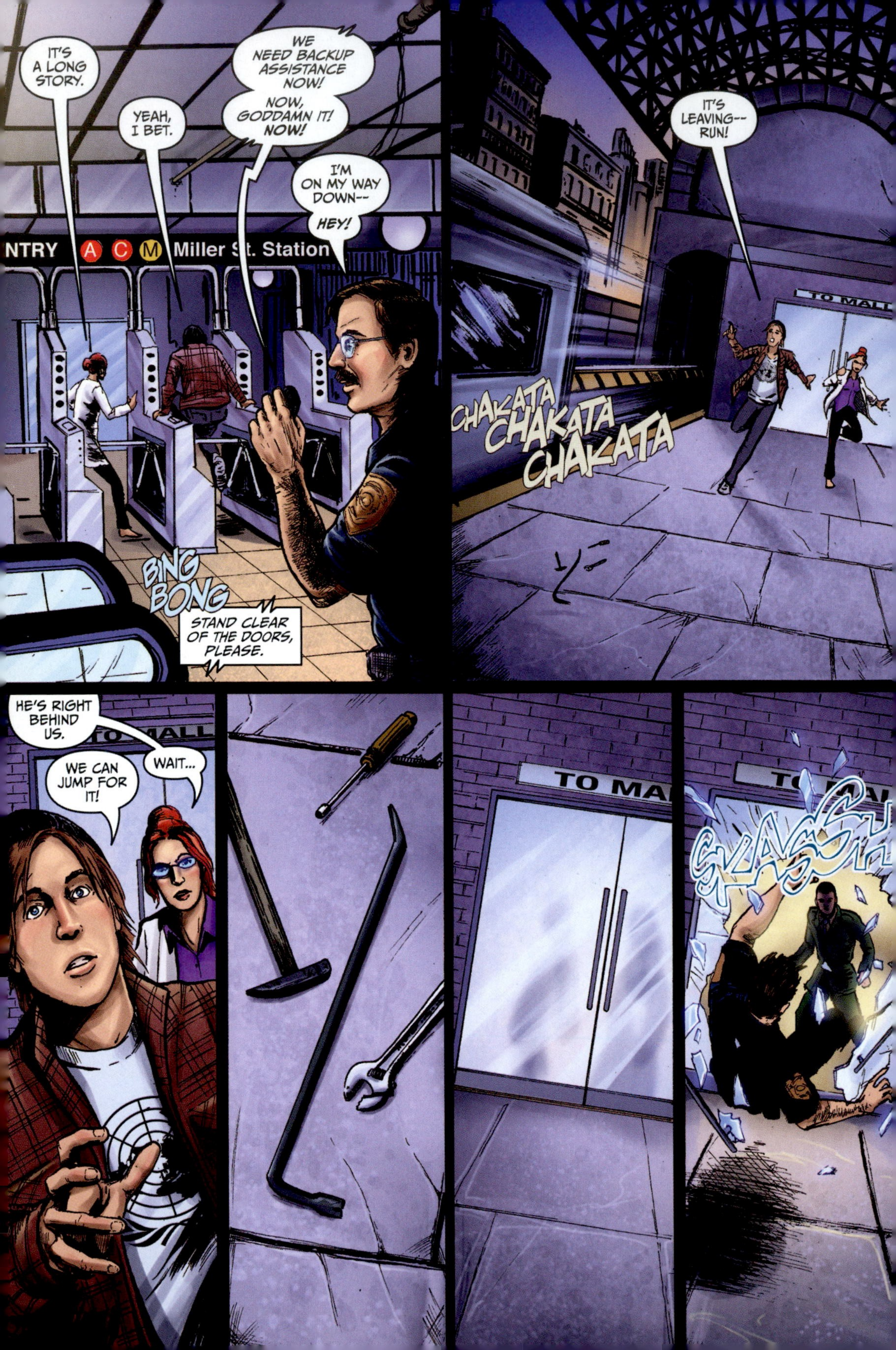
IT'S A LONG STORY.
YEAH, I BET.
WE NEED BACKUP ASSISTANCE NOW!
NOW, GODDAMN IT! NOW!
I'M ON MY WAY DOWN--
HEY!
NTRY A C M Miller St. Station
BING BONG
STAND CLEAR OF THE DOORS, PLEASE.
IT'S LEAVING-- RUN!
TO MALL
CHAKATA CHAKATA CHAKATA
HE'S RIGHT BEHIND US.
WE CAN JUMP FOR IT!
WAIT...
TO MALL
TO MA
SMASH

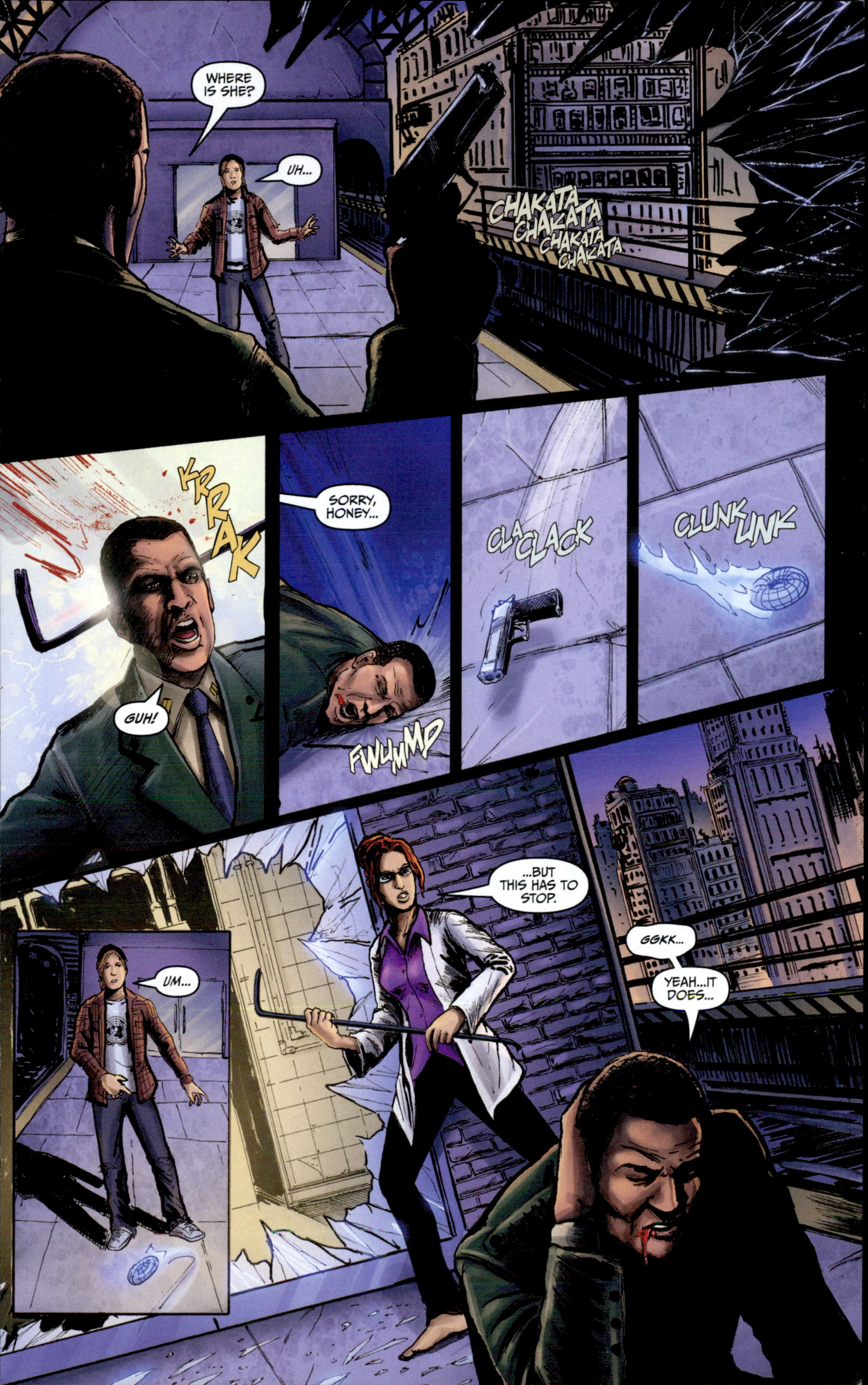
WHERE IS SHE?
UH...
CHAKATA CHAKATA CHAKATA CHAKATA
KRRAK
GUH!
SORRY, HONEY...
FWUMMP
CLACLACK
CLUNKUNK
...BUT THIS HAS TO STOP.
UM...
GGKK...
YEAH...IT DOES...

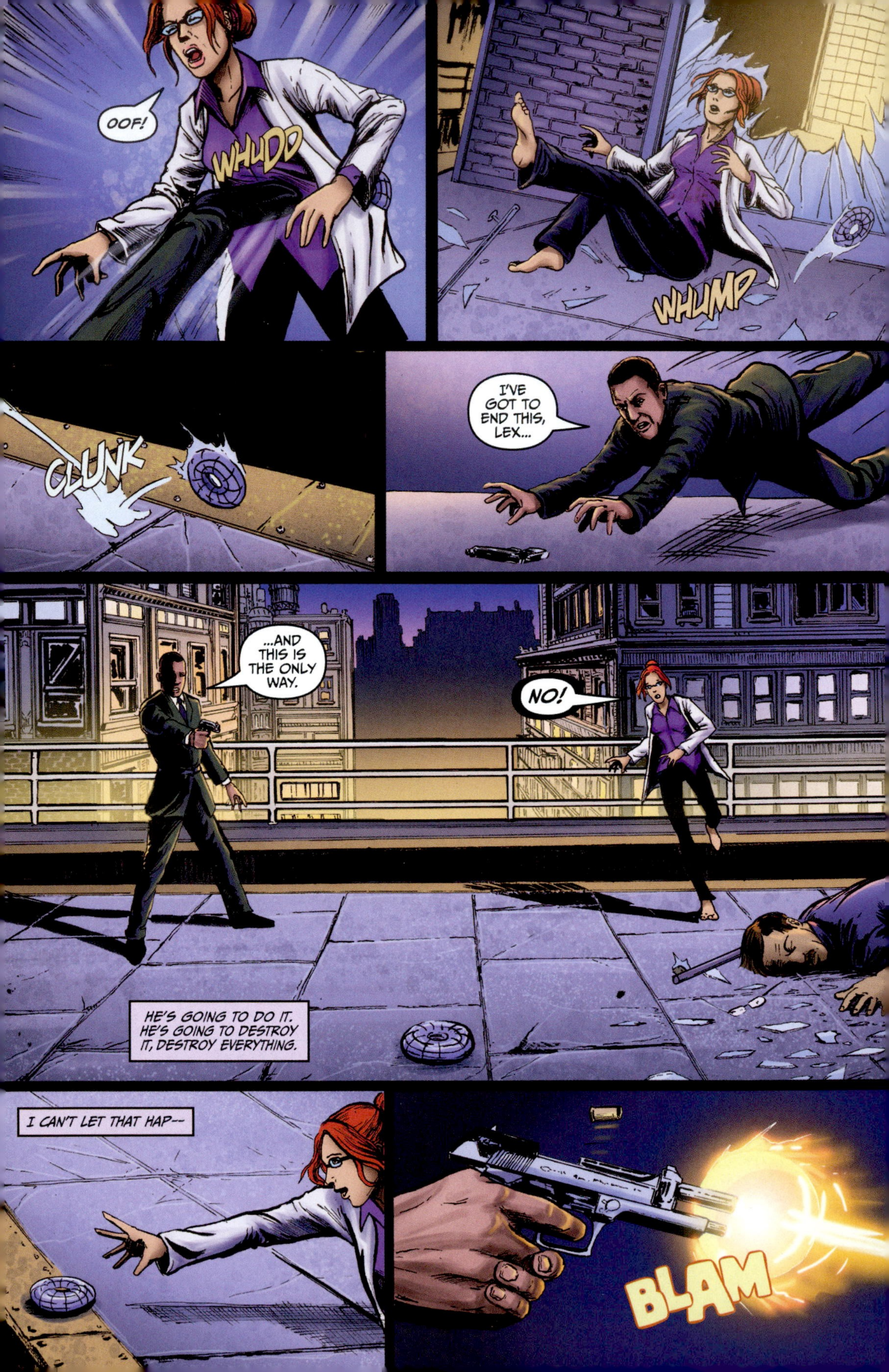
OOF!
WHUDD
WHUMP
CLUNK
I'VE GOT TO END THIS, LEX...
...AND THIS IS THE ONLY WAY.
NO!
HE'S GOING TO DO IT. HE'S GOING TO DESTROY IT, DESTROY EVERYTHING.
I CAN'T LET THAT HAP--
BLAM

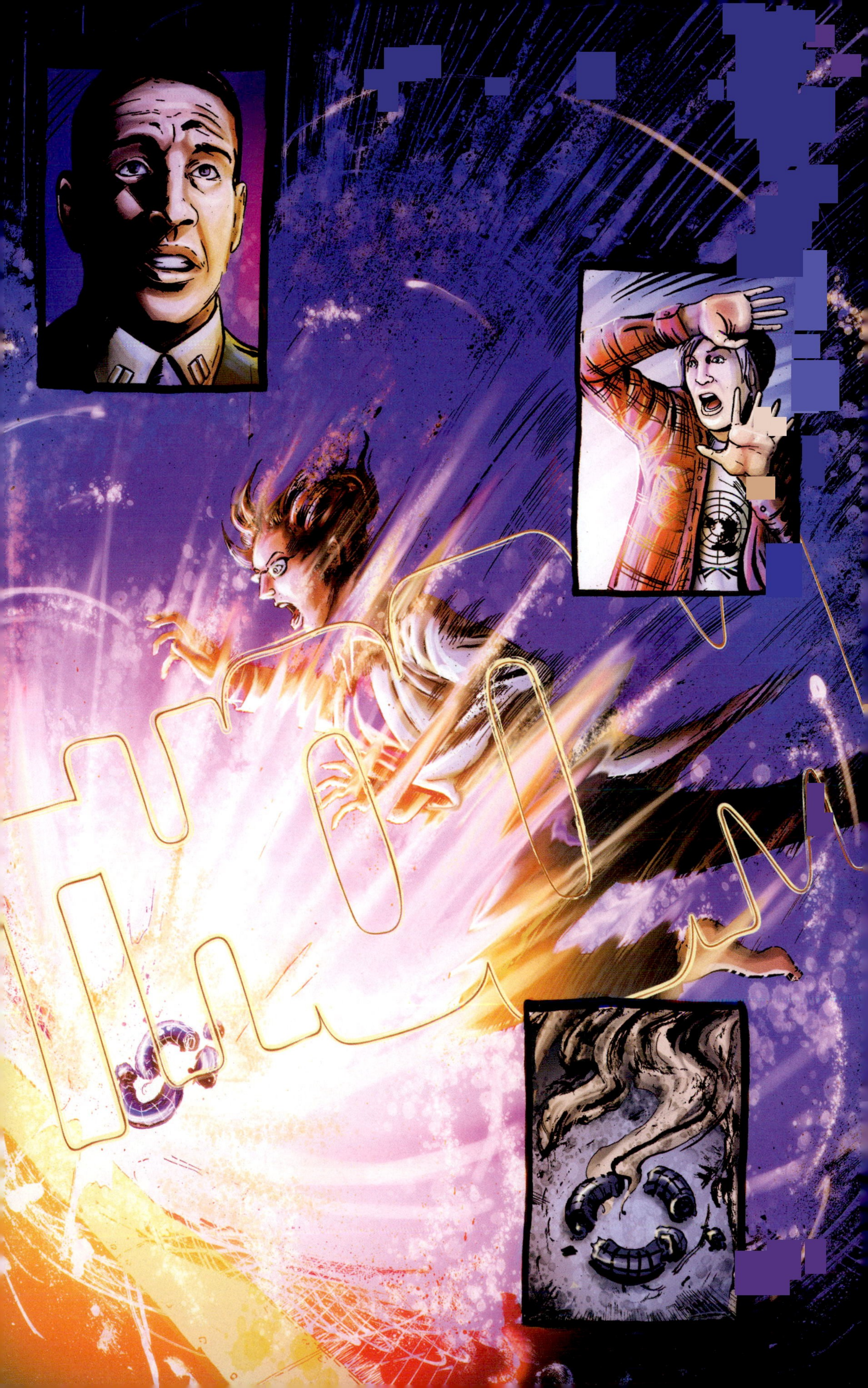

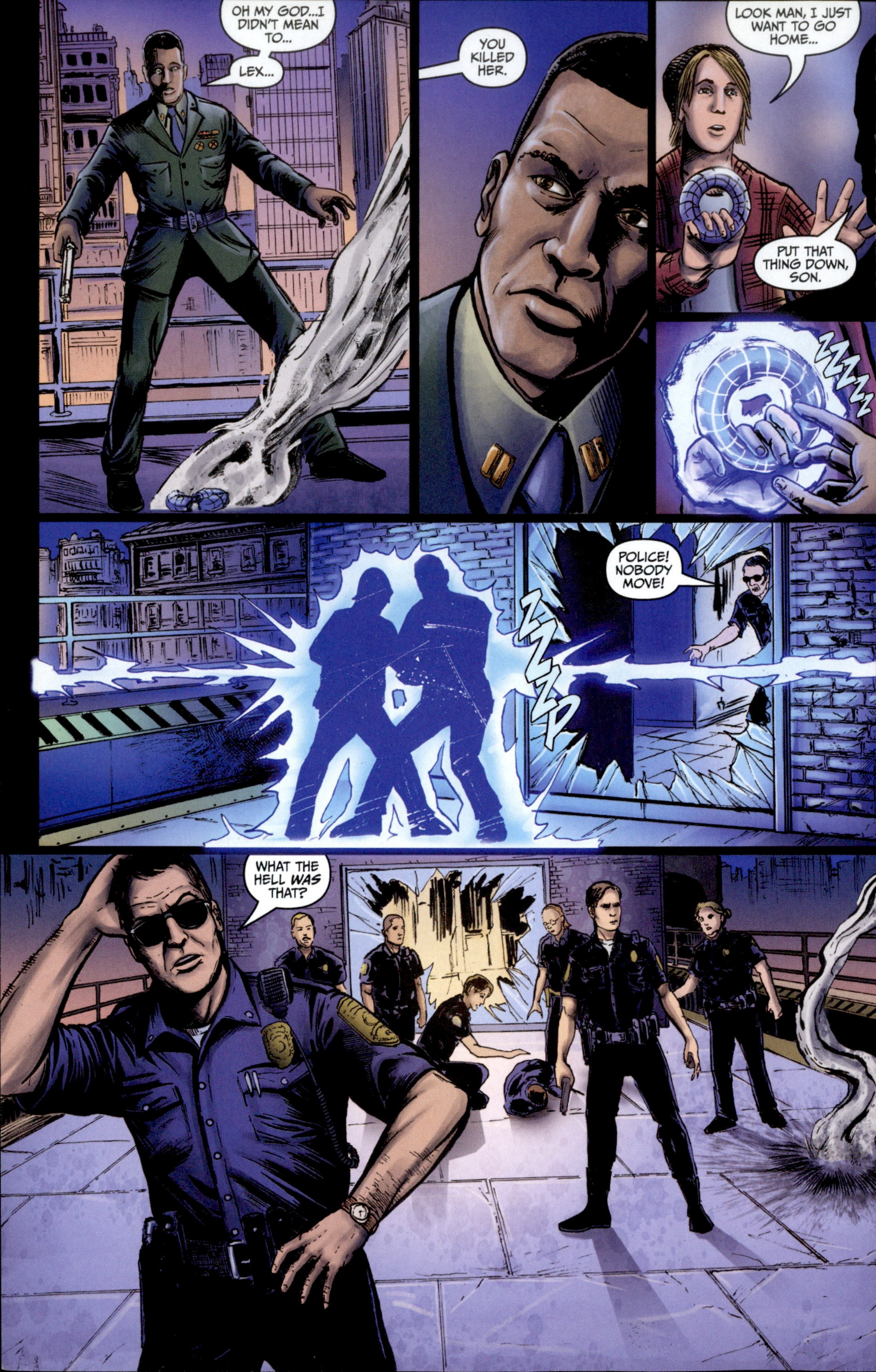
OH MY GOD...I DIDN'T MEAN TO...
LEX...
YOU KILLED HER.
LOOK MAN, I JUST WANT TO GO HOME...
PUT THAT THING DOWN, SON.
ZZZZ
ZZZZ
POLICE! NOBODY MOVE!
WHAT THE HELL *WAS* THAT?

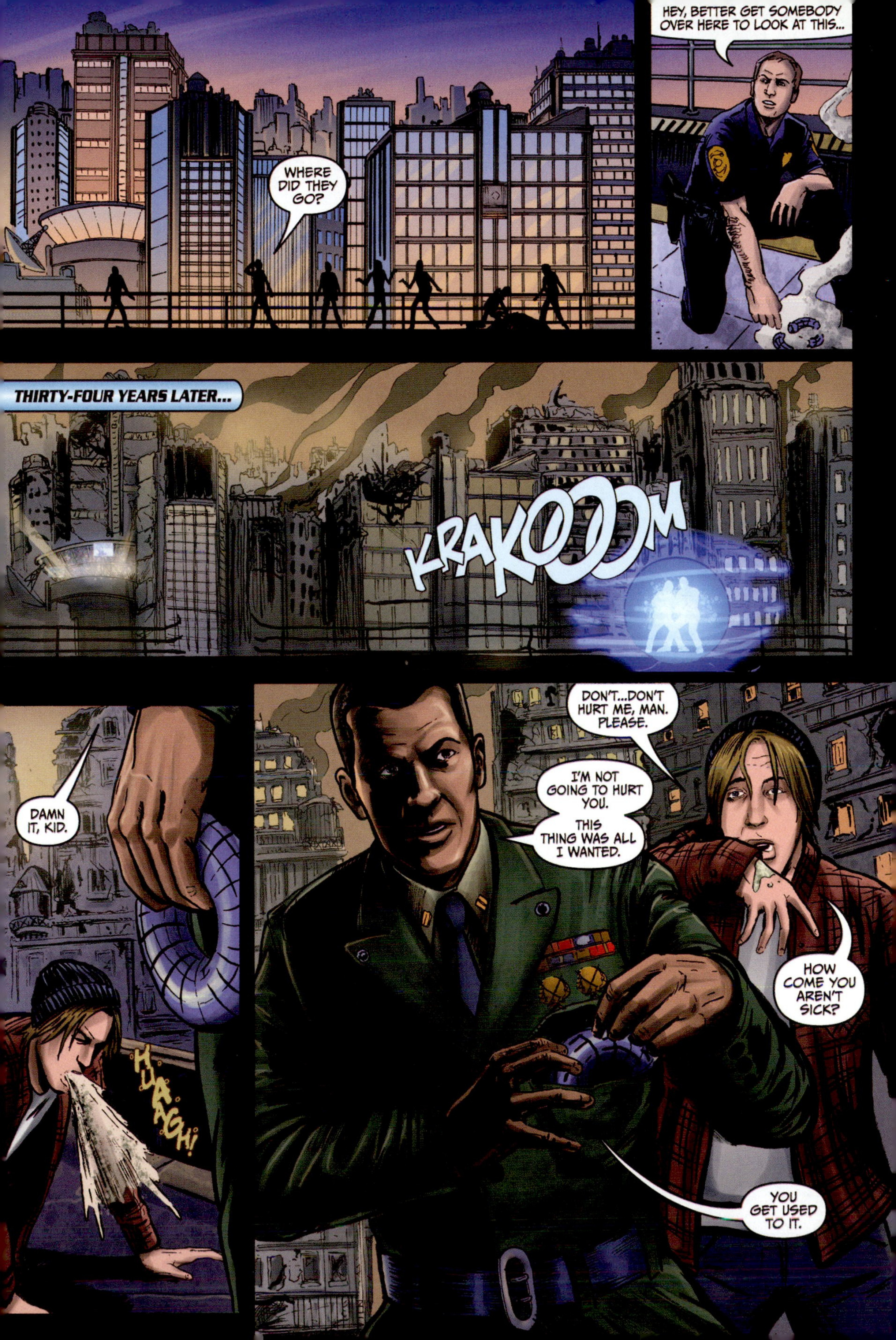
WHERE DID THEY GO?
HEY, BETTER GET SOMEBODY OVER HERE TO LOOK AT THIS...
THIRTY-FOUR YEARS LATER...
KRAKOOOM
DAMN IT, KID.
HUAAGH!
DON'T...DON'T HURT ME, MAN. PLEASE.
I'M NOT GOING TO HURT YOU.
THIS THING WAS ALL I WANTED.
HOW COME YOU AREN'T SICK?
YOU GET USED TO IT.

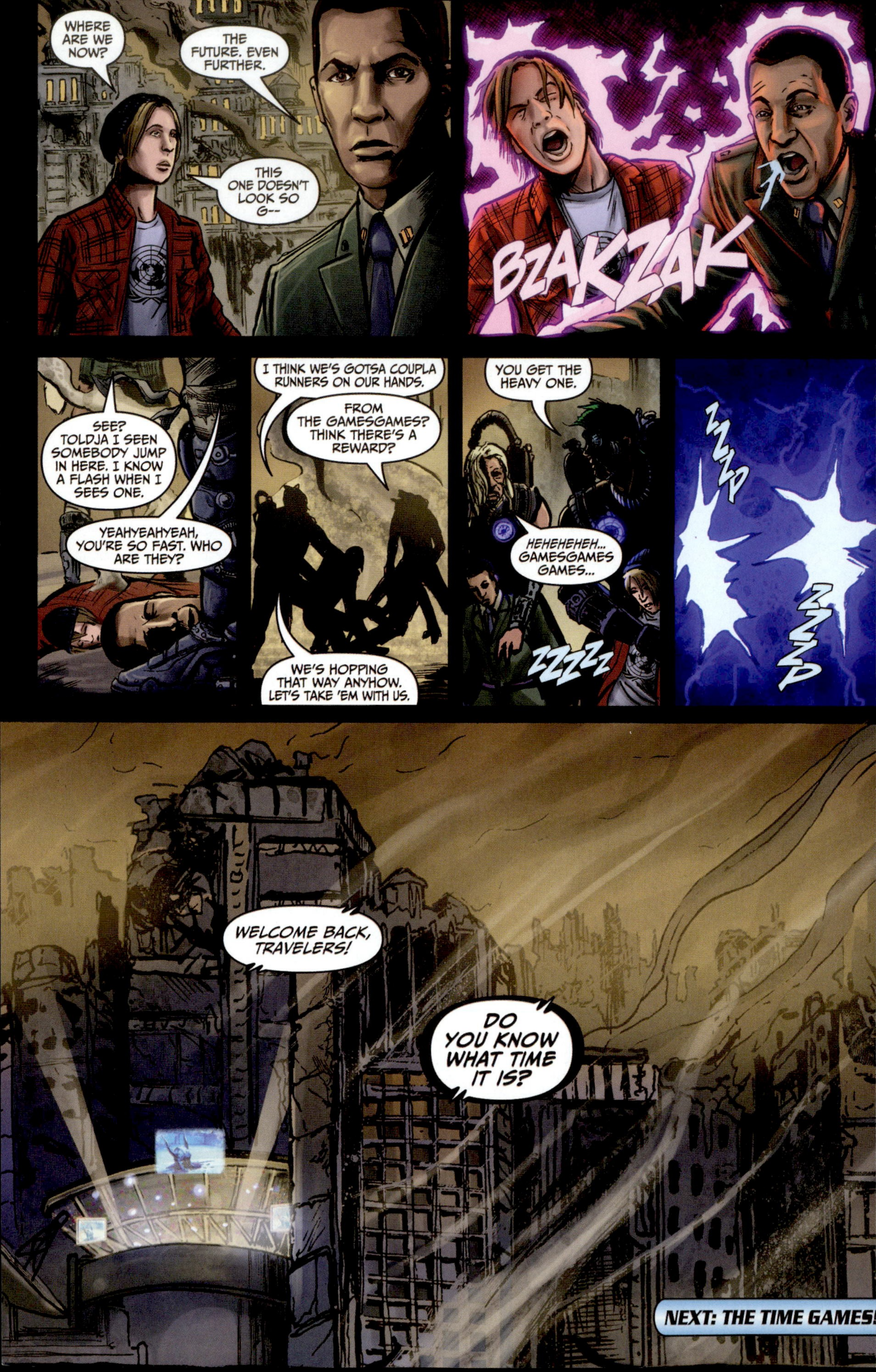
WHERE ARE WE NOW?
THE FUTURE. EVEN FURTHER.
THIS ONE DOESN'T LOOK SO G--
BZAKZAK
SEE? TOLDJA I SEEN SOMEBODY JUMP IN HERE. I KNOW A FLASH WHEN I SEES ONE.
YEAHYEAHYEAH, YOU'RE SO FAST. WHO ARE THEY?
I THINK WE'S GOTSA COUPLA RUNNERS ON OUR HANDS.
FROM THE GAMESGAMES? THINK THERE'S A REWARD?
WE'S HOPPING THAT WAY ANYHOW. LET'S TAKE 'EM WITH US.
YOU GET THE HEAVY ONE.
HEHEHEHEH... GAMESGAMES GAMES...
ZZZZZ
ZZZZP
ZZZZP
WELCOME BACK, TRAVELERS!
DO YOU KNOW WHAT TIME IT IS?
NEXT: THE TIME GAMES!

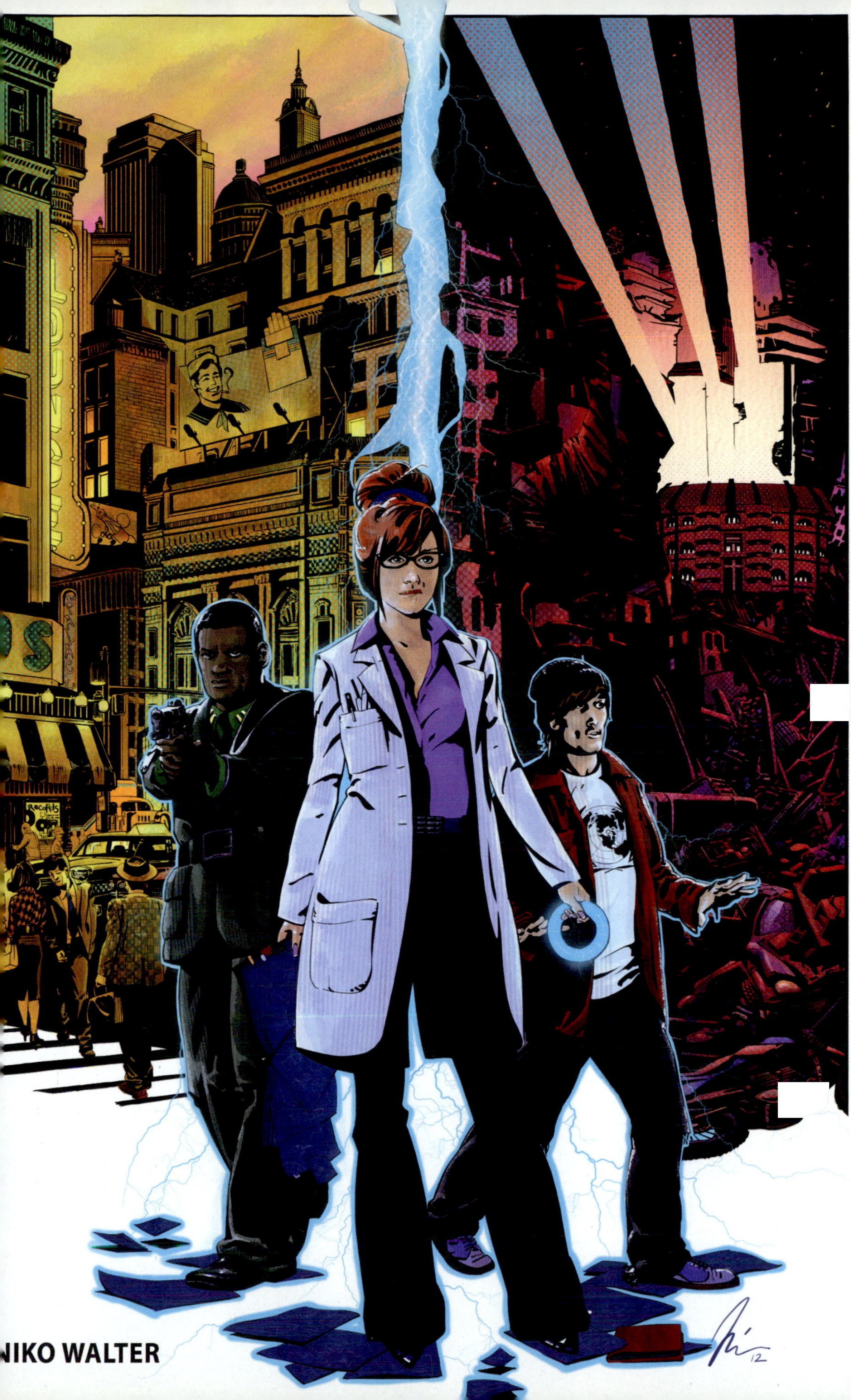

NIKO WALTER

2

Time To Kill

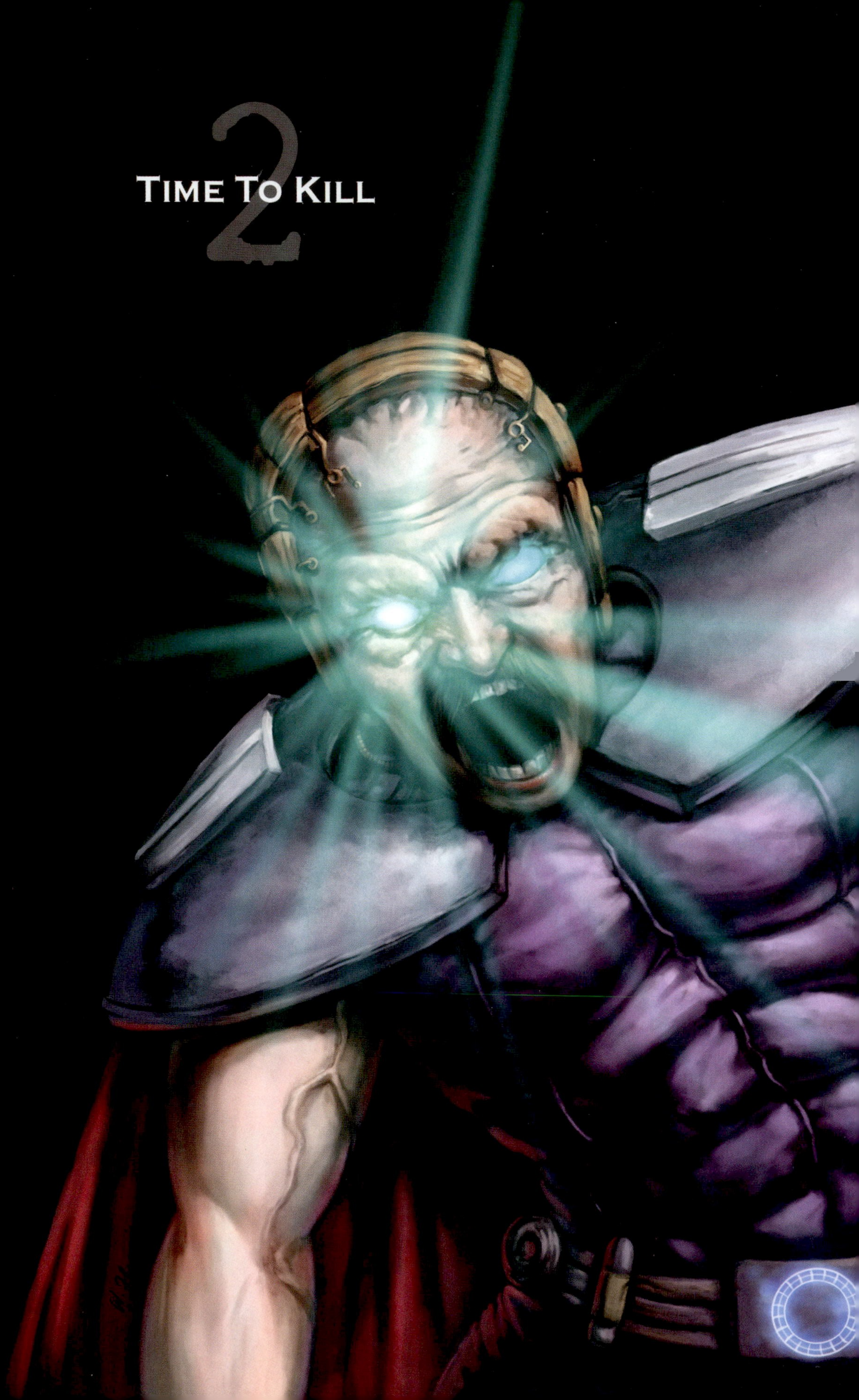

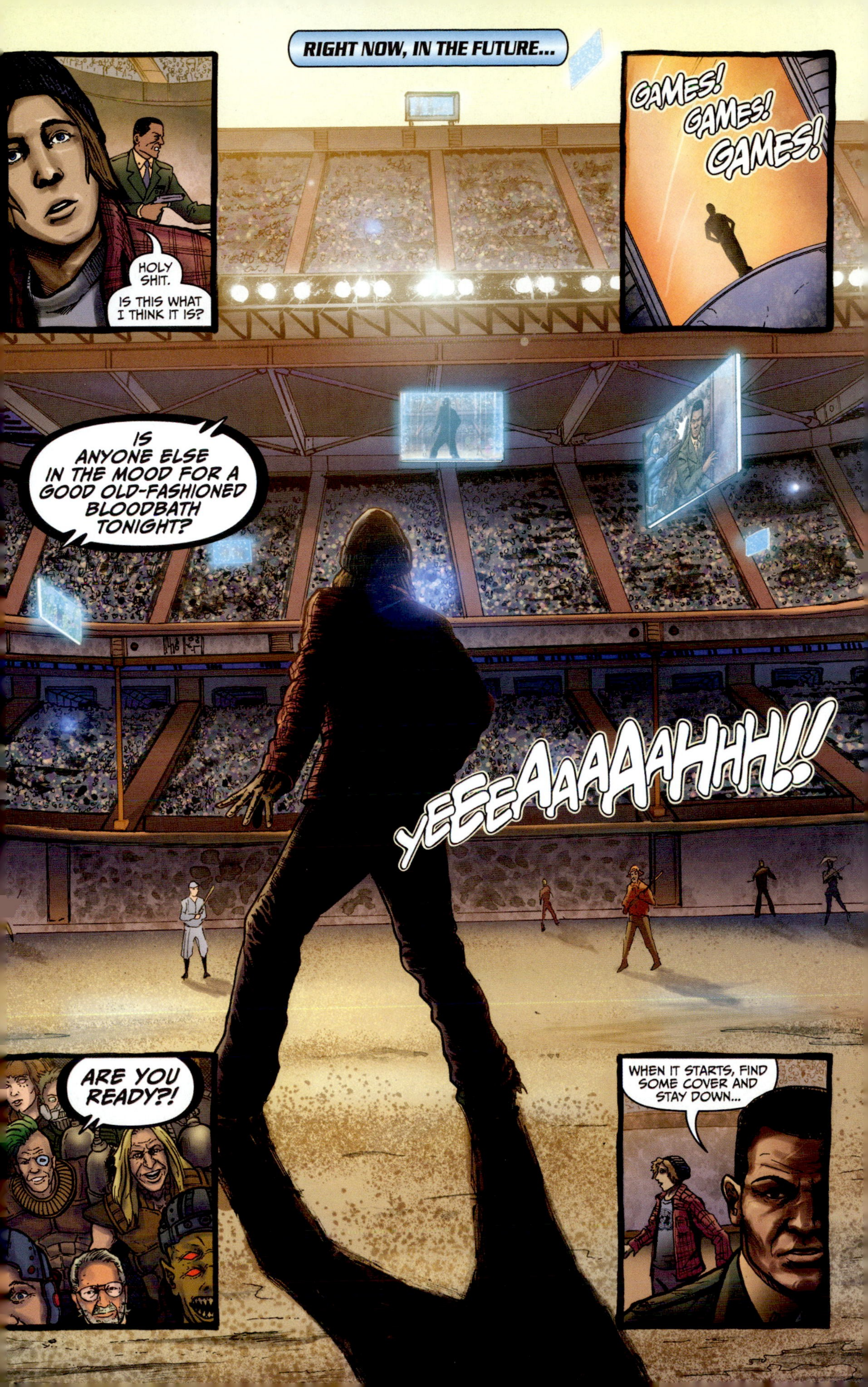
RIGHT NOW, IN THE FUTURE...
HOLY SHIT.
IS THIS WHAT I THINK IT IS?
GAMES! GAMES! GAMES!
IS ANYONE ELSE IN THE MOOD FOR A GOOD OLD-FASHIONED BLOODBATH TONIGHT?
YEEEAAAAAHHH!!
ARE YOU READY?!
WHEN IT STARTS, FIND SOME COVER AND STAY DOWN...

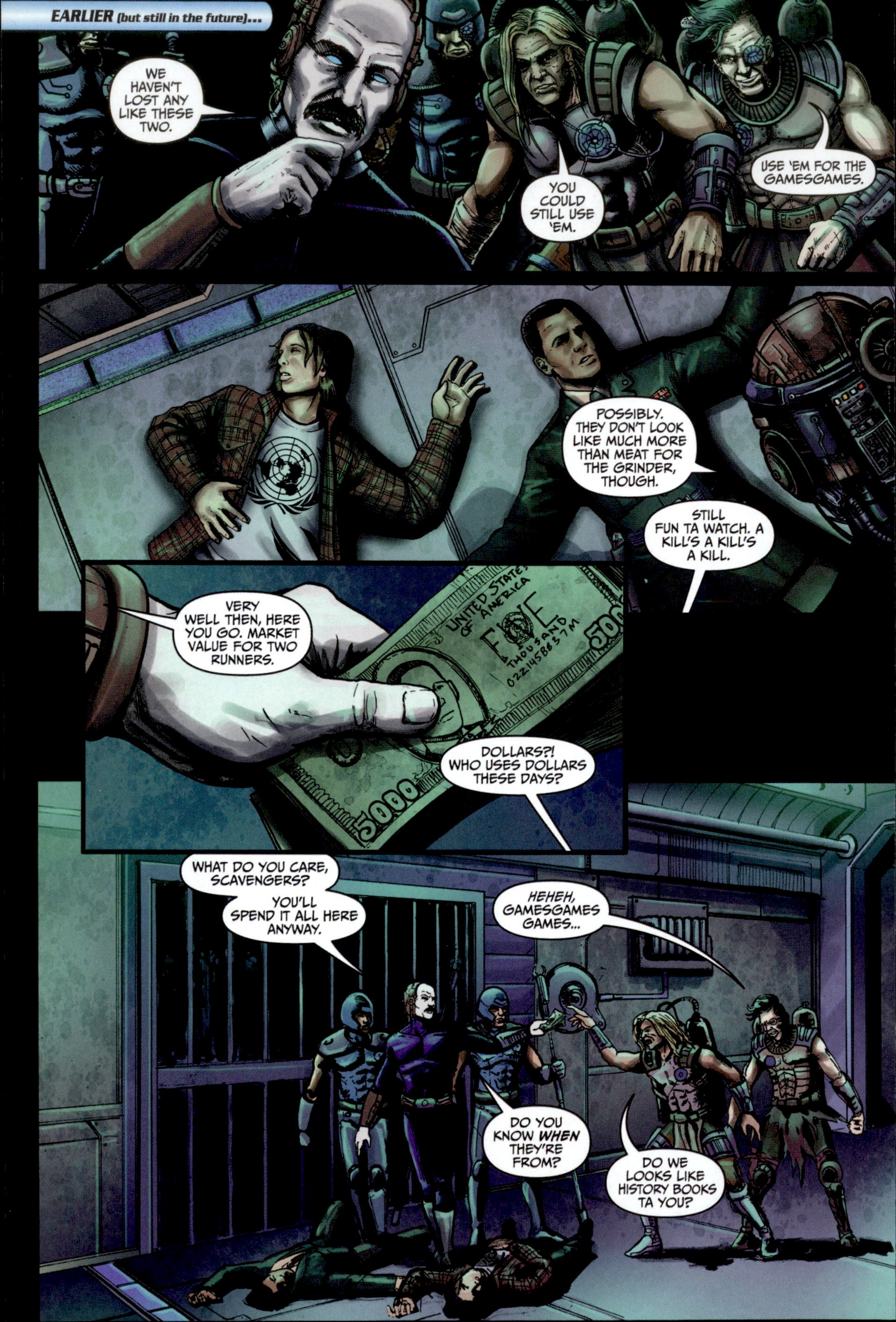
EARLIER (but still in the future)...
WE HAVEN'T LOST ANY LIKE THESE TWO.
YOU COULD STILL USE 'EM.
USE 'EM FOR THE GAMESGAMES.
POSSIBLY. THEY DON'T LOOK LIKE MUCH MORE THAN MEAT FOR THE GRINDER, THOUGH.
STILL FUN TA WATCH. A KILL'S A KILL'S A KILL.
VERY WELL THEN, HERE YOU GO. MARKET VALUE FOR TWO RUNNERS.
DOLLARS?! WHO USES DOLLARS THESE DAYS?
WHAT DO YOU CARE, SCAVENGERS?
YOU'LL SPEND IT ALL HERE ANYWAY.
HEHEH, GAMESGAMES GAMES...
DO YOU KNOW WHEN THEY'RE FROM?
DO WE LOOKS LIKE HISTORY BOOKS TA YOU?

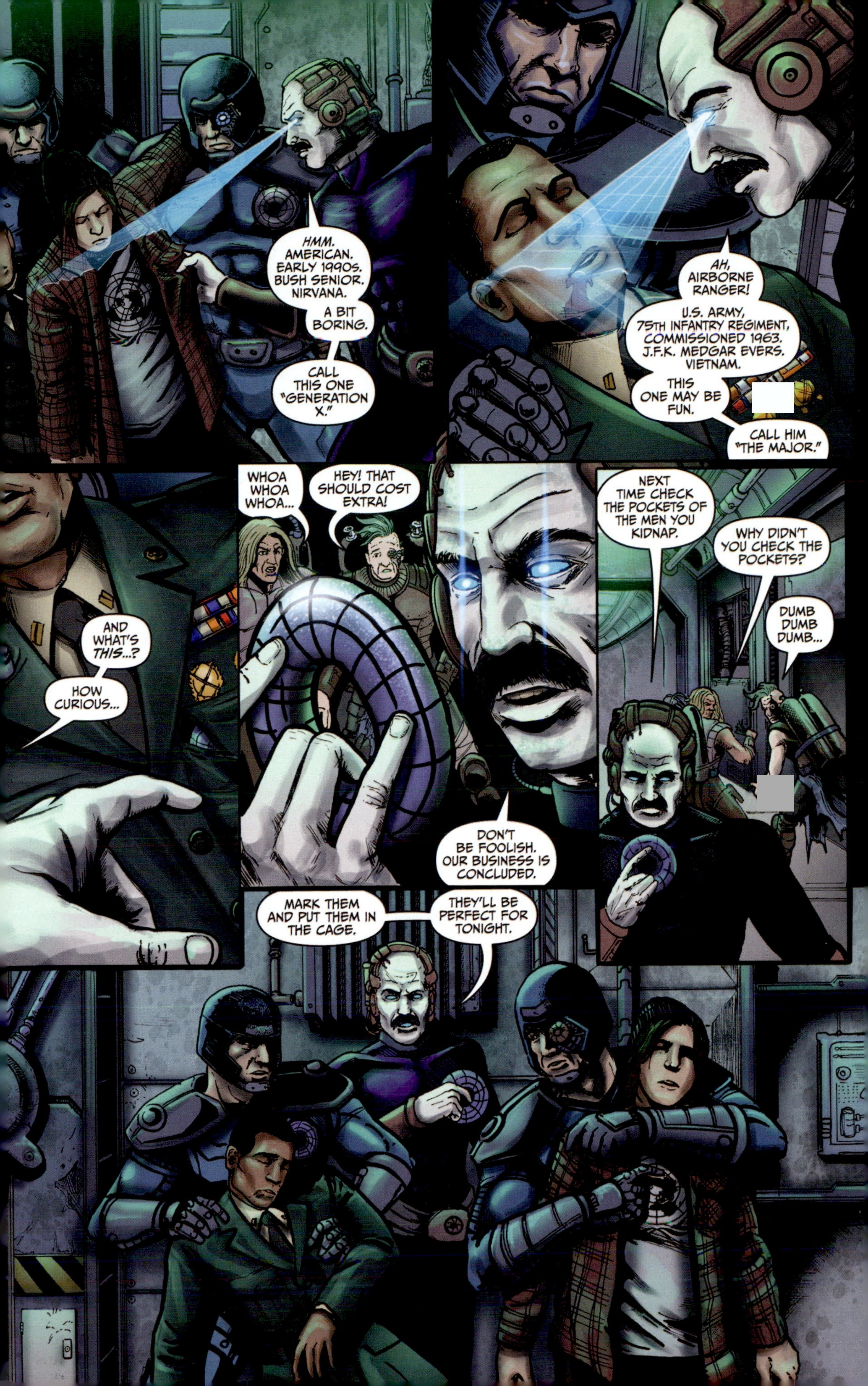
HMM. AMERICAN. EARLY 1990s. BUSH SENIOR. NIRVANA.
A BIT BORING.
CALL THIS ONE "GENERATION X."
AH, AIRBORNE RANGER!
U.S. ARMY, 75TH INFANTRY REGIMENT, COMMISSIONED 1963. J.F.K. MEDGAR EVERS. VIETNAM.
THIS ONE MAY BE FUN.
CALL HIM "THE MAJOR."
AND WHAT'S THIS...?
HOW CURIOUS...
WHOA WHOA WHOA...
HEY! THAT SHOULD COST EXTRA!
DON'T BE FOOLISH. OUR BUSINESS IS CONCLUDED.
NEXT TIME CHECK THE POCKETS OF THE MEN YOU KIDNAP.
WHY DIDN'T YOU CHECK THE POCKETS?
DUMB DUMB DUMB...
MARK THEM AND PUT THEM IN THE CAGE.
THEY'LL BE PERFECT FOR TONIGHT.

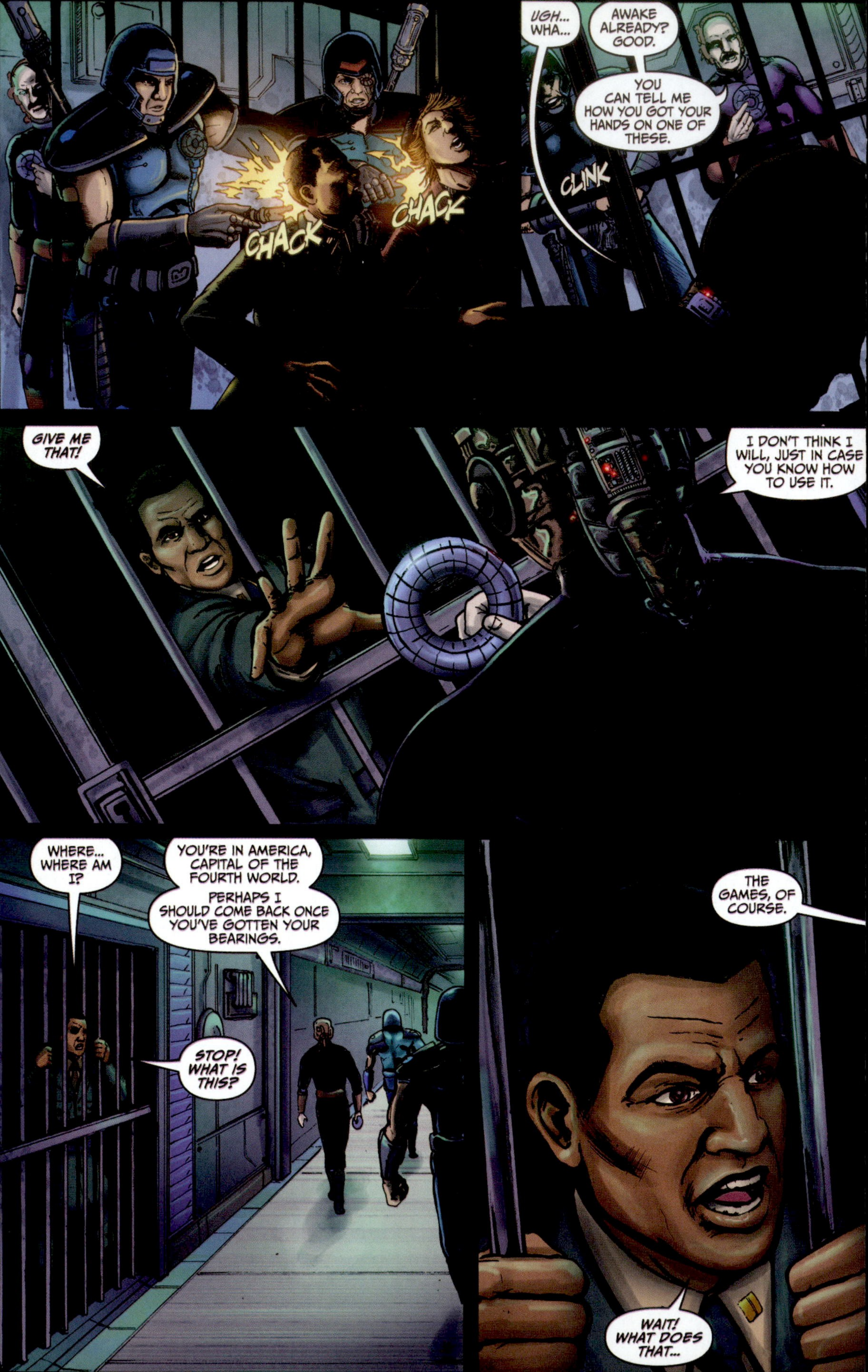
CHACK
CHACK
UGH... WHA...
AWAKE ALREADY? GOOD.
YOU CAN TELL ME HOW YOU GOT YOUR HANDS ON ONE OF THESE.
CLINK
GIVE ME THAT!
I DON'T THINK I WILL, JUST IN CASE YOU KNOW HOW TO USE IT.
WHERE... WHERE AM I?
YOU'RE IN AMERICA, CAPITAL OF THE FOURTH WORLD.
PERHAPS I SHOULD COME BACK ONCE YOU'VE GOTTEN YOUR BEARINGS.
STOP! WHAT IS THIS?
THE GAMES, OF COURSE.
WAIT! WHAT DOES THAT...

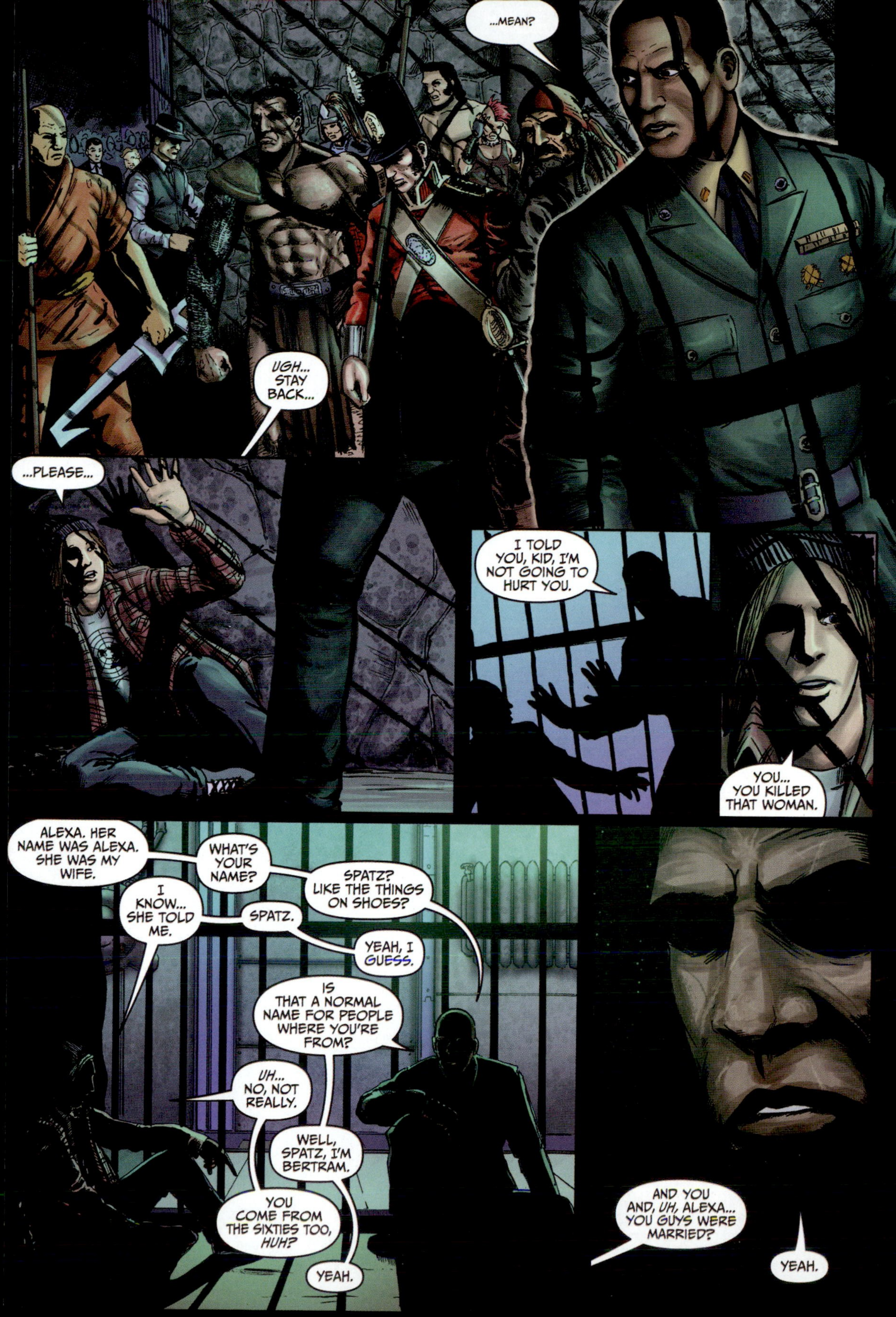
...MEAN?
UGH... STAY BACK...
...PLEASE...
I TOLD YOU, KID, I'M NOT GOING TO HURT YOU.
YOU... YOU KILLED THAT WOMAN.
ALEXA. HER NAME WAS ALEXA. SHE WAS MY WIFE.
I KNOW... SHE TOLD ME.
WHAT'S YOUR NAME?
SPATZ.
SPATZ? LIKE THE THINGS ON SHOES?
YEAH, I GUESS.
IS THAT A NORMAL NAME FOR PEOPLE WHERE YOU'RE FROM?
UH... NO, NOT REALLY.
WELL, SPATZ, I'M BERTRAM.
YOU COME FROM THE SIXTIES TOO, HUH?
YEAH.
AND YOU AND, UH, ALEXA... YOU GUYS WERE MARRIED?
YEAH.

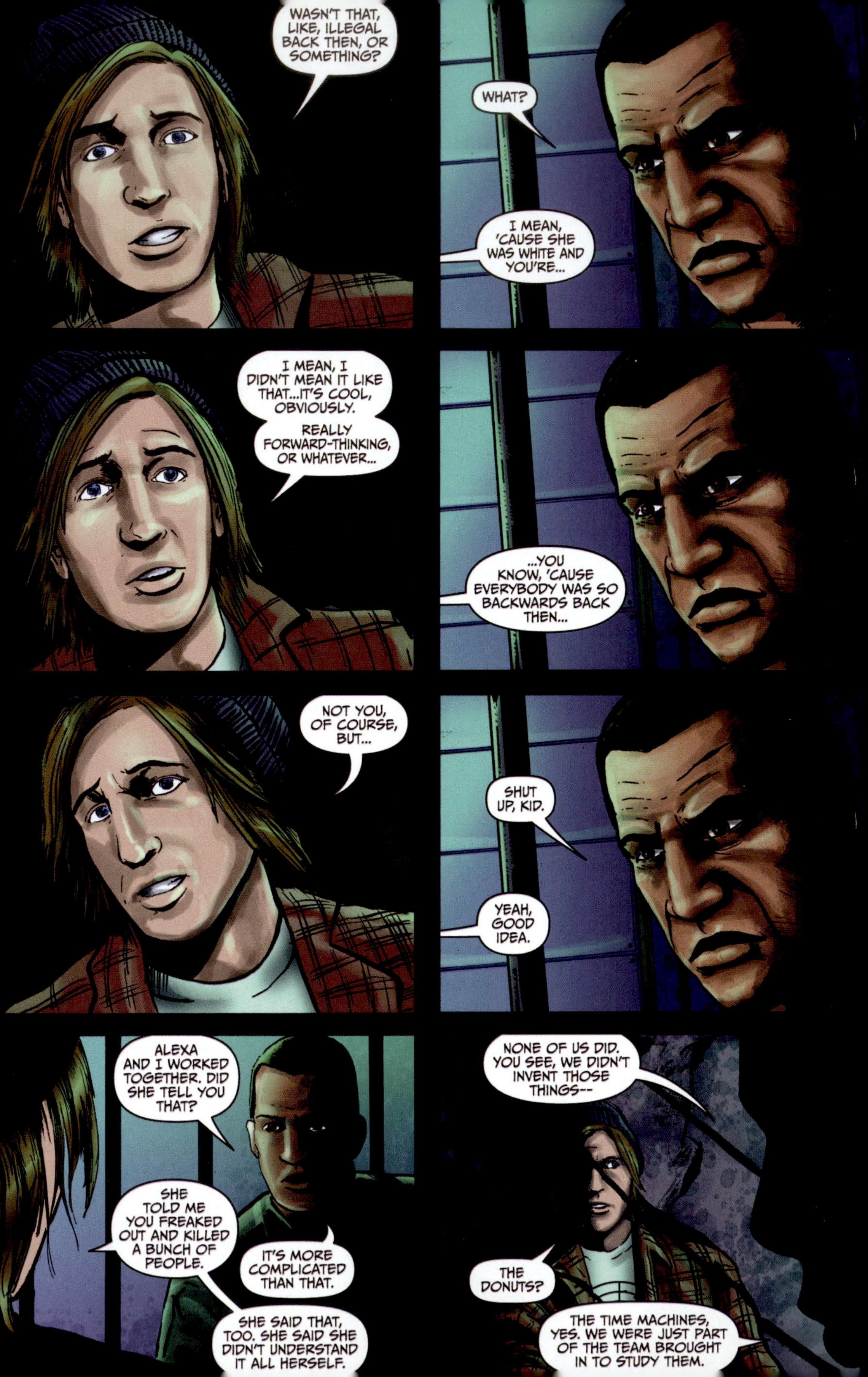
WASN'T THAT, LIKE, ILLEGAL BACK THEN, OR SOMETHING?
WHAT?
I MEAN, 'CAUSE SHE WAS WHITE AND YOU'RE...
I MEAN, I DIDN'T MEAN IT LIKE THAT...IT'S COOL, OBVIOUSLY.
REALLY FORWARD-THINKING, OR WHATEVER...
...YOU KNOW, 'CAUSE EVERYBODY WAS SO BACKWARDS BACK THEN...
NOT YOU, OF COURSE, BUT...
SHUT UP, KID.
YEAH, GOOD IDEA.
ALEXA AND I WORKED TOGETHER. DID SHE TELL YOU THAT?
SHE TOLD ME YOU FREAKED OUT AND KILLED A BUNCH OF PEOPLE.
IT'S MORE COMPLICATED THAN THAT.
SHE SAID THAT, TOO. SHE SAID SHE DIDN'T UNDERSTAND IT ALL HERSELF.
NONE OF US DID. YOU SEE, WE DIDN'T INVENT THOSE THINGS--
THE DONUTS?
THE TIME MACHINES, YES. WE WERE JUST PART OF THE TEAM BROUGHT IN TO STUDY THEM.

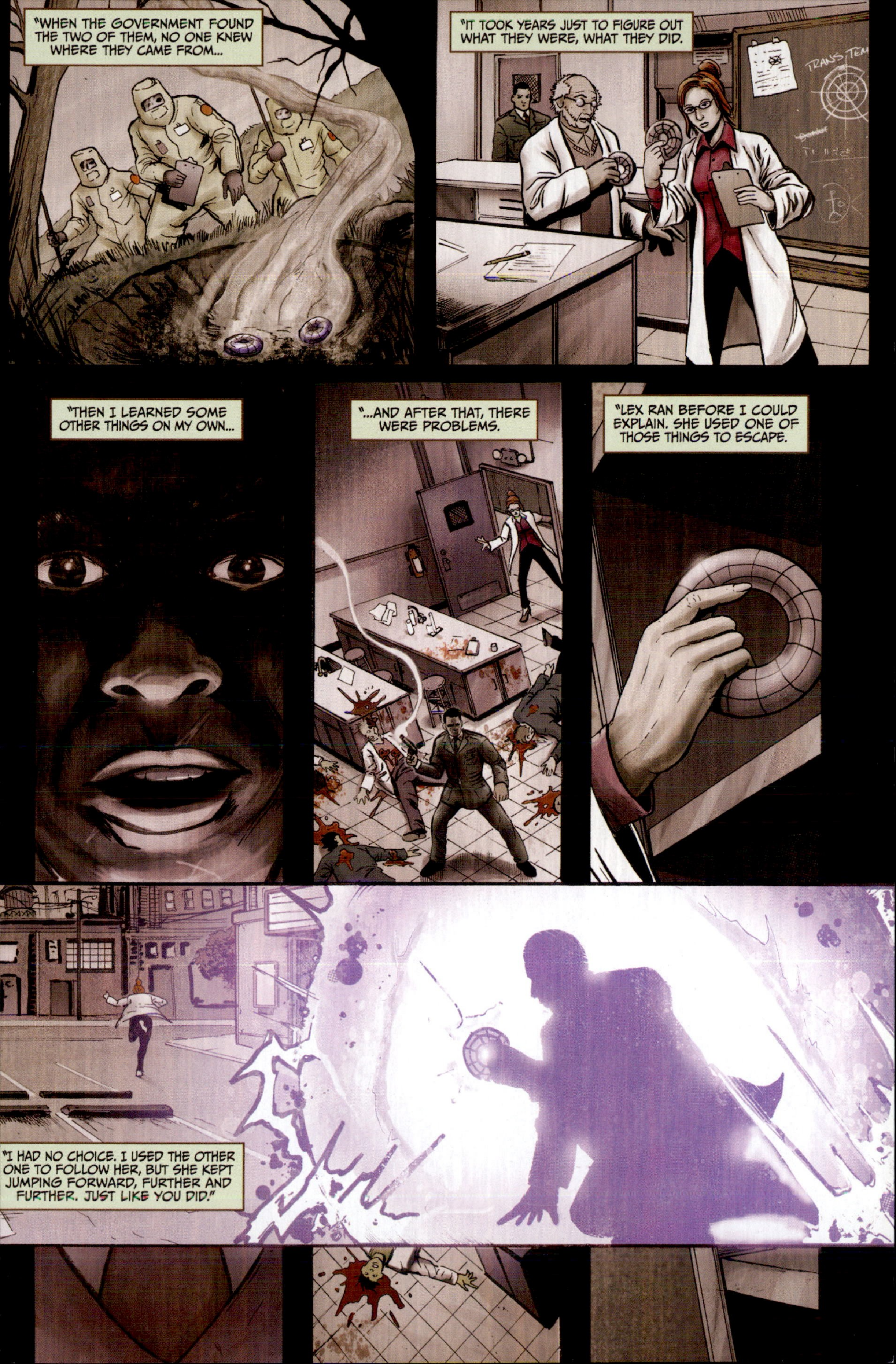
"WHEN THE GOVERNMENT FOUND THE TWO OF THEM, NO ONE KNEW WHERE THEY CAME FROM...
"IT TOOK YEARS JUST TO FIGURE OUT WHAT THEY WERE, WHAT THEY DID.
"THEN I LEARNED SOME OTHER THINGS ON MY OWN...
"...AND AFTER THAT, THERE WERE PROBLEMS.
"LEX RAN BEFORE I COULD EXPLAIN. SHE USED ONE OF THOSE THINGS TO ESCAPE.
"I HAD NO CHOICE. I USED THE OTHER ONE TO FOLLOW HER, BUT SHE KEPT JUMPING FORWARD, FURTHER AND FURTHER. JUST LIKE YOU DID."

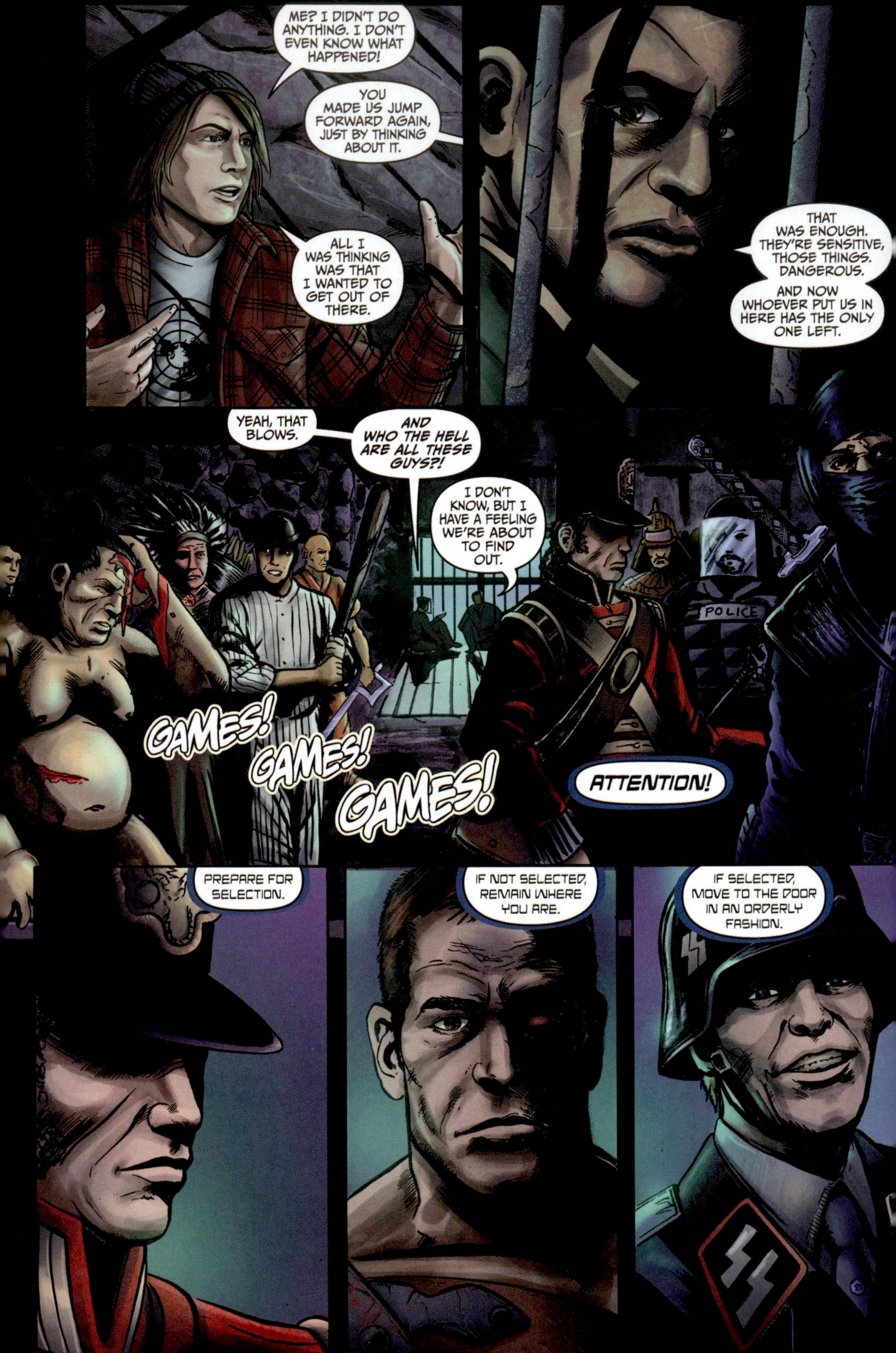
ME? I DIDN'T DO ANYTHING. I DON'T EVEN KNOW WHAT HAPPENED!
YOU MADE US JUMP FORWARD AGAIN, JUST BY THINKING ABOUT IT.
ALL I WAS THINKING WAS THAT I WANTED TO GET OUT OF THERE.
THAT WAS ENOUGH. THEY'RE SENSITIVE, THOSE THINGS. DANGEROUS.
AND NOW WHOEVER PUT US IN HERE HAS THE ONLY ONE LEFT.
YEAH, THAT BLOWS.
AND WHO THE HELL ARE ALL THESE GUYS?!
I DON'T KNOW, BUT I HAVE A FEELING WE'RE ABOUT TO FIND OUT.
POLICE
GAMES! GAMES! GAMES!
ATTENTION!
PREPARE FOR SELECTION.
IF NOT SELECTED, REMAIN WHERE YOU ARE.
IF SELECTED, MOVE TO THE DOOR IN AN ORDERLY FASHION.

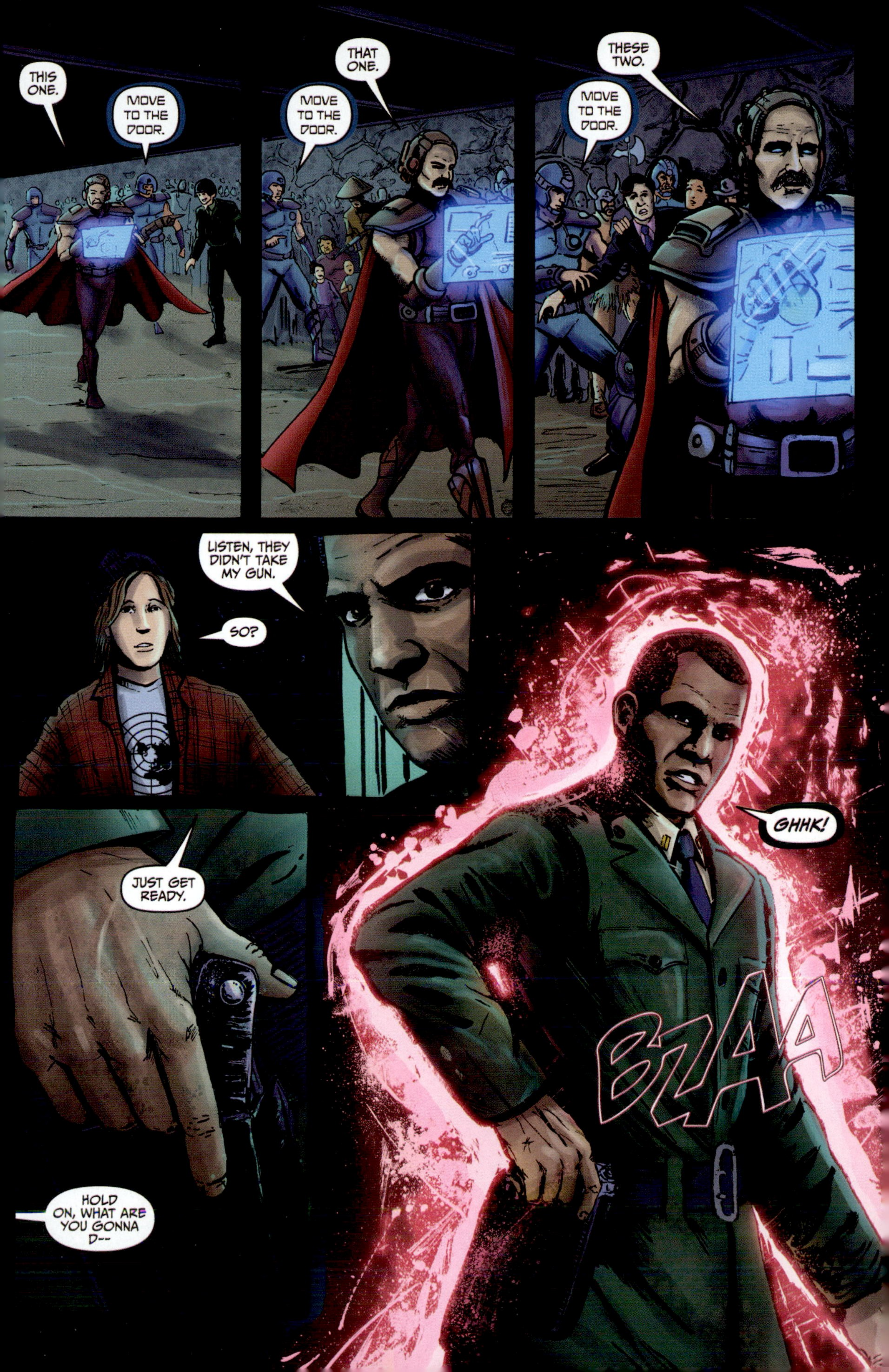
THIS ONE.
MOVE TO THE DOOR.
THAT ONE.
MOVE TO THE DOOR.
THESE TWO.
MOVE TO THE DOOR.
LISTEN, THEY DIDN'T TAKE MY GUN.
SO?
JUST GET READY.
HOLD ON, WHAT ARE YOU GONNA D--
GHHK!
BZAA

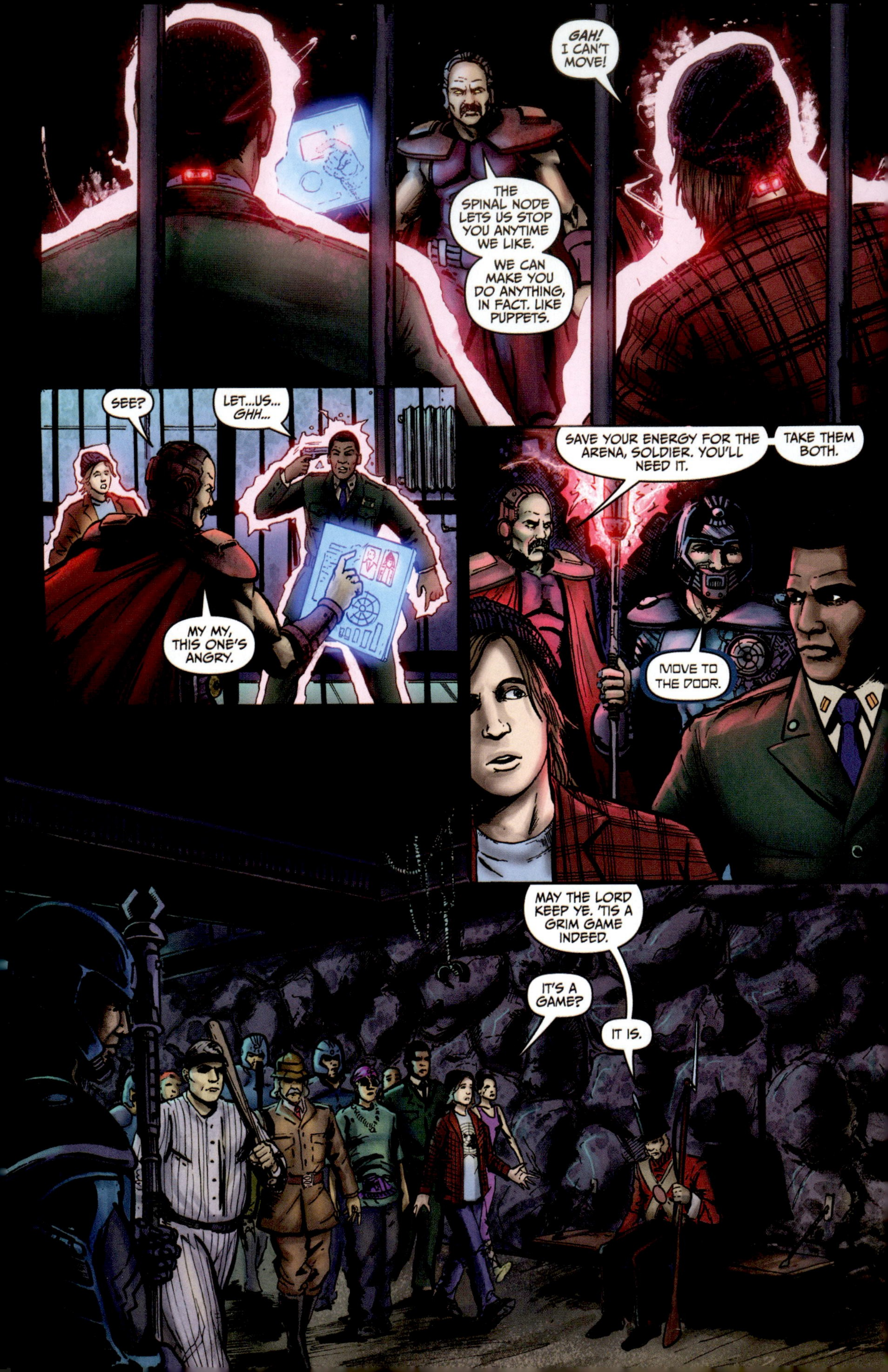
GAH! I CAN'T MOVE!
THE SPINAL NODE LETS US STOP YOU ANYTIME WE LIKE.
WE CAN MAKE YOU DO ANYTHING, IN FACT. LIKE PUPPETS.
SEE?
LET...US... GHH...
MY MY, THIS ONE'S ANGRY.
SAVE YOUR ENERGY FOR THE ARENA, SOLDIER. YOU'LL NEED IT.
TAKE THEM BOTH.
MOVE TO THE DOOR.
MAY THE LORD KEEP YE. 'TIS A GRIM GAME INDEED.
IT'S A GAME?
IT IS.

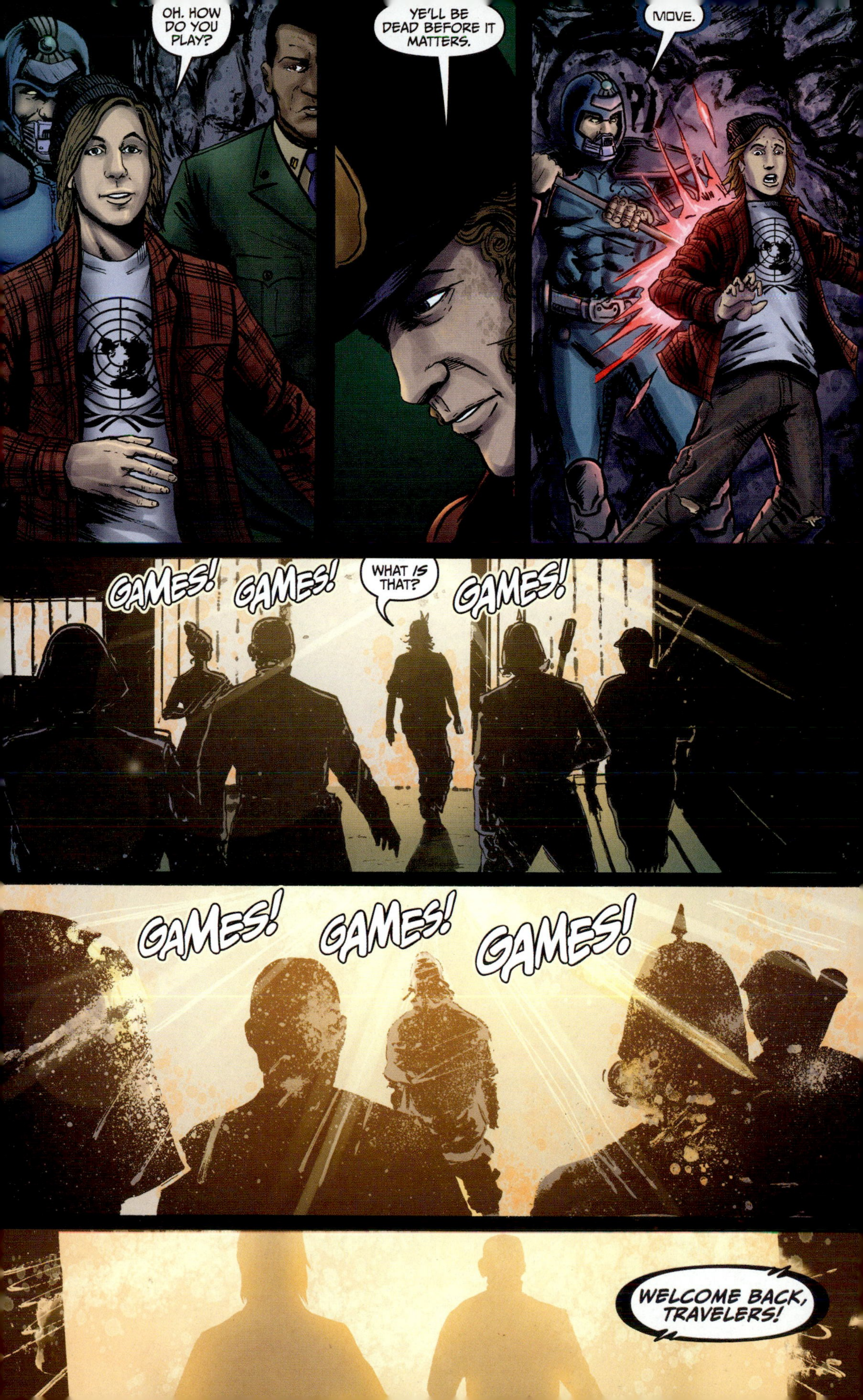
OH. HOW DO YOU PLAY?
YE'LL BE DEAD BEFORE IT MATTERS.
MOVE.
GAMES! GAMES!
WHAT IS THAT?
GAMES!
GAMES! GAMES! GAMES!
WELCOME BACK, TRAVELERS!

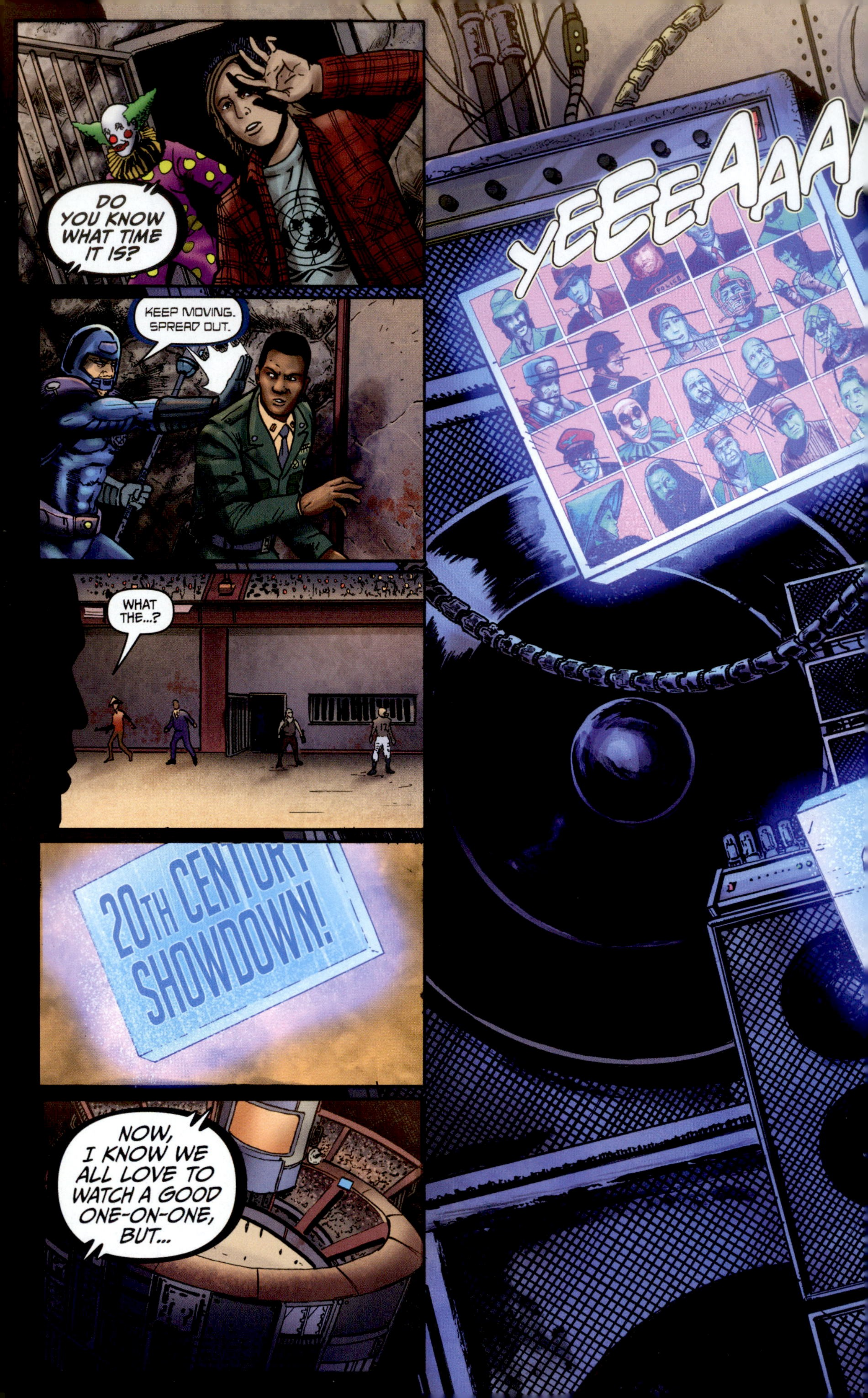
DO YOU KNOW WHAT TIME IT IS?
KEEP MOVING. SPREAD OUT.
WHAT THE...?
20TH CENTURY SHOWDOWN!
NOW, I KNOW WE ALL LOVE TO WATCH A GOOD ONE-ON-ONE, BUT...
YEEEAAA

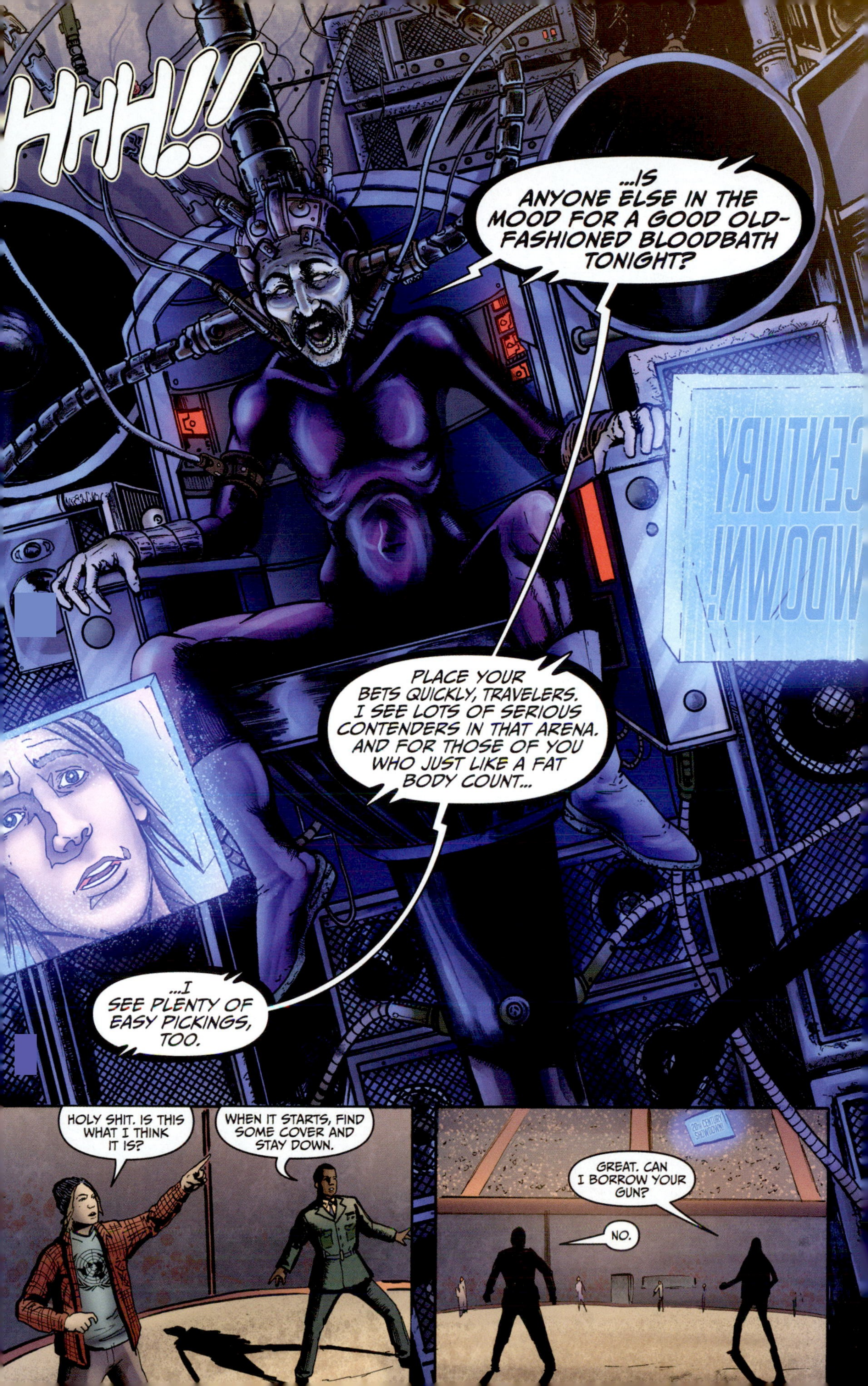
HHH!!
...IS ANYONE ELSE IN THE MOOD FOR A GOOD OLD-FASHIONED BLOODBATH TONIGHT?
PLACE YOUR BETS QUICKLY, TRAVELERS. I SEE LOTS OF SERIOUS CONTENDERS IN THAT ARENA. AND FOR THOSE OF YOU WHO JUST LIKE A FAT BODY COUNT...
...I SEE PLENTY OF EASY PICKINGS, TOO.
HOLY SHIT. IS THIS WHAT I THINK IT IS?
WHEN IT STARTS, FIND SOME COVER AND STAY DOWN.
GREAT. CAN I BORROW YOUR GUN?
NO.

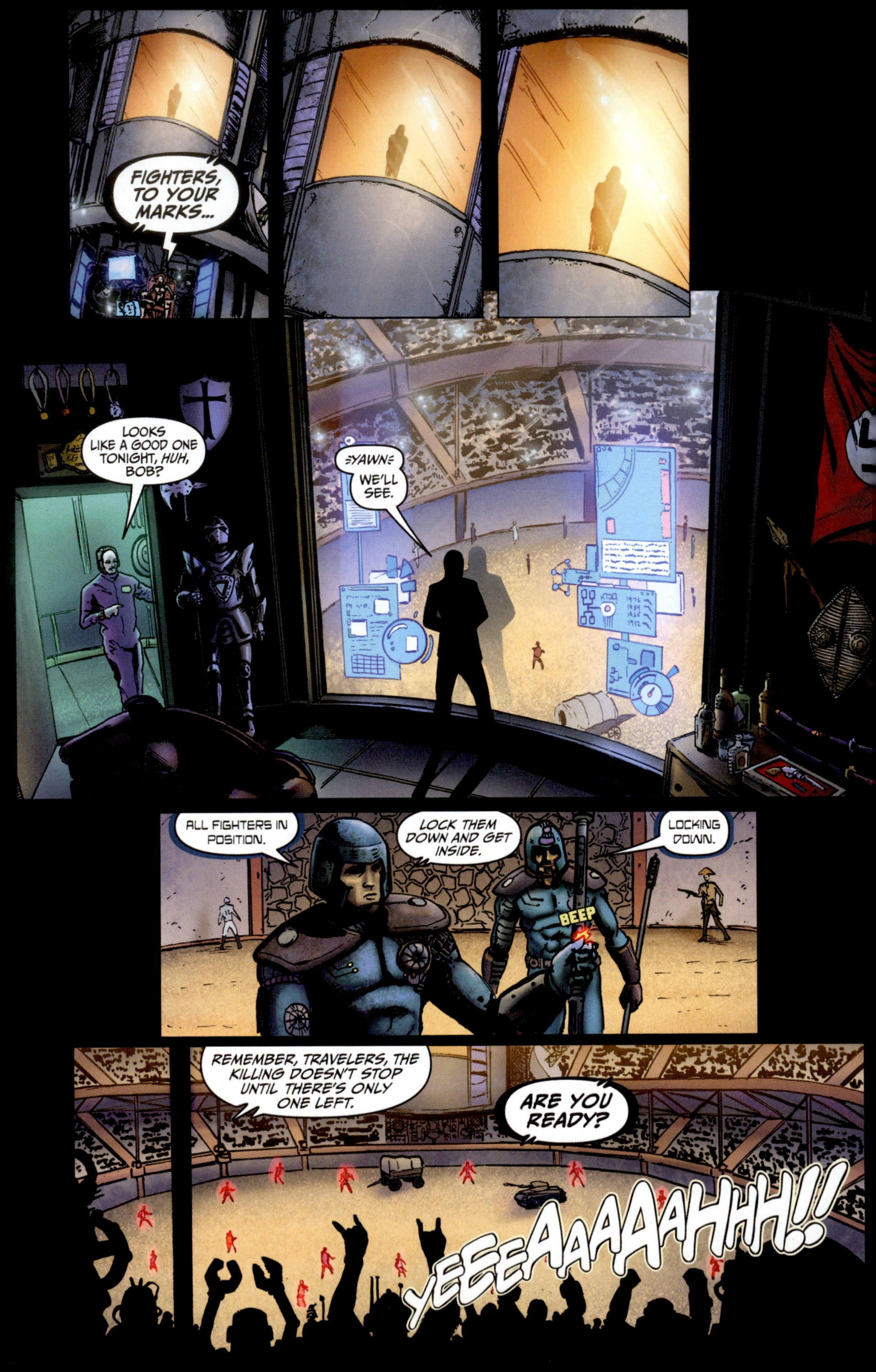
FIGHTERS, TO YOUR MARKS...
LOOKS LIKE A GOOD ONE TONIGHT, HUH, BOB?
=YAWN= WE'LL SEE.
ALL FIGHTERS IN POSITION.
LOCK THEM DOWN AND GET INSIDE.
LOCKING DOWN.
BEEP
REMEMBER, TRAVELERS, THE KILLING DOESN'T STOP UNTIL THERE'S ONLY ONE LEFT.
ARE YOU READY?
YEEEAAAAAHHH!!

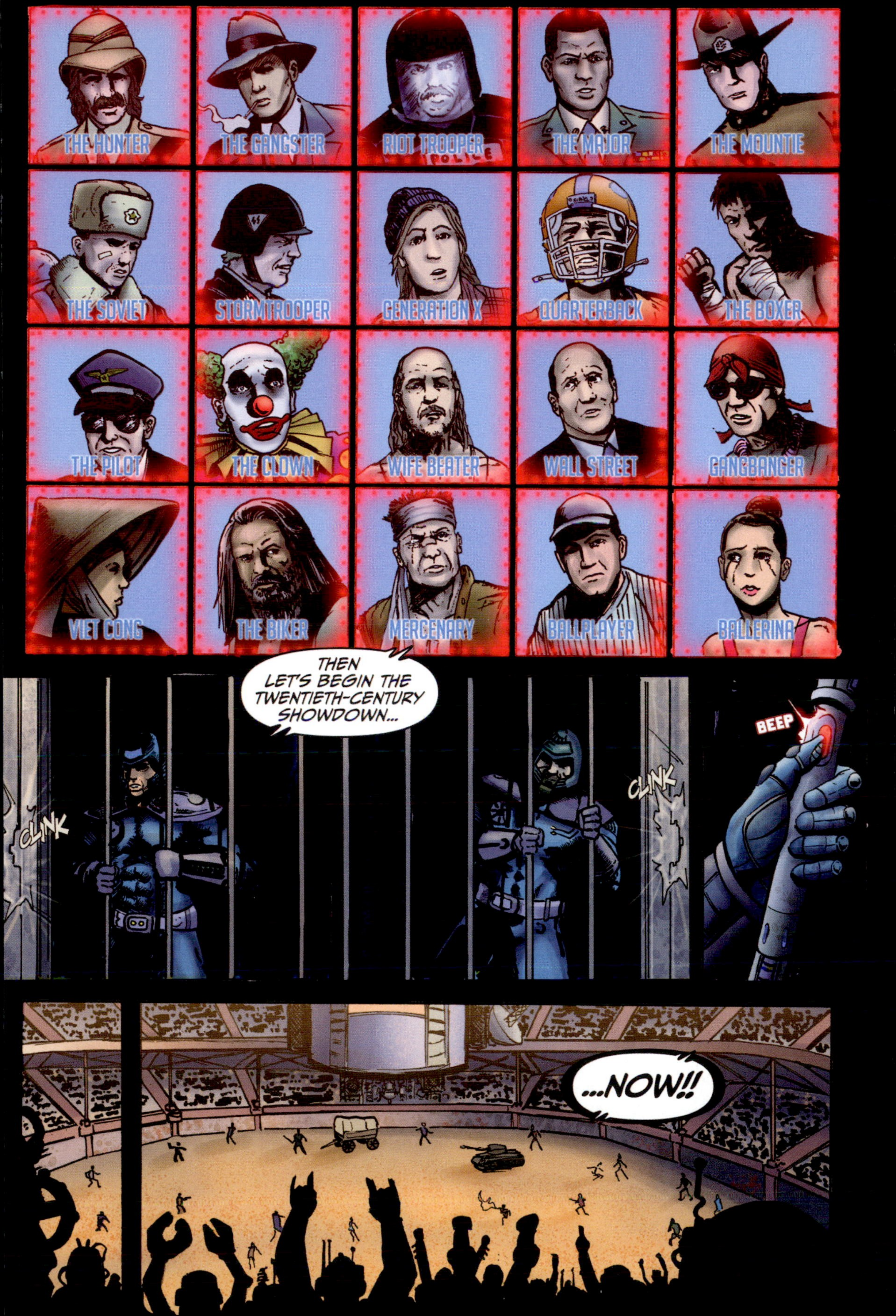
THE HUNTER
THE GANGSTER
RIOT TROOPER
POLICE
THE MAJOR
THE MOUNTIE
THE SOVIET
STORMTROOPER
GENERATION X
QUARTERBACK
THE BOXER
THE PILOT
THE CLOWN
WIFE BEATER
WALL STREET
GANGBANGER
VIET CONG
THE BIKER
MERCENARY
BALLPLAYER
BALLERINA
THEN LET'S BEGIN THE TWENTIETH-CENTURY SHOWDOWN...
CLINK
CLINK
BEEP
...NOW!!

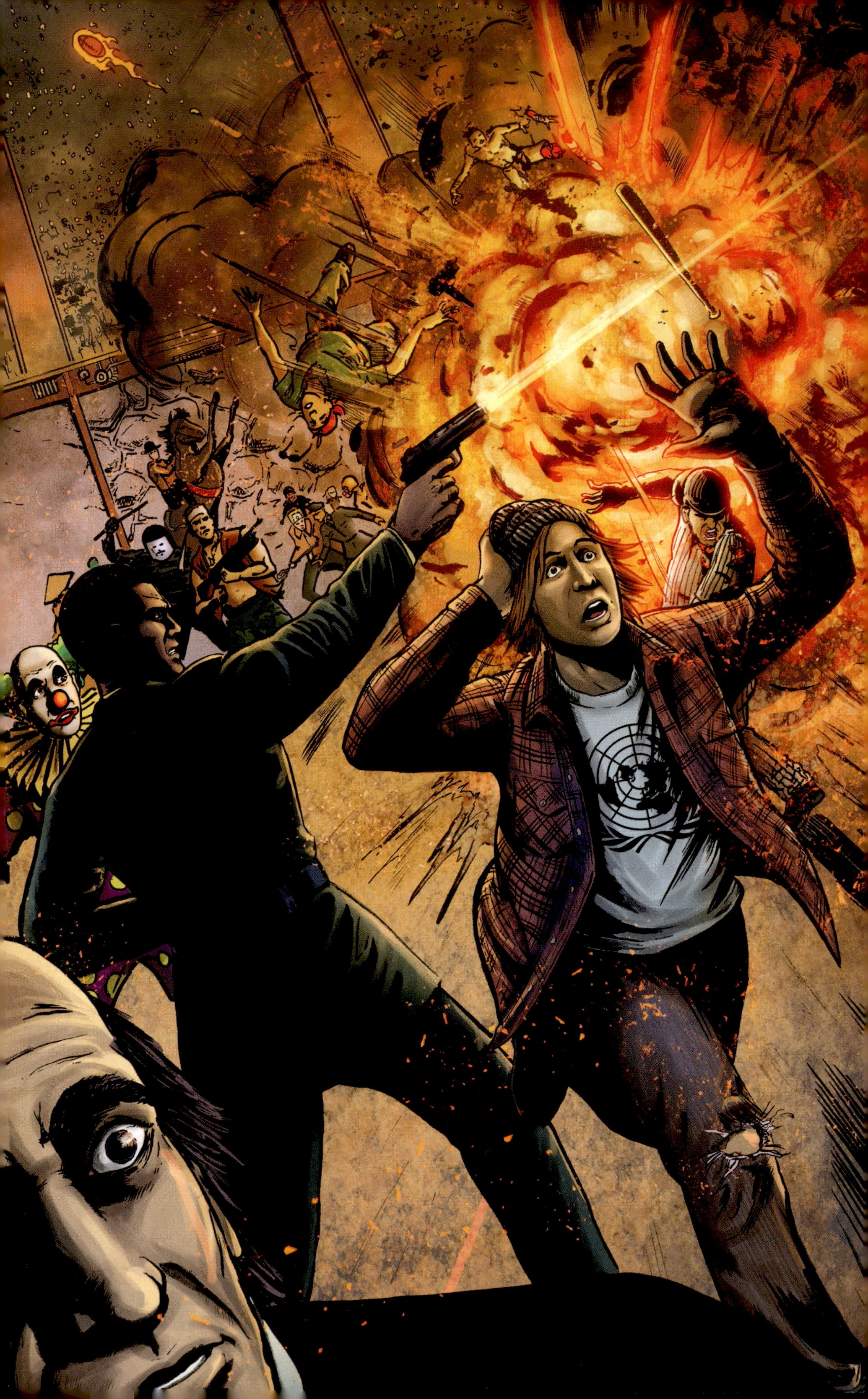

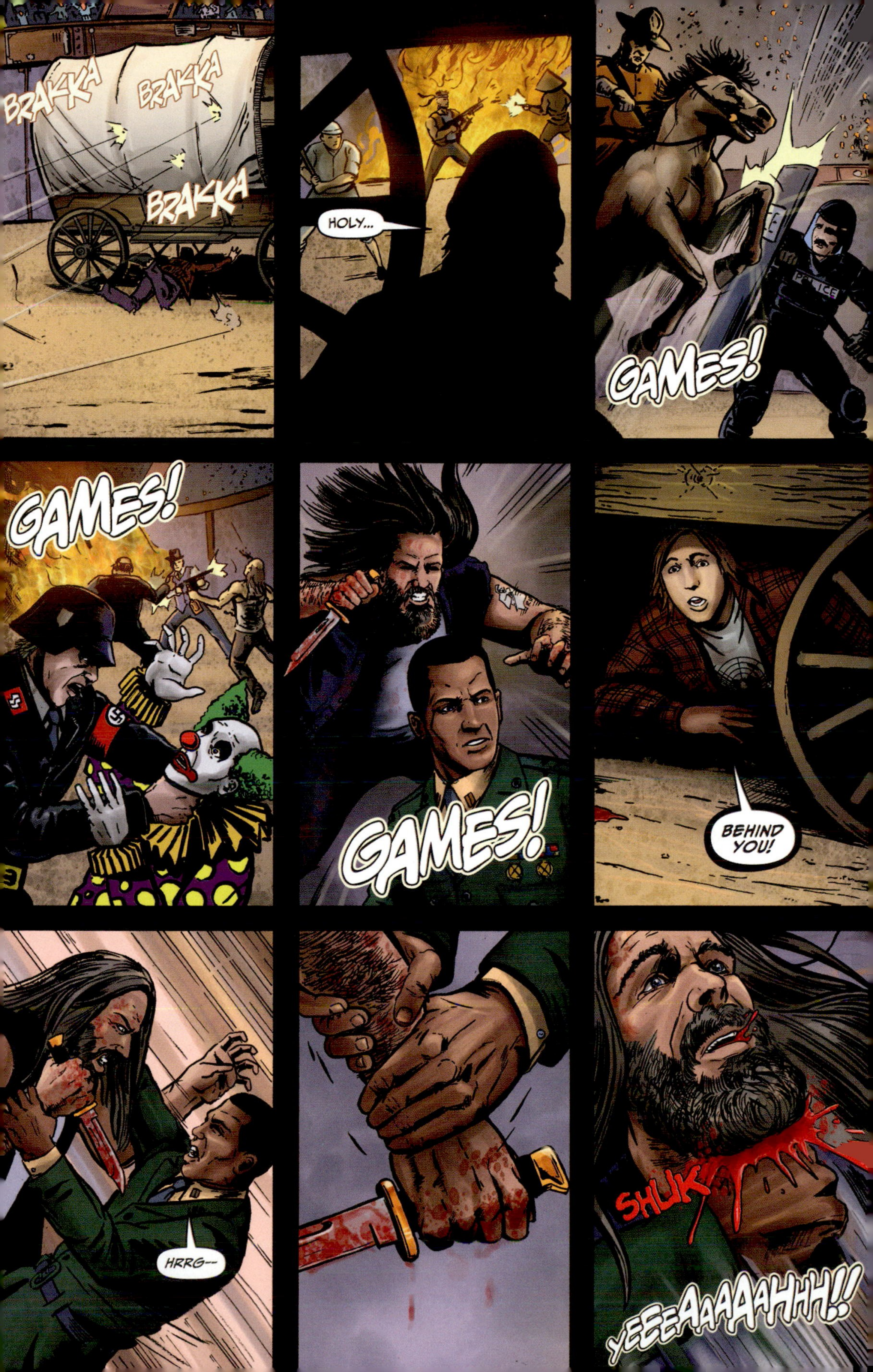
BRAKKA
BRAKKA
BRAKKA
HOLY...
GAMES!
GAMES!
GAMES!
BEHIND YOU!
HRRG--
SHUK
YEEEAAAAAHHH!!

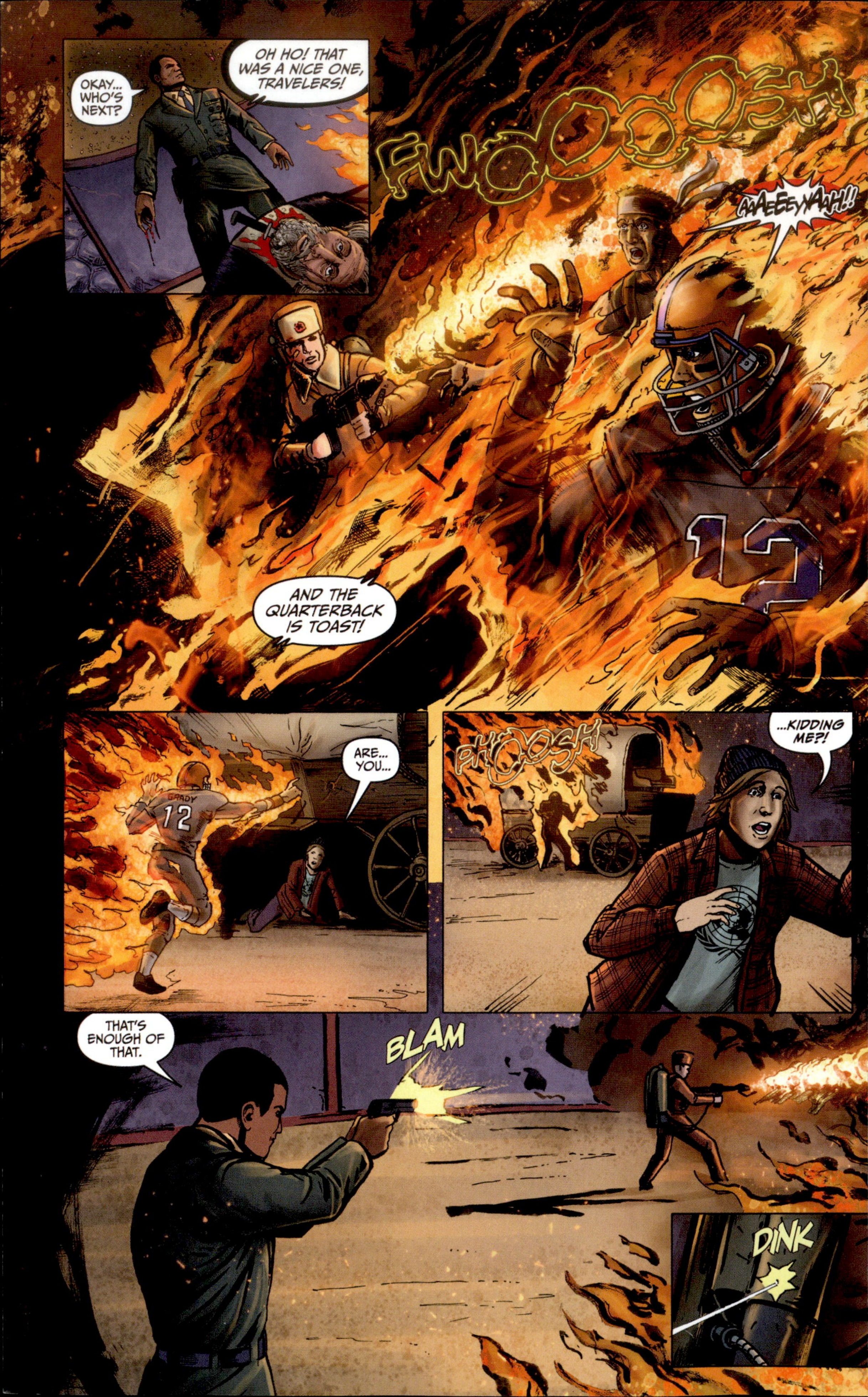
OKAY... WHO'S NEXT?
OH HO! THAT WAS A NICE ONE, TRAVELERS!
FWOOOOOSH
AAAEEEYAAH!!
AND THE QUARTERBACK IS TOAST!
BRADY
12
ARE... YOU...
PHOOSH
...KIDDING ME?!
THAT'S ENOUGH OF THAT.
BLAM
DINK

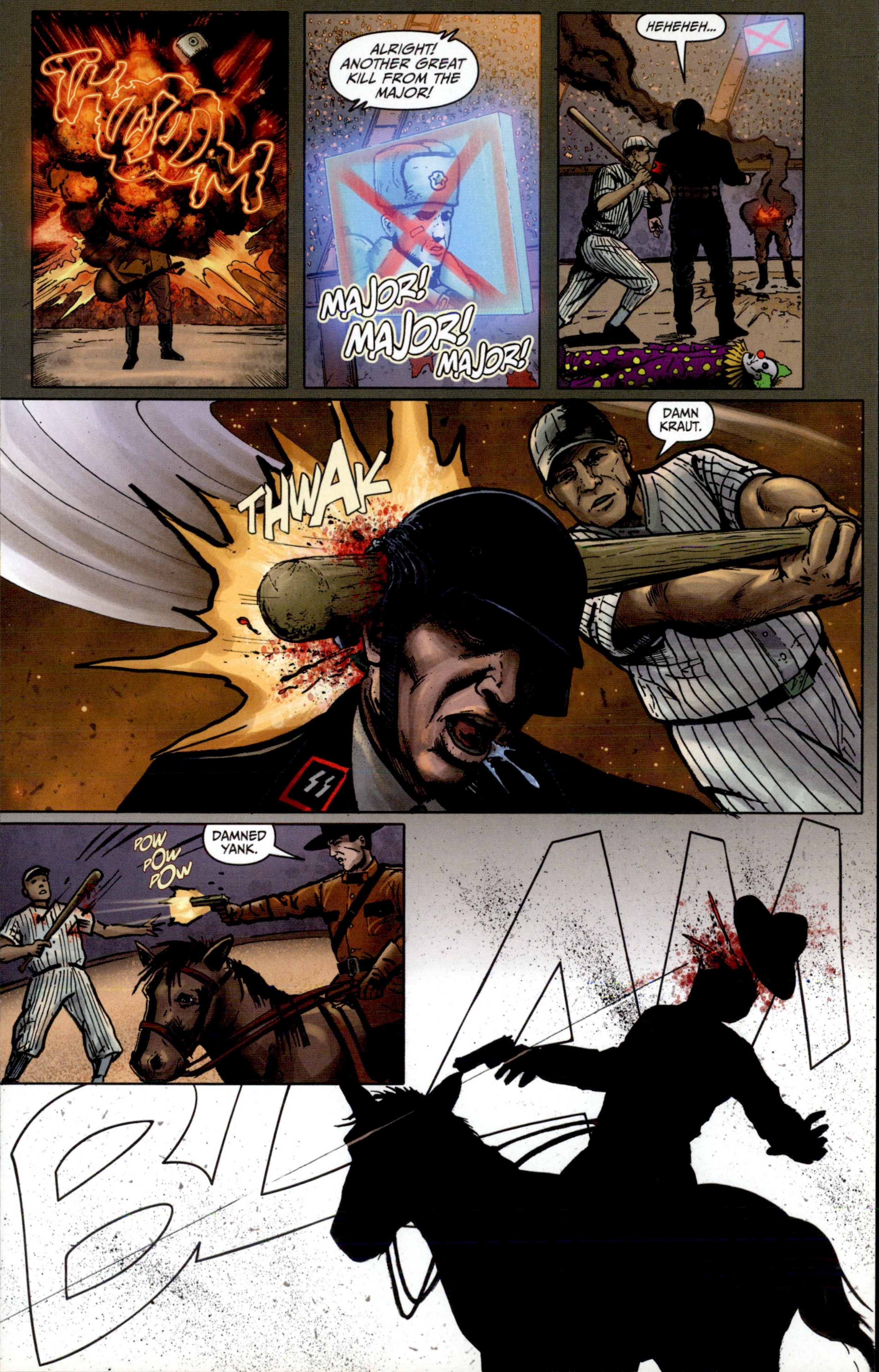
THOOM
ALRIGHT! ANOTHER GREAT KILL FROM THE MAJOR!
MAJOR! MAJOR! MAJOR!
HEHEHEH...
THWAK
DAMN KRAUT.
POW POW POW
DAMNED YANK.
BLAM

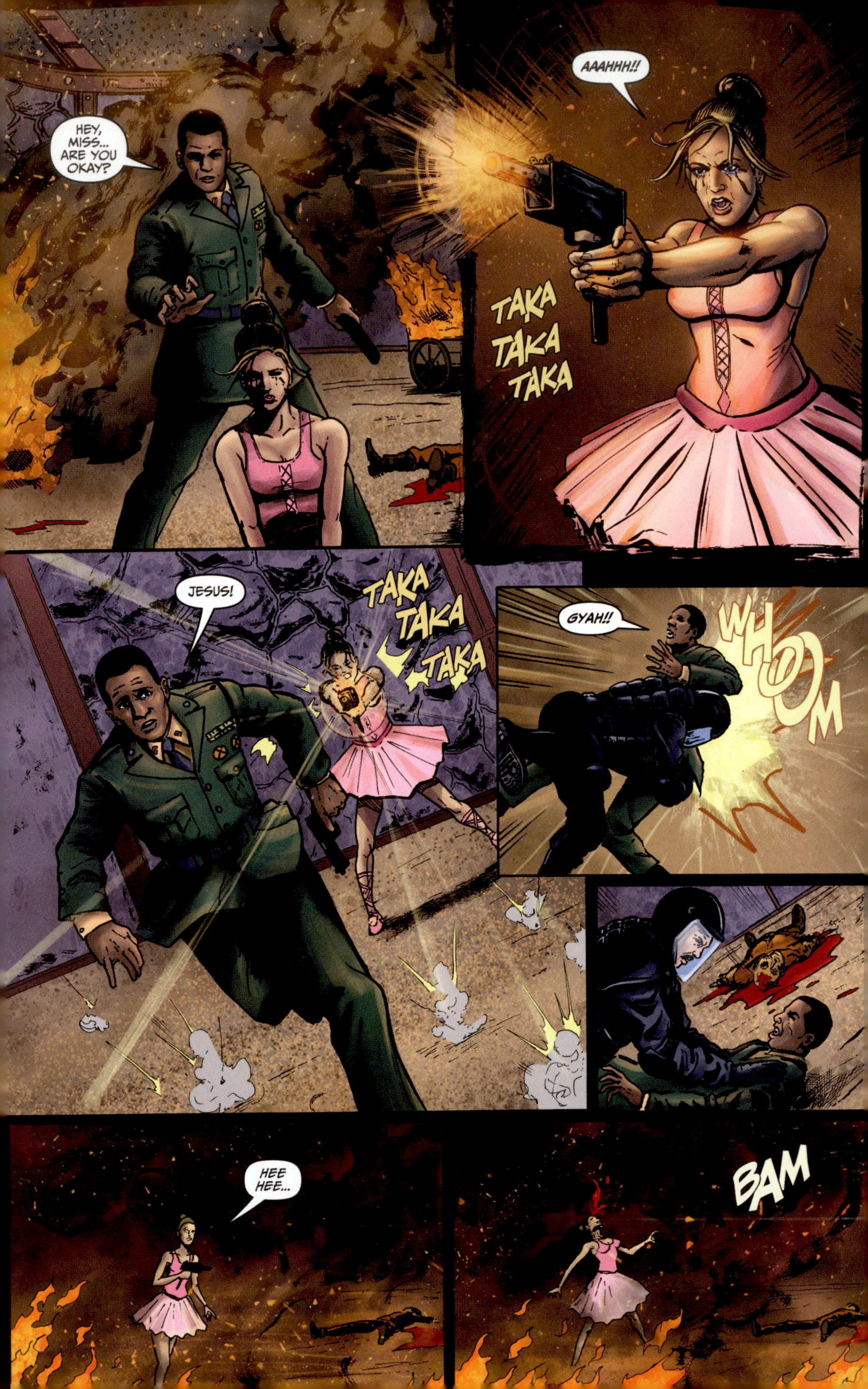
HEY, MISS... ARE YOU OKAY?
AAAHHH!!
TAKA TAKA TAKA
JESUS!
TAKA TAKA TAKA
GYAH!!
WHOOM
HEE HEE...
BAM

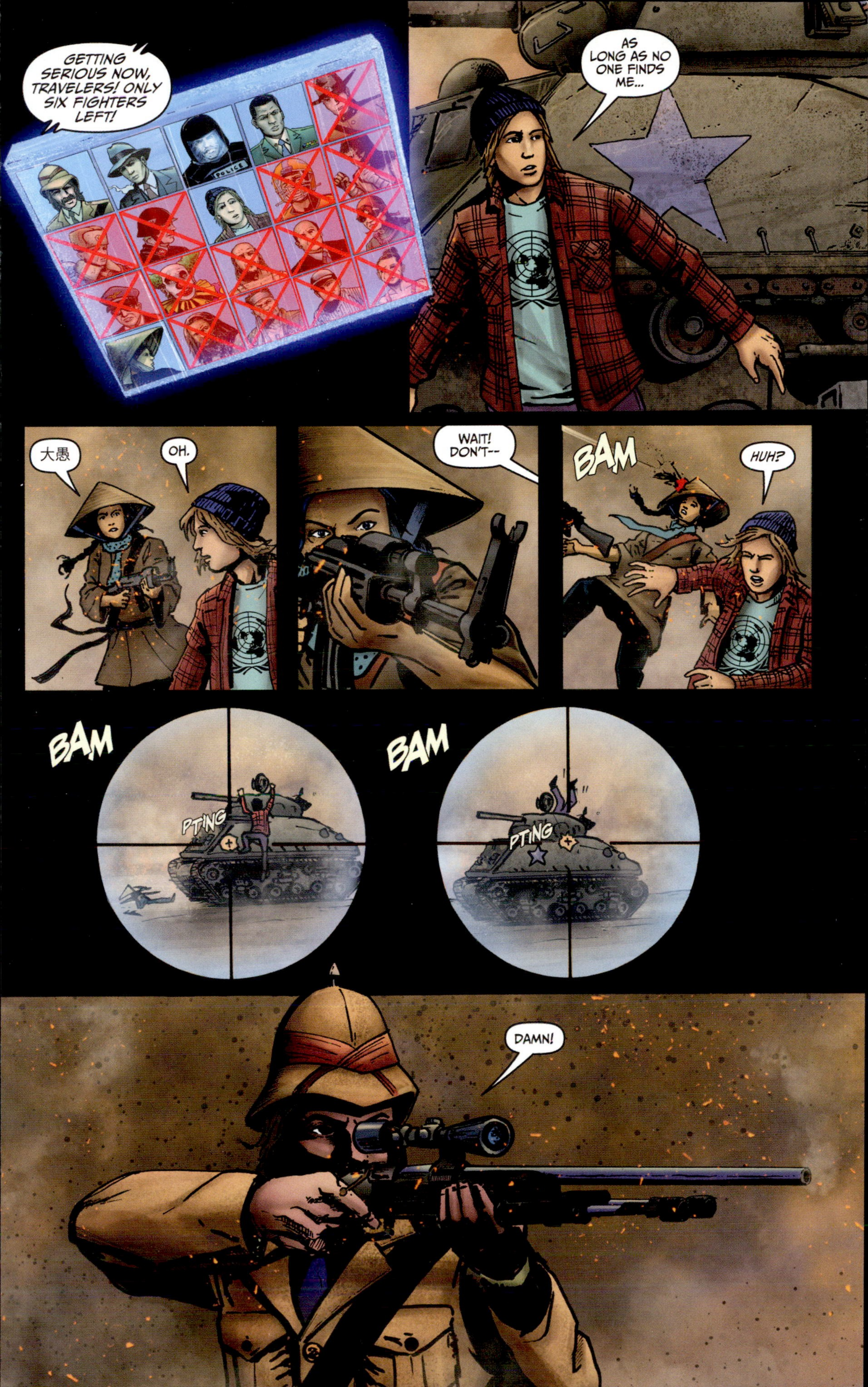
GETTING SERIOUS NOW, TRAVELERS! ONLY SIX FIGHTERS LEFT!
POLICE
AS LONG AS NO ONE FINDS ME...
大愚
OH.
WAIT! DON'T--
BAM
HUH?
BAM
PTING
BAM
PTING
DAMN!

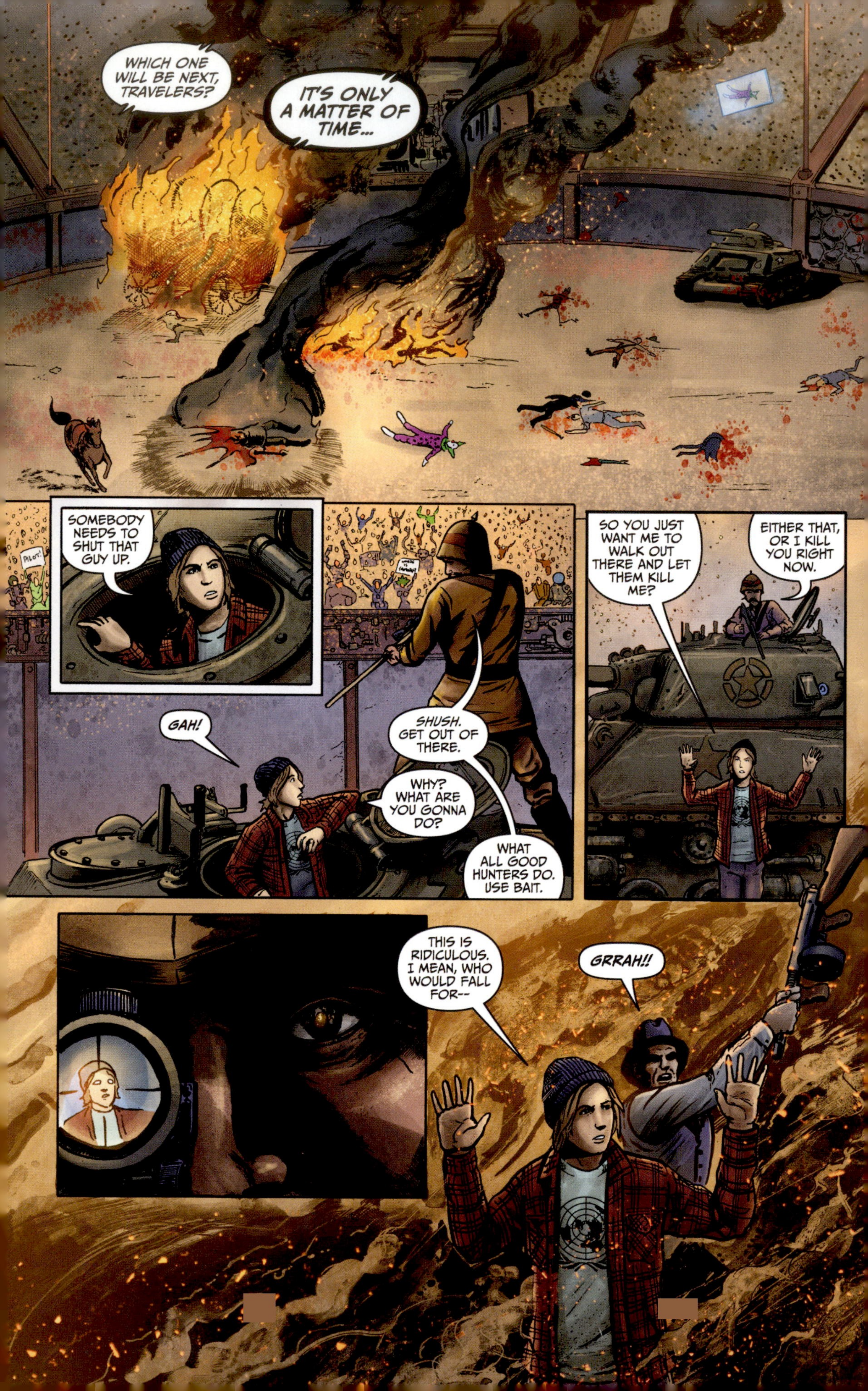
WHICH ONE WILL BE NEXT, TRAVELERS?
IT'S ONLY A MATTER OF TIME...
SOMEBODY NEEDS TO SHUT THAT GUY UP.
PILOT!
GAH!
SHUSH. GET OUT OF THERE.
WHY? WHAT ARE YOU GONNA DO?
WHAT ALL GOOD HUNTERS DO. USE BAIT.
SO YOU JUST WANT ME TO WALK OUT THERE AND LET THEM KILL ME?
EITHER THAT, OR I KILL YOU RIGHT NOW.
THIS IS RIDICULOUS. I MEAN, WHO WOULD FALL FOR--
GRRAH!!

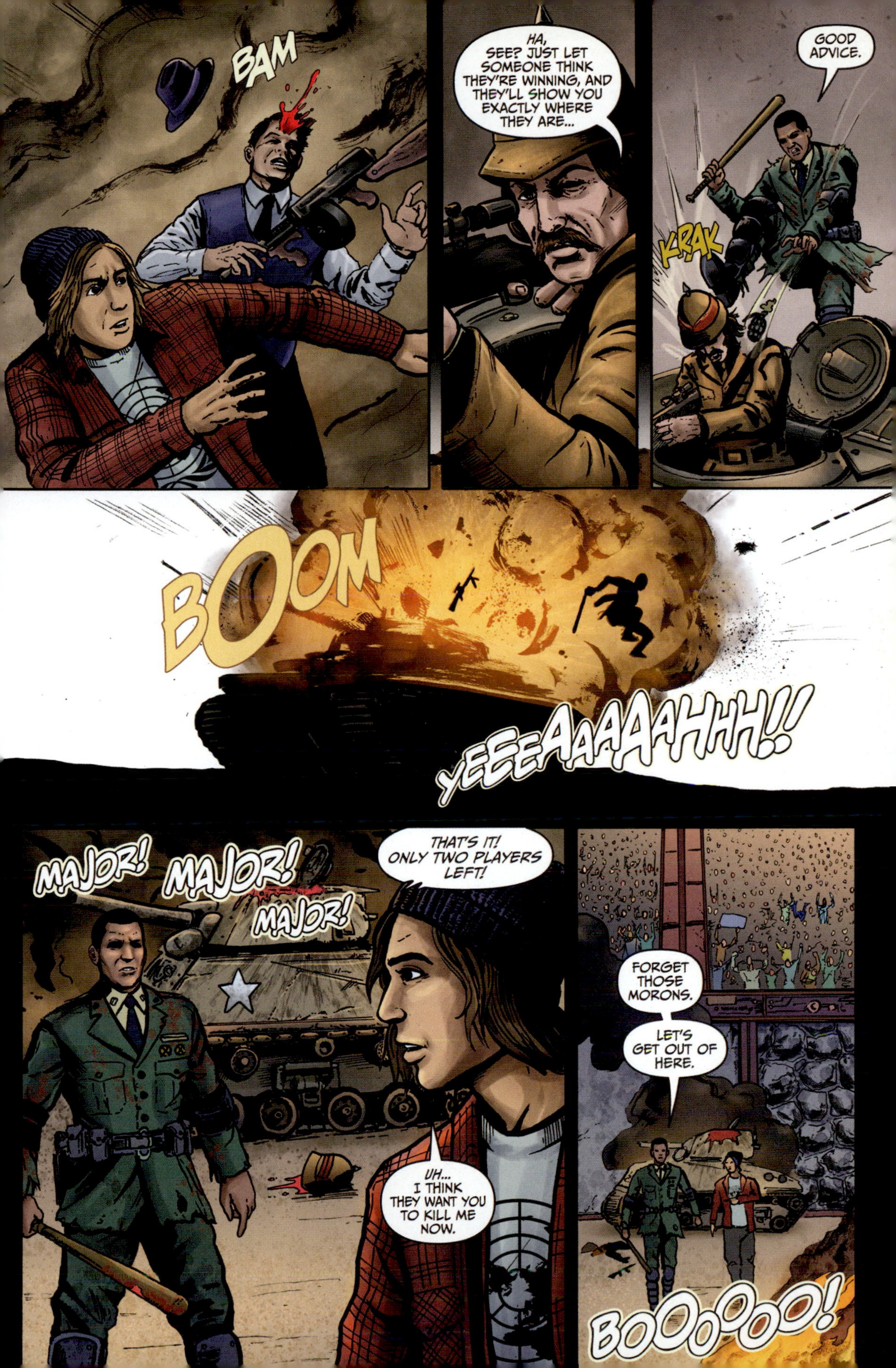
BAM
HA, SEE? JUST LET SOMEONE THINK THEY'RE WINNING, AND THEY'LL SHOW YOU EXACTLY WHERE THEY ARE...
GOOD ADVICE.
KRAK
BOOM
YEEEAAAAAHHH!!
MAJOR! MAJOR! MAJOR!
THAT'S IT! ONLY TWO PLAYERS LEFT!
UH... I THINK THEY WANT YOU TO KILL ME NOW.
FORGET THOSE MORONS.
LET'S GET OUT OF HERE.
BOOOOOOO!

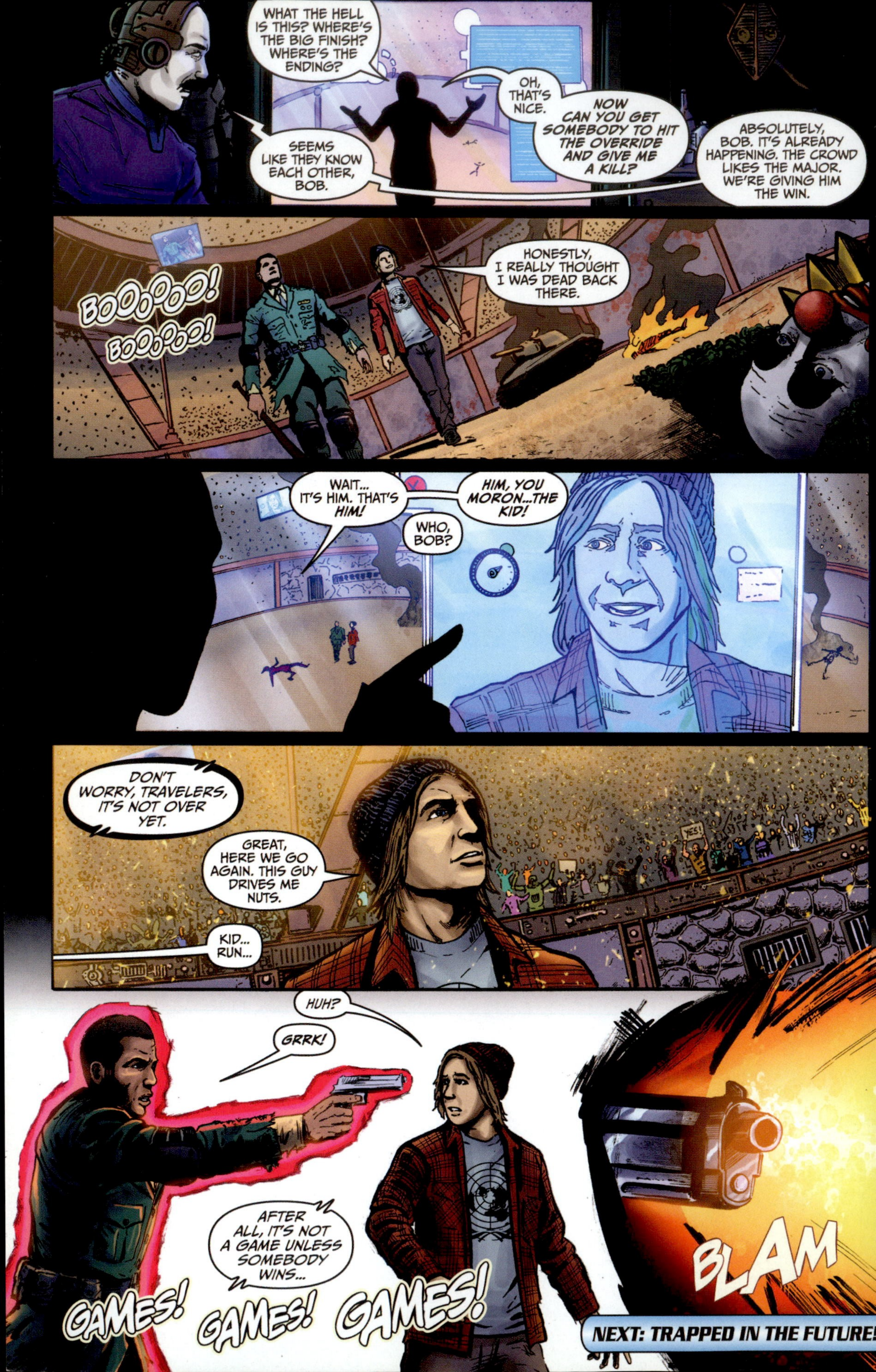
WHAT THE HELL IS THIS? WHERE'S THE BIG FINISH? WHERE'S THE ENDING?
OH, THAT'S NICE.
SEEMS LIKE THEY KNOW EACH OTHER, BOB.
NOW CAN YOU GET SOMEBODY TO HIT THE OVERRIDE AND GIVE ME A KILL?
ABSOLUTELY, BOB. IT'S ALREADY HAPPENING. THE CROWD LIKES THE MAJOR. WE'RE GIVING HIM THE WIN.
BOOOOOO!
BOOOOO!
HONESTLY, I REALLY THOUGHT I WAS DEAD BACK THERE.
WAIT... IT'S HIM. THAT'S HIM!
WHO, BOB?
HIM, YOU MORON...THE KID!
DON'T WORRY, TRAVELERS, IT'S NOT OVER YET.
GREAT, HERE WE GO AGAIN. THIS GUY DRIVES ME NUTS.
KID... RUN...
HUH?
GRRK!
AFTER ALL, IT'S NOT A GAME UNLESS SOMEBODY WINS...
GAMES! GAMES! GAMES!
BLAM
NEXT: TRAPPED IN THE FUTURE!

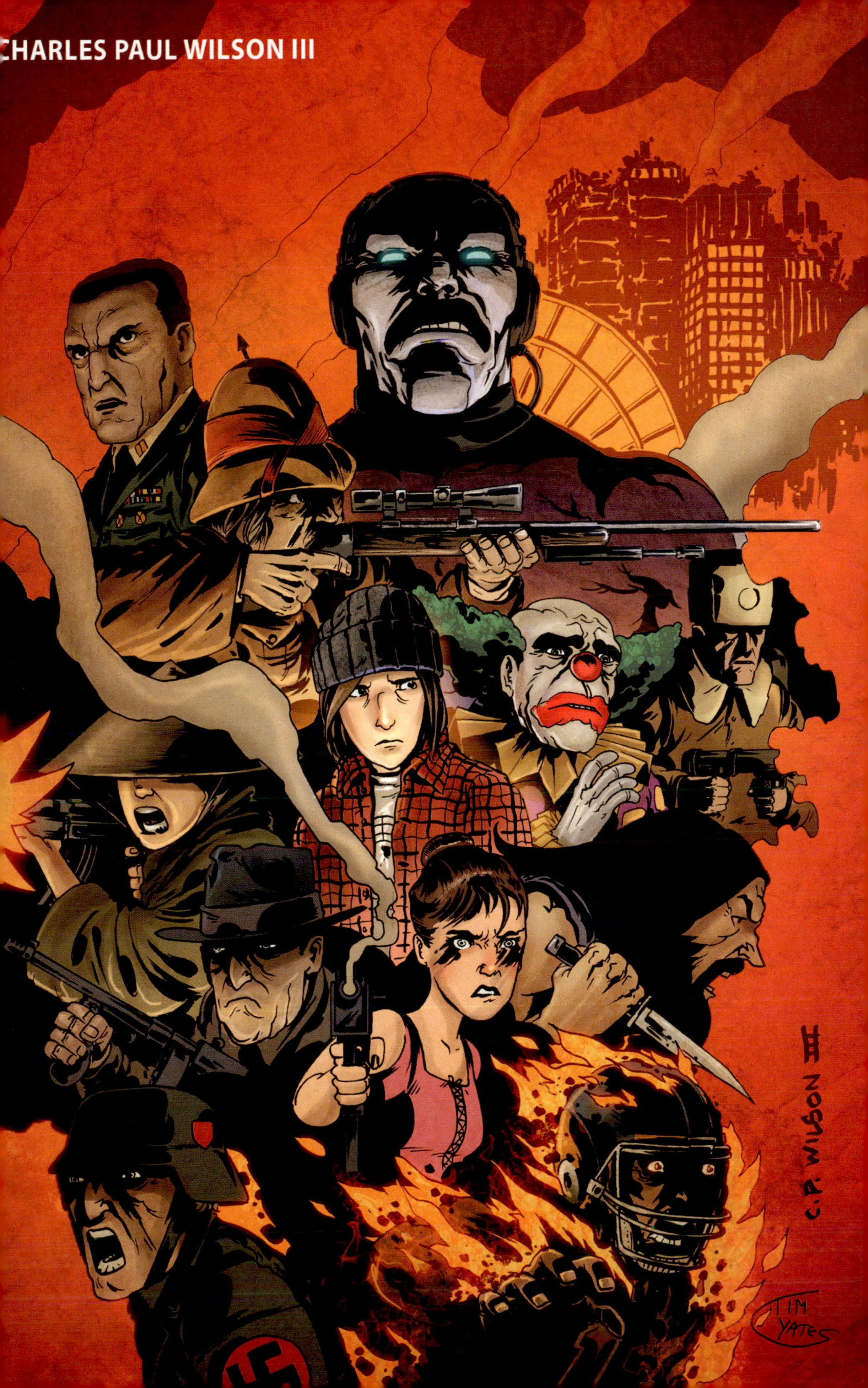
CHARLES PAUL WILSON III
C.P. WILSON III
TIM YATES

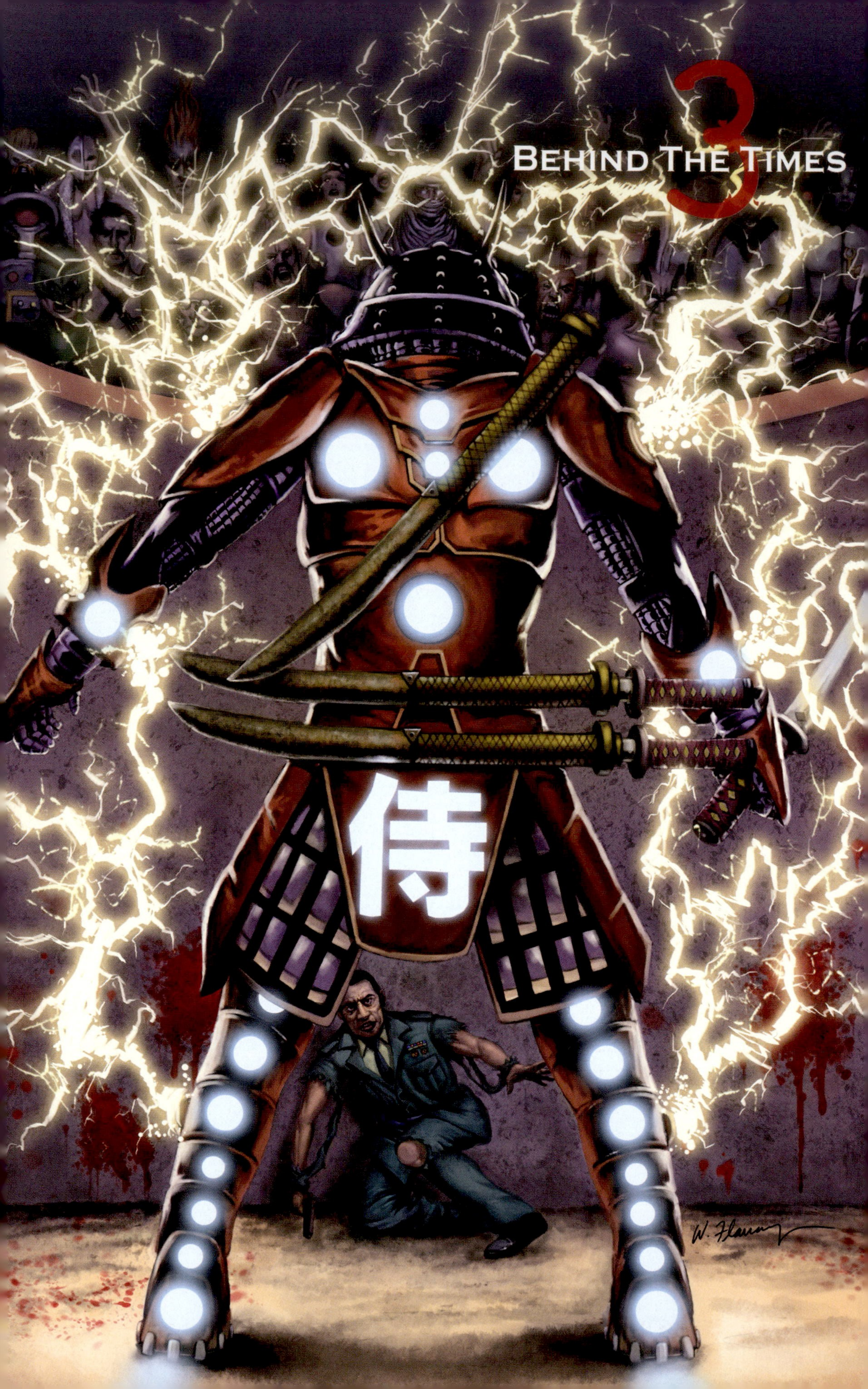
3
BEHIND THE TIMES
侍
W. Flauraa

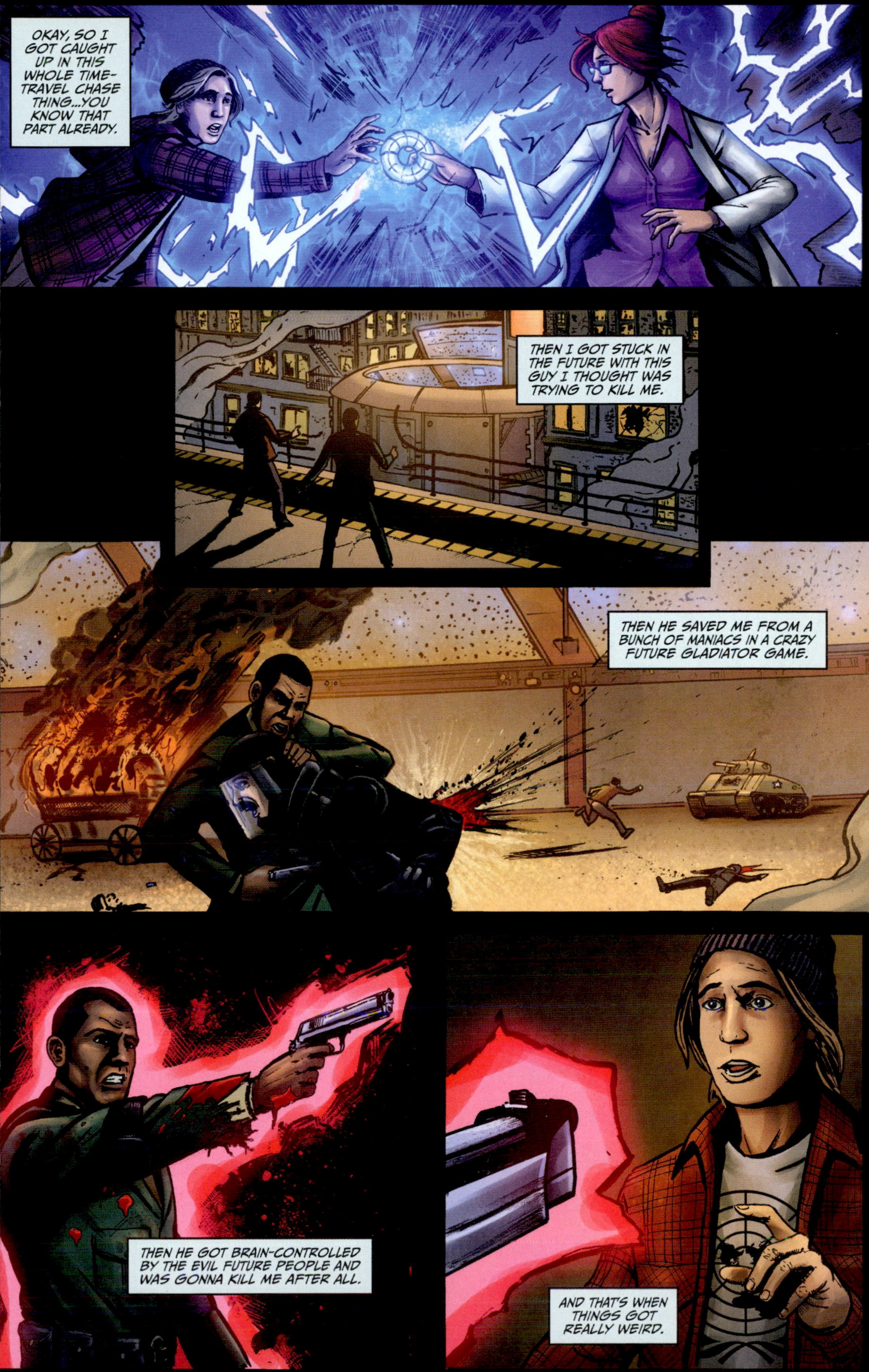
OKAY, SO I GOT CAUGHT UP IN THIS WHOLE TIME-TRAVEL CHASE THING...YOU KNOW THAT PART ALREADY.
THEN I GOT STUCK IN THE FUTURE WITH THIS GUY I THOUGHT WAS TRYING TO KILL ME.
THEN HE SAVED ME FROM A BUNCH OF MANIACS IN A CRAZY FUTURE GLADIATOR GAME.
THEN HE GOT BRAIN-CONTROLLED BY THE EVIL FUTURE PEOPLE AND WAS GONNA KILL ME AFTER ALL.
AND THAT'S WHEN THINGS GOT REALLY WEIRD.

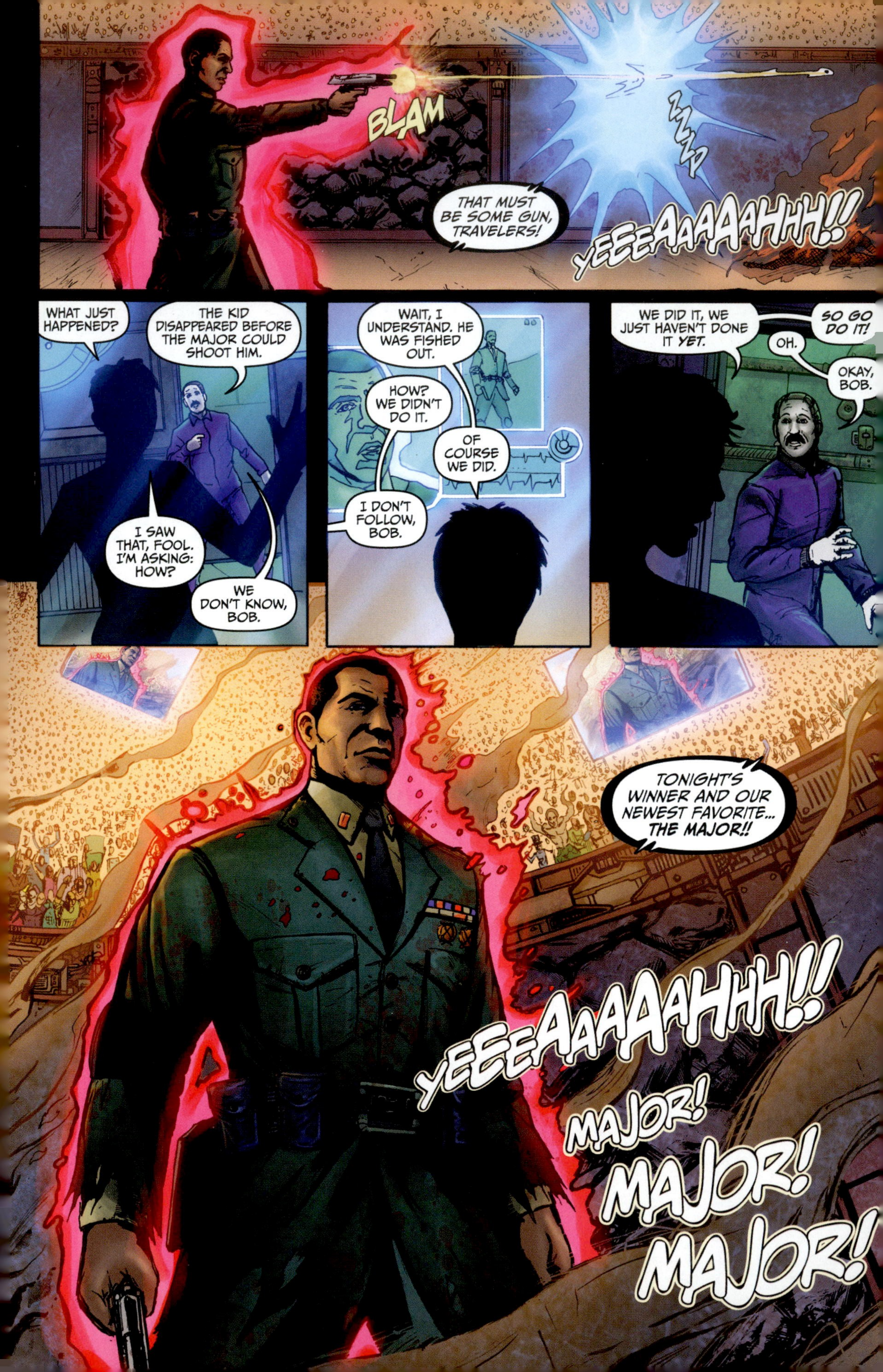
BLAM
ZZZZ
THAT MUST BE SOME GUN, TRAVELERS!
YEEEAAAAAHHH!!
WHAT JUST HAPPENED?
THE KID DISAPPEARED BEFORE THE MAJOR COULD SHOOT HIM.
I SAW THAT, FOOL. I'M ASKING: HOW?
WE DON'T KNOW, BOB.
WAIT, I UNDERSTAND. HE WAS FISHED OUT.
HOW? WE DIDN'T DO IT.
OF COURSE WE DID.
I DON'T FOLLOW, BOB.
WE DID IT, WE JUST HAVEN'T DONE IT YET.
OH.
SO GO DO IT!
OKAY, BOB.
TONIGHT'S WINNER AND OUR NEWEST FAVORITE... THE MAJOR!!
YEEEAAAAAHHH!!
MAJOR!
MAJOR!
MAJOR!

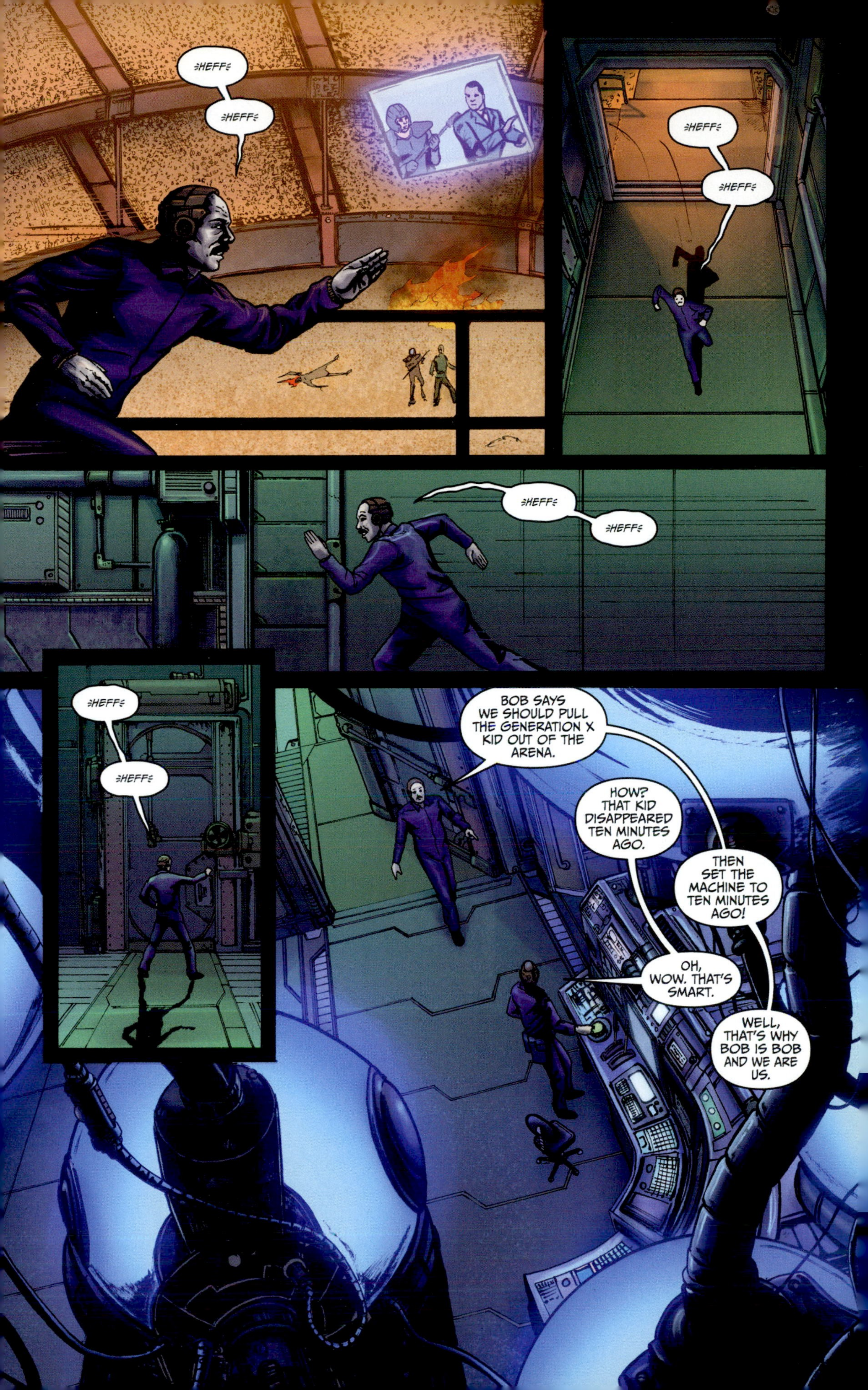

HEFF
HEFF
HEFF
HEFF
HEFF
HEFF
HEFF
HEFF
BOB SAYS WE SHOULD PULL THE GENERATION X KID OUT OF THE ARENA.
HOW? THAT KID DISAPPEARED TEN MINUTES AGO.
THEN SET THE MACHINE TO TEN MINUTES AGO!
OH, WOW. THAT'S SMART.
WELL, THAT'S WHY BOB IS BOB AND WE ARE US.

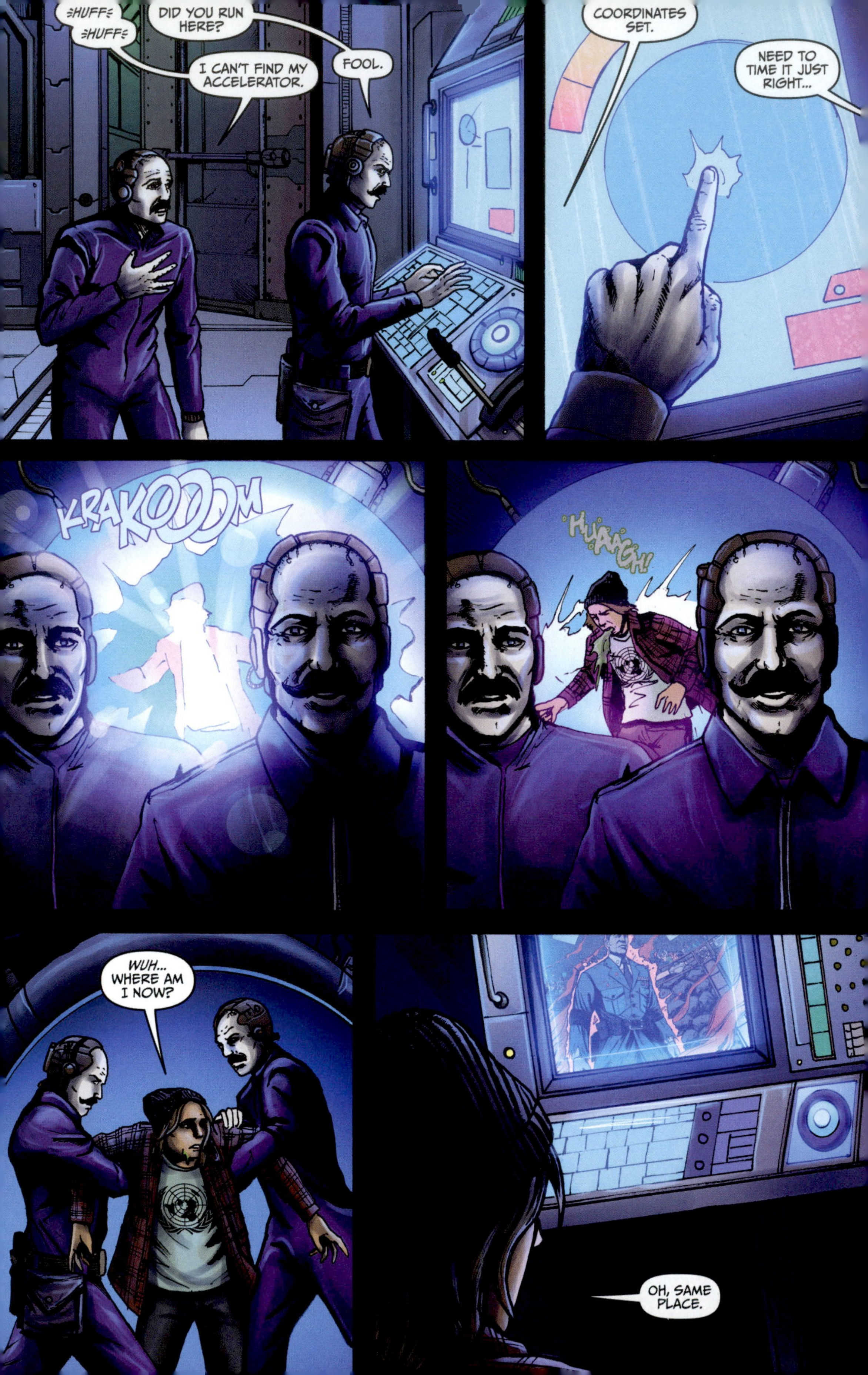
HUFF
HUFF
DID YOU RUN HERE?
I CAN'T FIND MY ACCELERATOR.
FOOL.
COORDINATES SET.
NEED TO TIME IT JUST RIGHT...
KRAKOOOOM
HUAAAGH!
WUH... WHERE AM I NOW?
OH, SAME PLACE.

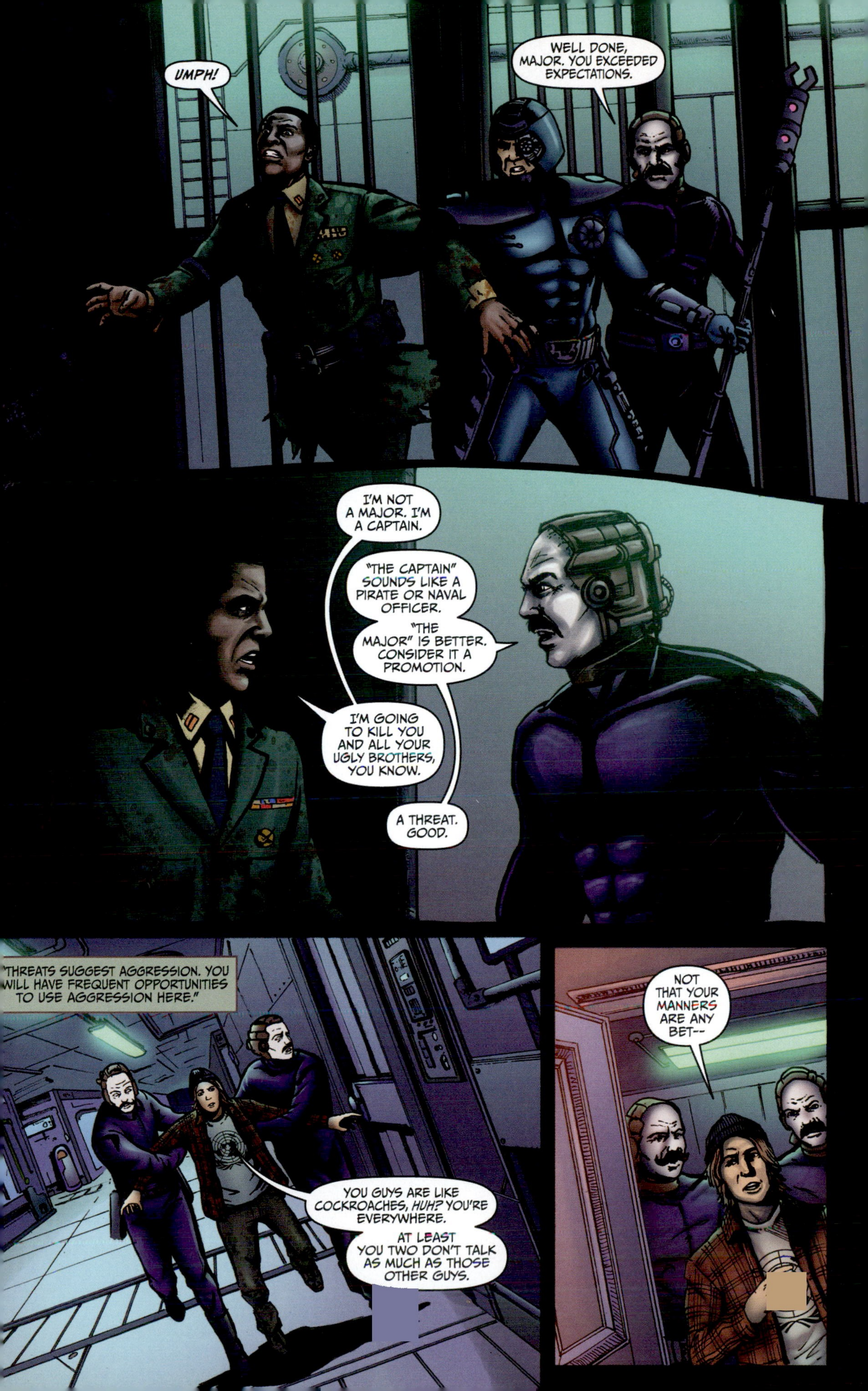
UMPH!
WELL DONE, MAJOR. YOU EXCEEDED EXPECTATIONS.
I'M NOT A MAJOR. I'M A CAPTAIN.
"THE CAPTAIN" SOUNDS LIKE A PIRATE OR NAVAL OFFICER.
"THE MAJOR" IS BETTER. CONSIDER IT A PROMOTION.
I'M GOING TO KILL YOU AND ALL YOUR UGLY BROTHERS, YOU KNOW.
A THREAT. GOOD.
"THREATS SUGGEST AGGRESSION. YOU WILL HAVE FREQUENT OPPORTUNITIES TO USE AGGRESSION HERE."
YOU GUYS ARE LIKE COCKROACHES, HUH? YOU'RE EVERYWHERE.
AT LEAST YOU TWO DON'T TALK AS MUCH AS THOSE OTHER GUYS.
NOT THAT YOUR MANNERS ARE ANY BET--

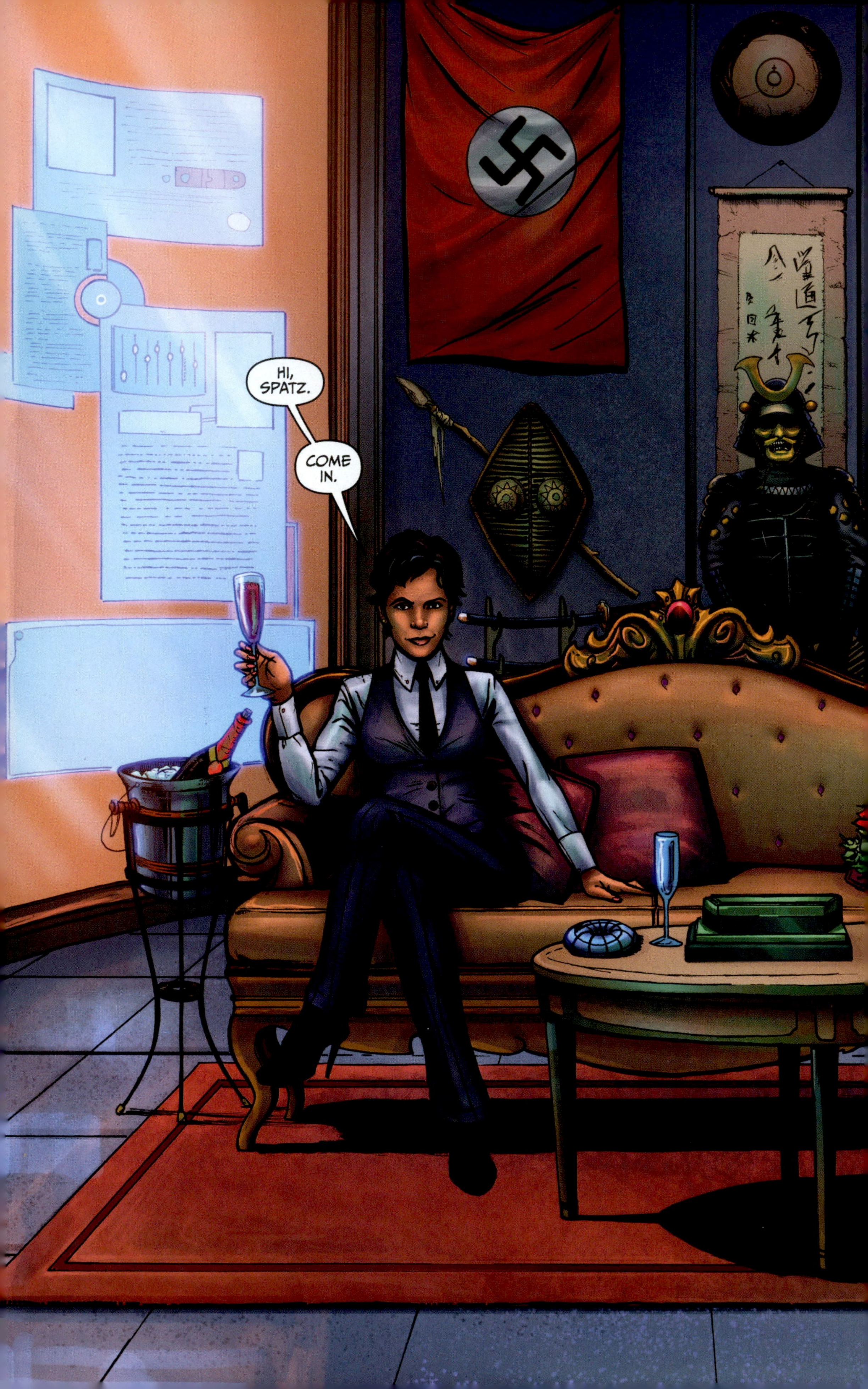
HI, SPATZ.
COME IN.

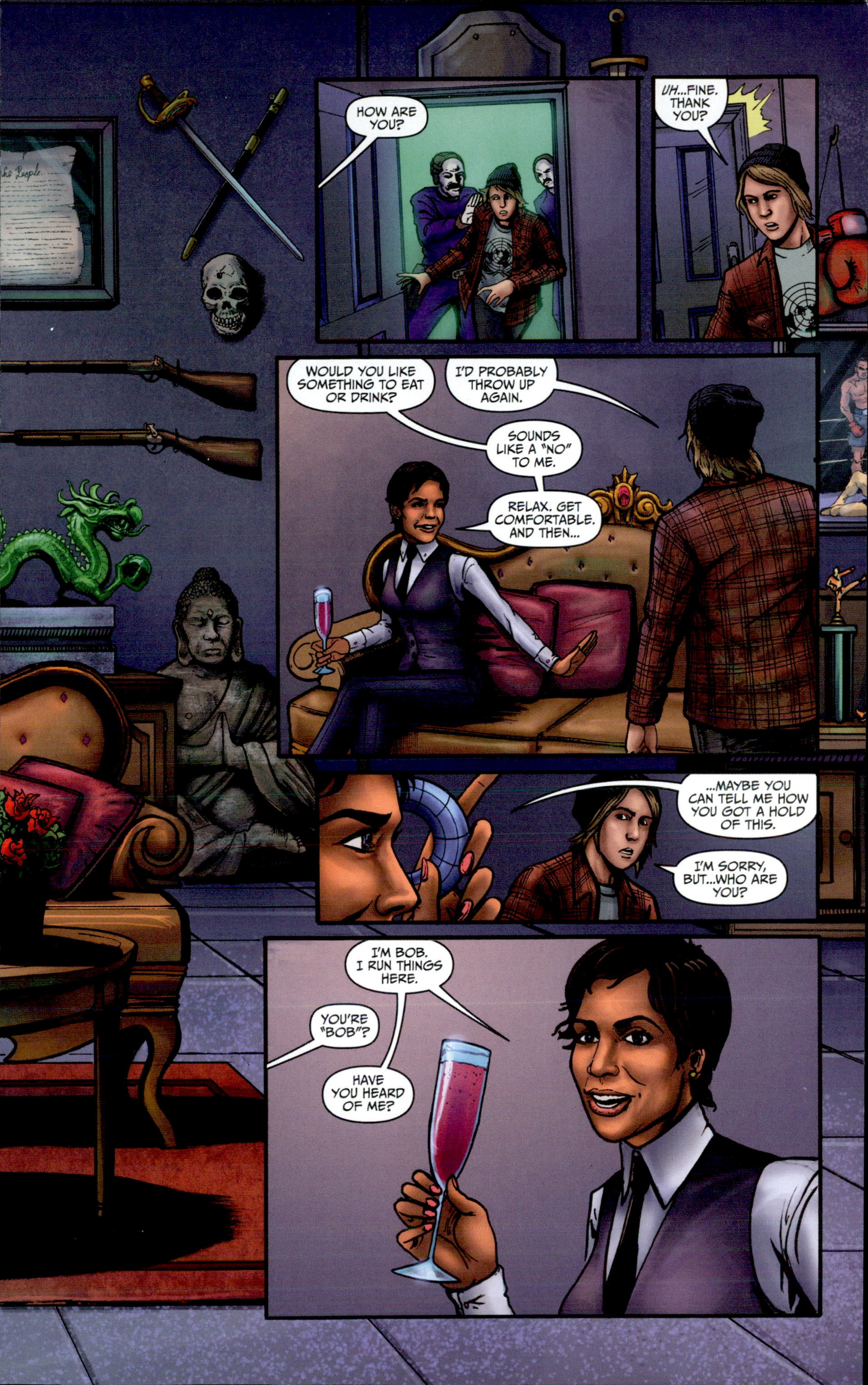
HOW ARE YOU?
UH...FINE. THANK YOU?
WOULD YOU LIKE SOMETHING TO EAT OR DRINK?
I'D PROBABLY THROW UP AGAIN.
SOUNDS LIKE A "NO" TO ME.
RELAX. GET COMFORTABLE. AND THEN...
...MAYBE YOU CAN TELL ME HOW YOU GOT A HOLD OF THIS.
I'M SORRY, BUT...WHO ARE YOU?
I'M BOB. I RUN THINGS HERE.
YOU'RE "BOB"?
HAVE YOU HEARD OF ME?

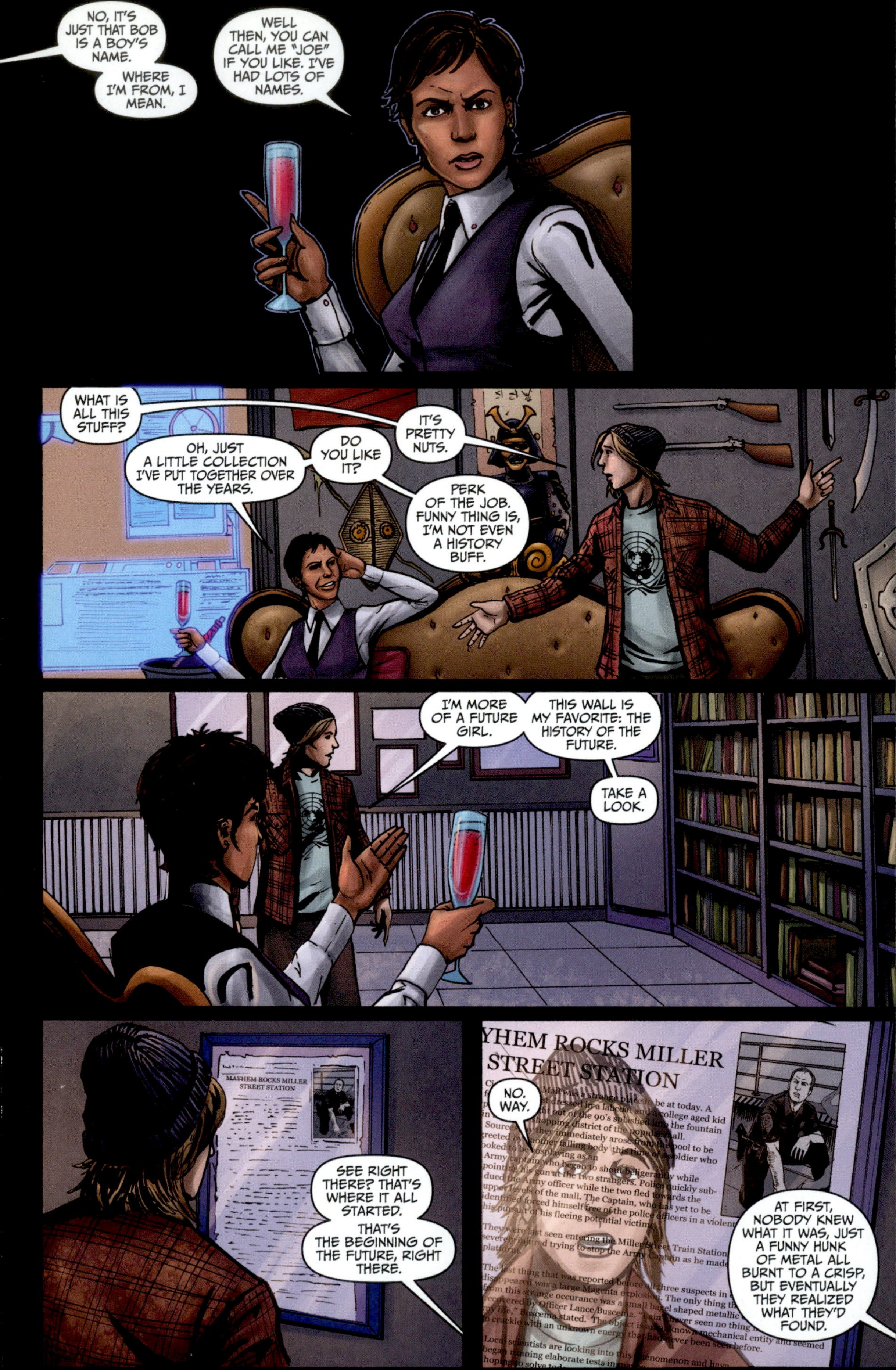
NO, IT'S JUST THAT BOB IS A BOY'S NAME.
WHERE I'M FROM, I MEAN.
WELL THEN, YOU CAN CALL ME "JOE" IF YOU LIKE. I'VE HAD LOTS OF NAMES.
WHAT IS ALL THIS STUFF?
OH, JUST A LITTLE COLLECTION I'VE PUT TOGETHER OVER THE YEARS.
DO YOU LIKE IT?
IT'S PRETTY NUTS.
PERK OF THE JOB. FUNNY THING IS, I'M NOT EVEN A HISTORY BUFF.
I'M MORE OF A FUTURE GIRL.
THIS WALL IS MY FAVORITE: THE HISTORY OF THE FUTURE.
TAKE A LOOK.
MAYHEM ROCKS MILLER STREET STATION
SEE RIGHT THERE? THAT'S WHERE IT ALL STARTED.
THAT'S THE BEGINNING OF THE FUTURE, RIGHT THERE.
YHEM ROCKS MILLER STREET STATION
NO. WAY.
AT FIRST, NOBODY KNEW WHAT IT WAS, JUST A FUNNY HUNK OF METAL ALL BURNT TO A CRISP, BUT EVENTUALLY THEY REALIZED WHAT THEY'D FOUND.

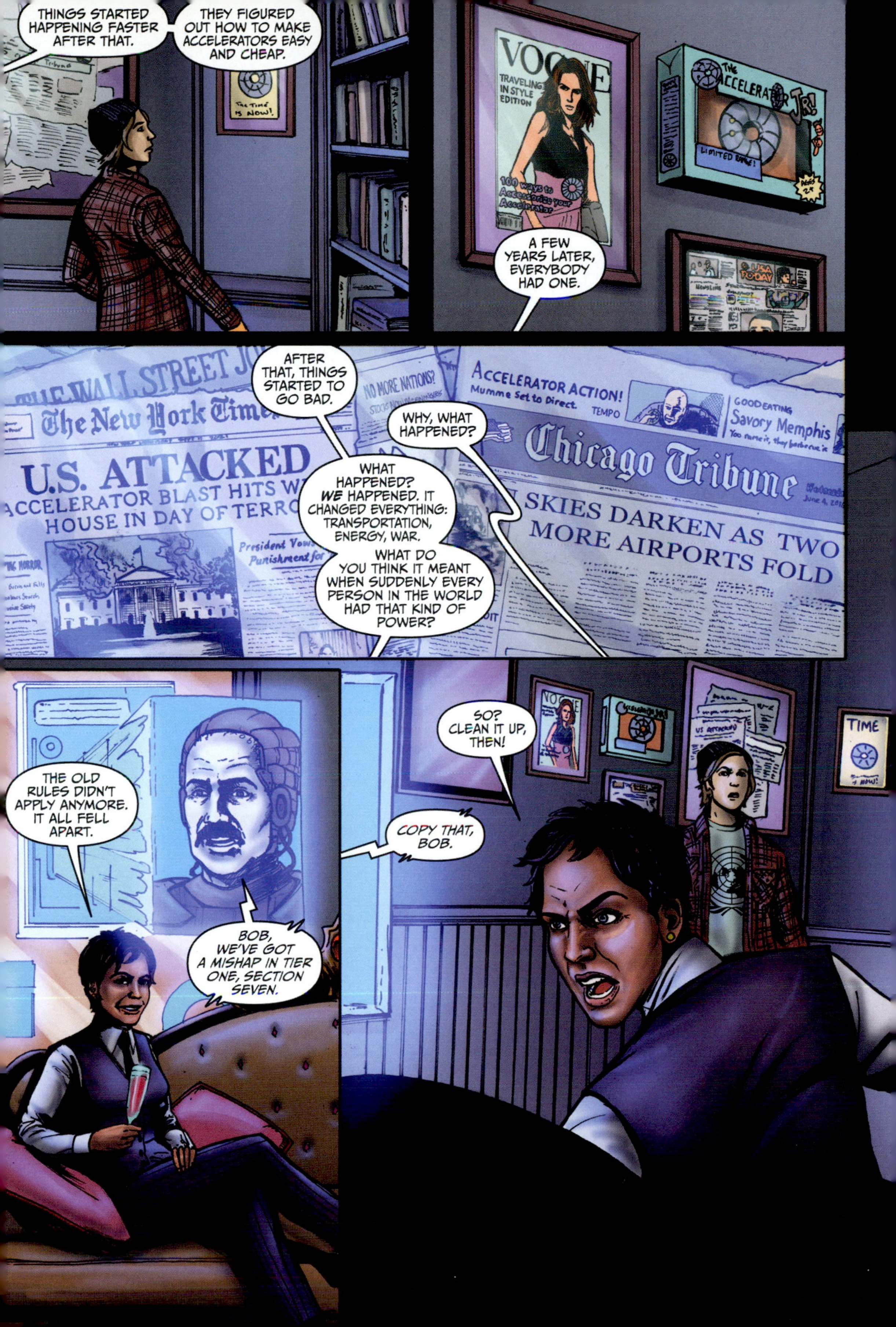
THINGS STARTED HAPPENING FASTER AFTER THAT.
THEY FIGURED OUT HOW TO MAKE ACCELERATORS EASY AND CHEAP.
A FEW YEARS LATER, EVERYBODY HAD ONE.
AFTER THAT, THINGS STARTED TO GO BAD.
WHY, WHAT HAPPENED?
WHAT HAPPENED? WE HAPPENED. IT CHANGED EVERYTHING: TRANSPORTATION, ENERGY, WAR.
WHAT DO YOU THINK IT MEANT WHEN SUDDENLY EVERY PERSON IN THE WORLD HAD THAT KIND OF POWER?
The New York Times
U.S. ATTACKED
ACCELERATOR BLAST HITS W
HOUSE IN DAY OF TERRO
Chicago Tribune
SKIES DARKEN AS TWO MORE AIRPORTS FOLD
ACCELERATOR ACTION!
Savory Memphis
THE OLD RULES DIDN'T APPLY ANYMORE. IT ALL FELL APART.
BOB, WE'VE GOT A MISHAP IN TIER ONE, SECTION SEVEN.
COPY THAT, BOB.
SO? CLEAN IT UP, THEN!

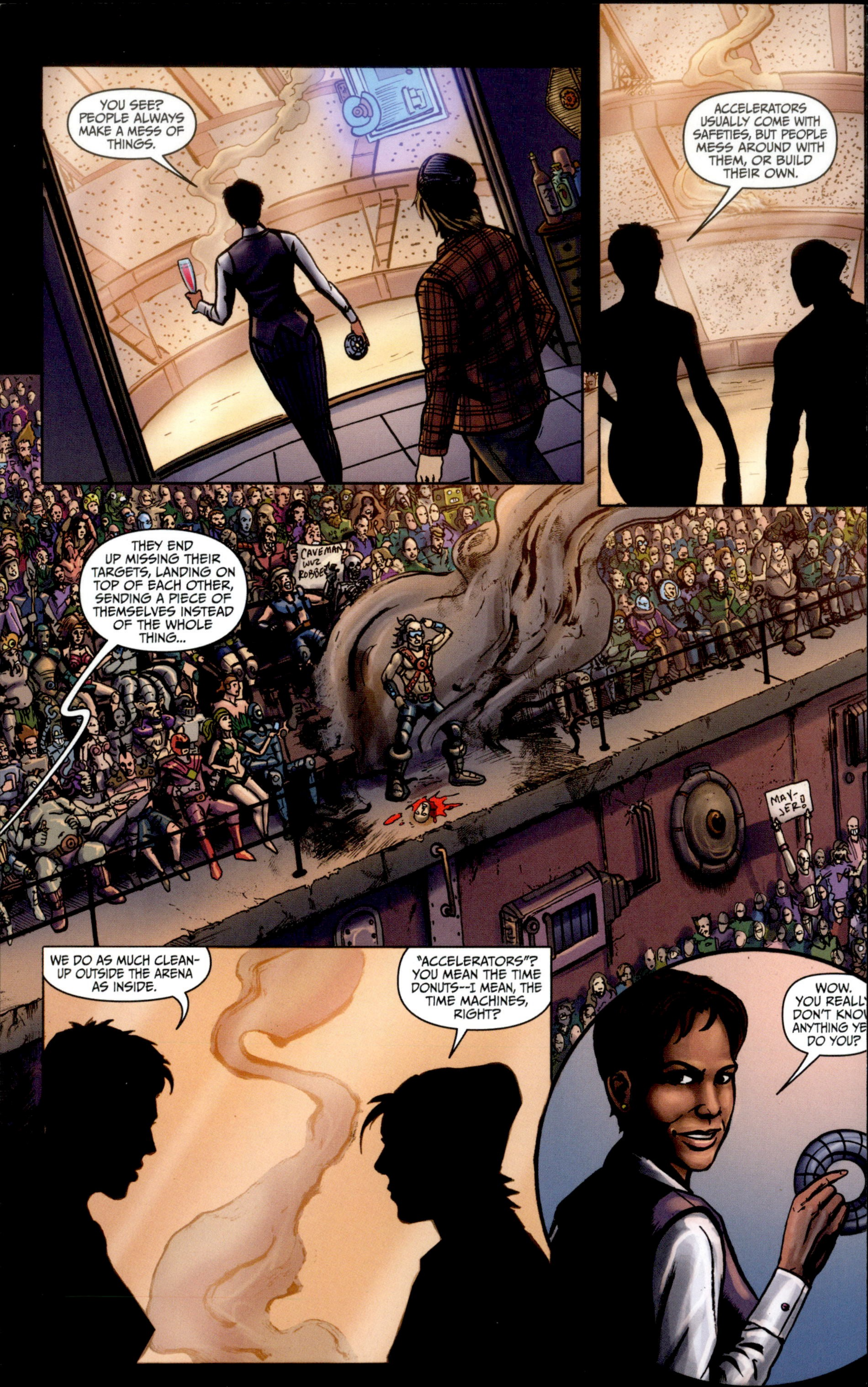
YOU SEE? PEOPLE ALWAYS MAKE A MESS OF THINGS.
ACCELERATORS USUALLY COME WITH SAFETIES, BUT PEOPLE MESS AROUND WITH THEM, OR BUILD THEIR OWN.
THEY END UP MISSING THEIR TARGETS, LANDING ON TOP OF EACH OTHER, SENDING A PIECE OF THEMSELVES INSTEAD OF THE WHOLE THING...
CAVEMAN WUZ ROBBED
MAY-JER!
WE DO AS MUCH CLEAN-UP OUTSIDE THE ARENA AS INSIDE.
"ACCELERATORS"? YOU MEAN THE TIME DONUTS--I MEAN, THE TIME MACHINES, RIGHT?
WOW. YOU REALL DON'T KNO ANYTHING YE DO YOU?

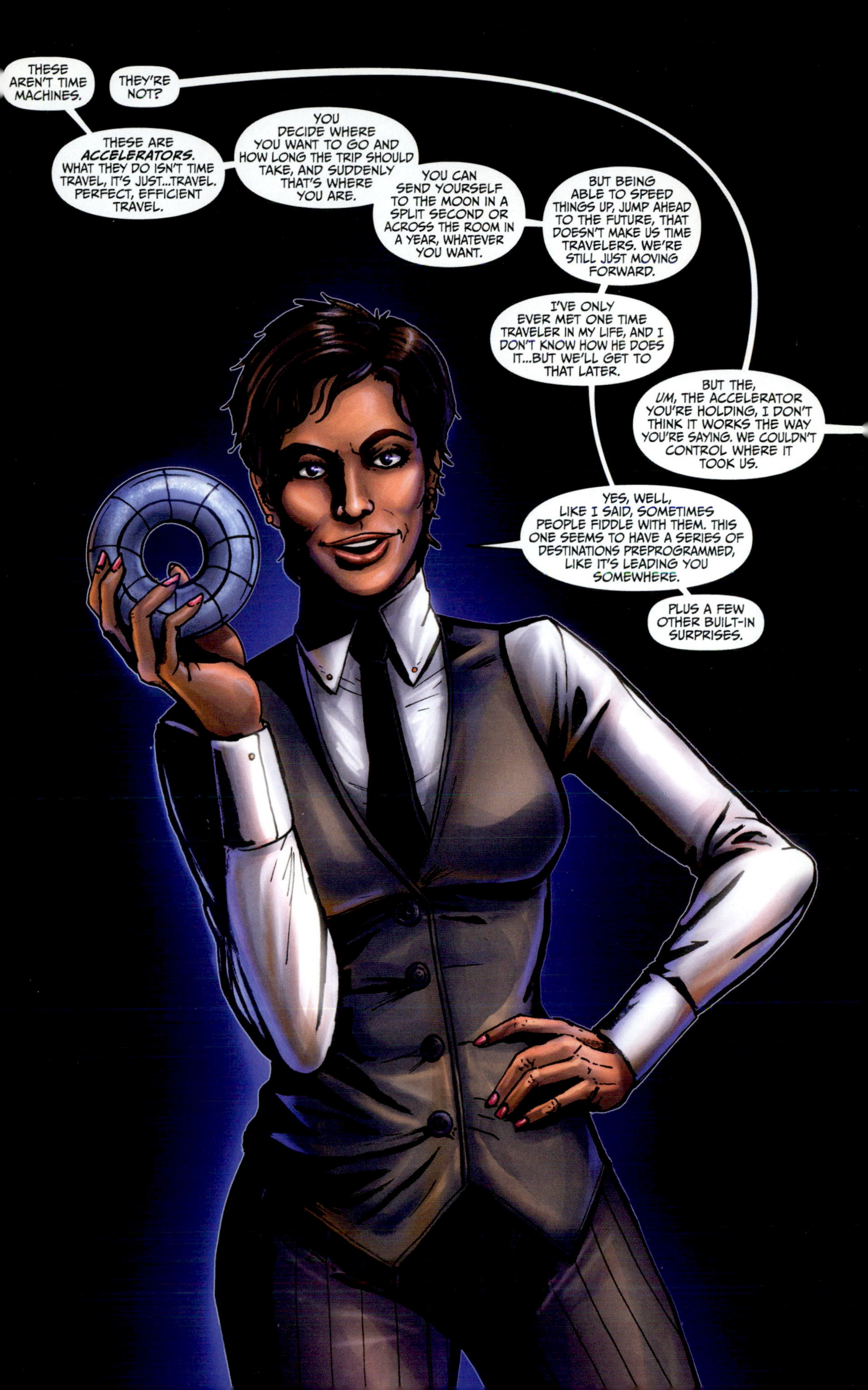
THESE AREN'T TIME MACHINES.
THEY'RE NOT?
THESE ARE ***ACCELERATORS.*** WHAT THEY DO ISN'T TIME TRAVEL, IT'S JUST...TRAVEL. PERFECT, EFFICIENT TRAVEL.
YOU DECIDE WHERE YOU WANT TO GO AND HOW LONG THE TRIP SHOULD TAKE, AND SUDDENLY THAT'S WHERE YOU ARE.
YOU CAN SEND YOURSELF TO THE MOON IN A SPLIT SECOND OR ACROSS THE ROOM IN A YEAR, WHATEVER YOU WANT.
BUT BEING ABLE TO SPEED THINGS UP, JUMP AHEAD TO THE FUTURE, THAT DOESN'T MAKE US TIME TRAVELERS. WE'RE STILL JUST MOVING FORWARD.
I'VE ONLY EVER MET ONE TIME TRAVELER IN MY LIFE, AND I DON'T KNOW HOW HE DOES IT...BUT WE'LL GET TO THAT LATER.
BUT THE, *UM,* THE ACCELERATOR YOU'RE HOLDING, I DON'T THINK IT WORKS THE WAY YOU'RE SAYING. WE COULDN'T CONTROL WHERE IT TOOK US.
YES, WELL, LIKE I SAID, SOMETIMES PEOPLE FIDDLE WITH THEM. THIS ONE SEEMS TO HAVE A SERIES OF DESTINATIONS PREPROGRAMMED, LIKE IT'S LEADING YOU SOMEWHERE.
PLUS A FEW OTHER BUILT-IN SURPRISES.

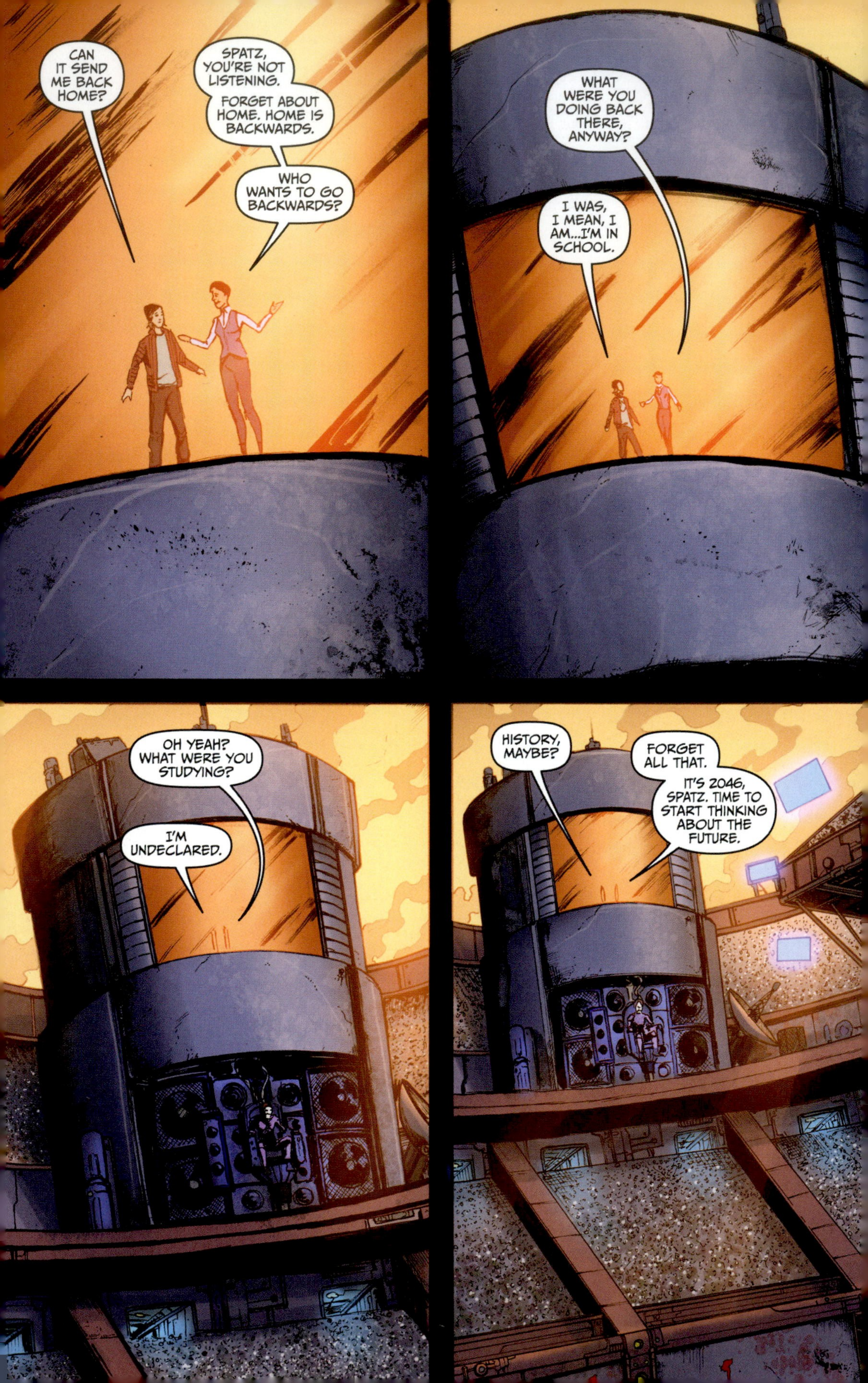
CAN IT SEND ME BACK HOME?
SPATZ, YOU'RE NOT LISTENING.
FORGET ABOUT HOME. HOME IS BACKWARDS.
WHO WANTS TO GO BACKWARDS?
WHAT WERE YOU DOING BACK THERE, ANYWAY?
I WAS, I MEAN, I AM...I'M IN SCHOOL.
OH YEAH? WHAT WERE YOU STUDYING?
I'M UNDECLARED.
HISTORY, MAYBE?
FORGET ALL THAT.
IT'S 2046, SPATZ. TIME TO START THINKING ABOUT THE FUTURE.

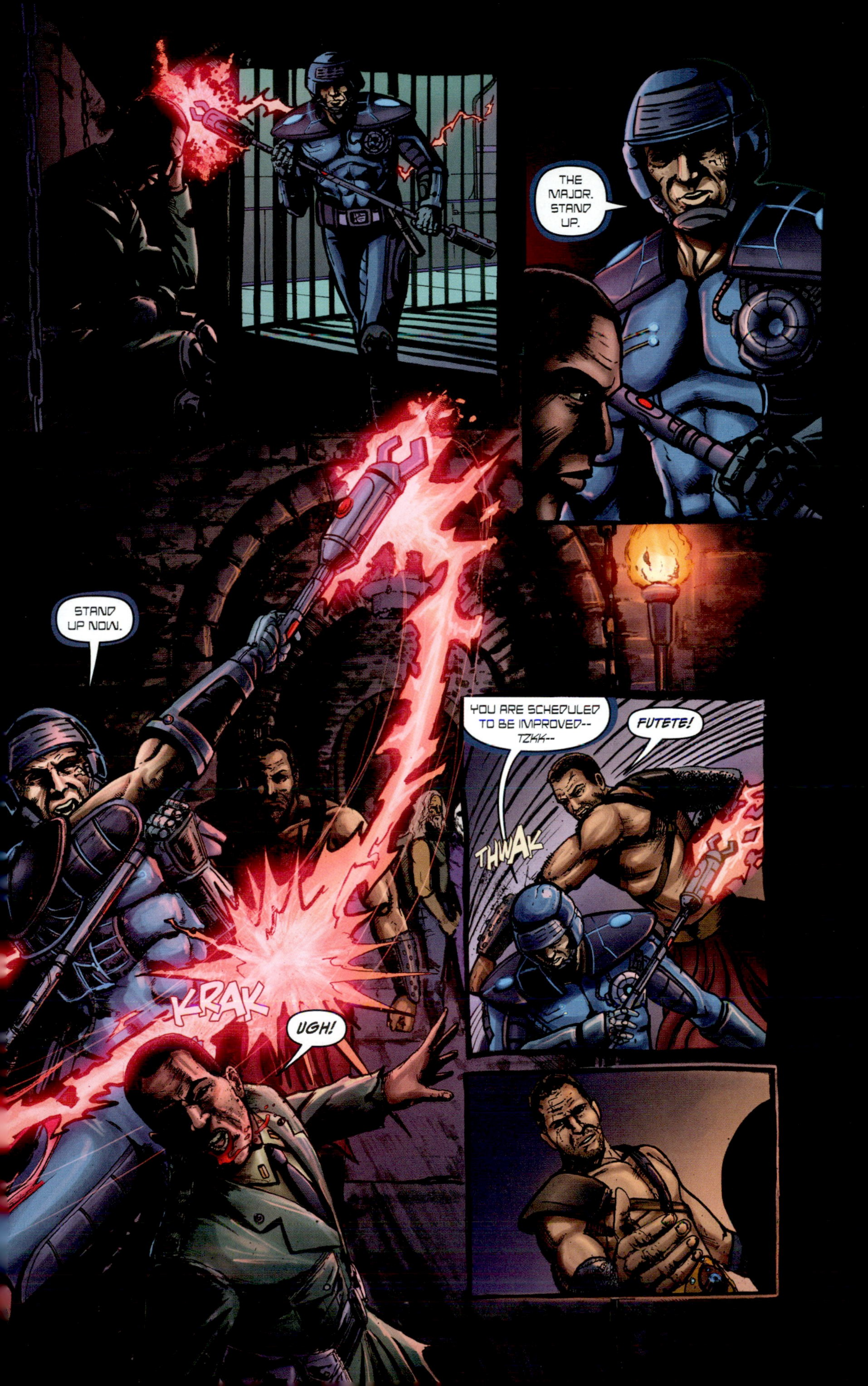
THE MAJOR. STAND UP.
STAND UP NOW.
KRAK
UGH!
YOU ARE SCHEDULED TO BE IMPROVED-- TZKK--
FUTETE!
THWAK

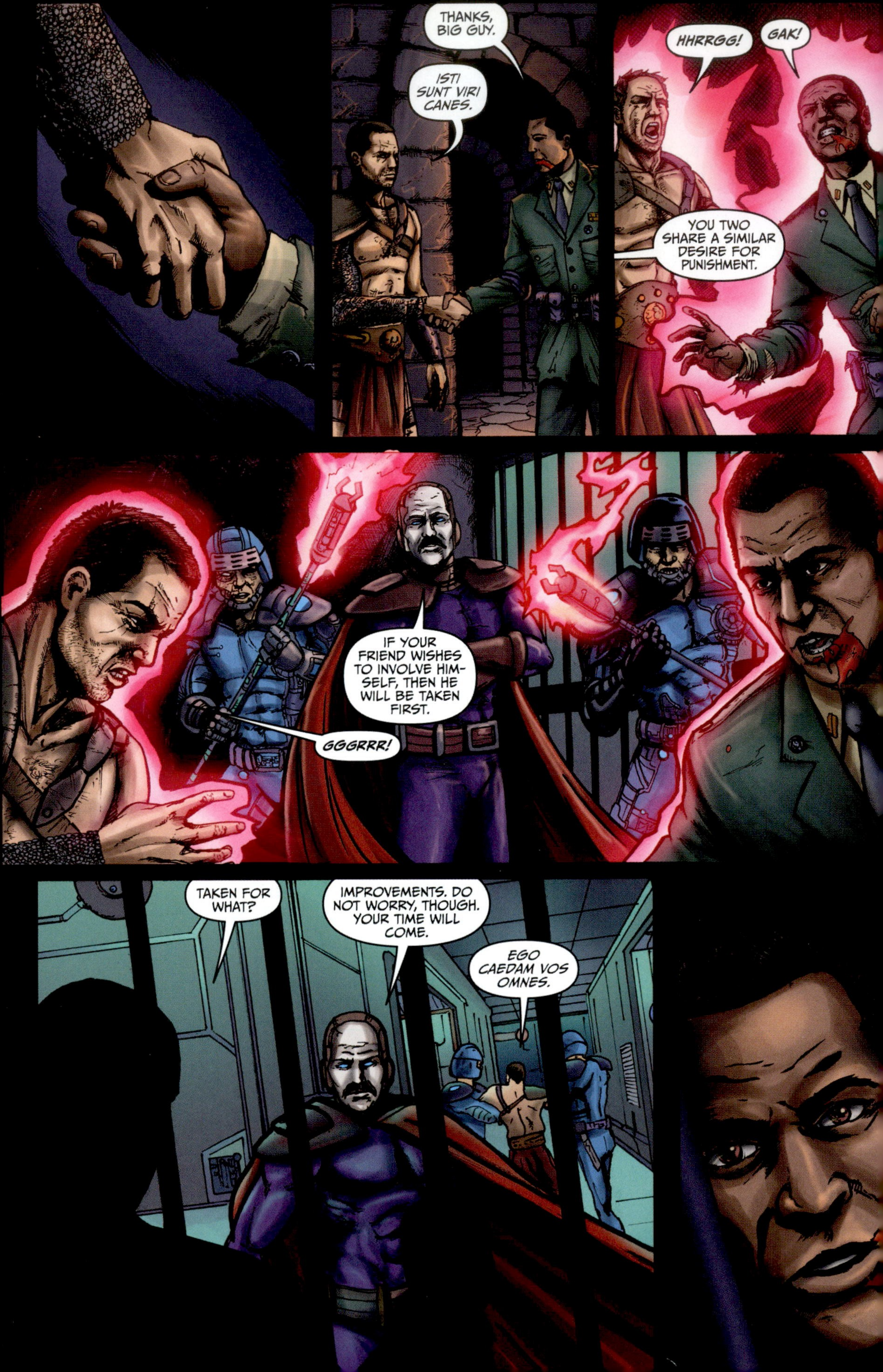
THANKS, BIG GUY.
ISTI SUNT VIRI CANES.
HHRRGG!
GAK!
YOU TWO SHARE A SIMILAR DESIRE FOR PUNISHMENT.
IF YOUR FRIEND WISHES TO INVOLVE HIM-SELF, THEN HE WILL BE TAKEN FIRST.
GGGRRR!
TAKEN FOR WHAT?
IMPROVEMENTS. DO NOT WORRY, THOUGH. YOUR TIME WILL COME.
EGO CAEDAM VOS OMNES.

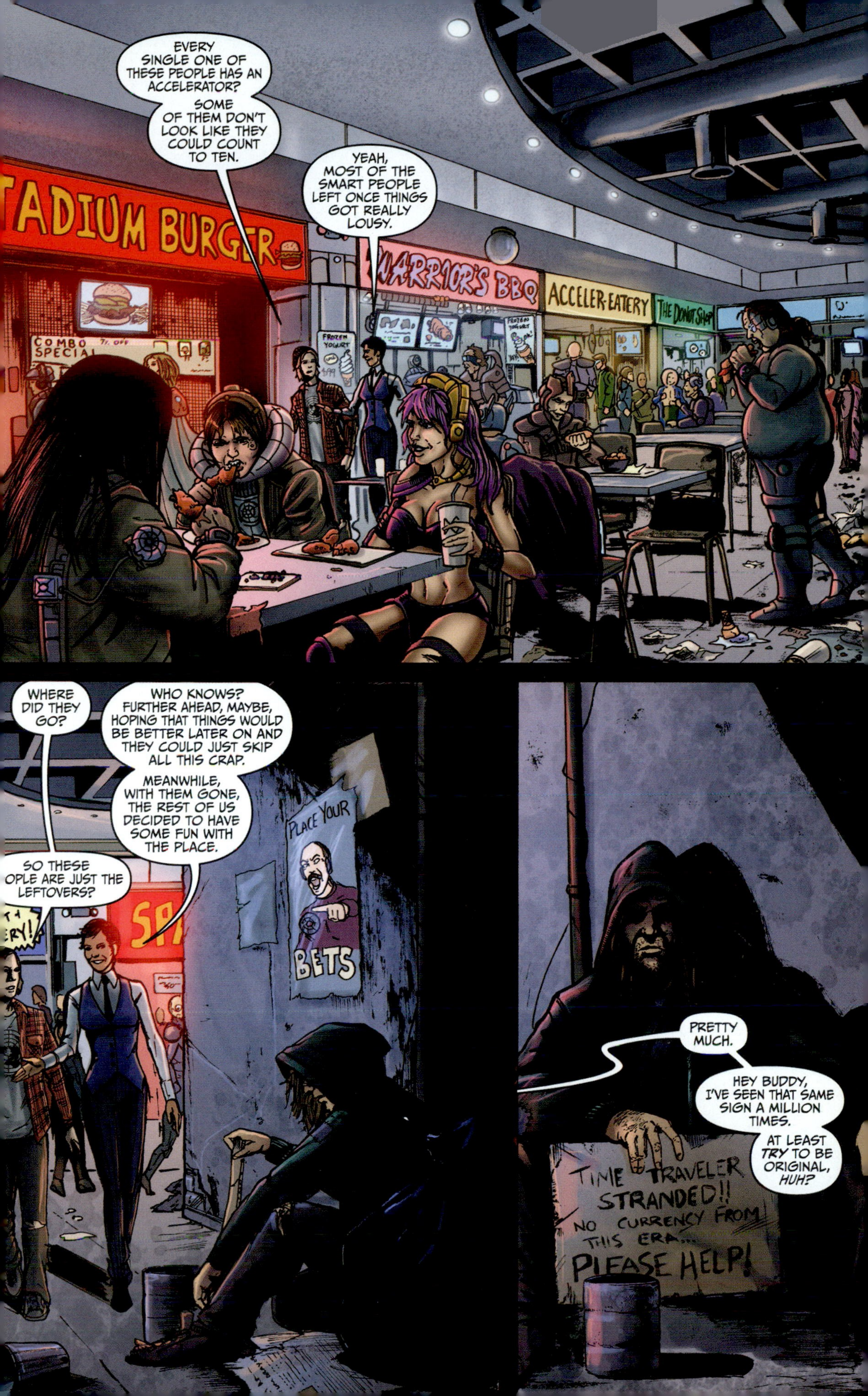
EVERY SINGLE ONE OF THESE PEOPLE HAS AN ACCELERATOR?
SOME OF THEM DON'T LOOK LIKE THEY COULD COUNT TO TEN.
YEAH, MOST OF THE SMART PEOPLE LEFT ONCE THINGS GOT REALLY LOUSY.
TADIUM BURGER
WARRIOR'S BBQ
ACCELER-EATERY
THE DONUT SHOP
COMBO SPECIAL
FROZEN YOGURT
WHERE DID THEY GO?
WHO KNOWS? FURTHER AHEAD, MAYBE, HOPING THAT THINGS WOULD BE BETTER LATER ON AND THEY COULD JUST SKIP ALL THIS CRAP.
MEANWHILE, WITH THEM GONE, THE REST OF US DECIDED TO HAVE SOME FUN WITH THE PLACE.
SO THESE OPLE ARE JUST THE LEFTOVERS?
PLACE YOUR BETS
PRETTY MUCH.
HEY BUDDY, I'VE SEEN THAT SAME SIGN A MILLION TIMES.
AT LEAST *TRY* TO BE ORIGINAL, *HUH?*
TIME TRAVELER STRANDED!! NO CURRENCY FROM THIS ERA... PLEASE HELP!

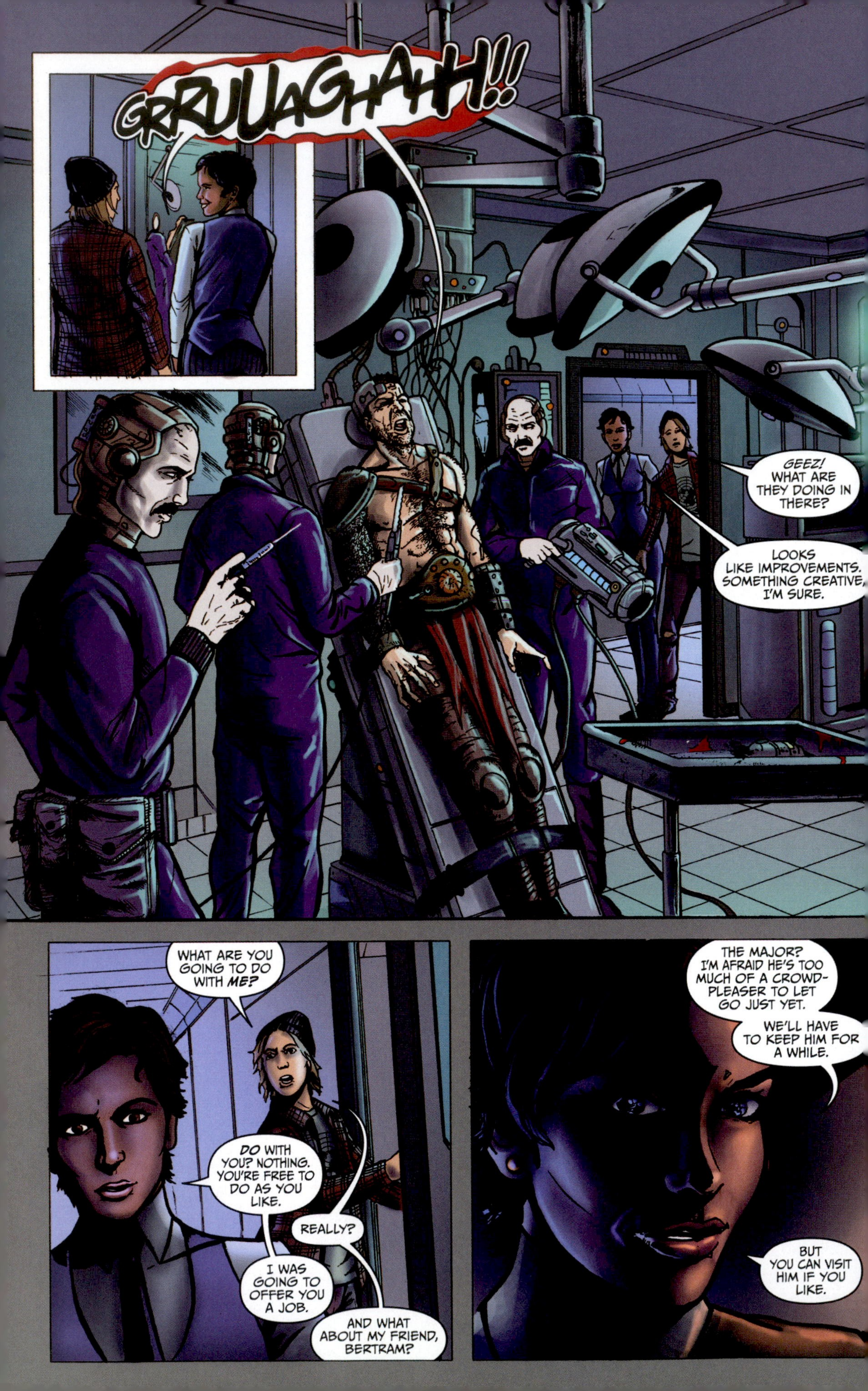
GRRUUAGHAHH!!
GEEZ! WHAT ARE THEY DOING IN THERE?
LOOKS LIKE IMPROVEMENTS. SOMETHING CREATIVE, I'M SURE.
WHAT ARE YOU GOING TO DO WITH *ME?*
DO WITH YOU? NOTHING. YOU'RE FREE TO DO AS YOU LIKE.
REALLY?
I WAS GOING TO OFFER YOU A JOB.
AND WHAT ABOUT MY FRIEND, BERTRAM?
THE MAJOR? I'M AFRAID HE'S TOO MUCH OF A CROWD-PLEASER TO LET GO JUST YET.
WE'LL HAVE TO KEEP HIM FOR A WHILE.
BUT YOU CAN VISIT HIM IF YOU LIKE.

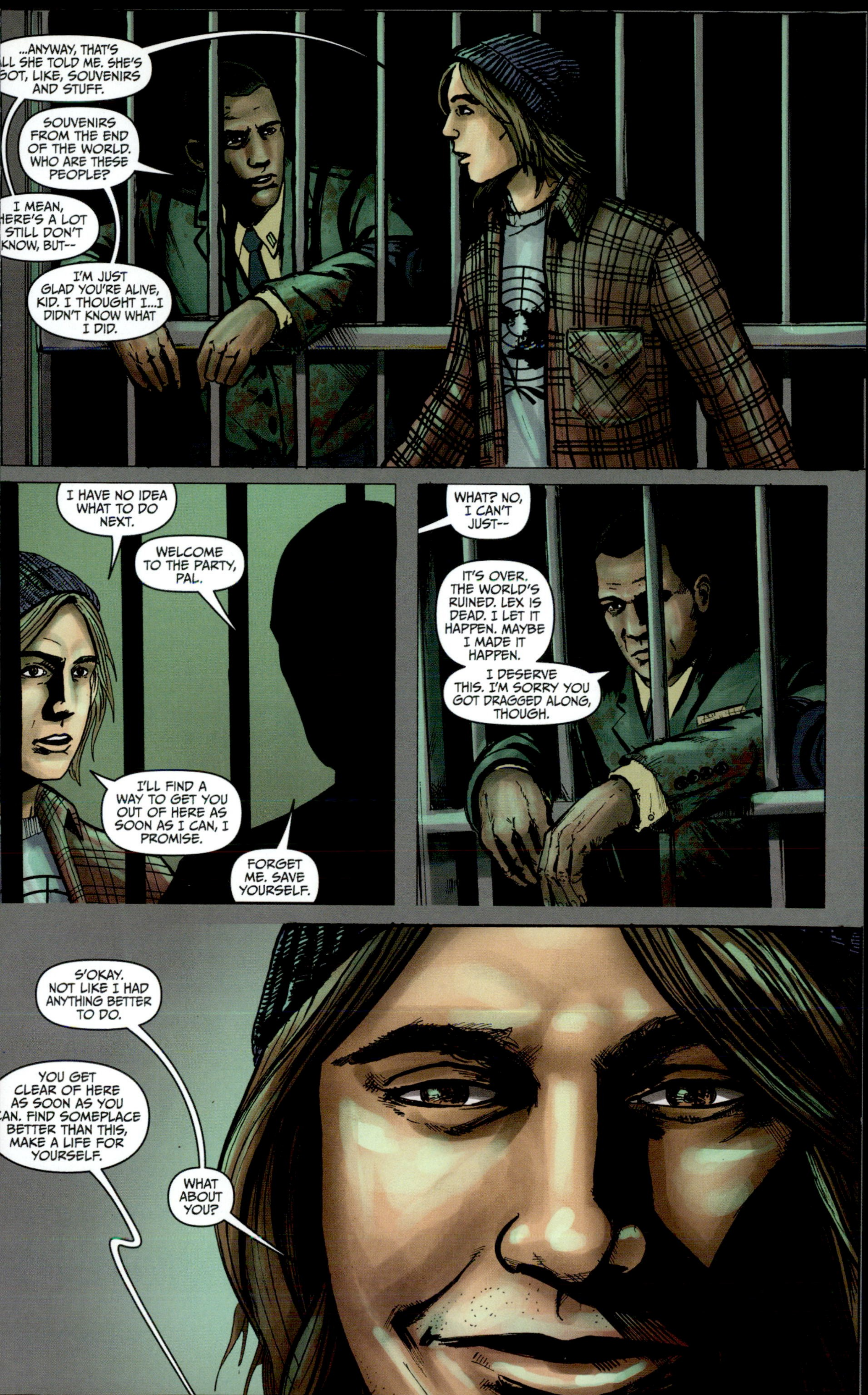
...ANYWAY, THAT'S ALL SHE TOLD ME. SHE'S GOT, LIKE, SOUVENIRS AND STUFF.
SOUVENIRS FROM THE END OF THE WORLD. WHO ARE THESE PEOPLE?
I MEAN, THERE'S A LOT I STILL DON'T KNOW, BUT--
I'M JUST GLAD YOU'RE ALIVE, KID. I THOUGHT I...I DIDN'T KNOW WHAT I DID.
I HAVE NO IDEA WHAT TO DO NEXT.
WELCOME TO THE PARTY, PAL.
I'LL FIND A WAY TO GET YOU OUT OF HERE AS SOON AS I CAN, I PROMISE.
FORGET ME. SAVE YOURSELF.
WHAT? NO, I CAN'T JUST--
IT'S OVER. THE WORLD'S RUINED. LEX IS DEAD. I LET IT HAPPEN. MAYBE I MADE IT HAPPEN.
I DESERVE THIS. I'M SORRY YOU GOT DRAGGED ALONG, THOUGH.
S'OKAY. NOT LIKE I HAD ANYTHING BETTER TO DO.
YOU GET CLEAR OF HERE AS SOON AS YOU CAN. FIND SOMEPLACE BETTER THAN THIS, MAKE A LIFE FOR YOURSELF.
WHAT ABOUT YOU?

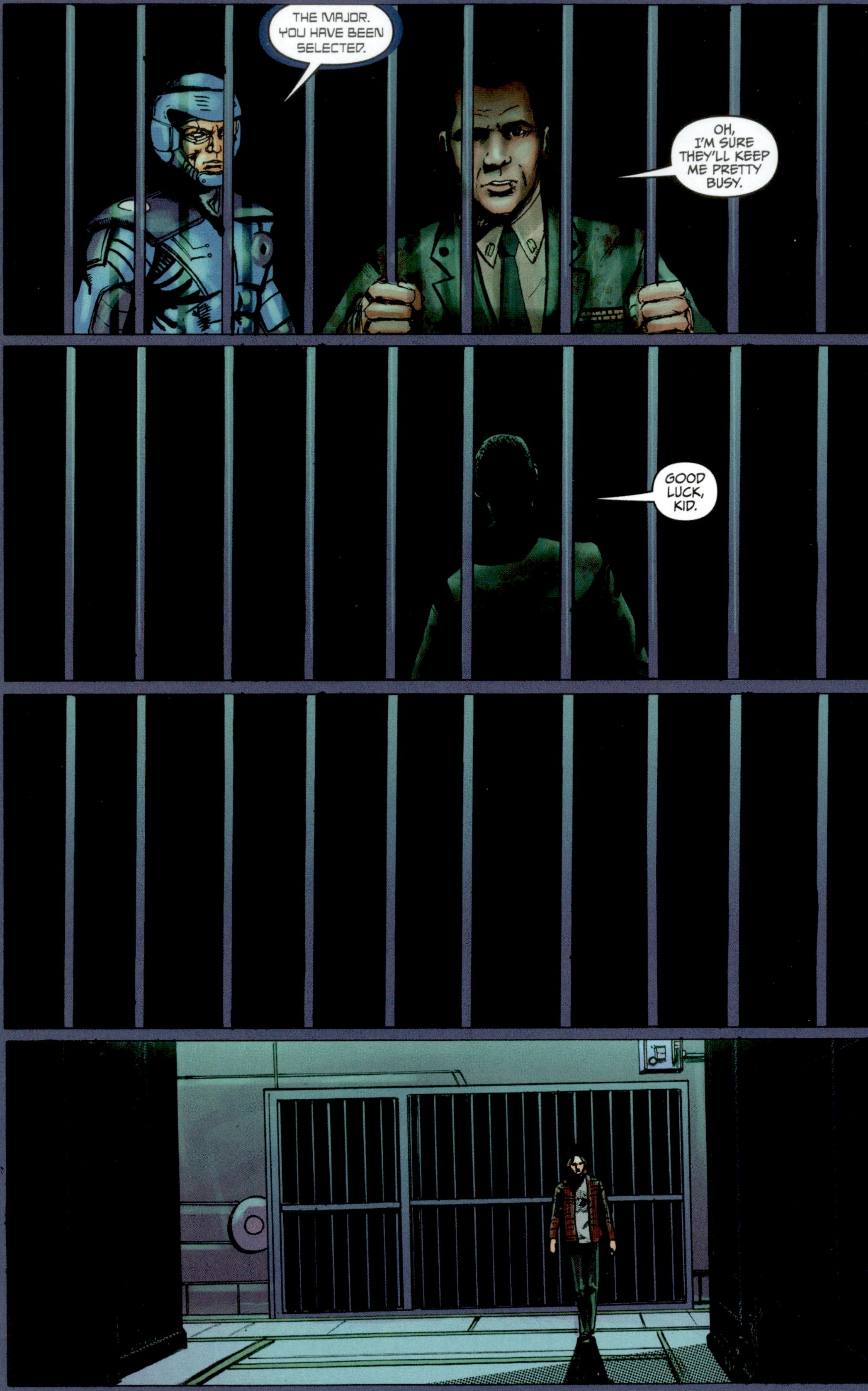
THE MAJOR. YOU HAVE BEEN SELECTED.
OH, I'M SURE THEY'LL KEEP ME PRETTY BUSY.
GOOD LUCK, KID.

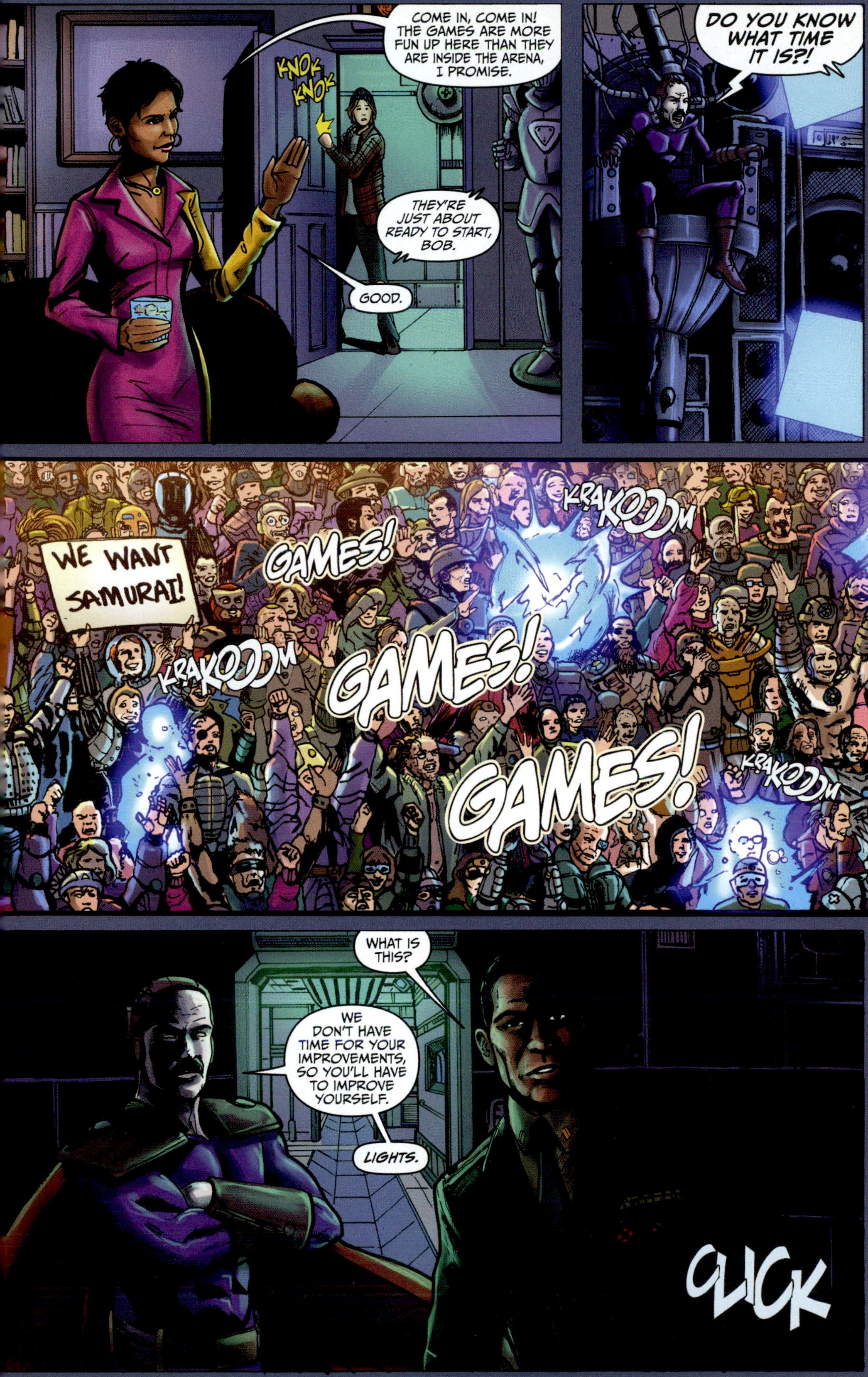
COME IN, COME IN! THE GAMES ARE MORE FUN UP HERE THAN THEY ARE INSIDE THE ARENA, I PROMISE.
KNOK KNOK
THEY'RE JUST ABOUT READY TO START, BOB.
GOOD.
DO YOU KNOW WHAT TIME IT IS?!
WE WANT SAMURAI!
GAMES!
KRAKOOOM
KRAKOOOM
GAMES!
GAMES!
KRAKOOOM
WHAT IS THIS?
WE DON'T HAVE TIME FOR YOUR IMPROVEMENTS, SO YOU'LL HAVE TO IMPROVE YOURSELF.
LIGHTS.
CLICK

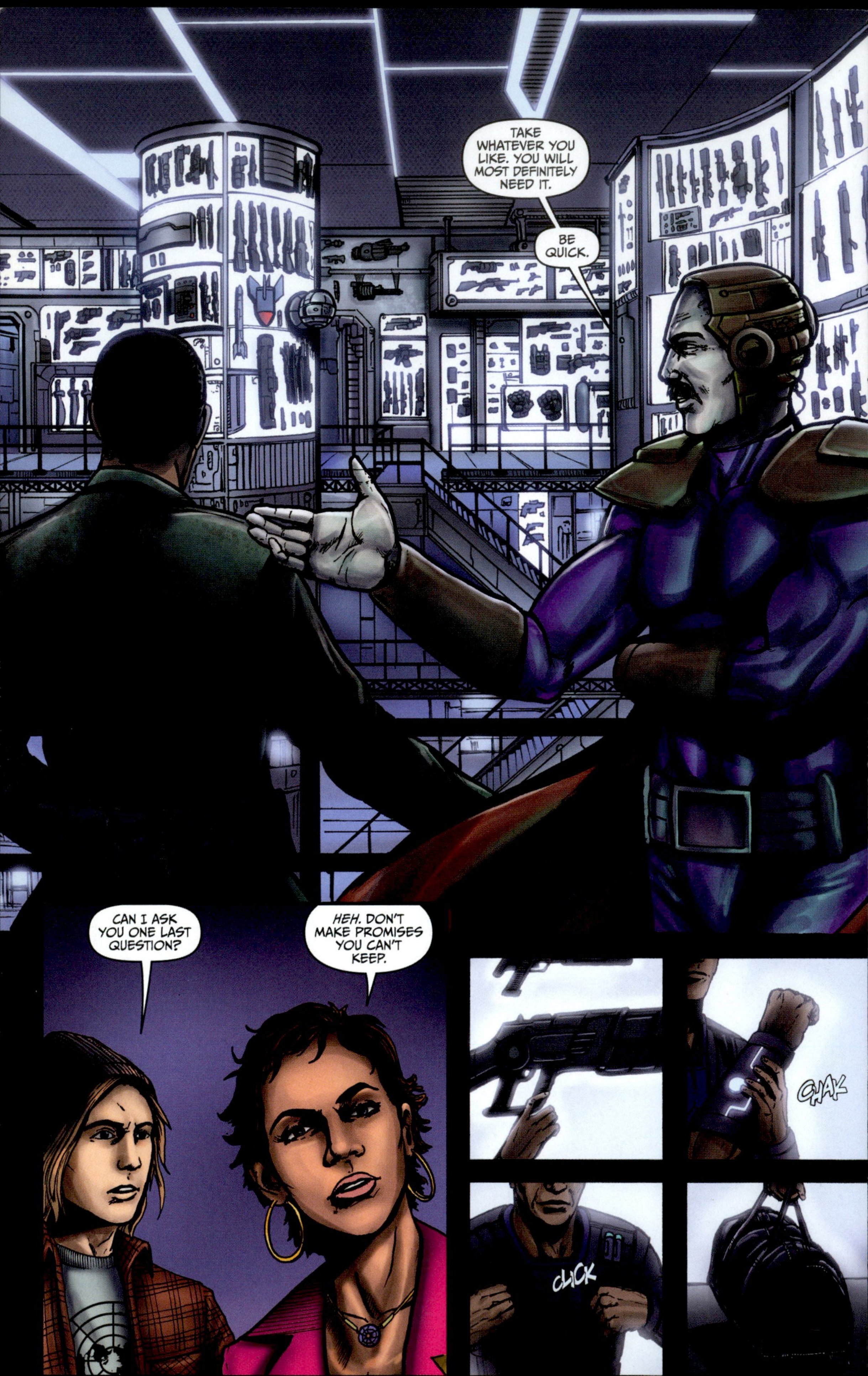
TAKE WHATEVER YOU LIKE. YOU WILL MOST DEFINITELY NEED IT.
BE QUICK.
CAN I ASK YOU ONE LAST QUESTION?
HEH. DON'T MAKE PROMISES YOU CAN'T KEEP.
CHAK
CLICK

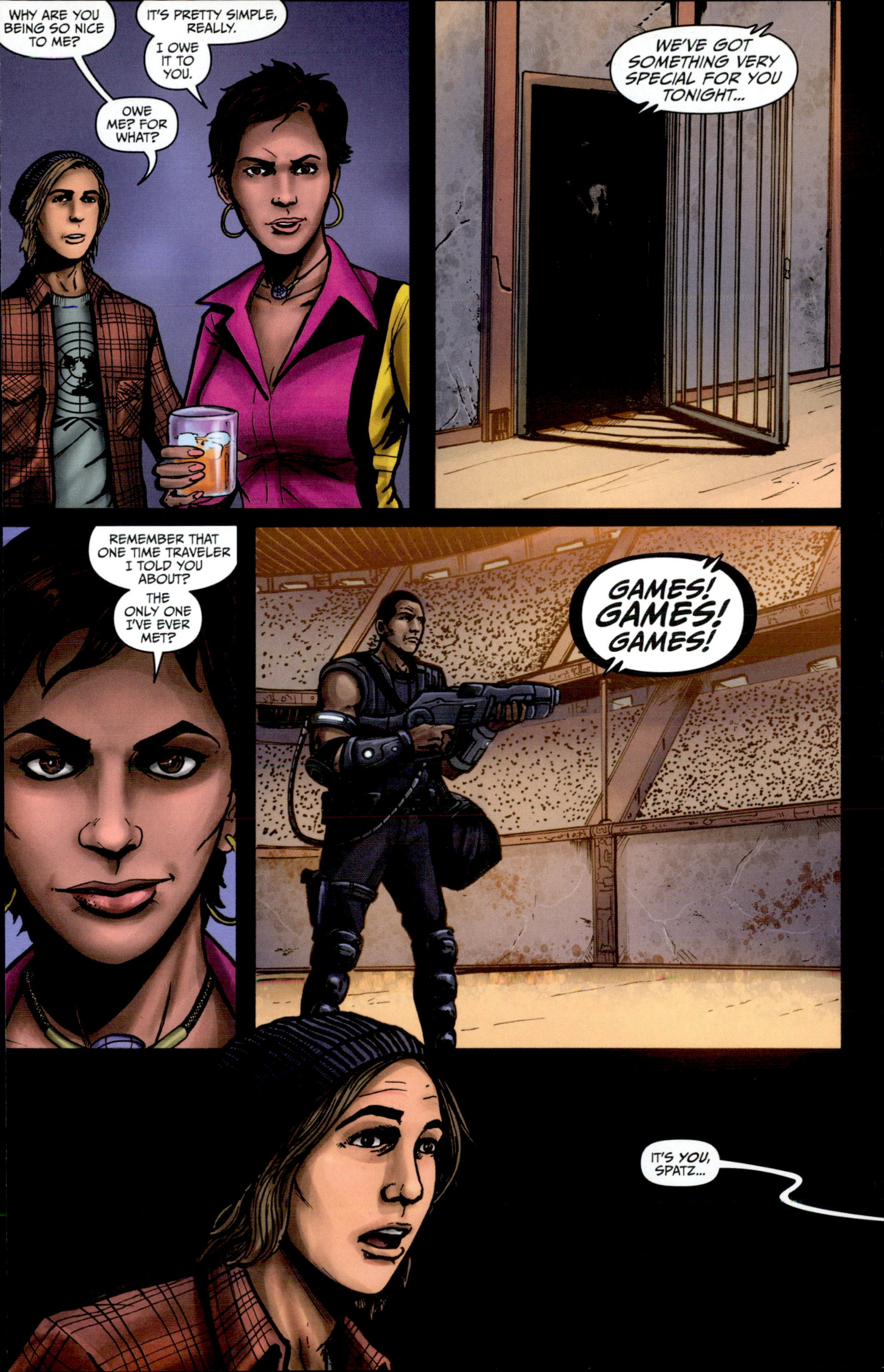
WHY ARE YOU BEING SO NICE TO ME?
IT'S PRETTY SIMPLE, REALLY.
I OWE IT TO YOU.
OWE ME? FOR WHAT?
WE'VE GOT SOMETHING VERY SPECIAL FOR YOU TONIGHT...
REMEMBER THAT ONE TIME TRAVELER I TOLD YOU ABOUT?
THE ONLY ONE I'VE EVER MET?
GAMES! GAMES! GAMES!
IT'S YOU, SPATZ...

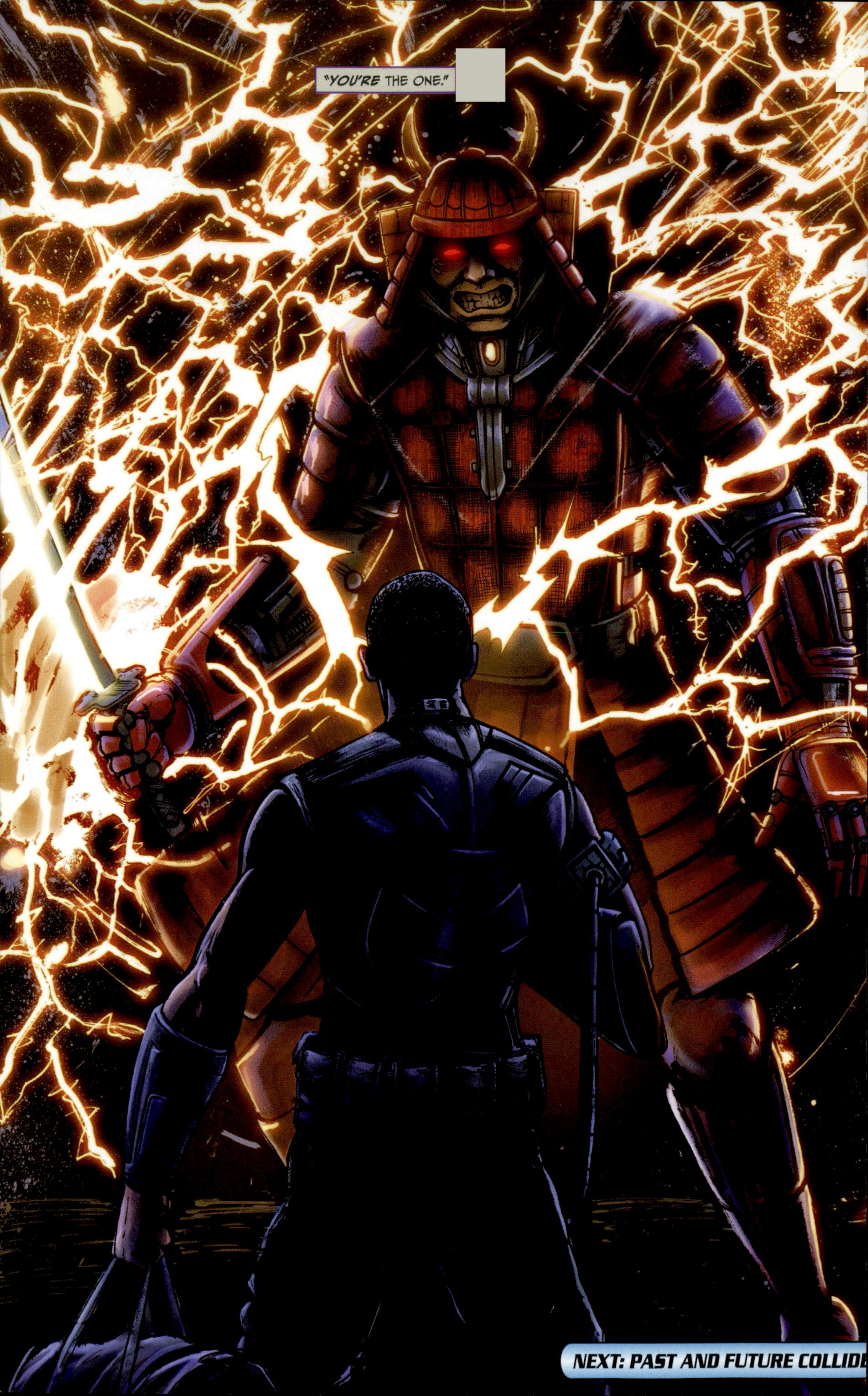
"YOU'RE THE ONE."
NEXT: PAST AND FUTURE COLLIDE

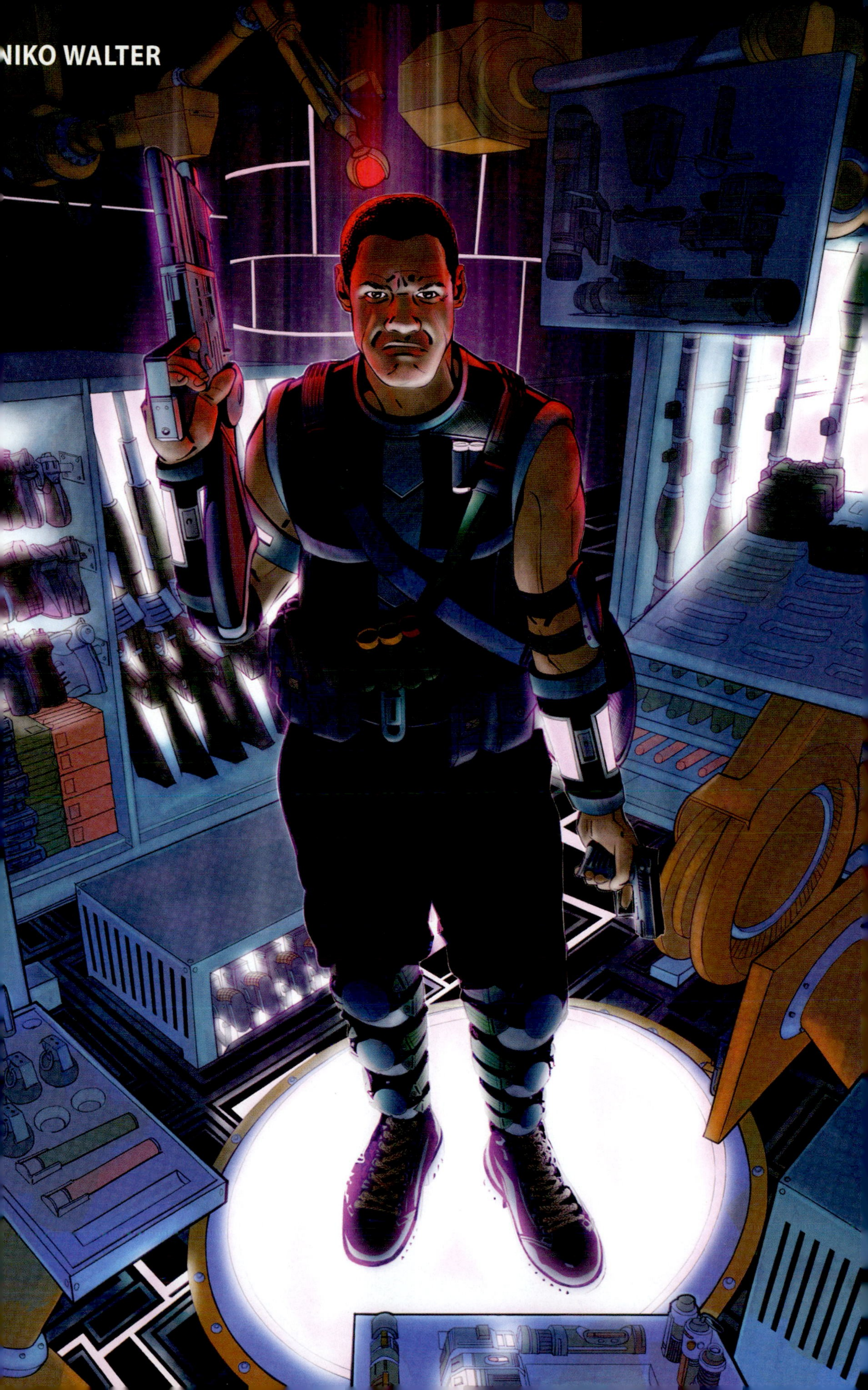
NIKO WALTER

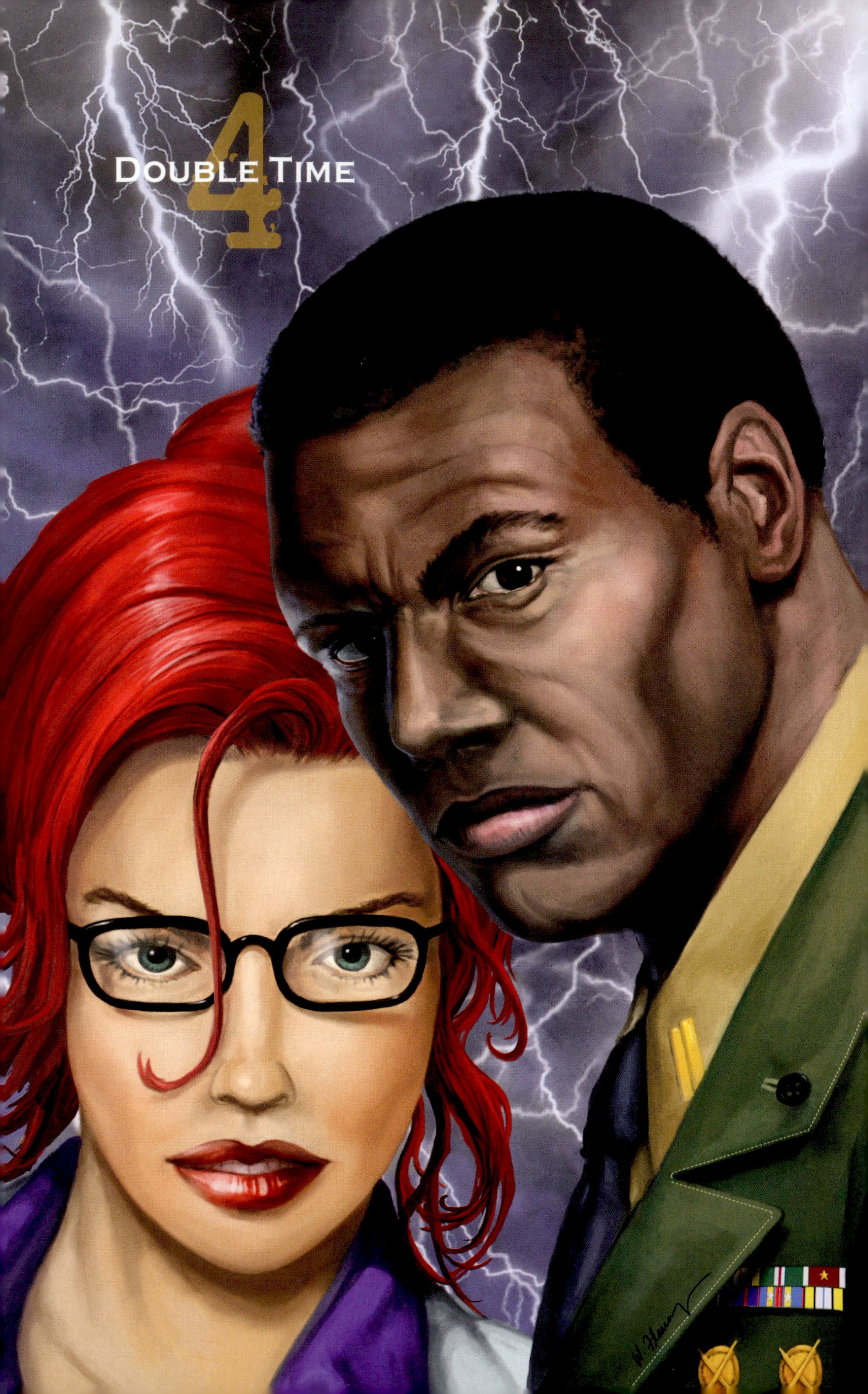
DOUBLE TIME
4

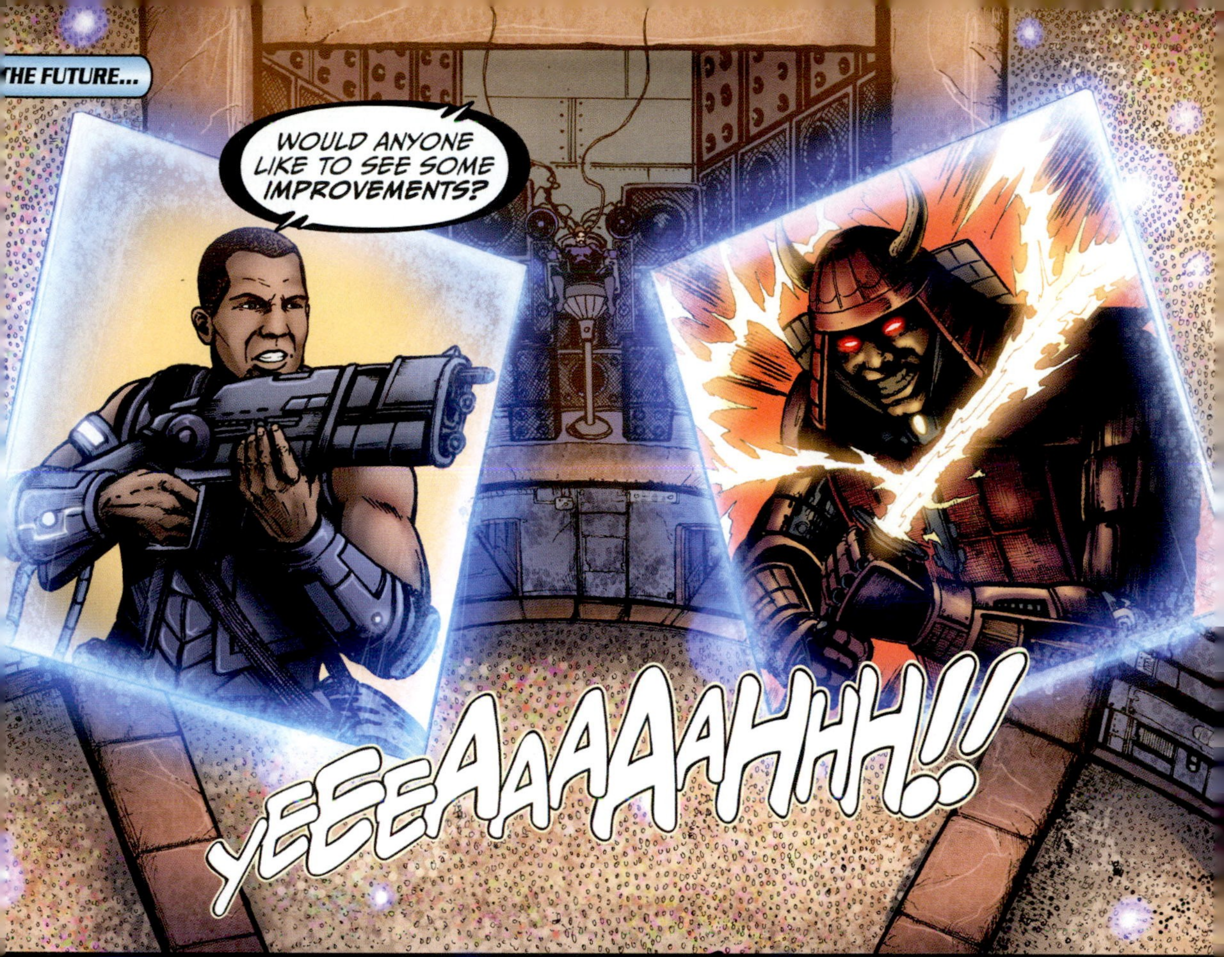

HE FUTURE...
WOULD ANYONE LIKE TO SEE SOME IMPROVEMENTS?
YEEEAAAAAAHHH!!

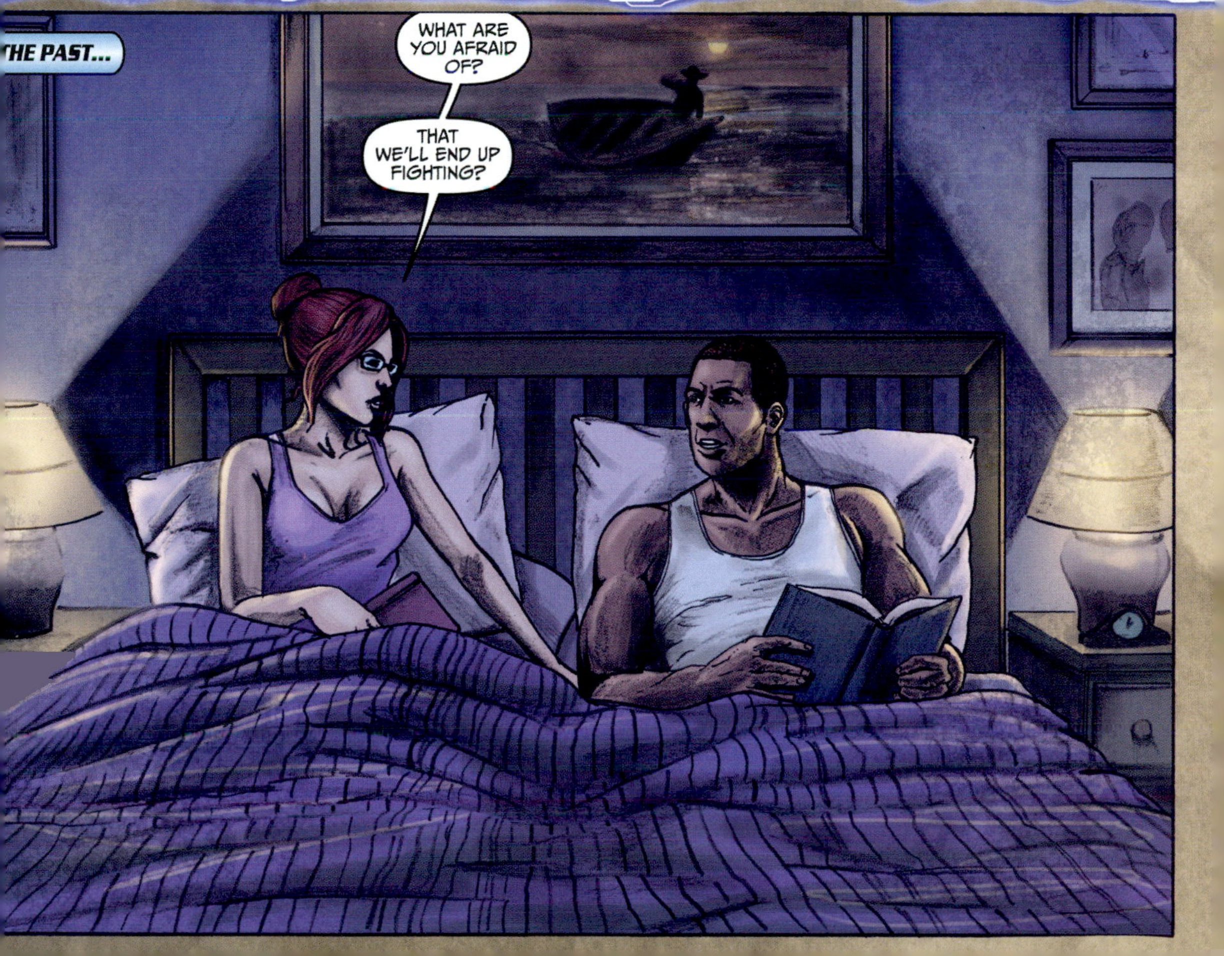

HE PAST...
WHAT ARE YOU AFRAID OF?
THAT WE'LL END UP FIGHTING?

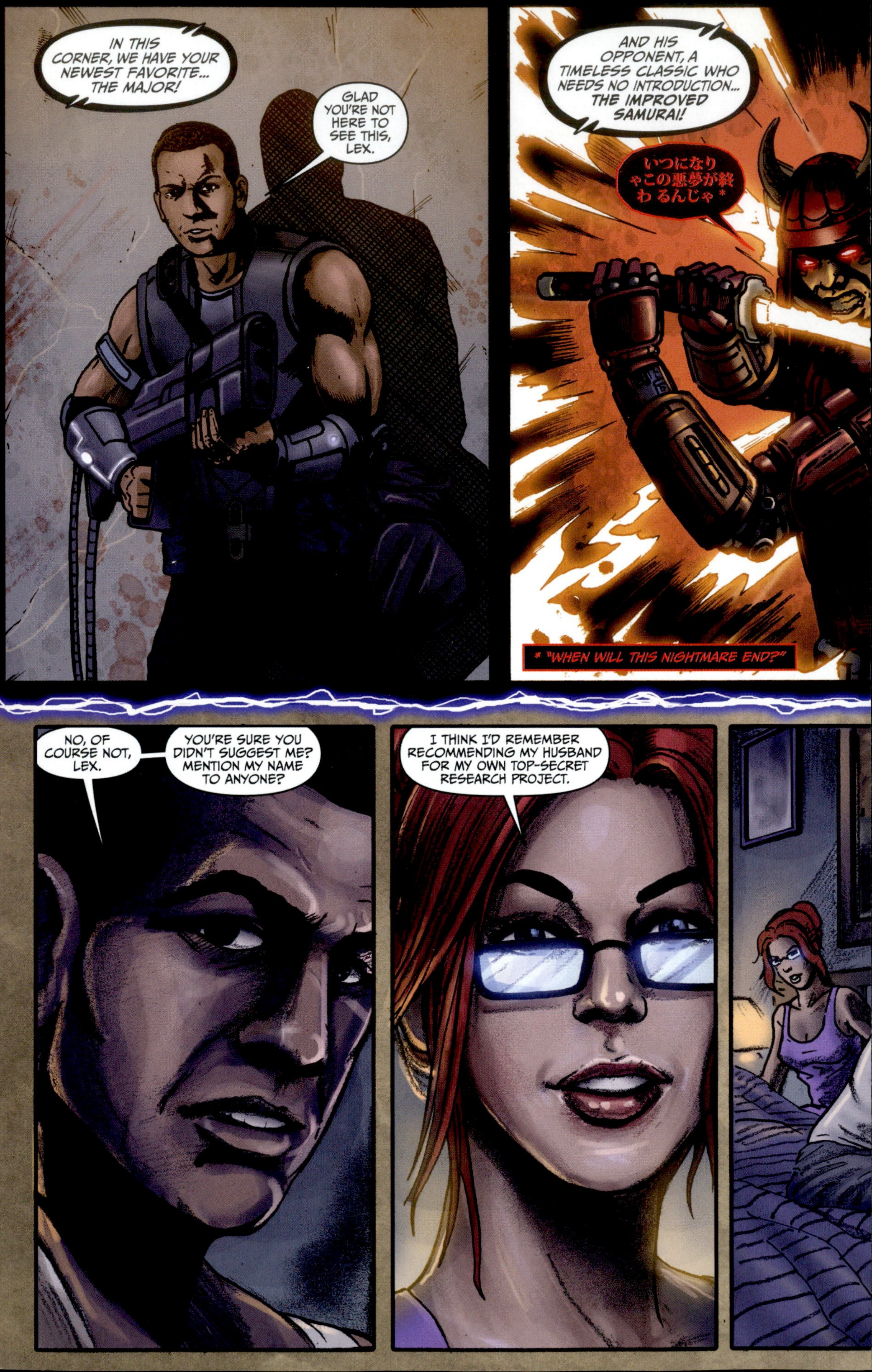
IN THIS CORNER, WE HAVE YOUR NEWEST FAVORITE... THE MAJOR!
GLAD YOU'RE NOT HERE TO SEE THIS, LEX.
AND HIS OPPONENT, A TIMELESS CLASSIC WHO NEEDS NO INTRODUCTION... THE IMPROVED SAMURAI!
いつになりゃこの悪夢が終わるんじゃ *
* "WHEN WILL THIS NIGHTMARE END?"
YOU'RE SURE YOU DIDN'T SUGGEST ME? MENTION MY NAME TO ANYONE?
NO, OF COURSE NOT, LEX.
I THINK I'D REMEMBER RECOMMENDING MY HUSBAND FOR MY OWN TOP-SECRET RESEARCH PROJECT.

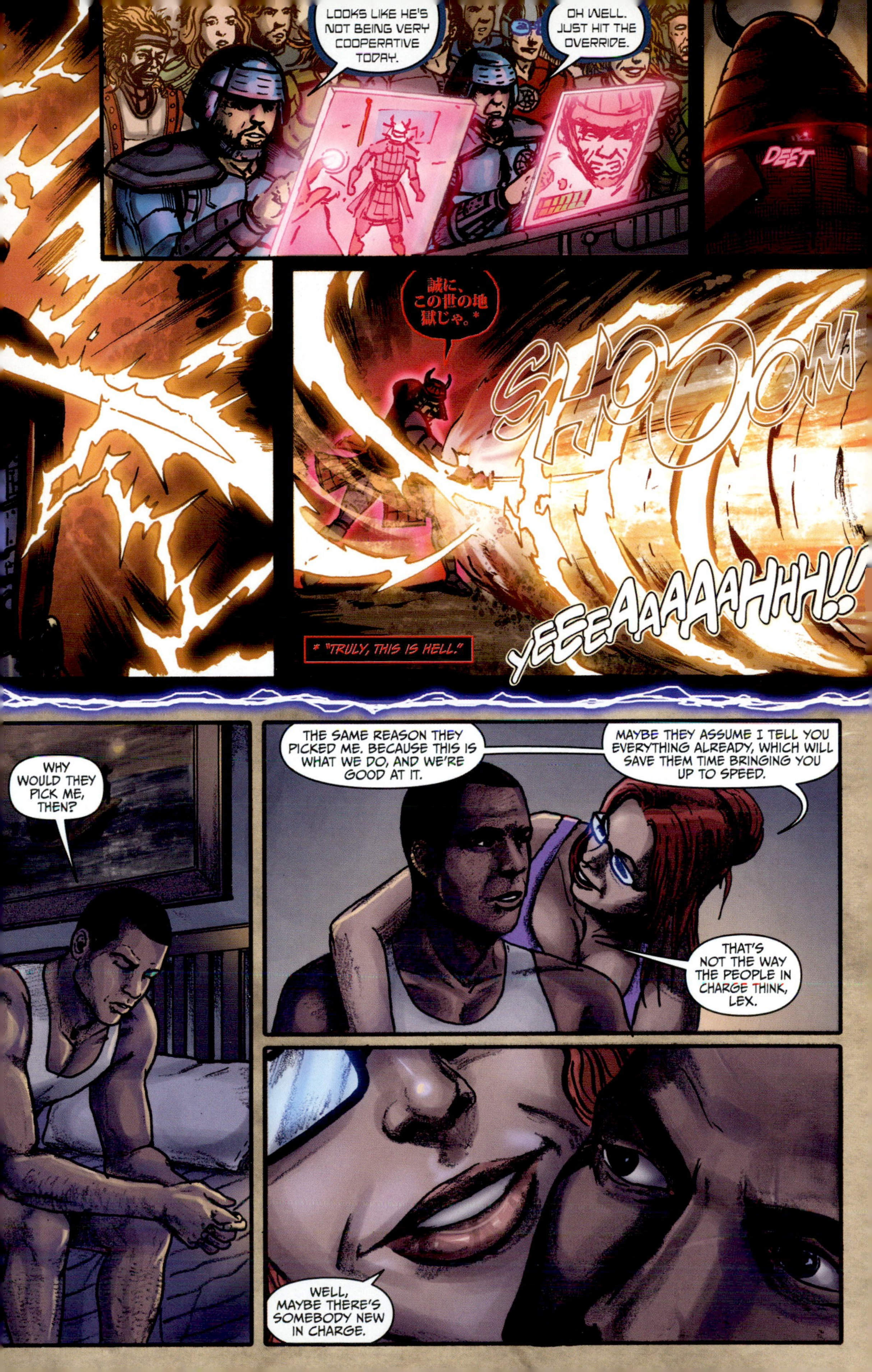

LOOKS LIKE HE'S NOT BEING VERY COOPERATIVE TODAY.
OH WELL. JUST HIT THE OVERRIDE.
DEET
誠に、この世の地獄じゃ。*
SHOOOOM
YEEEAAAAAHHH!!
* "TRULY, THIS IS HELL."
WHY WOULD THEY PICK ME, THEN?
THE SAME REASON THEY PICKED ME. BECAUSE THIS IS WHAT WE DO, AND WE'RE GOOD AT IT.
MAYBE THEY ASSUME I TELL YOU EVERYTHING ALREADY, WHICH WILL SAVE THEM TIME BRINGING YOU UP TO SPEED.
THAT'S NOT THE WAY THE PEOPLE IN CHARGE THINK, LEX.
WELL, MAYBE THERE'S SOMEBODY NEW IN CHARGE.

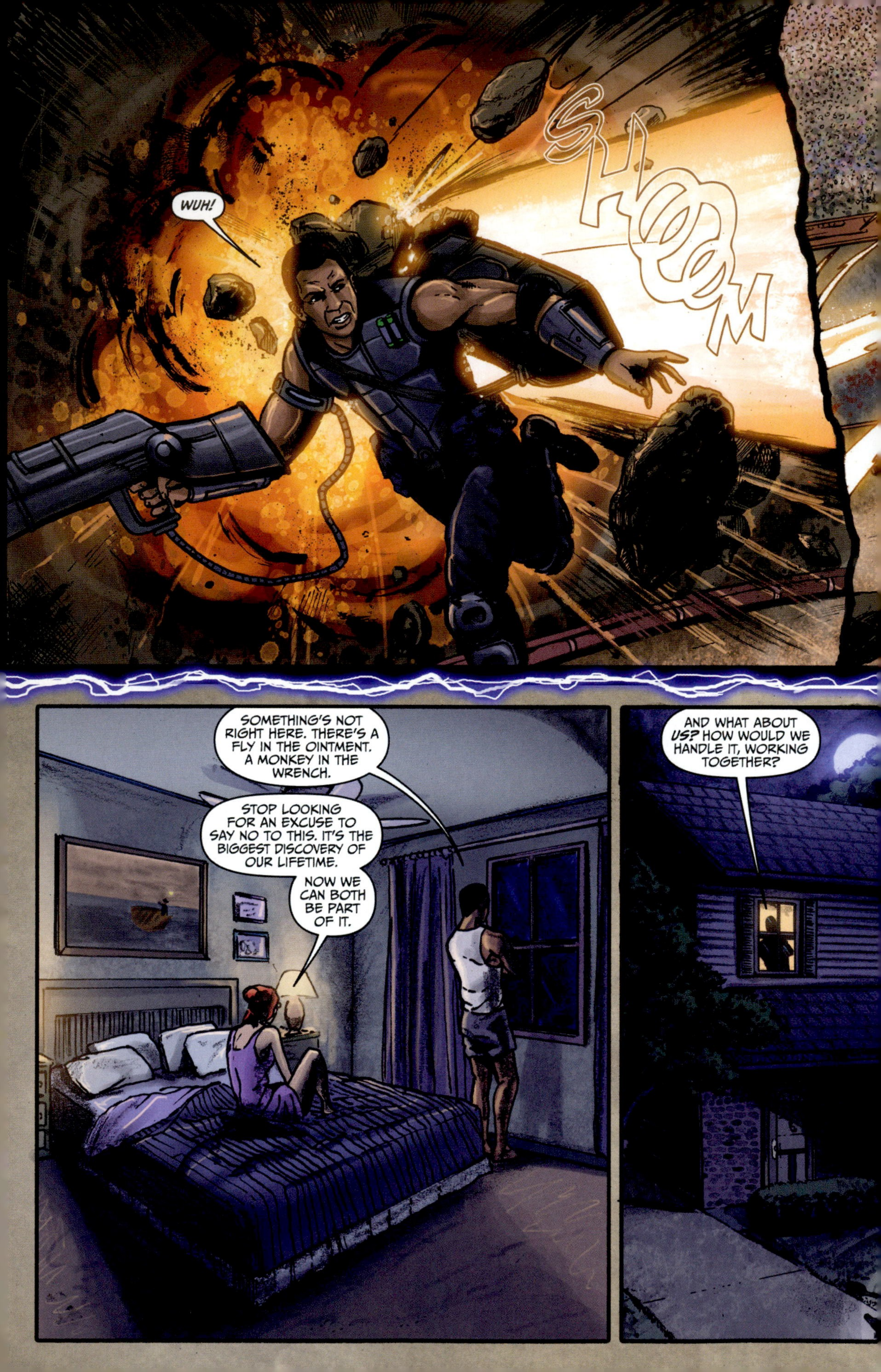
WUH!
SHOOOM
SOMETHING'S NOT RIGHT HERE. THERE'S A FLY IN THE OINTMENT. A MONKEY IN THE WRENCH.
STOP LOOKING FOR AN EXCUSE TO SAY NO TO THIS. IT'S THE BIGGEST DISCOVERY OF OUR LIFETIME.
NOW WE CAN BOTH BE PART OF IT.
AND WHAT ABOUT US? HOW WOULD WE HANDLE IT, WORKING TOGETHER?

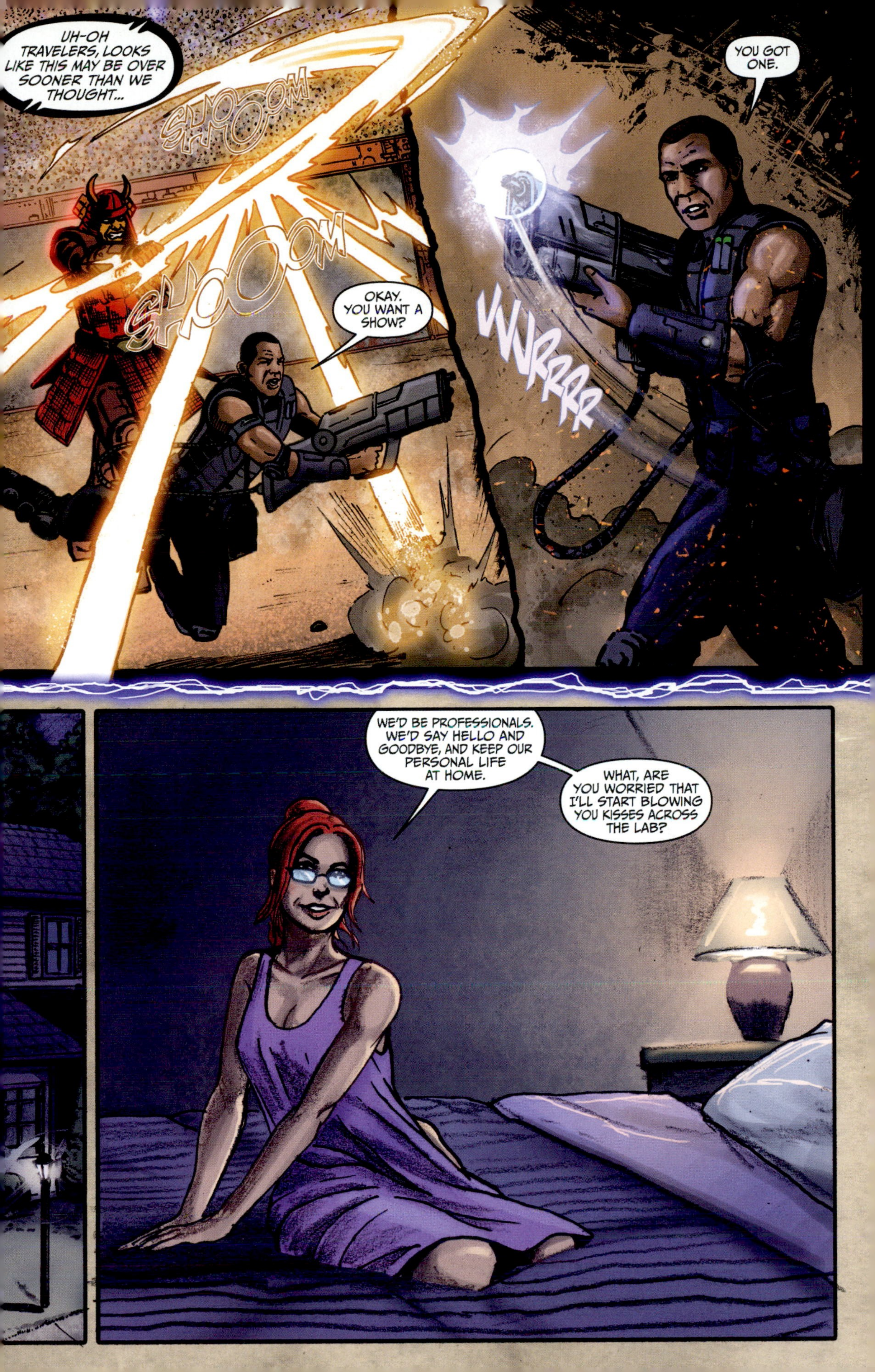
UH-OH TRAVELERS, LOOKS LIKE THIS MAY BE OVER SOONER THAN WE THOUGHT...
SHOOOOM
SHOOOOM
OKAY. YOU WANT A SHOW?
YOU GOT ONE.
WE'D BE PROFESSIONALS. WE'D SAY HELLO AND GOODBYE, AND KEEP OUR PERSONAL LIFE AT HOME.
WHAT, ARE YOU WORRIED THAT I'LL START BLOWING YOU KISSES ACROSS THE LAB?

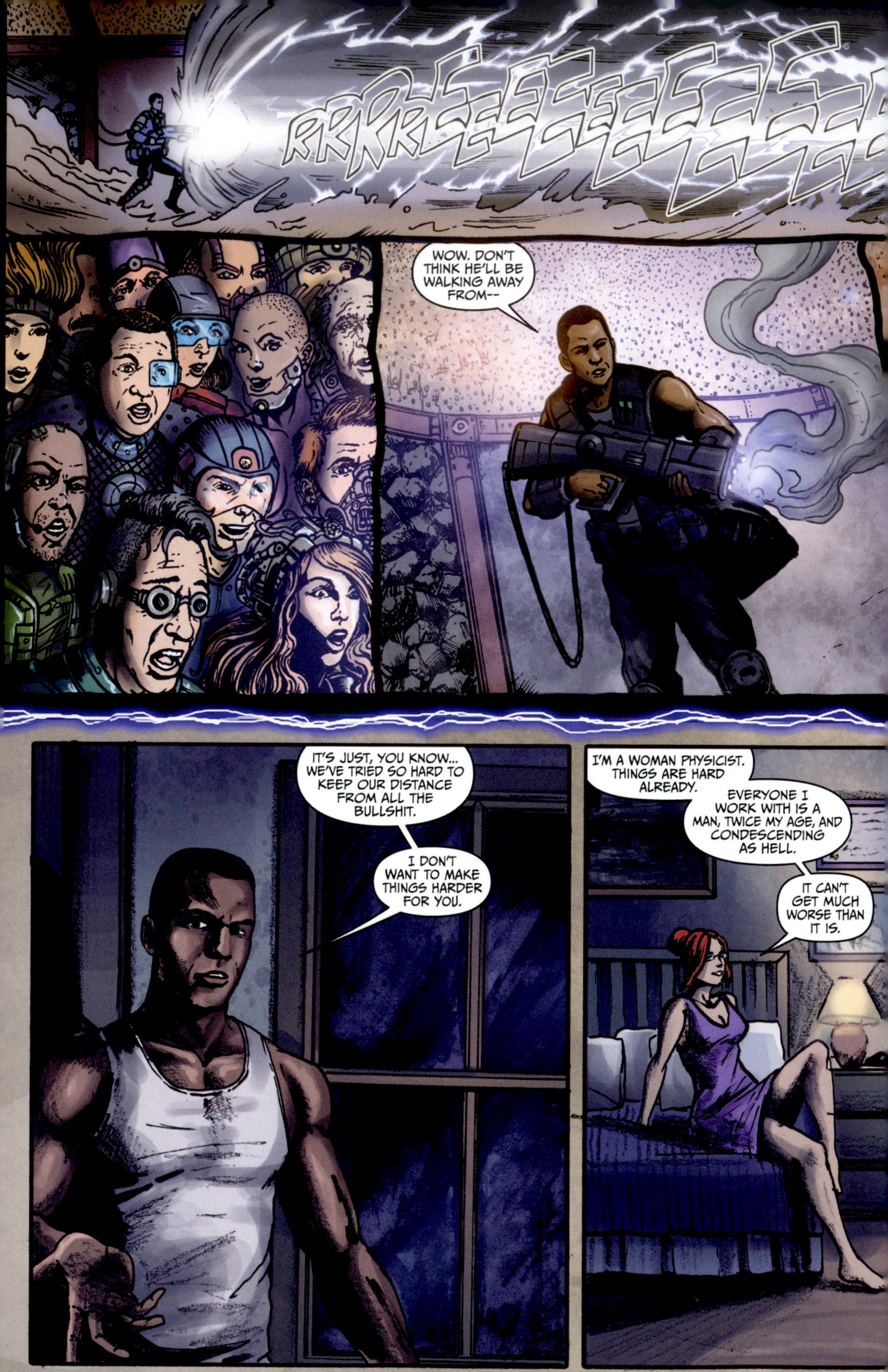
RRRRREEEEEEEEEEEEEEE
WOW. DON'T THINK HE'LL BE WALKING AWAY FROM--
IT'S JUST, YOU KNOW... WE'VE TRIED SO HARD TO KEEP OUR DISTANCE FROM ALL THE BULLSHIT.
I DON'T WANT TO MAKE THINGS HARDER FOR YOU.
I'M A WOMAN PHYSICIST. THINGS ARE HARD ALREADY.
EVERYONE I WORK WITH IS A MAN, TWICE MY AGE, AND CONDESCENDING AS HELL.
IT CAN'T GET MUCH WORSE THAN IT IS.

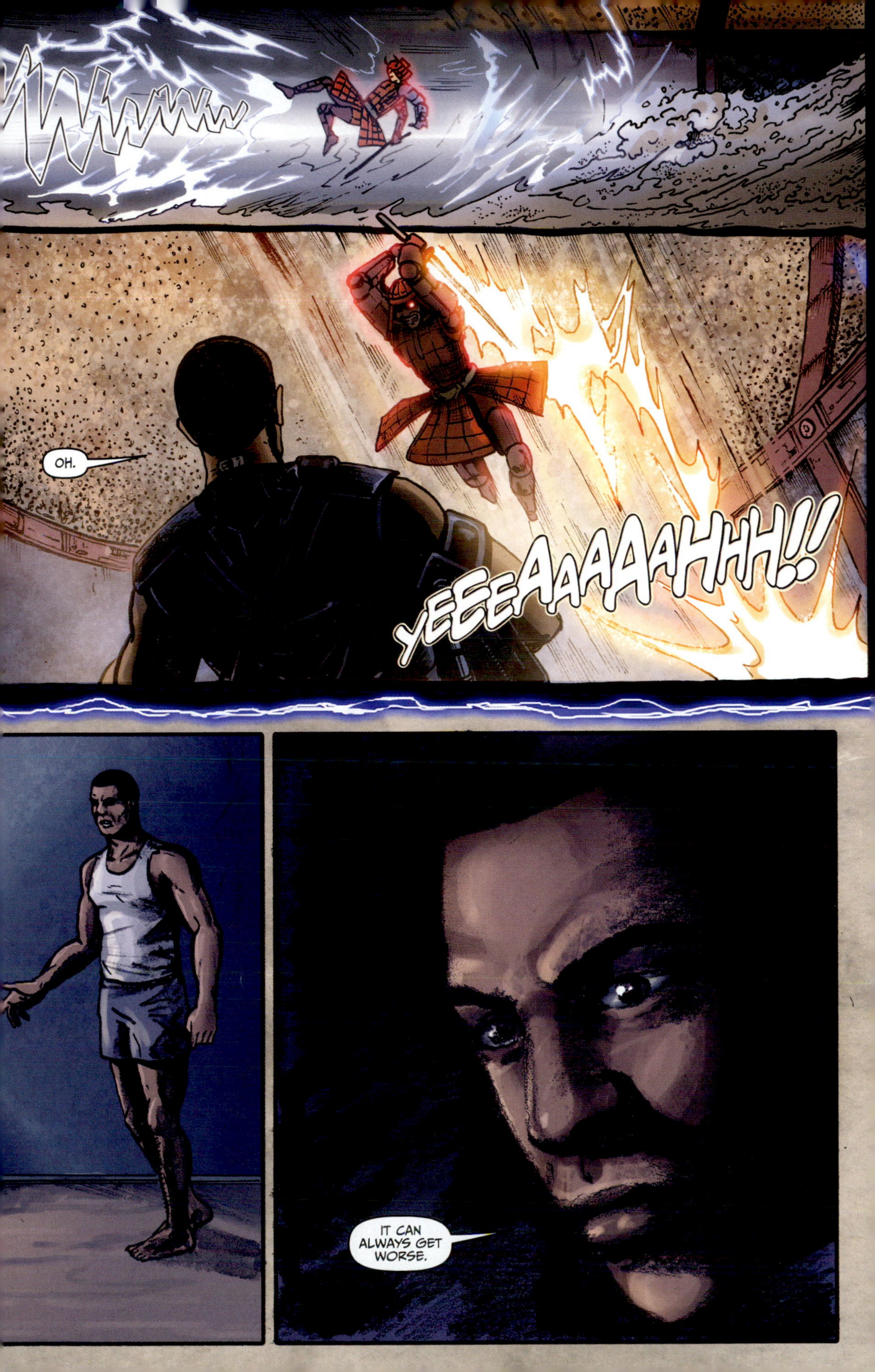
WHAAAA
OH.
YEEEAAAAAHHH!!
IT CAN ALWAYS GET WORSE.

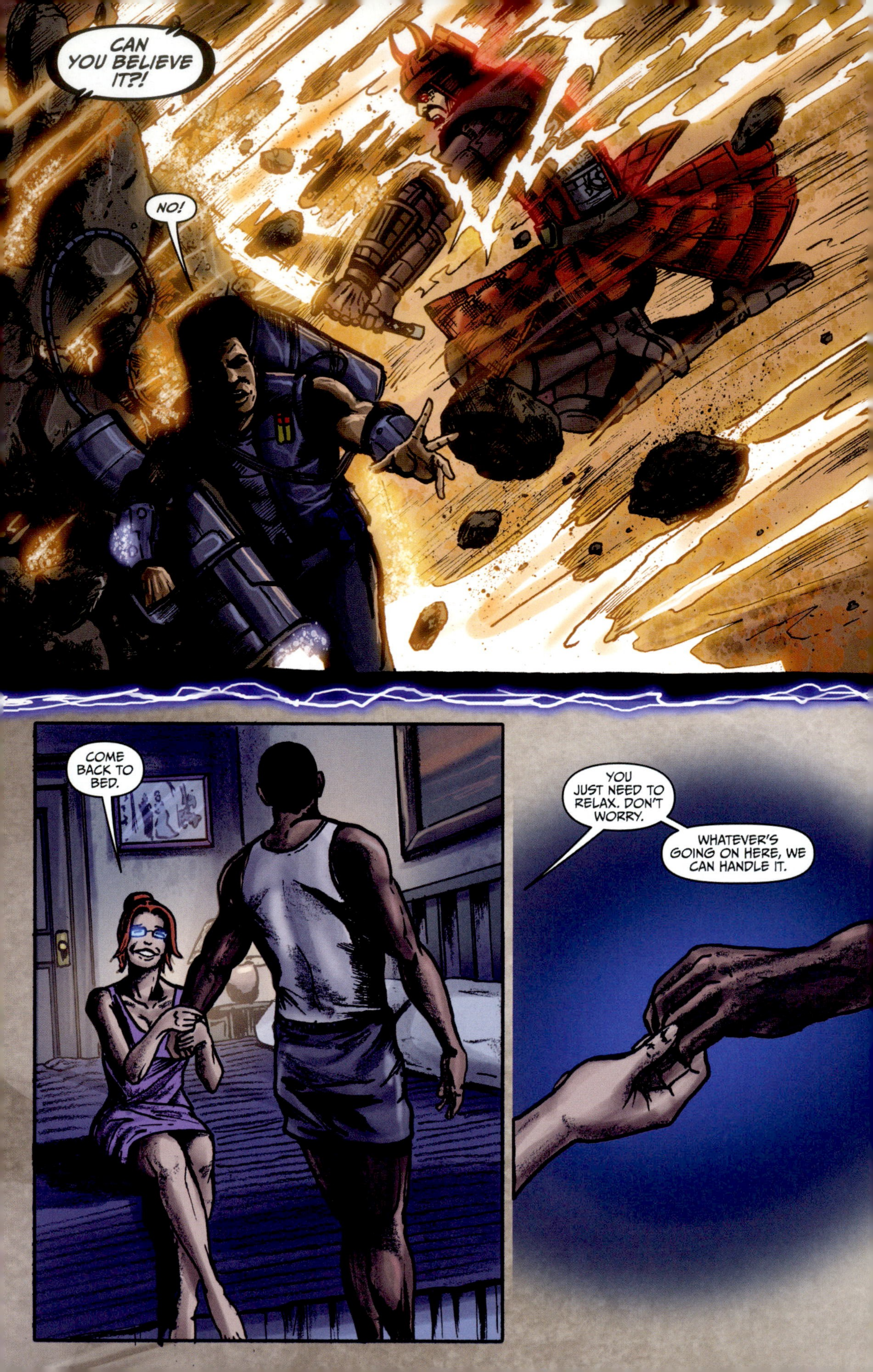
CAN YOU BELIEVE IT?!
NO!
COME BACK TO BED.
YOU JUST NEED TO RELAX. DON'T WORRY.
WHATEVER'S GOING ON HERE, WE CAN HANDLE IT.

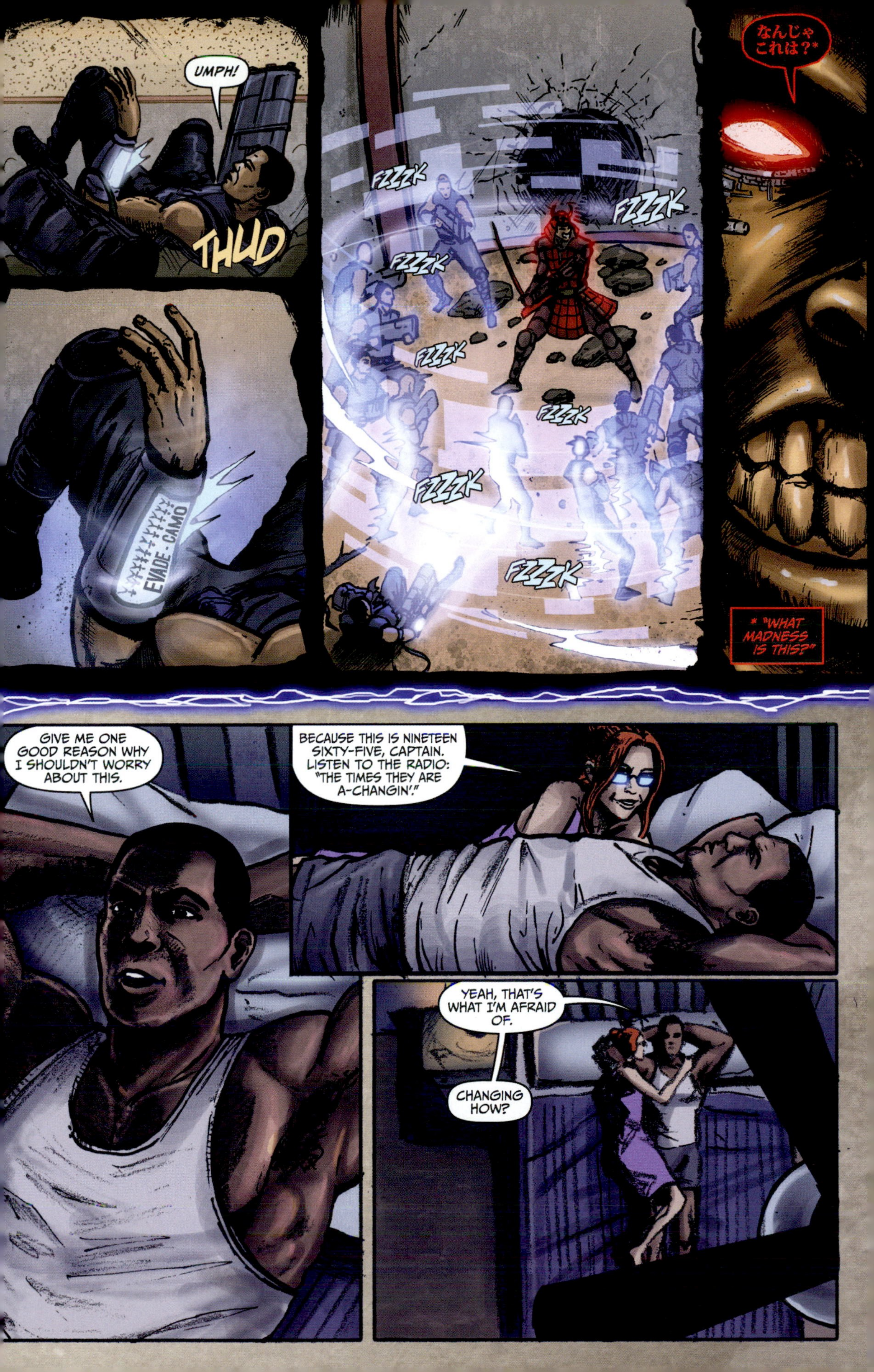
UMPH!
THUD
EVADE-CAMO
FZZZK
FZZZK
FZZZK
FZZZK
FZZZK
FZZZK
FZZZK
なんじゃ これは?*
* "WHAT MADNESS IS THIS?"
GIVE ME ONE GOOD REASON WHY I SHOULDN'T WORRY ABOUT THIS.
BECAUSE THIS IS NINETEEN SIXTY-FIVE, CAPTAIN. LISTEN TO THE RADIO: "THE TIMES THEY ARE A-CHANGIN'."
CHANGING HOW?
YEAH, THAT'S WHAT I'M AFRAID OF.

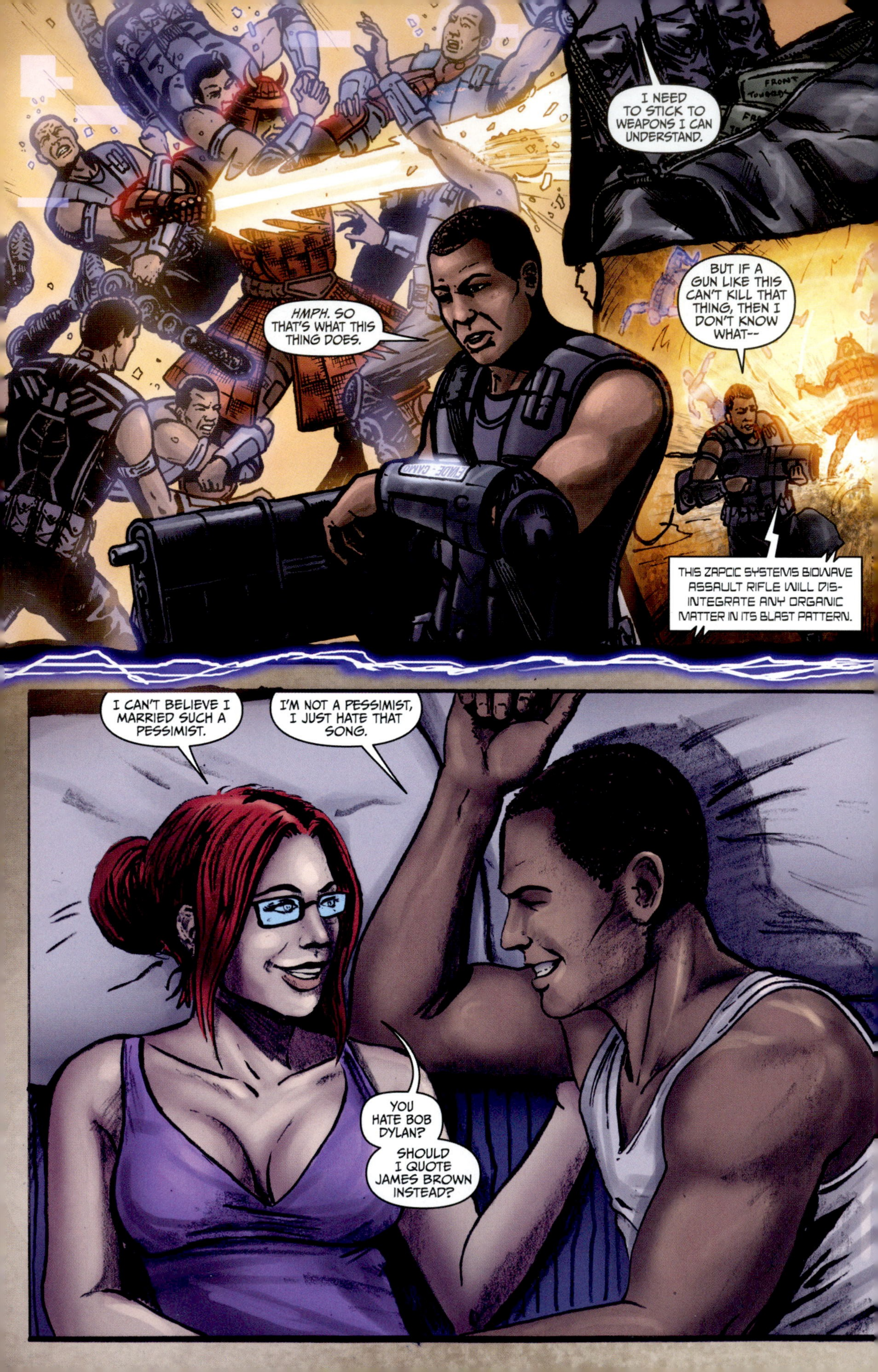
HMPH. SO THAT'S WHAT THIS THING DOES.
I NEED TO STICK TO WEAPONS I CAN UNDERSTAND.
BUT IF A GUN LIKE THIS CAN'T KILL THAT THING, THEN I DON'T KNOW WHAT--
THIS ZAPCIC SYSTEMS BIOWAVE ASSAULT RIFLE WILL DIS-INTEGRATE ANY ORGANIC MATTER IN ITS BLAST PATTERN.
I CAN'T BELIEVE I MARRIED SUCH A PESSIMIST.
I'M NOT A PESSIMIST, I JUST HATE THAT SONG.
YOU HATE BOB DYLAN?
SHOULD I QUOTE JAMES BROWN INSTEAD?

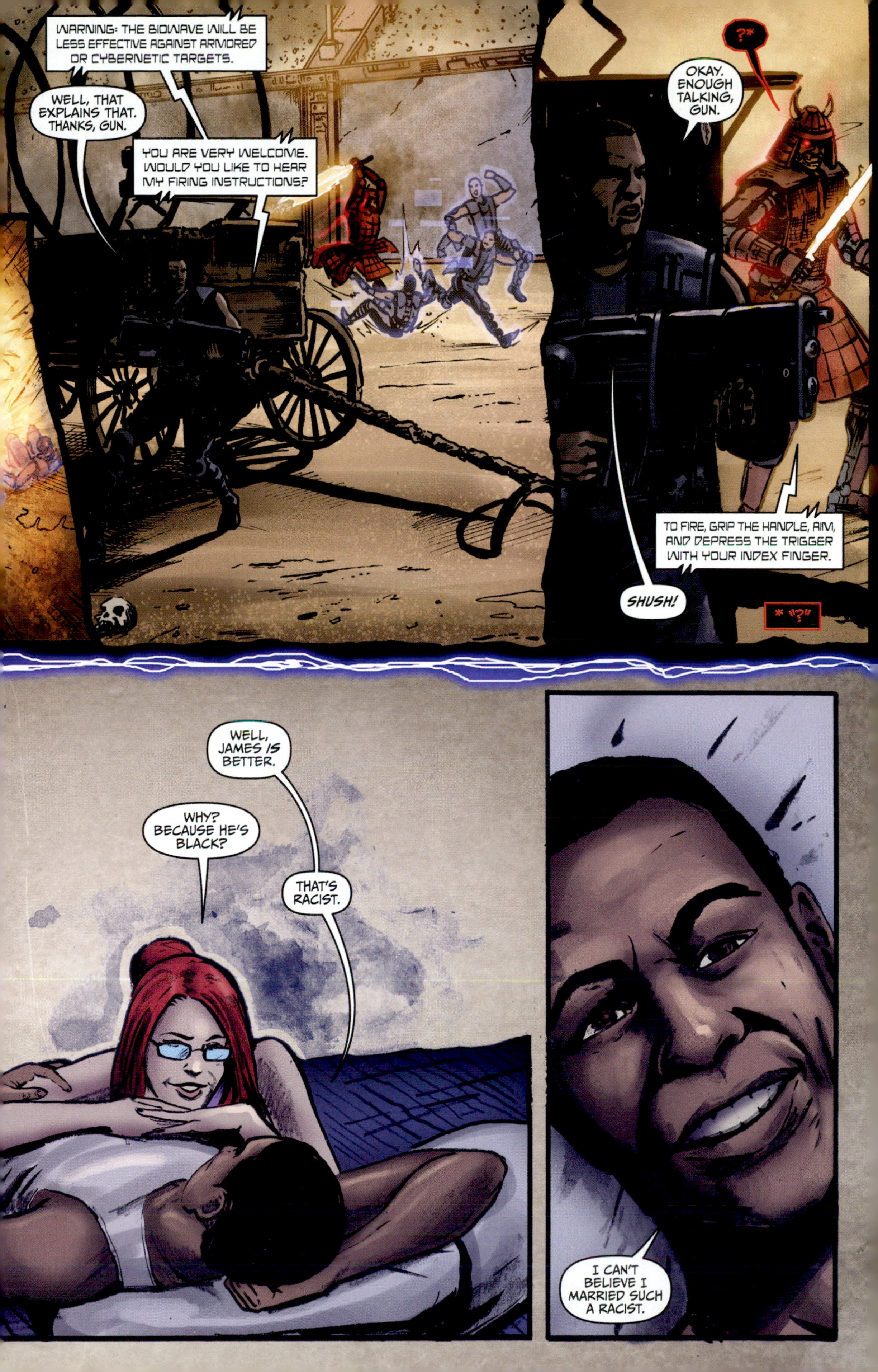
WARNING: THE BIOWAVE WILL BE LESS EFFECTIVE AGAINST ARMORED OR CYBERNETIC TARGETS.
WELL, THAT EXPLAINS THAT. THANKS, GUN.
YOU ARE VERY WELCOME. WOULD YOU LIKE TO HEAR MY FIRING INSTRUCTIONS?
?*
OKAY. ENOUGH TALKING, GUN.
TO FIRE, GRIP THE HANDLE, AIM, AND DEPRESS THE TRIGGER WITH YOUR INDEX FINGER.
SHUSH!
* "?"
WELL, JAMES *IS* BETTER.
WHY? BECAUSE HE'S BLACK?
THAT'S RACIST.
I CAN'T BELIEVE I MARRIED SUCH A RACIST.

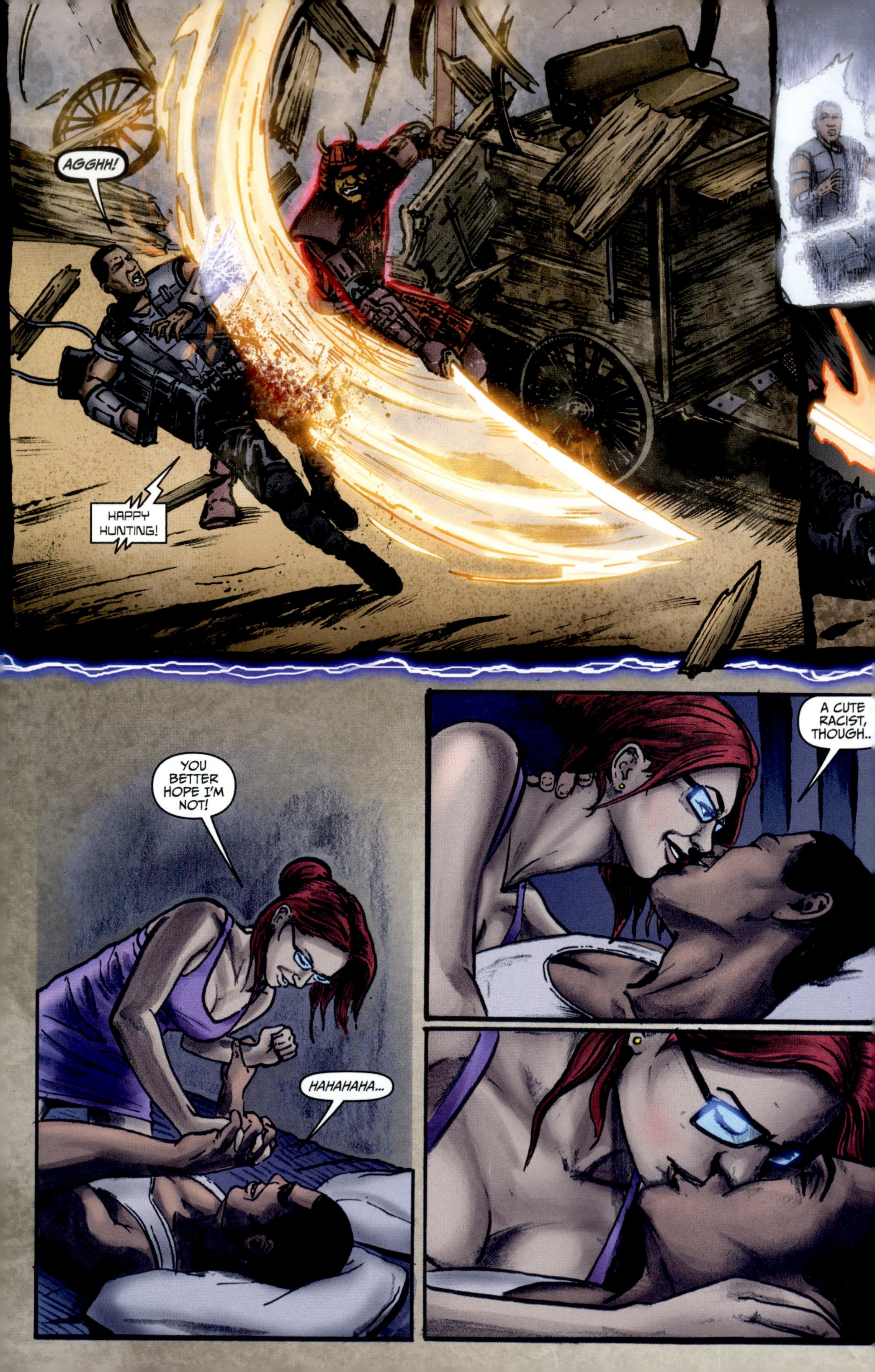
AGGHH!
HAPPY HUNTING!
YOU BETTER HOPE I'M NOT!
HAHAHAHA...
A CUTE RACIST, THOUGH..

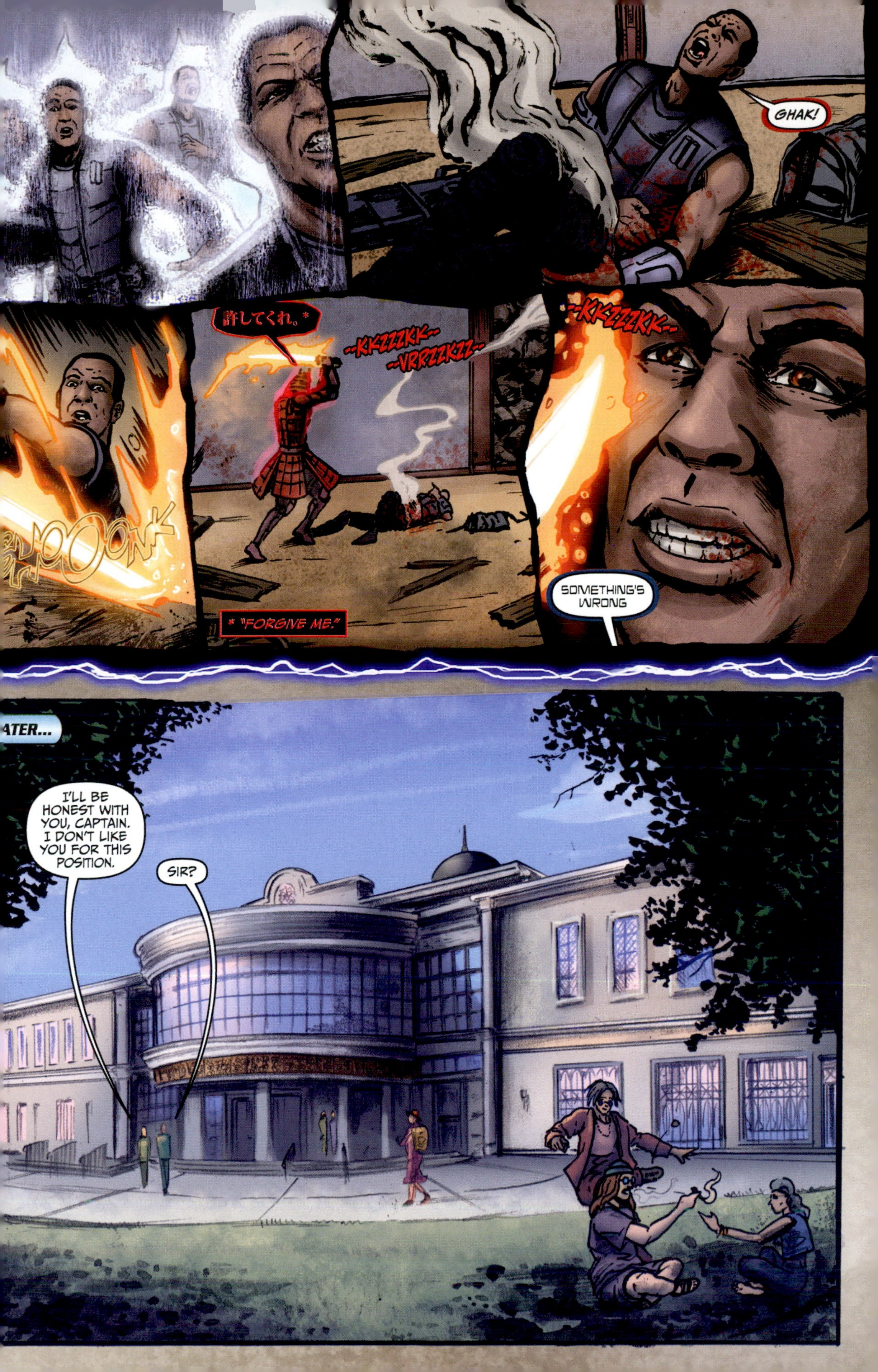
GHAK!
許してくれ。*
-KKZZZKK-
-VRRZZKZZ-
* "FORGIVE ME."
-KKZZZKK-
SOMETHING'S WRONG
ATER...
I'LL BE HONEST WITH YOU, CAPTAIN. I DON'T LIKE YOU FOR THIS POSITION.
SIR?

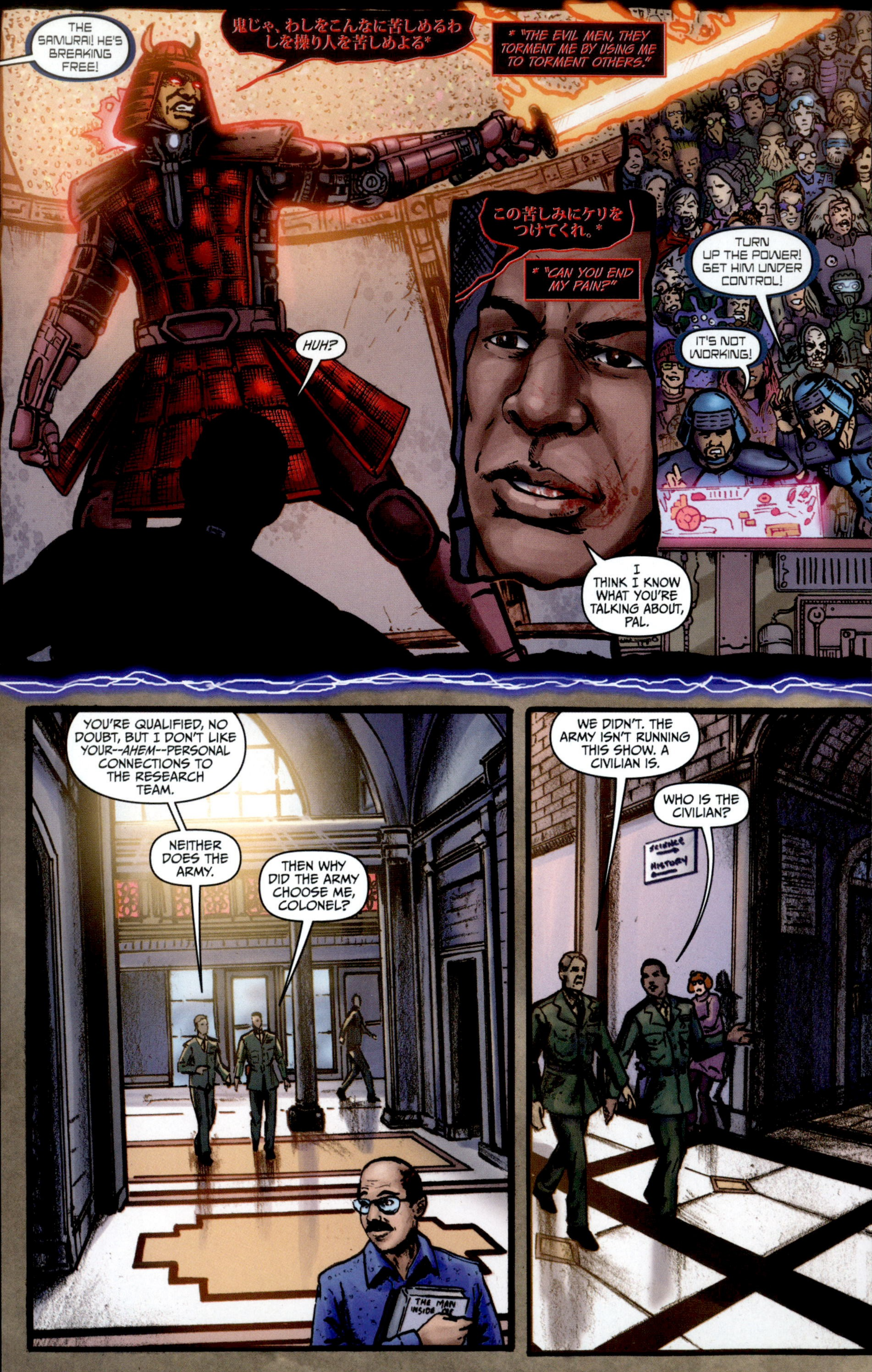
THE SAMURAI! HE'S BREAKING FREE!
鬼じゃ、わしをこんなに苦しめるわしを操り人を苦しめよる*
* "THE EVIL MEN, THEY TORMENT ME BY USING ME TO TORMENT OTHERS."
この苦しみにケリをつけてくれ。*
* "CAN YOU END MY PAIN?"
TURN UP THE POWER! GET HIM UNDER CONTROL!
HUH?
IT'S NOT WORKING!
I THINK I KNOW WHAT YOU'RE TALKING ABOUT, PAL.
YOU'RE QUALIFIED, NO DOUBT, BUT I DON'T LIKE YOUR--AHEM--PERSONAL CONNECTIONS TO THE RESEARCH TEAM.
NEITHER DOES THE ARMY.
THEN WHY DID THE ARMY CHOOSE ME, COLONEL?
WE DIDN'T. THE ARMY ISN'T RUNNING THIS SHOW. A CIVILIAN IS.
WHO IS THE CIVILIAN?

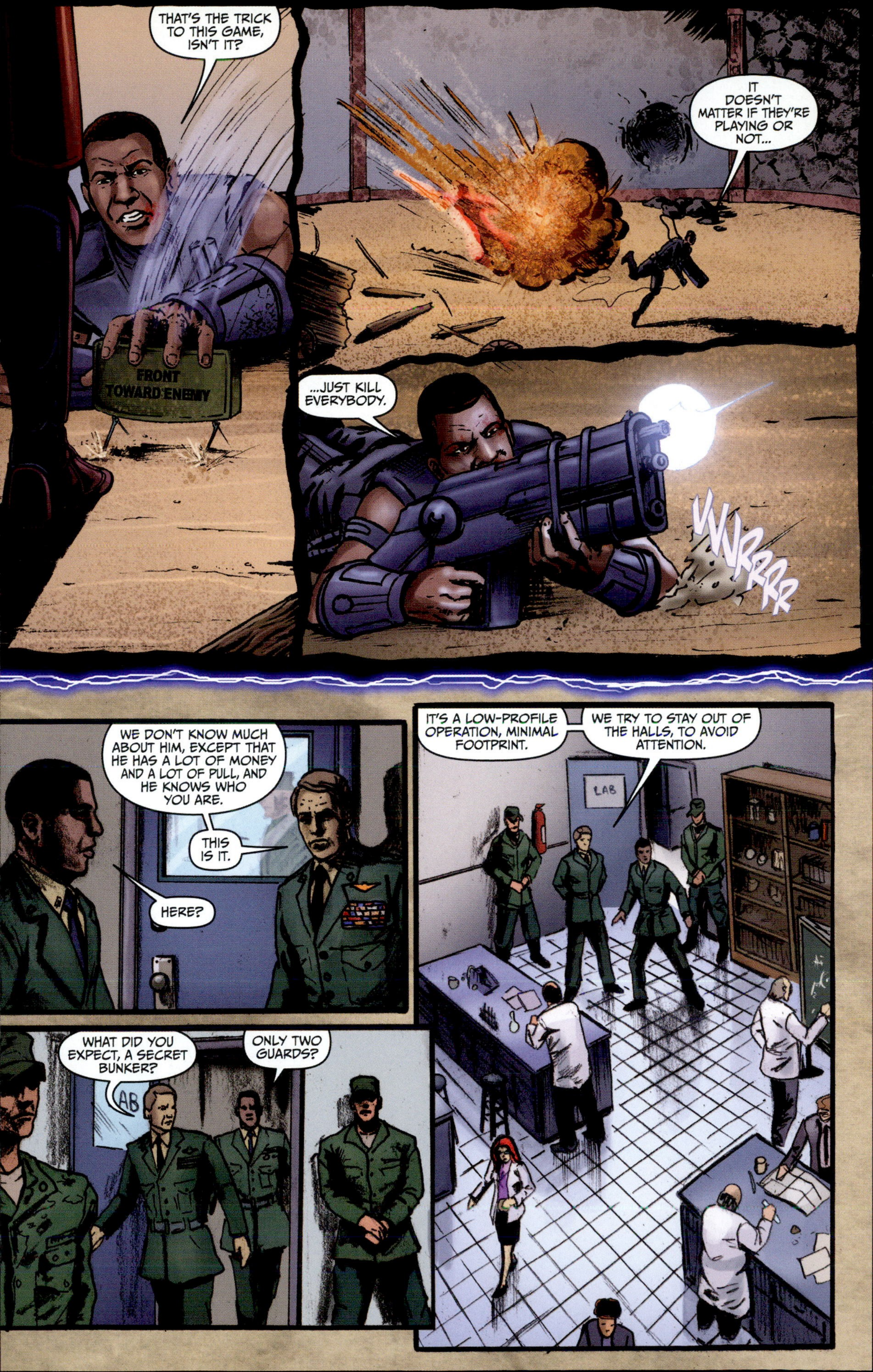

THAT'S THE TRICK TO THIS GAME, ISN'T IT?
FRONT TOWARD ENEMY
IT DOESN'T MATTER IF THEY'RE PLAYING OR NOT...
...JUST KILL EVERYBODY.
VVVRRRR
WE DON'T KNOW MUCH ABOUT HIM, EXCEPT THAT HE HAS A LOT OF MONEY AND A LOT OF PULL, AND HE KNOWS WHO YOU ARE.
THIS IS IT.
HERE?
WHAT DID YOU EXPECT, A SECRET BUNKER?
ONLY TWO GUARDS?
IT'S A LOW-PROFILE OPERATION, MINIMAL FOOTPRINT.
WE TRY TO STAY OUT OF THE HALLS, TO AVOID ATTENTION.
LAB

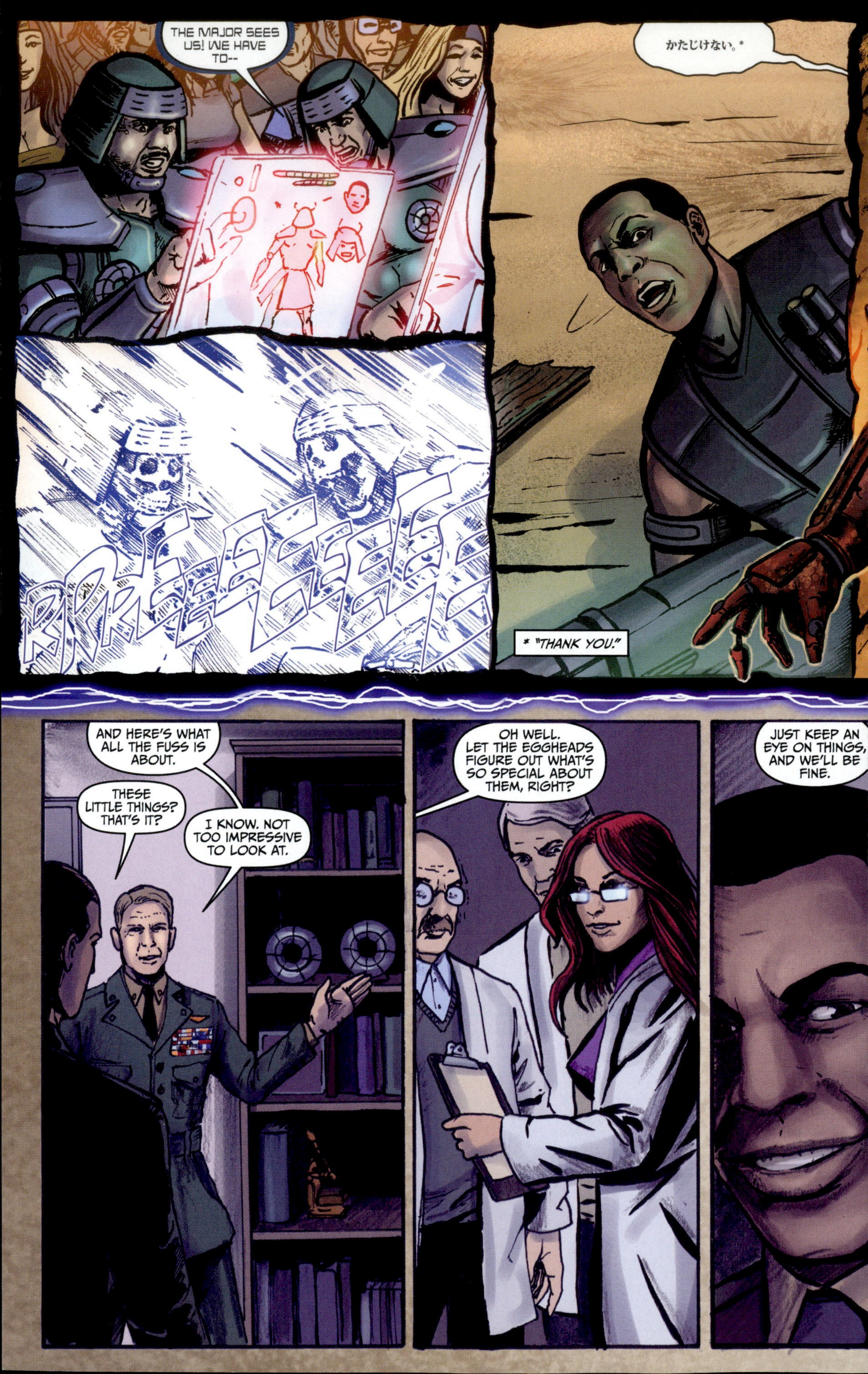
THE MAJOR SEES US! WE HAVE TO--
かたじけない。*
* "THANK YOU."
AND HERE'S WHAT ALL THE FUSS IS ABOUT.
THESE LITTLE THINGS? THAT'S IT?
I KNOW. NOT TOO IMPRESSIVE TO LOOK AT.
OH WELL. LET THE EGGHEADS FIGURE OUT WHAT'S SO SPECIAL ABOUT THEM, RIGHT?
JUST KEEP AN EYE ON THINGS, AND WE'LL BE FINE.

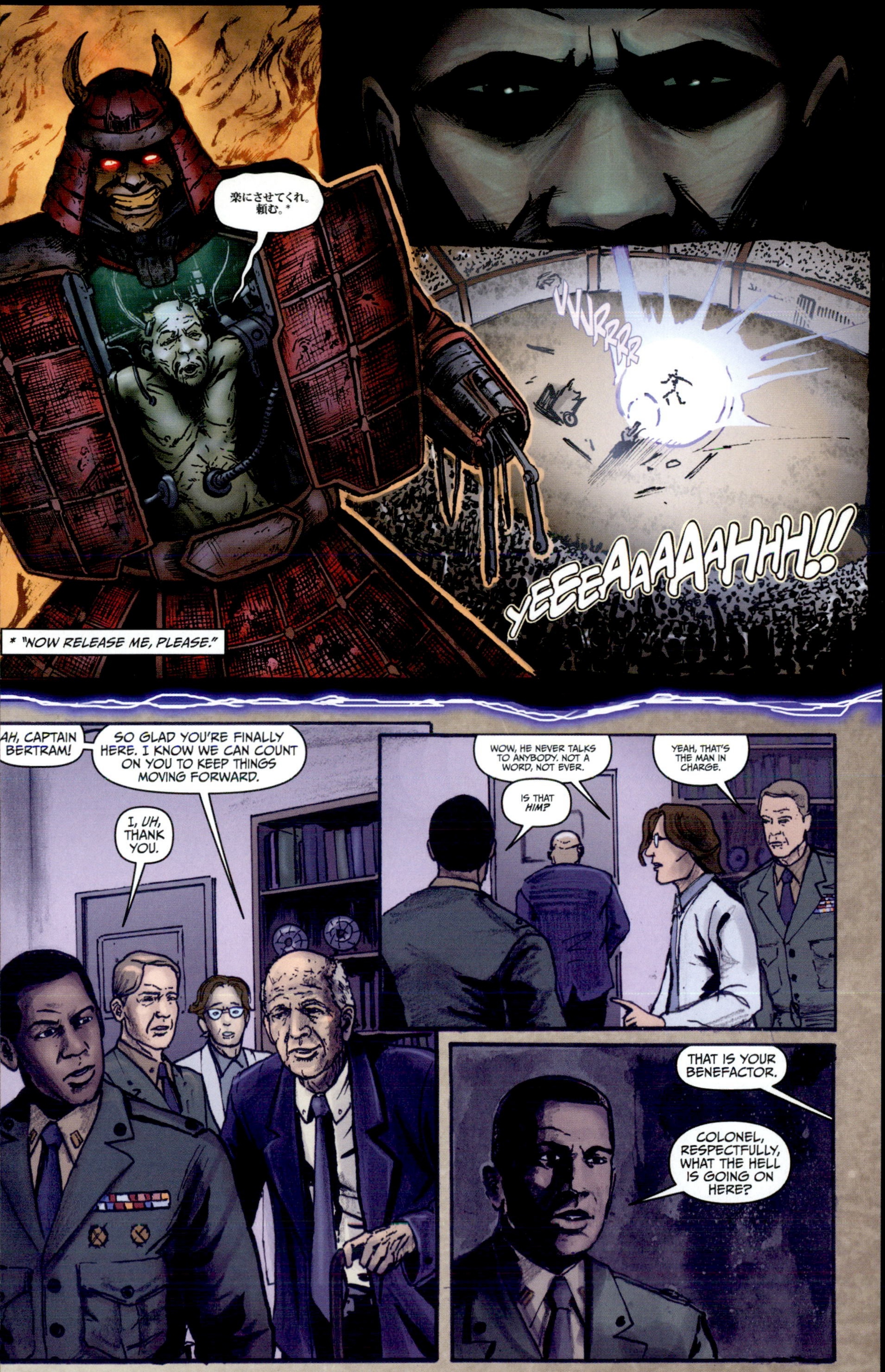

楽にさせてくれ。頼む。*
VVJRRRR
YEEEAAAAAHHH!!
* "NOW RELEASE ME, PLEASE."
AH, CAPTAIN BERTRAM!
SO GLAD YOU'RE FINALLY HERE. I KNOW WE CAN COUNT ON YOU TO KEEP THINGS MOVING FORWARD.
I, UH, THANK YOU.
IS THAT HIM?
WOW, HE NEVER TALKS TO ANYBODY. NOT A WORD, NOT EVER.
YEAH, THAT'S THE MAN IN CHARGE.
THAT IS YOUR BENEFACTOR.
COLONEL, RESPECTFULLY, WHAT THE HELL IS GOING ON HERE?

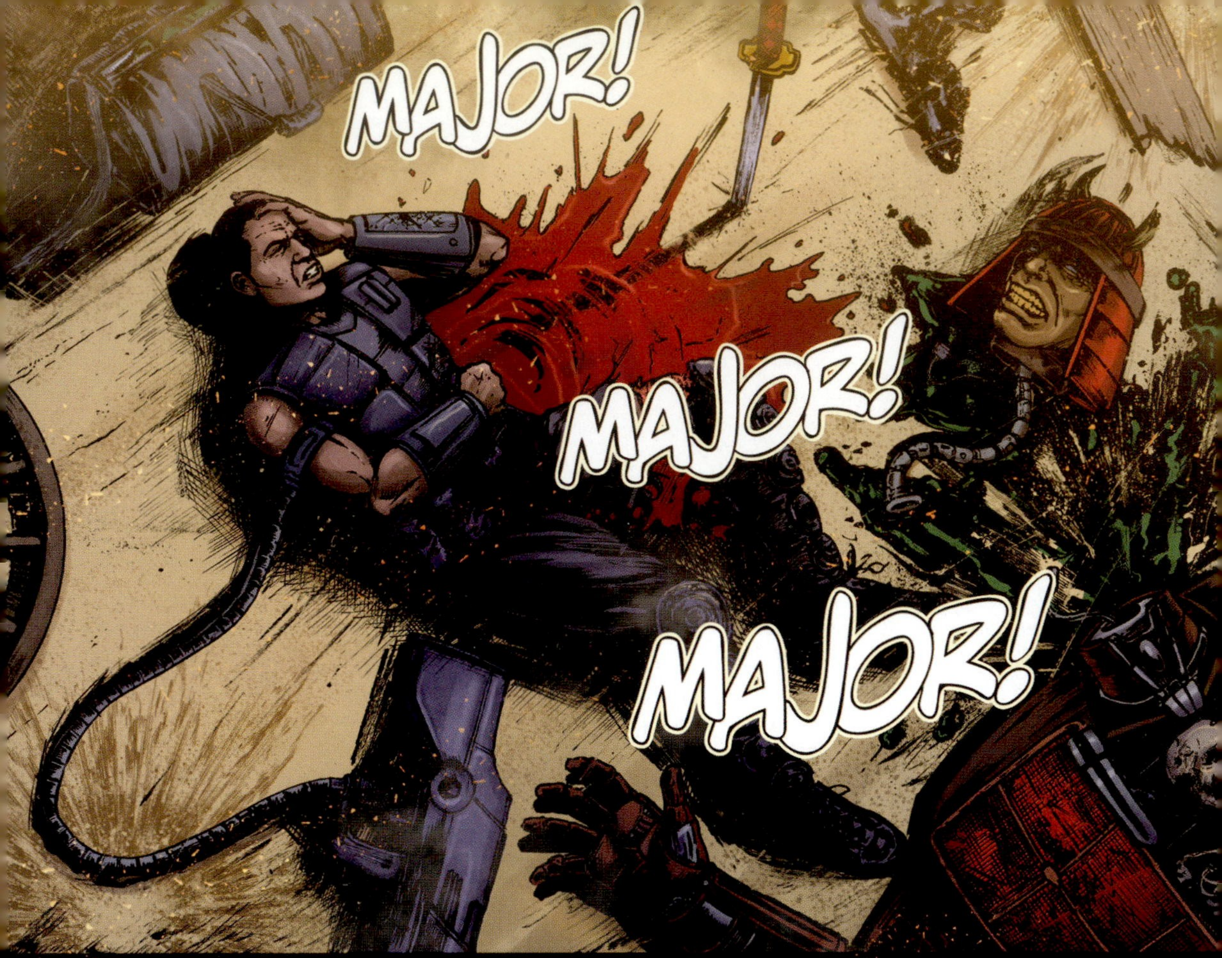
MAJOR!
MAJOR!
MAJOR!
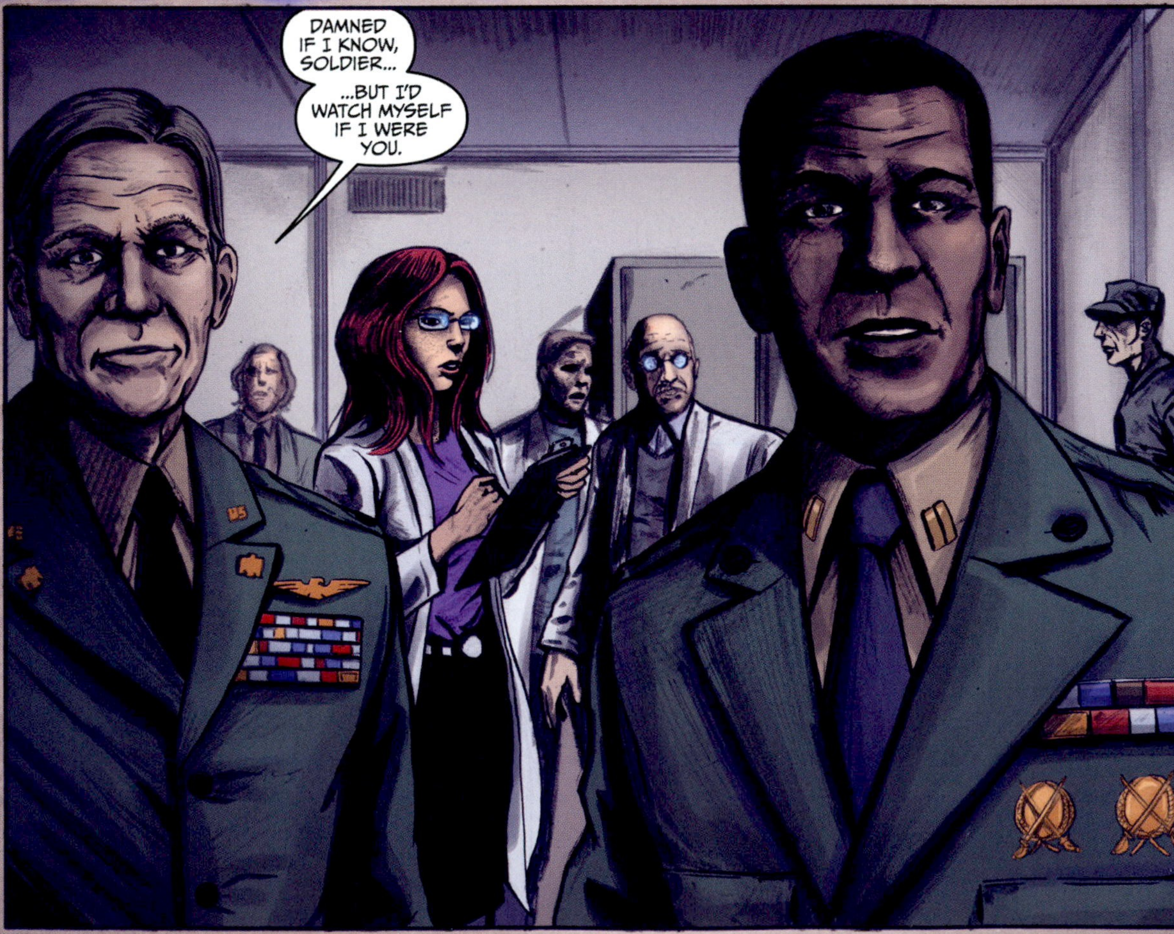
DAMNED IF I KNOW, SOLDIER...
...BUT I'D WATCH MYSELF IF I WERE YOU.

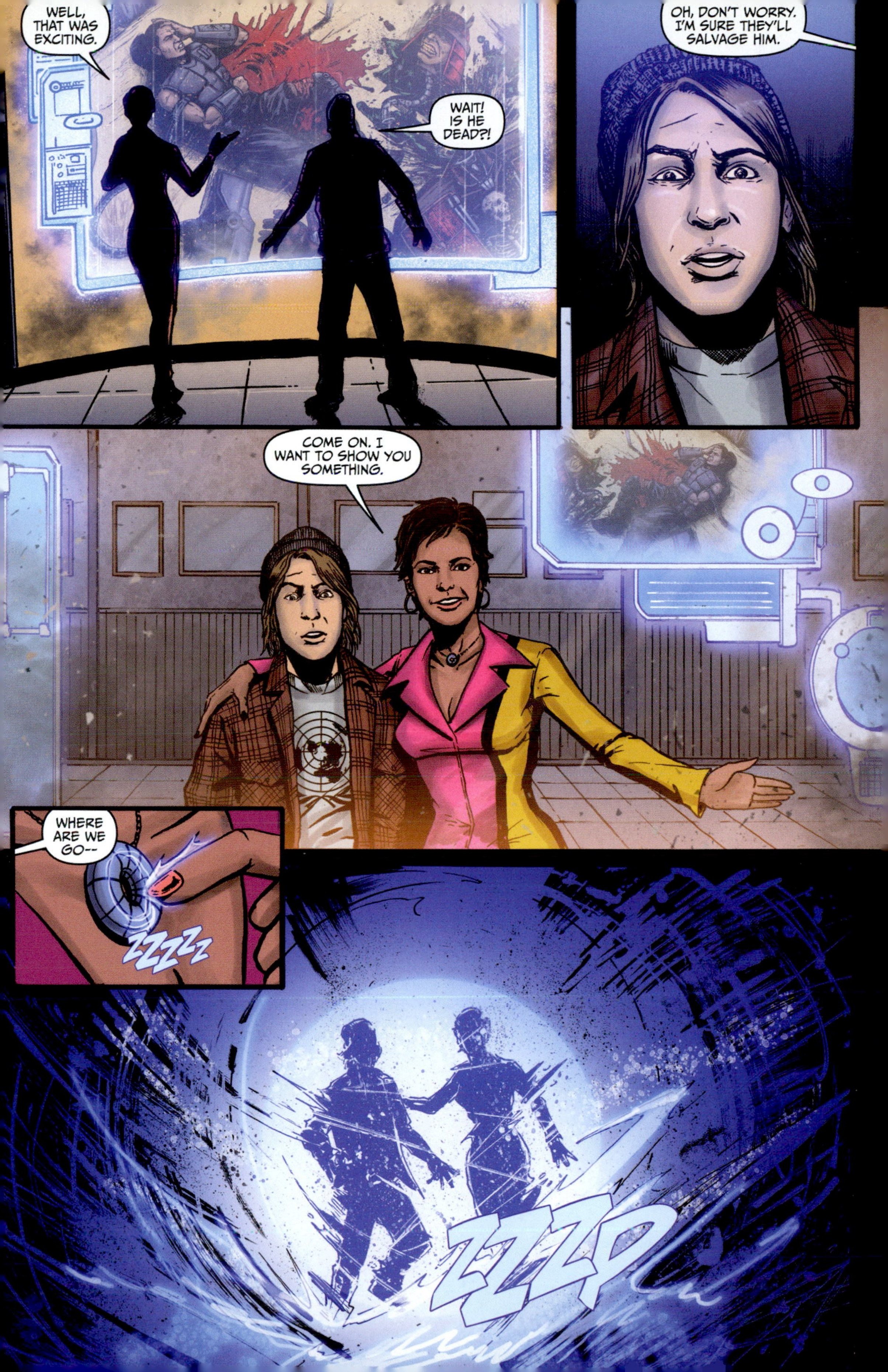
WELL, THAT WAS EXCITING.
WAIT! IS HE DEAD?!
OH, DON'T WORRY. I'M SURE THEY'LL SALVAGE HIM.
COME ON. I WANT TO SHOW YOU SOMETHING.
WHERE ARE WE GO--
ZZZZZ
ZZZP

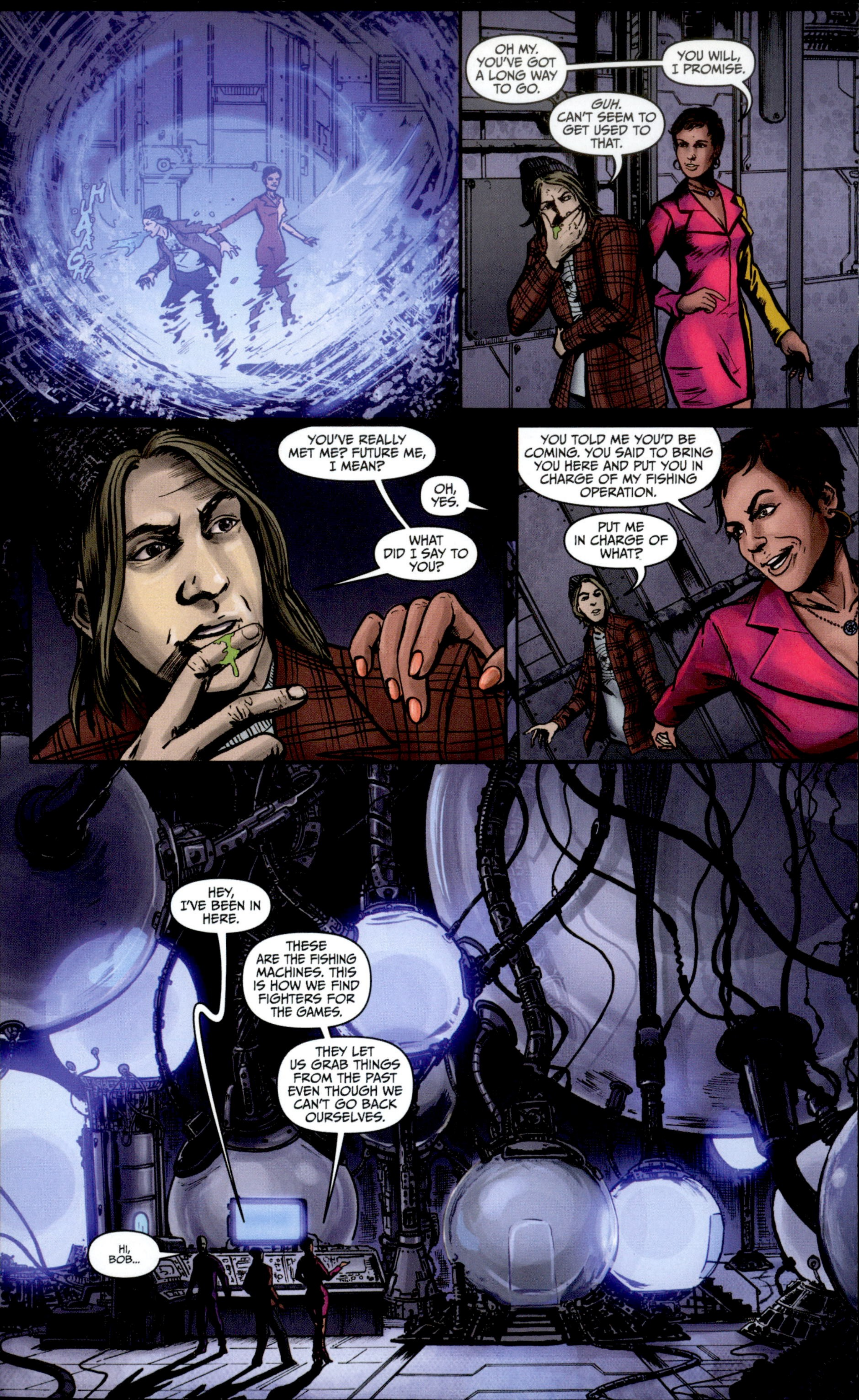
HHAAGH!
OH MY. YOU'VE GOT A LONG WAY TO GO.
GUH. CAN'T SEEM TO GET USED TO THAT.
YOU WILL, I PROMISE.
YOU'VE REALLY MET ME? FUTURE ME, I MEAN?
OH, YES.
WHAT DID I SAY TO YOU?
YOU TOLD ME YOU'D BE COMING. YOU SAID TO BRING YOU HERE AND PUT YOU IN CHARGE OF MY FISHING OPERATION.
PUT ME IN CHARGE OF WHAT?
HEY, I'VE BEEN IN HERE.
THESE ARE THE FISHING MACHINES. THIS IS HOW WE FIND FIGHTERS FOR THE GAMES.
THEY LET US GRAB THINGS FROM THE PAST EVEN THOUGH WE CAN'T GO BACK OURSELVES.
HI, BOB...

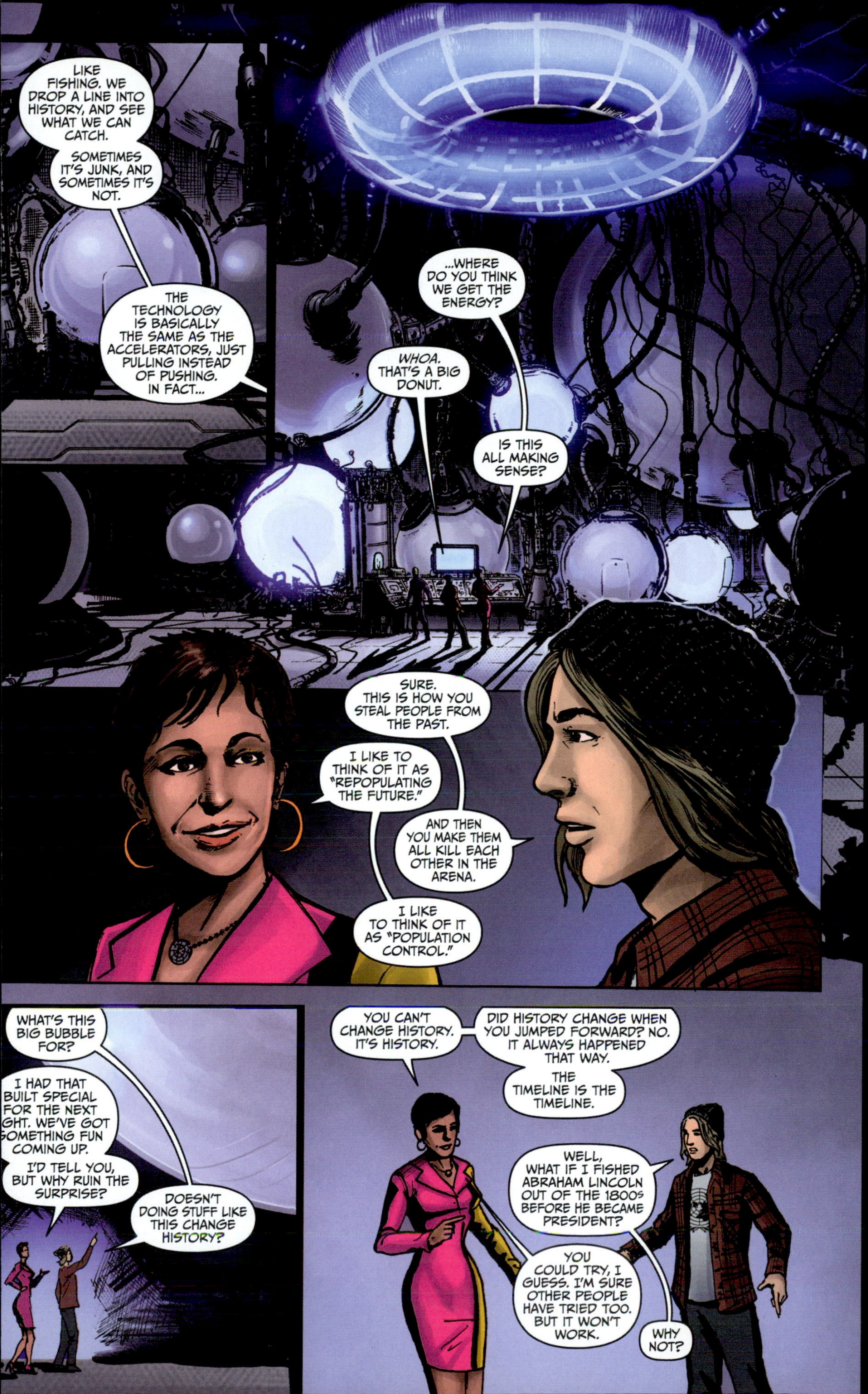
LIKE FISHING. WE DROP A LINE INTO HISTORY, AND SEE WHAT WE CAN CATCH.
SOMETIMES IT'S JUNK, AND SOMETIMES IT'S NOT.
THE TECHNOLOGY IS BASICALLY THE SAME AS THE ACCELERATORS, JUST PULLING INSTEAD OF PUSHING. IN FACT...
...WHERE DO YOU THINK WE GET THE ENERGY?
WHOA. THAT'S A BIG DONUT.
IS THIS ALL MAKING SENSE?
SURE. THIS IS HOW YOU STEAL PEOPLE FROM THE PAST.
I LIKE TO THINK OF IT AS "REPOPULATING THE FUTURE."
AND THEN YOU MAKE THEM ALL KILL EACH OTHER IN THE ARENA.
I LIKE TO THINK OF IT AS "POPULATION CONTROL."
WHAT'S THIS BIG BUBBLE FOR?
I HAD THAT BUILT SPECIAL FOR THE NEXT GHT. WE'VE GOT OMETHING FUN COMING UP.
I'D TELL YOU, BUT WHY RUIN THE SURPRISE?
DOESN'T DOING STUFF LIKE THIS CHANGE HISTORY?
YOU CAN'T CHANGE HISTORY. IT'S HISTORY.
DID HISTORY CHANGE WHEN YOU JUMPED FORWARD? NO. IT ALWAYS HAPPENED THAT WAY.
THE TIMELINE IS THE TIMELINE.
WELL, WHAT IF I FISHED ABRAHAM LINCOLN OUT OF THE 1800s BEFORE HE BECAME PRESIDENT?
YOU COULD TRY, I GUESS. I'M SURE OTHER PEOPLE HAVE TRIED TOO. BUT IT WON'T WORK.
WHY NOT?

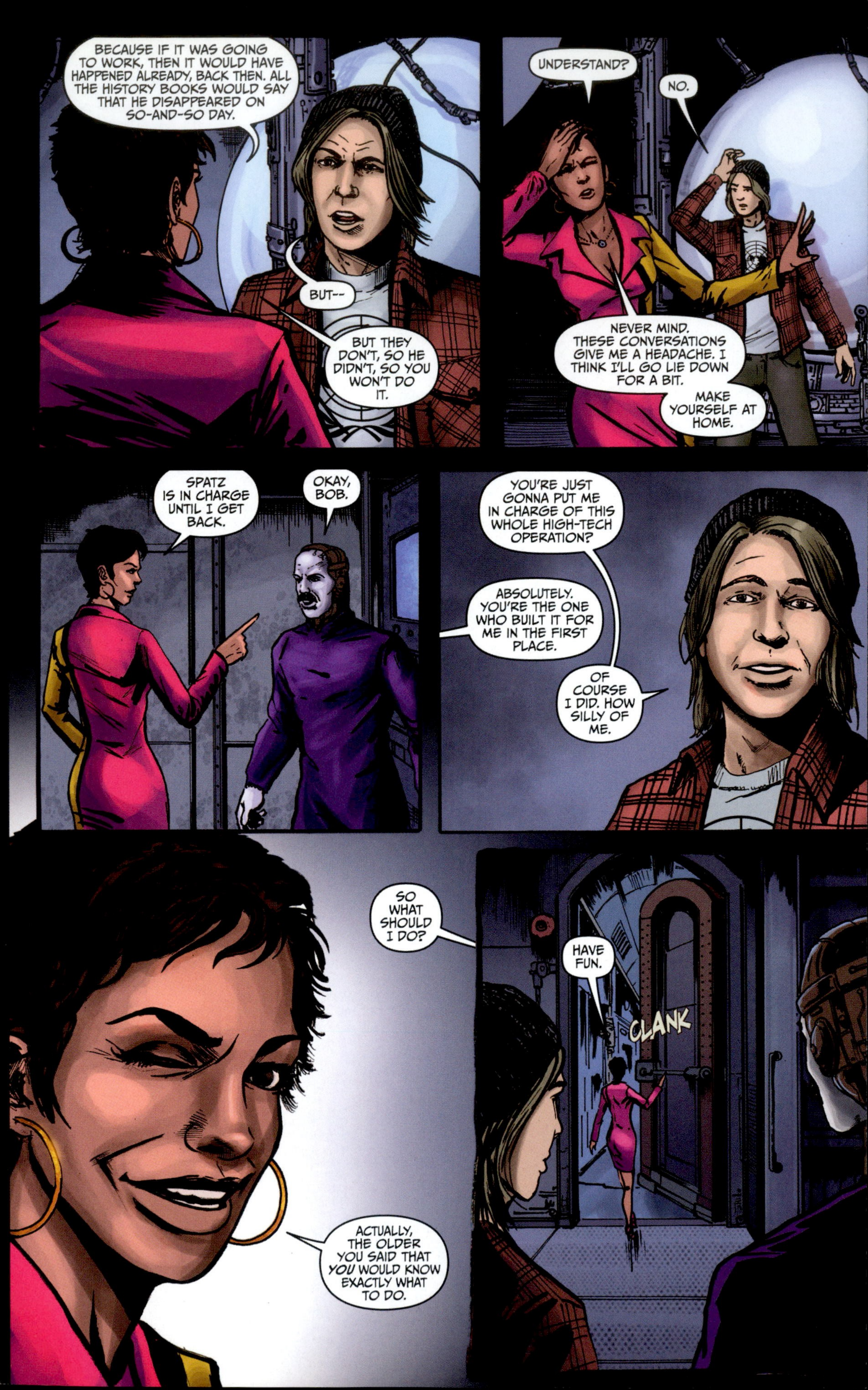

BECAUSE IF IT WAS GOING TO WORK, THEN IT WOULD HAVE HAPPENED ALREADY, BACK THEN. ALL THE HISTORY BOOKS WOULD SAY THAT HE DISAPPEARED ON SO-AND-SO DAY.
BUT--
BUT THEY DON'T, SO HE DIDN'T, SO YOU WON'T DO IT.
UNDERSTAND?
NO.
NEVER MIND. THESE CONVERSATIONS GIVE ME A HEADACHE. I THINK I'LL GO LIE DOWN FOR A BIT.
MAKE YOURSELF AT HOME.
SPATZ IS IN CHARGE UNTIL I GET BACK.
OKAY, BOB.
YOU'RE JUST GONNA PUT ME IN CHARGE OF THIS WHOLE HIGH-TECH OPERATION?
ABSOLUTELY. YOU'RE THE ONE WHO BUILT IT FOR ME IN THE FIRST PLACE.
OF COURSE I DID. HOW SILLY OF ME.
SO WHAT SHOULD I DO?
ACTUALLY, THE OLDER YOU SAID THAT *YOU* WOULD KNOW EXACTLY WHAT TO DO.
HAVE FUN.
CLANK

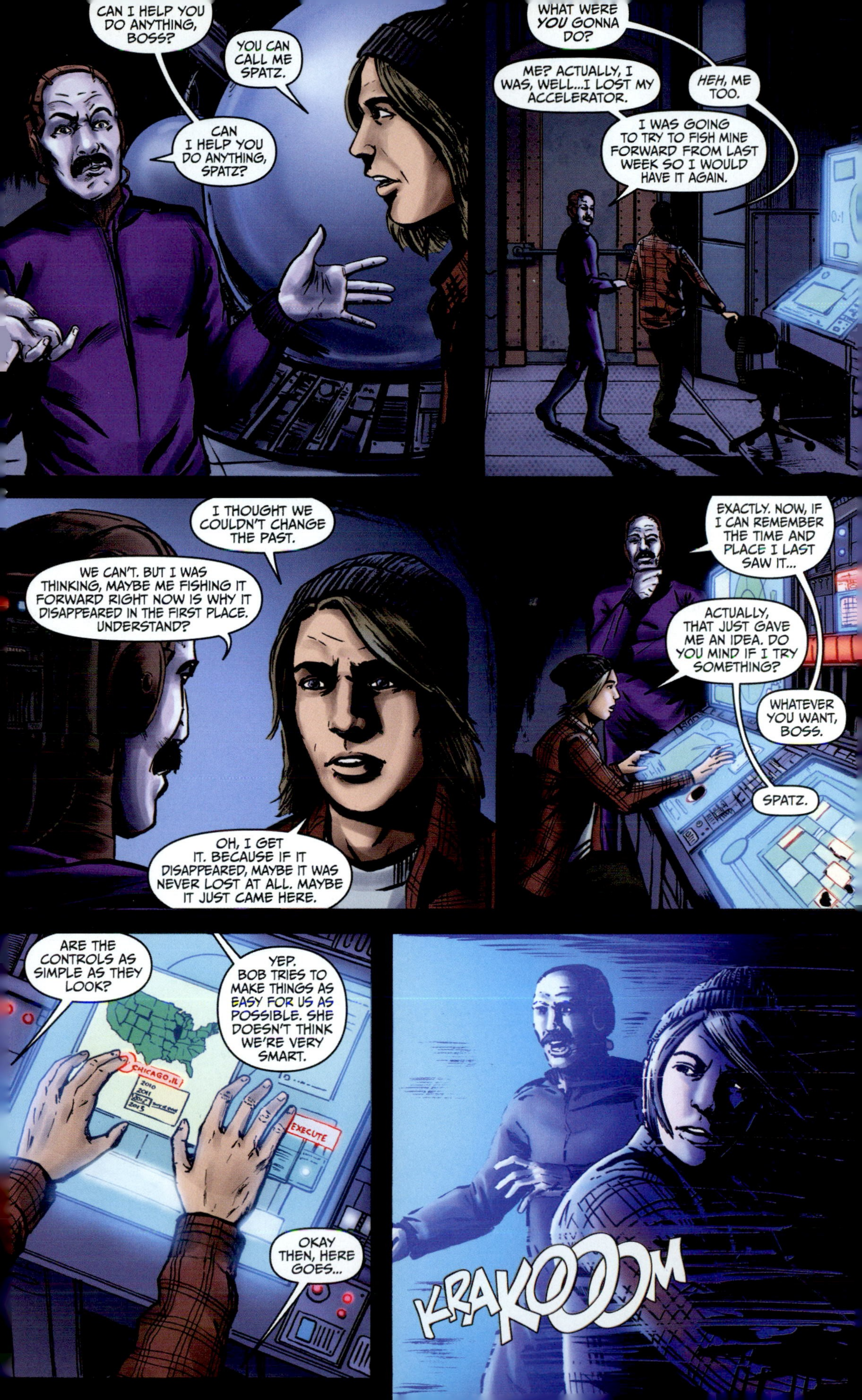
CAN I HELP YOU DO ANYTHING, BOSS?
YOU CAN CALL ME SPATZ.
CAN I HELP YOU DO ANYTHING, SPATZ?
WHAT WERE YOU GONNA DO?
ME? ACTUALLY, I WAS, WELL...I LOST MY ACCELERATOR.
HEH, ME TOO.
I WAS GOING TO TRY TO FISH MINE FORWARD FROM LAST WEEK SO I WOULD HAVE IT AGAIN.
I THOUGHT WE COULDN'T CHANGE THE PAST.
WE CAN'T. BUT I WAS THINKING, MAYBE ME FISHING IT FORWARD RIGHT NOW IS WHY IT DISAPPEARED IN THE FIRST PLACE. UNDERSTAND?
OH, I GET IT. BECAUSE IF IT DISAPPEARED, MAYBE IT WAS NEVER LOST AT ALL. MAYBE IT JUST CAME HERE.
EXACTLY. NOW, IF I CAN REMEMBER THE TIME AND PLACE I LAST SAW IT...
ACTUALLY, THAT JUST GAVE ME AN IDEA. DO YOU MIND IF I TRY SOMETHING?
WHATEVER YOU WANT, BOSS.
SPATZ.
ARE THE CONTROLS AS SIMPLE AS THEY LOOK?
YEP. BOB TRIES TO MAKE THINGS AS EASY FOR US AS POSSIBLE. SHE DOESN'T THINK WE'RE VERY SMART.
CHICAGO, IL
2010
2011
2013
EXECUTE
OKAY THEN, HERE GOES...
KRAKOOOM

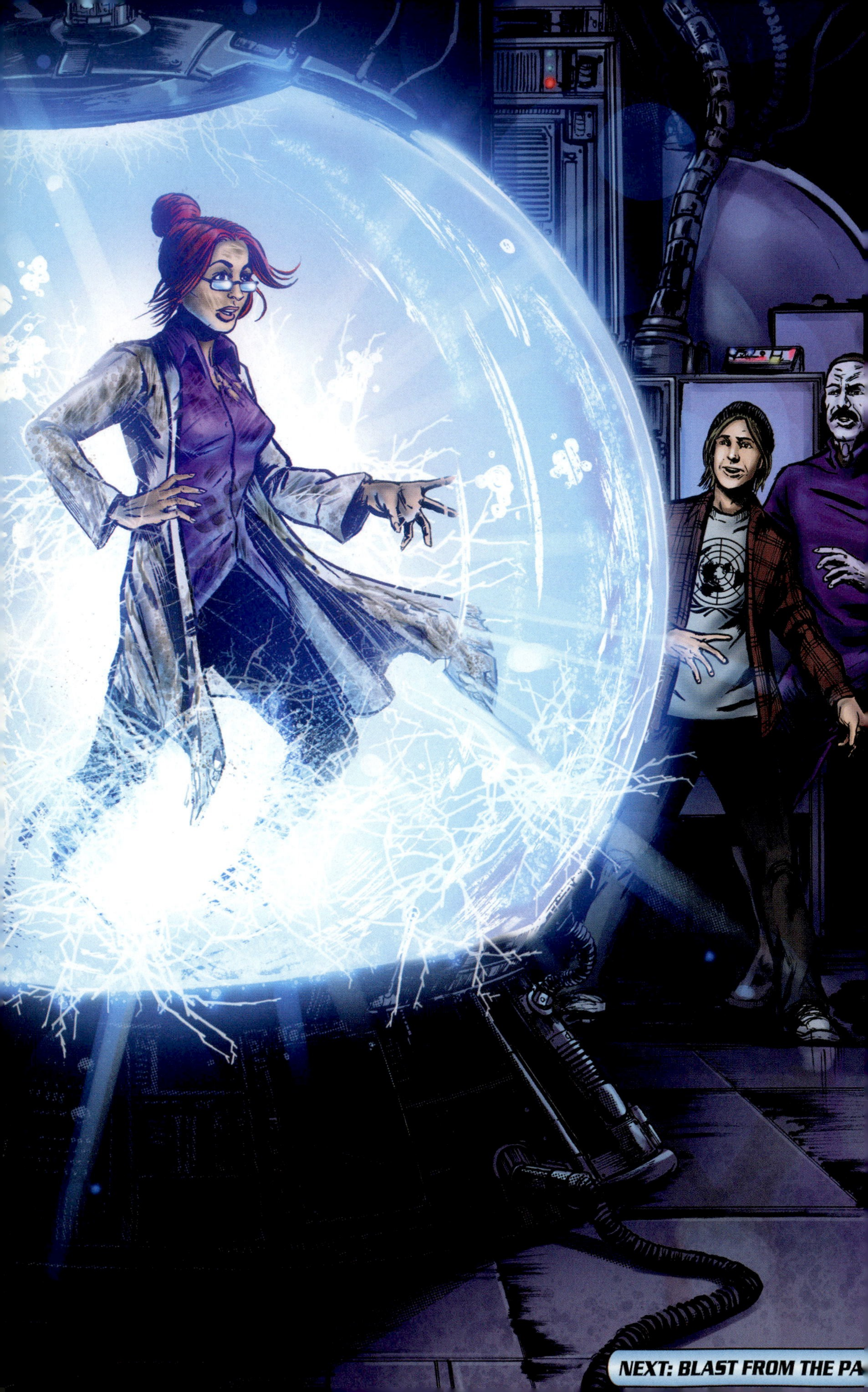
NEXT: BLAST FROM THE PA

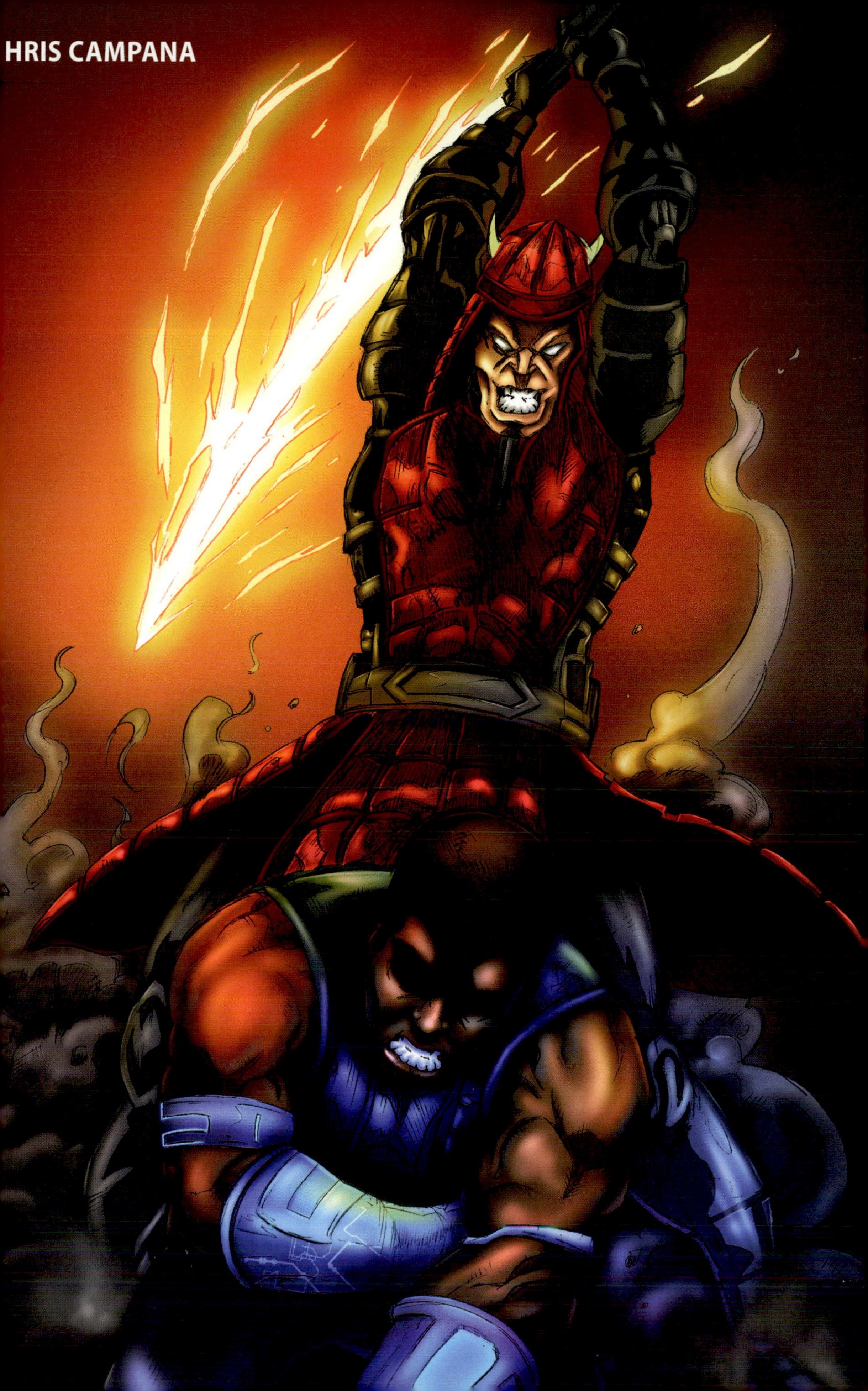
HRIS CAMPANA

5
Out Of Time

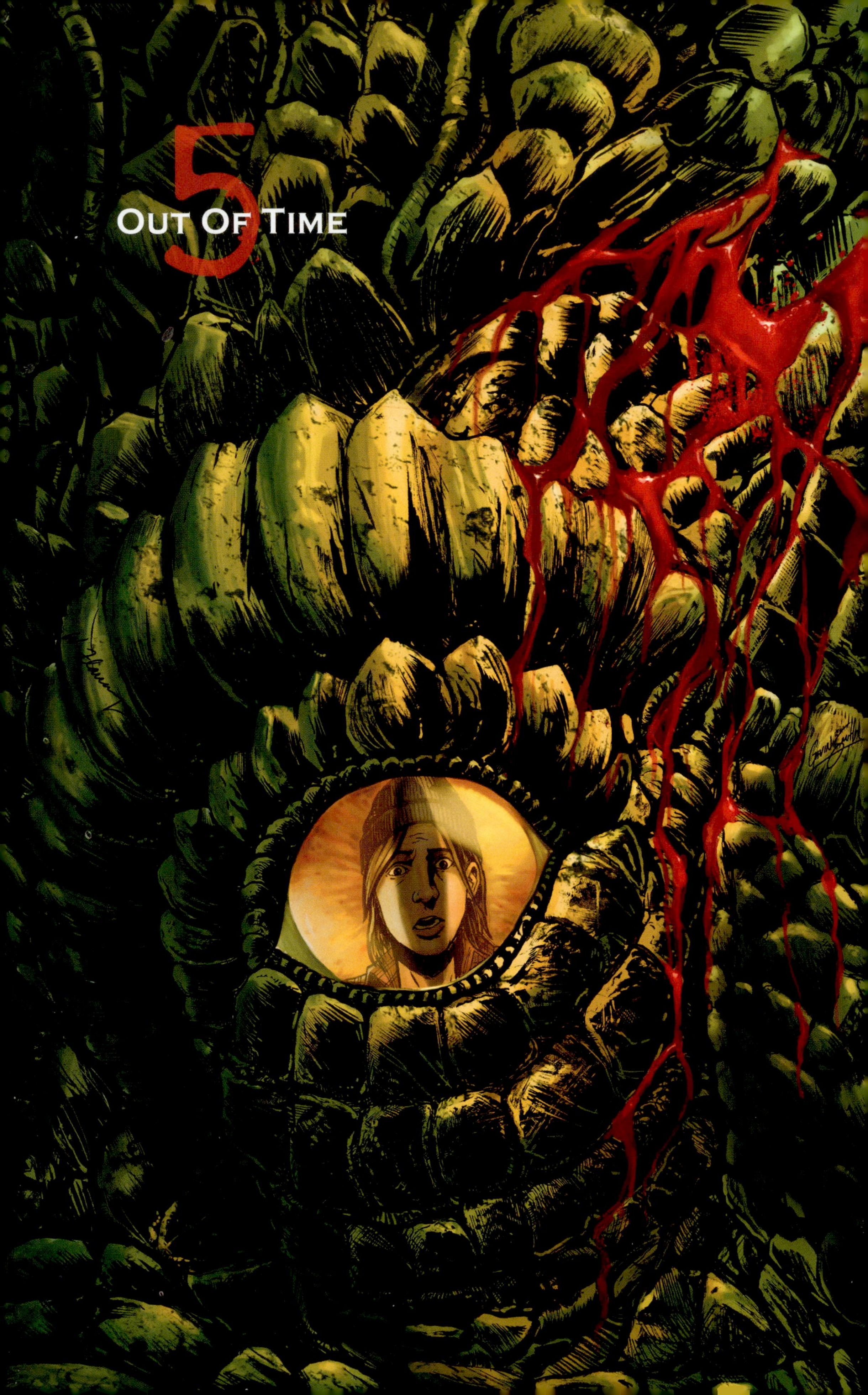

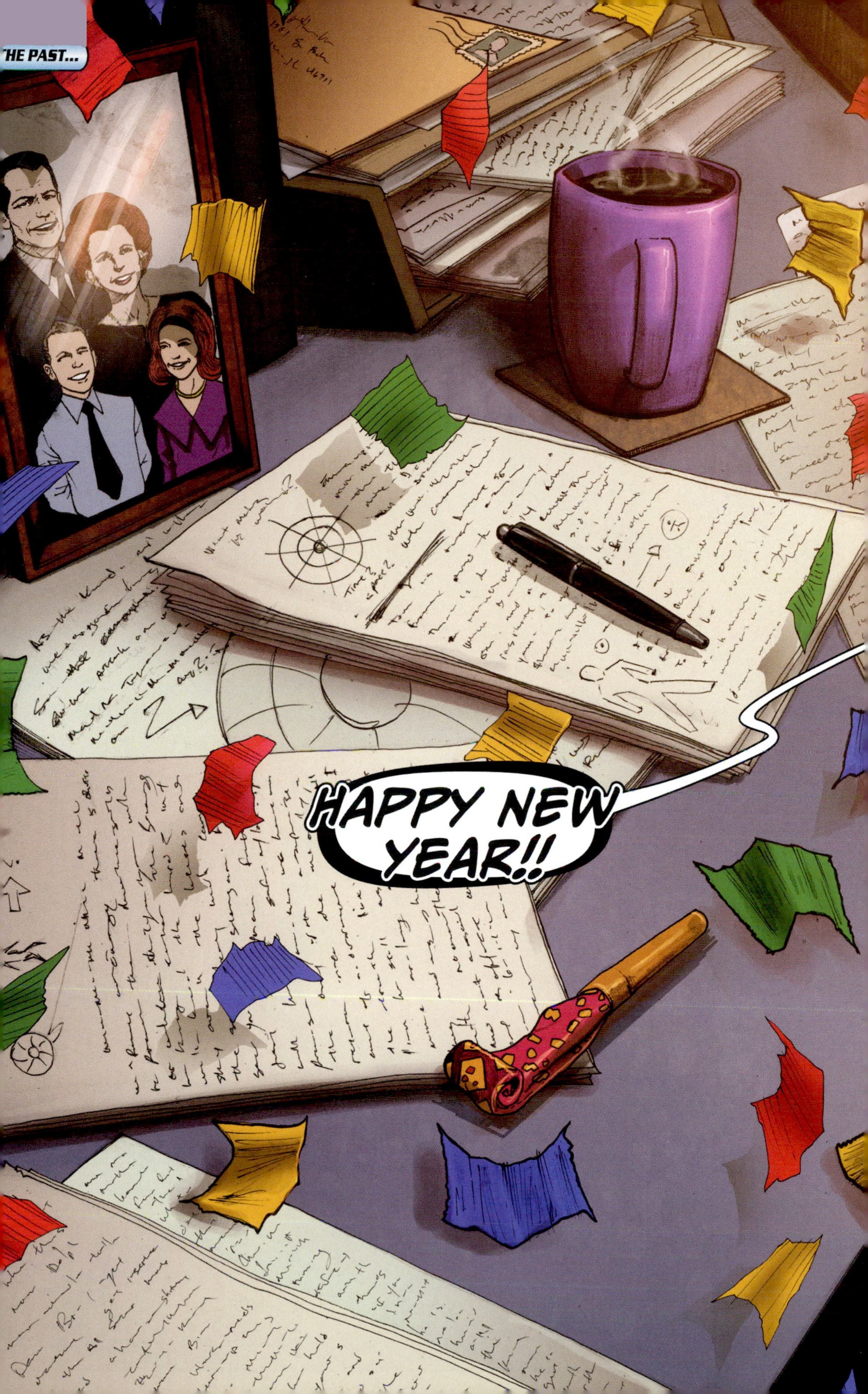

HE PAST...
HAPPY NEW YEAR!!

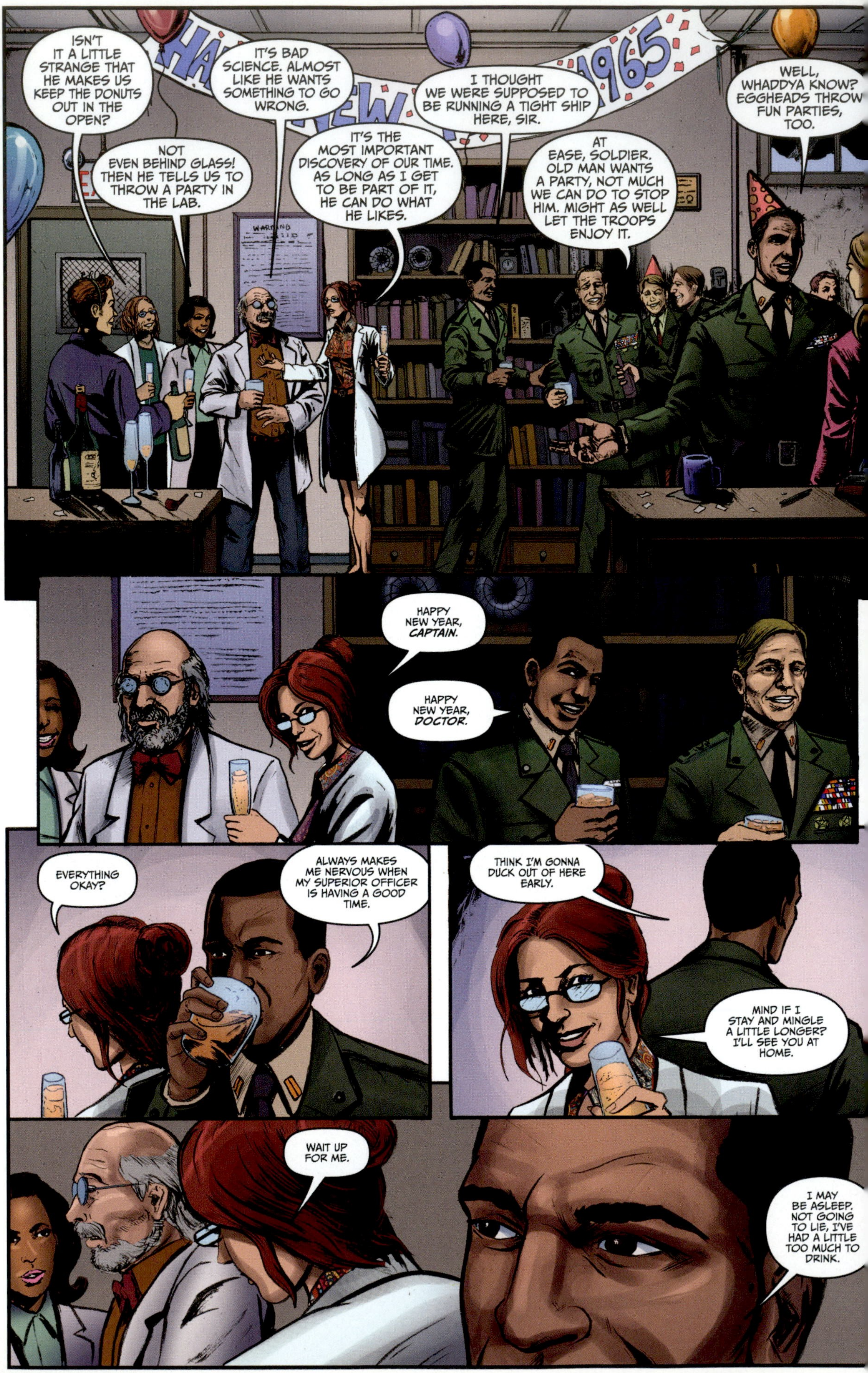
HA... NEW... 1965
ISN'T IT A LITTLE STRANGE THAT HE MAKES US KEEP THE DONUTS OUT IN THE OPEN?
NOT EVEN BEHIND GLASS! THEN HE TELLS US TO THROW A PARTY IN THE LAB.
IT'S BAD SCIENCE. ALMOST LIKE HE WANTS SOMETHING TO GO WRONG.
IT'S THE MOST IMPORTANT DISCOVERY OF OUR TIME. AS LONG AS I GET TO BE PART OF IT, HE CAN DO WHAT HE LIKES.
I THOUGHT WE WERE SUPPOSED TO BE RUNNING A TIGHT SHIP HERE, SIR.
AT EASE, SOLDIER. OLD MAN WANTS A PARTY, NOT MUCH WE CAN DO TO STOP HIM. MIGHT AS WELL LET THE TROOPS ENJOY IT.
WELL, WHADDYA KNOW? EGGHEADS THROW FUN PARTIES, TOO.
HAPPY NEW YEAR, *CAPTAIN.*
HAPPY NEW YEAR, *DOCTOR.*
EVERYTHING OKAY?
ALWAYS MAKES ME NERVOUS WHEN MY SUPERIOR OFFICER IS HAVING A GOOD TIME.
THINK I'M GONNA DUCK OUT OF HERE EARLY.
MIND IF I STAY AND MINGLE A LITTLE LONGER? I'LL SEE YOU AT HOME.
WAIT UP FOR ME.
I MAY BE ASLEEP. NOT GOING TO LIE, I'VE HAD A LITTLE TOO MUCH TO DRINK.

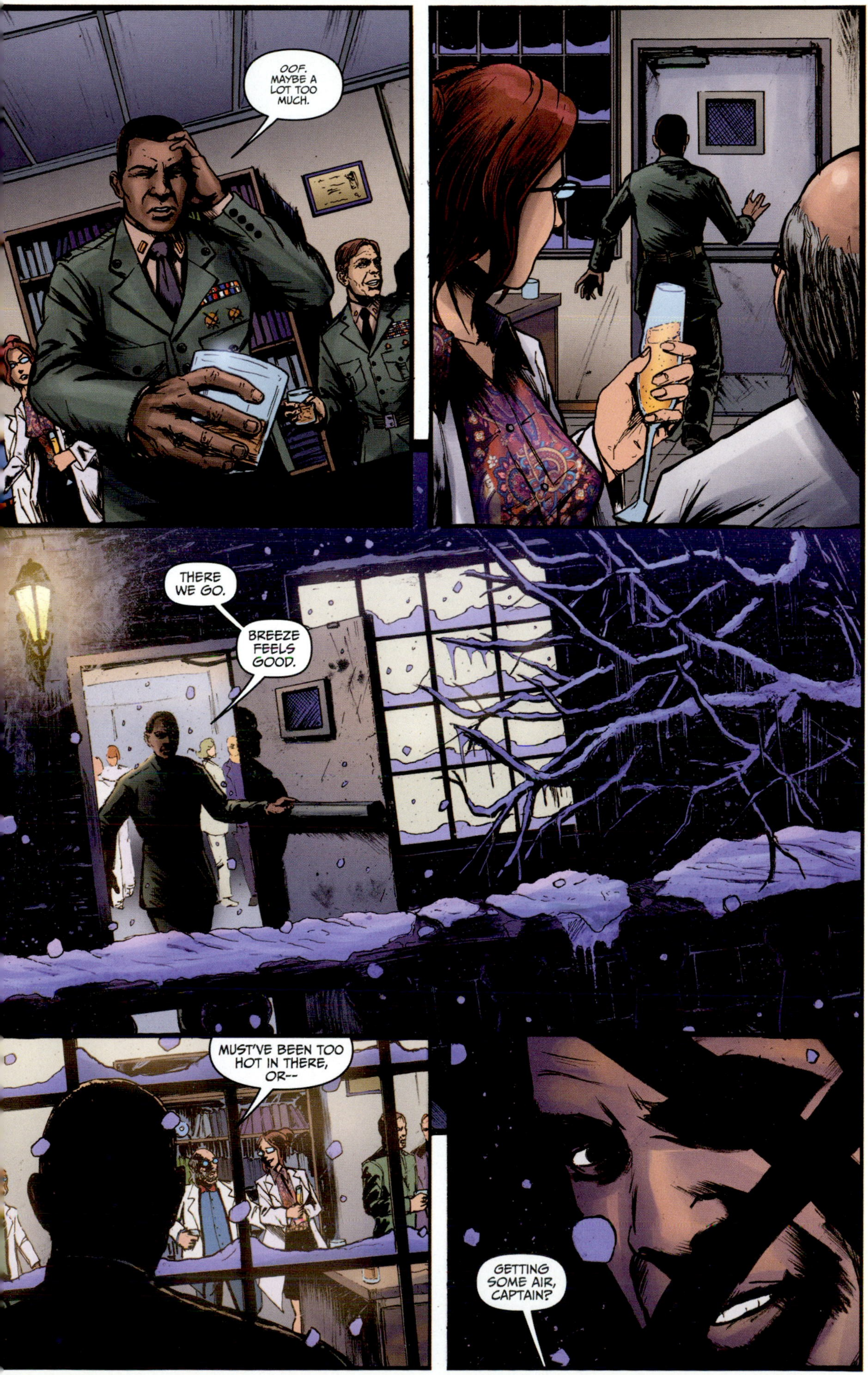
OOF. MAYBE A LOT TOO MUCH.
THERE WE GO.
BREEZE FEELS GOOD.
MUST'VE BEEN TOO HOT IN THERE, OR--
GETTING SOME AIR, CAPTAIN?

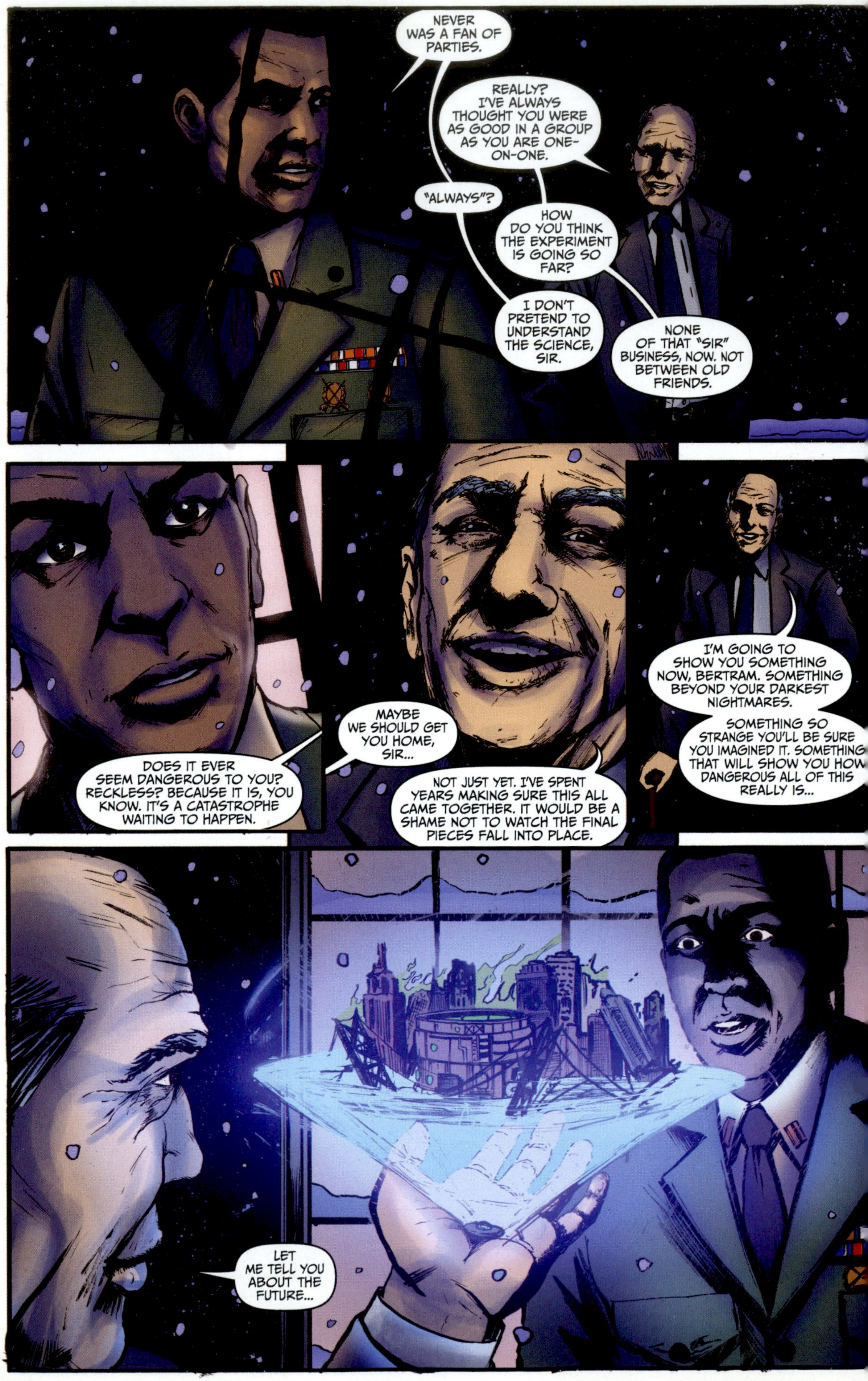
NEVER WAS A FAN OF PARTIES.
REALLY? I'VE ALWAYS THOUGHT YOU WERE AS GOOD IN A GROUP AS YOU ARE ONE-ON-ONE.
"ALWAYS"?
HOW DO YOU THINK THE EXPERIMENT IS GOING SO FAR?
I DON'T PRETEND TO UNDERSTAND THE SCIENCE, SIR.
NONE OF THAT "SIR" BUSINESS, NOW. NOT BETWEEN OLD FRIENDS.
DOES IT EVER SEEM DANGEROUS TO YOU? RECKLESS? BECAUSE IT IS, YOU KNOW. IT'S A CATASTROPHE WAITING TO HAPPEN.
MAYBE WE SHOULD GET YOU HOME, SIR...
NOT JUST YET. I'VE SPENT YEARS MAKING SURE THIS ALL CAME TOGETHER. IT WOULD BE A SHAME NOT TO WATCH THE FINAL PIECES FALL INTO PLACE.
I'M GOING TO SHOW YOU SOMETHING NOW, BERTRAM. SOMETHING BEYOND YOUR DARKEST NIGHTMARES.
SOMETHING SO STRANGE YOU'LL BE SURE YOU IMAGINED IT. SOMETHING THAT WILL SHOW YOU HOW DANGEROUS ALL OF THIS REALLY IS...
LET ME TELL YOU ABOUT THE FUTURE...

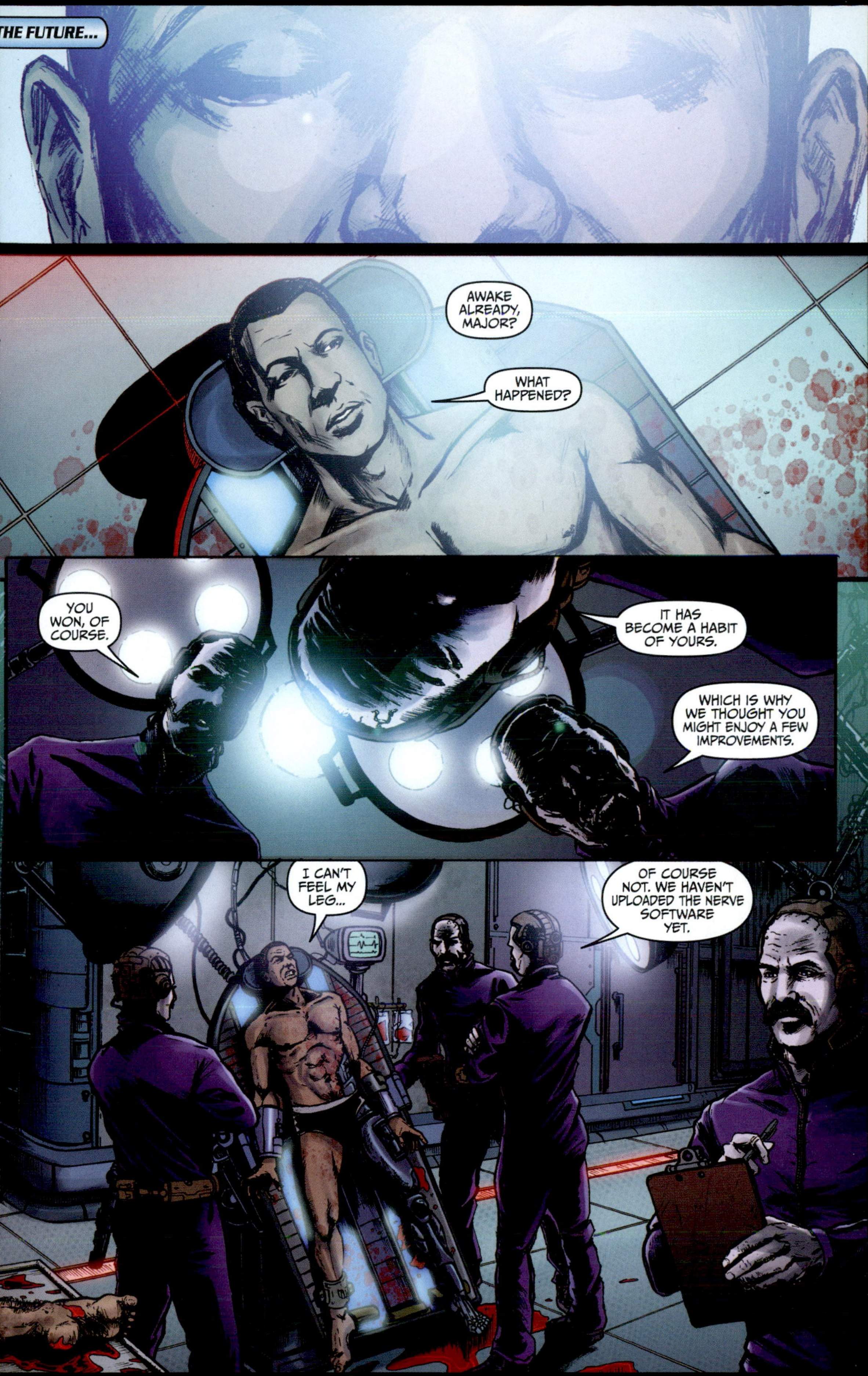
THE FUTURE...
AWAKE ALREADY, MAJOR?
WHAT HAPPENED?
YOU WON, OF COURSE.
IT HAS BECOME A HABIT OF YOURS.
WHICH IS WHY WE THOUGHT YOU MIGHT ENJOY A FEW IMPROVEMENTS.
I CAN'T FEEL MY LEG...
OF COURSE NOT. WE HAVEN'T UPLOADED THE NERVE SOFTWARE YET.

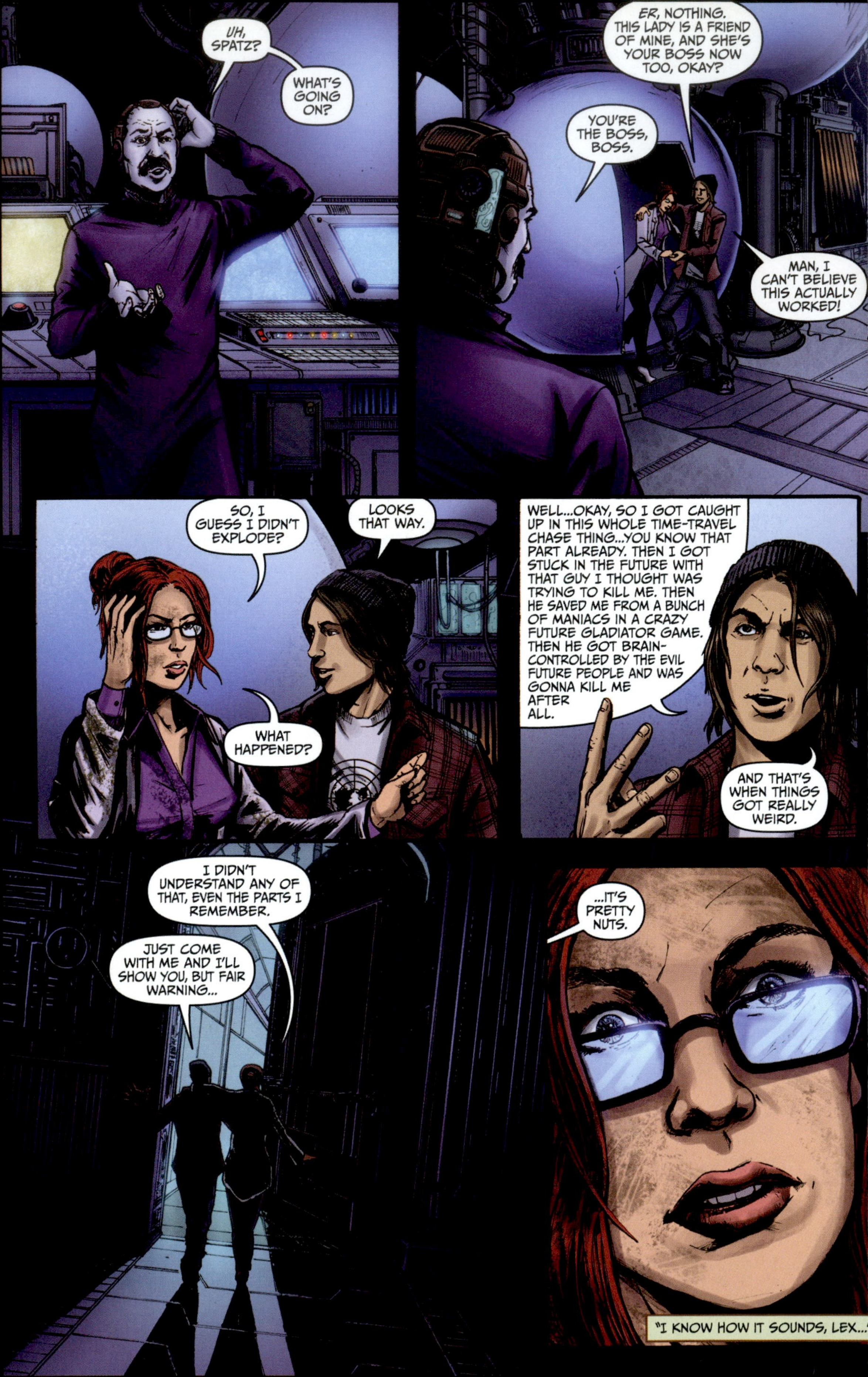
UH, SPATZ?
WHAT'S GOING ON?
ER, NOTHING. THIS LADY IS A FRIEND OF MINE, AND SHE'S YOUR BOSS NOW TOO, OKAY?
YOU'RE THE BOSS, BOSS.
MAN, I CAN'T BELIEVE THIS ACTUALLY WORKED!
SO, I GUESS I DIDN'T EXPLODE?
LOOKS THAT WAY.
WHAT HAPPENED?
WELL...OKAY, SO I GOT CAUGHT UP IN THIS WHOLE TIME-TRAVEL CHASE THING...YOU KNOW THAT PART ALREADY. THEN I GOT STUCK IN THE FUTURE WITH THAT GUY I THOUGHT WAS TRYING TO KILL ME. THEN HE SAVED ME FROM A BUNCH OF MANIACS IN A CRAZY FUTURE GLADIATOR GAME. THEN HE GOT BRAIN-CONTROLLED BY THE EVIL FUTURE PEOPLE AND WAS GONNA KILL ME AFTER ALL.
AND THAT'S WHEN THINGS GOT REALLY WEIRD.
I DIDN'T UNDERSTAND ANY OF THAT, EVEN THE PARTS I REMEMBER.
JUST COME WITH ME AND I'LL SHOW YOU, BUT FAIR WARNING...
...IT'S PRETTY NUTS.
"I KNOW HOW IT SOUNDS, LEX..."

IT SOUNDS LIKE YOU WERE DRUNK.

I DIDN'T THINK I WAS *THAT* DRUNK.

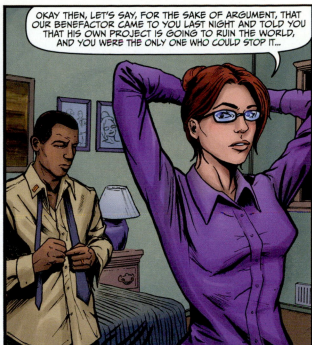

OKAY THEN, LET'S SAY, FOR THE SAKE OF ARGUMENT, THAT OUR BENEFACTOR CAME TO YOU LAST NIGHT AND TOLD YOU THAT HIS OWN PROJECT IS GOING TO RUIN THE WORLD, AND YOU WERE THE ONLY ONE WHO COULD STOP IT...

IF HE KNEW THERE WAS A PROBLEM WITH THE PROJECT, THEN WHY WOULDN'T HE JUST DO SOMETHING ABOUT IT HIMSELF?

I DON'T KNOW. HEY, IT'S RIDICULOUS, BUT I JUST CAN'T SHAKE THE FEELING THAT SOMETHING'S REALLY WRONG.

I MEAN, THE ARMY HAS ALWAYS BEEN NERVOUS ABOUT THIS THING, ESPECIALLY IN THE HANDS OF CIVILIANS...

IS THAT WHAT THIS IS ABOUT? THE MILITARY-VERSUS-CIVILIAN THING? REALLY?

YOUR COLONEL IS FINALLY STARTING TO RELAX, AND NOW YOU'RE GETTING UPTIGHT ABOUT IT?

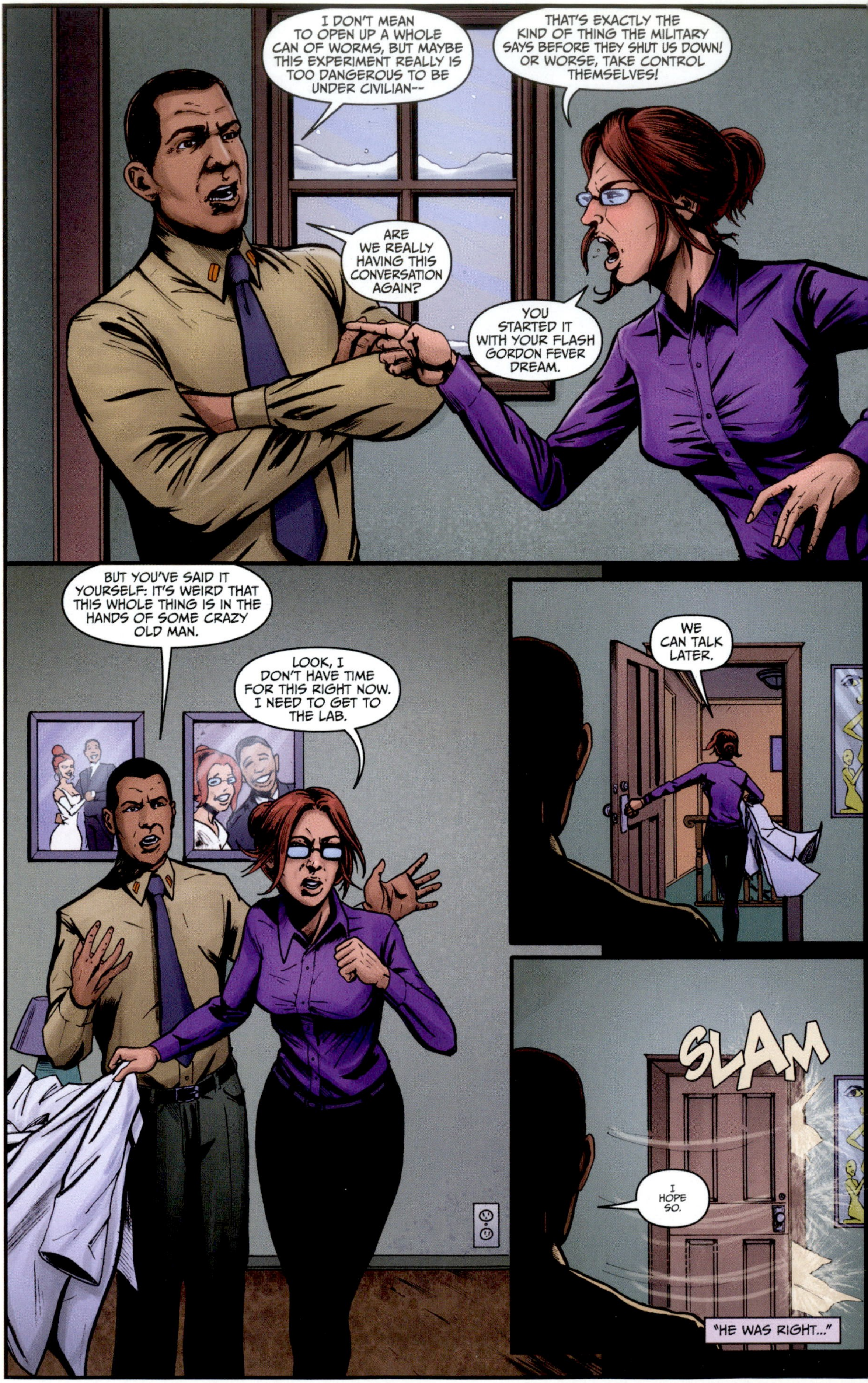
I DON'T MEAN TO OPEN UP A WHOLE CAN OF WORMS, BUT MAYBE THIS EXPERIMENT REALLY IS TOO DANGEROUS TO BE UNDER CIVILIAN--
THAT'S EXACTLY THE KIND OF THING THE MILITARY SAYS BEFORE THEY SHUT US DOWN! OR WORSE, TAKE CONTROL THEMSELVES!
ARE WE REALLY HAVING THIS CONVERSATION AGAIN?
YOU STARTED IT WITH YOUR FLASH GORDON FEVER DREAM.
BUT YOU'VE SAID IT YOURSELF: IT'S WEIRD THAT THIS WHOLE THING IS IN THE HANDS OF SOME CRAZY OLD MAN.
LOOK, I DON'T HAVE TIME FOR THIS RIGHT NOW. I NEED TO GET TO THE LAB.
WE CAN TALK LATER.
SLAM
I HOPE SO.
"HE WAS RIGHT..."

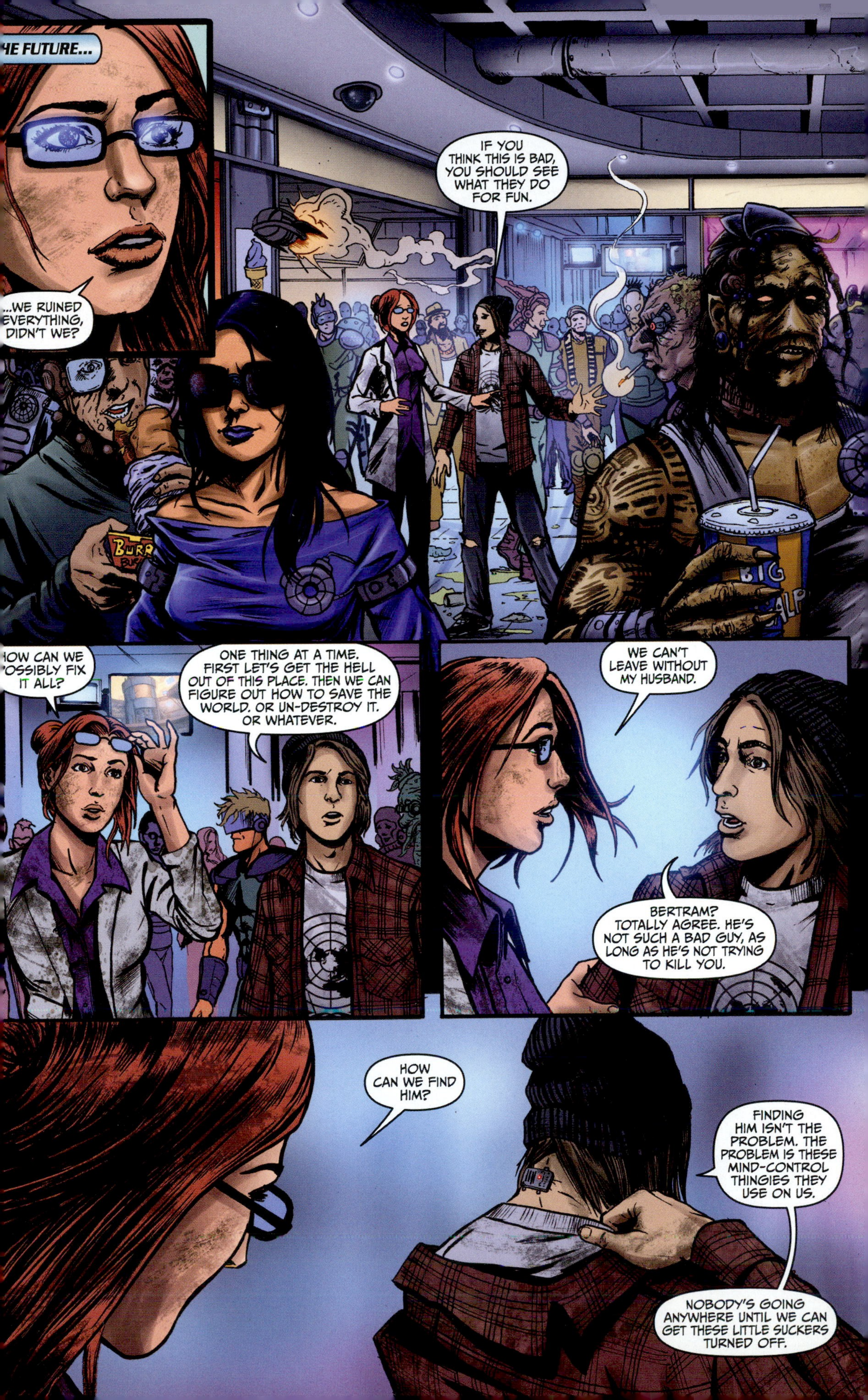

HE FUTURE...
...WE RUINED EVERYTHING, DIDN'T WE?
IF YOU THINK THIS IS BAD, YOU SHOULD SEE WHAT THEY DO FOR FUN.
HOW CAN WE POSSIBLY FIX IT ALL?
ONE THING AT A TIME. FIRST LET'S GET THE HELL OUT OF THIS PLACE. THEN WE CAN FIGURE OUT HOW TO SAVE THE WORLD. OR UN-DESTROY IT. OR WHATEVER.
WE CAN'T LEAVE WITHOUT MY HUSBAND.
BERTRAM? TOTALLY AGREE. HE'S NOT SUCH A BAD GUY, AS LONG AS HE'S NOT TRYING TO KILL YOU.
HOW CAN WE FIND HIM?
FINDING HIM ISN'T THE PROBLEM. THE PROBLEM IS THESE MIND-CONTROL THINGIES THEY USE ON US.
NOBODY'S GOING ANYWHERE UNTIL WE CAN GET THESE LITTLE SUCKERS TURNED OFF.

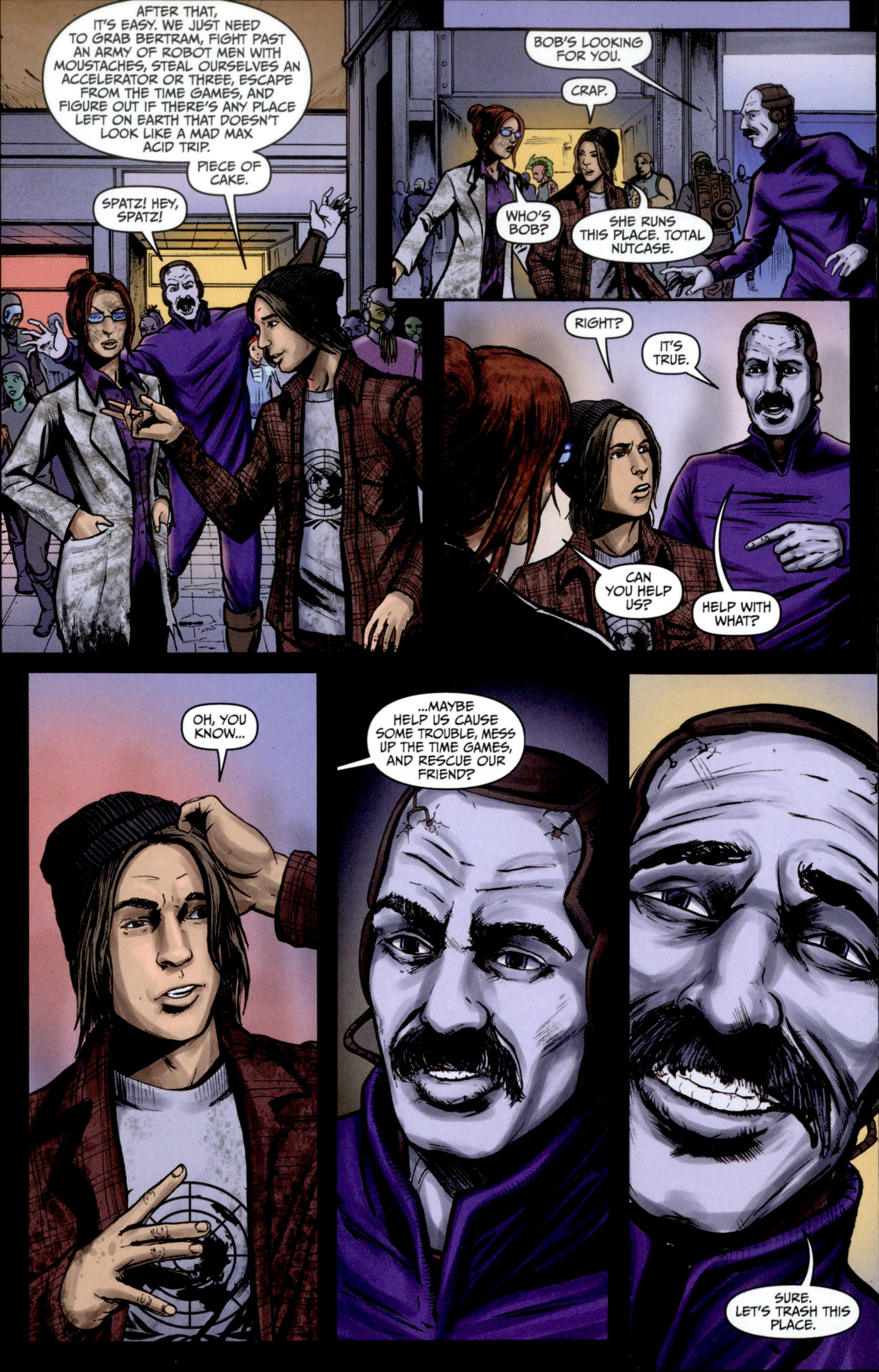
AFTER THAT, IT'S EASY. WE JUST NEED TO GRAB BERTRAM, FIGHT PAST AN ARMY OF ROBOT MEN WITH MOUSTACHES, STEAL OURSELVES AN ACCELERATOR OR THREE, ESCAPE FROM THE TIME GAMES, AND FIGURE OUT IF THERE'S ANY PLACE LEFT ON EARTH THAT DOESN'T LOOK LIKE A MAD MAX ACID TRIP.
PIECE OF CAKE.
SPATZ! HEY, SPATZ!
BOB'S LOOKING FOR YOU.
CRAP.
WHO'S BOB?
SHE RUNS THIS PLACE. TOTAL NUTCASE.
RIGHT?
IT'S TRUE.
CAN YOU HELP US?
HELP WITH WHAT?
OH, YOU KNOW...
...MAYBE HELP US CAUSE SOME TROUBLE, MESS UP THE TIME GAMES, AND RESCUE OUR FRIEND?
SURE. LET'S TRASH THIS PLACE.

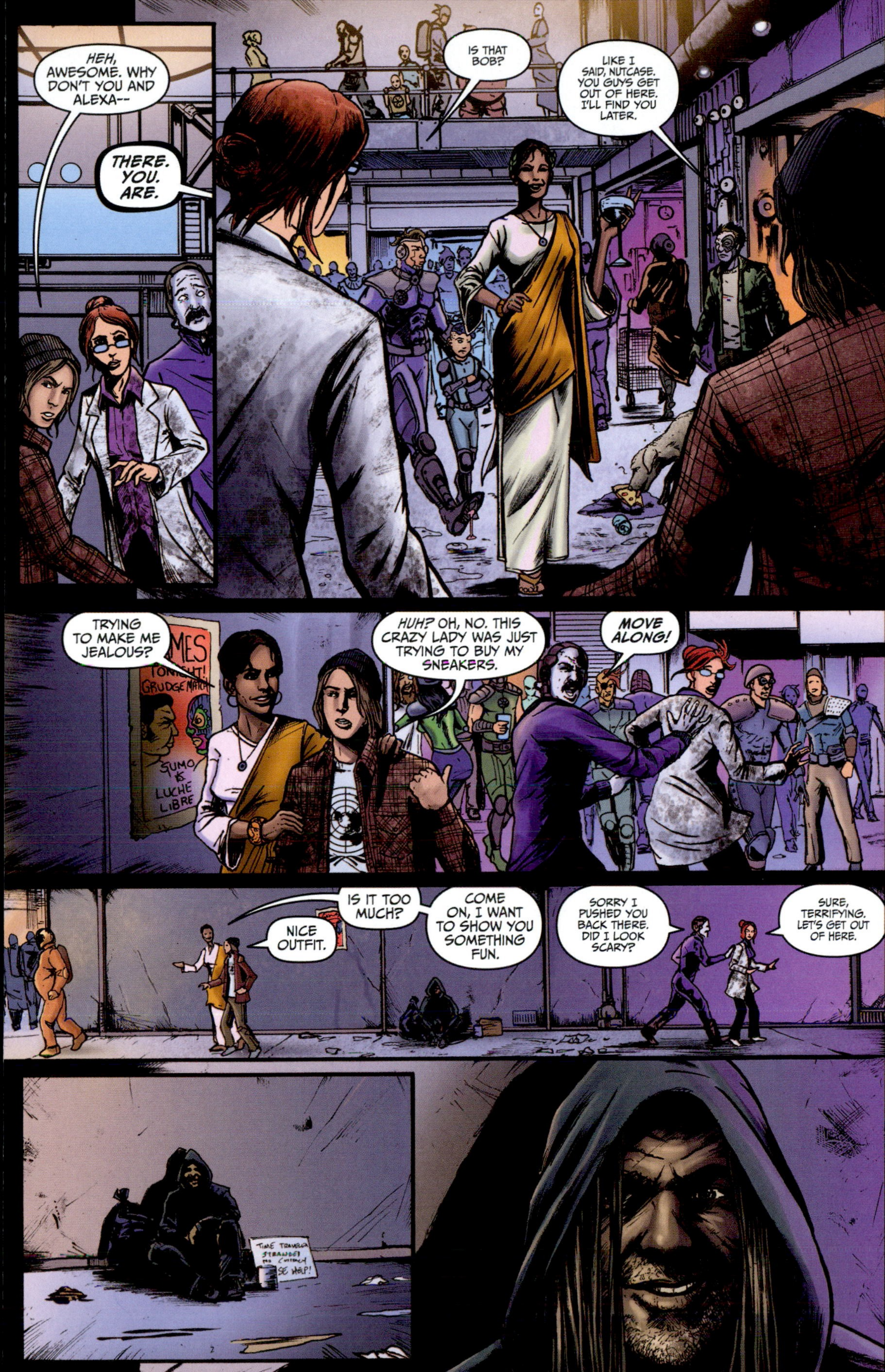
HEH, AWESOME. WHY DON'T YOU AND ALEXA--
THERE. YOU. ARE.
IS THAT BOB?
LIKE I SAID, NUTCASE. YOU GUYS GET OUT OF HERE. I'LL FIND YOU LATER.
TRYING TO MAKE ME JEALOUS?
TONIGHT!
GRUDGE MATCH
SUMO vs LUCHE LIBRE
HUH? OH, NO. THIS CRAZY LADY WAS JUST TRYING TO BUY MY SNEAKERS.
MOVE ALONG!
NICE OUTFIT.
IS IT TOO MUCH?
COME ON, I WANT TO SHOW YOU SOMETHING FUN.
SORRY I PUSHED YOU BACK THERE. DID I LOOK SCARY?
SURE, TERRIFYING. LET'S GET OUT OF HERE.

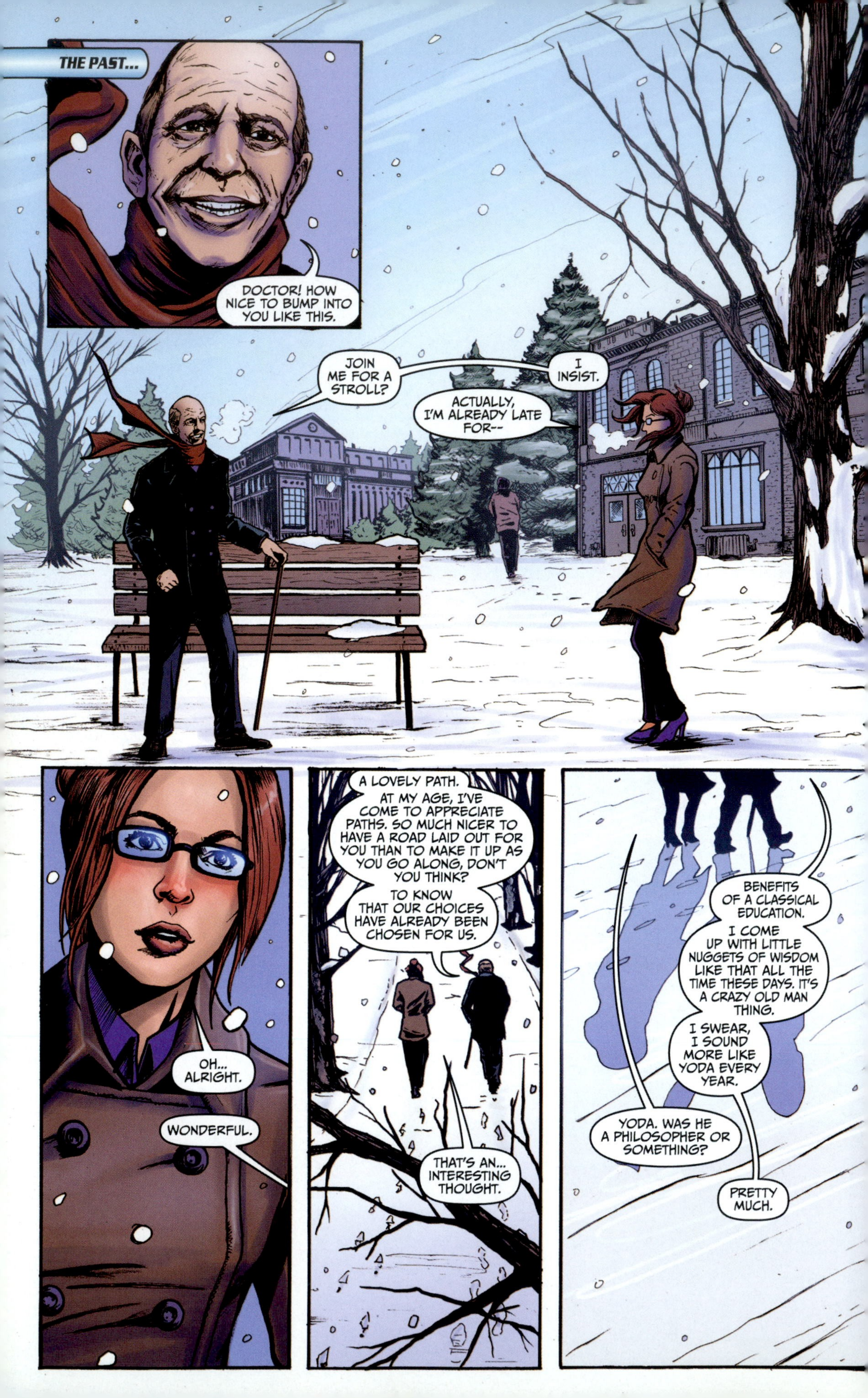
THE PAST...
DOCTOR! HOW NICE TO BUMP INTO YOU LIKE THIS.
JOIN ME FOR A STROLL?
I INSIST.
ACTUALLY, I'M ALREADY LATE FOR--
OH... ALRIGHT.
WONDERFUL.
A LOVELY PATH.
AT MY AGE, I'VE COME TO APPRECIATE PATHS. SO MUCH NICER TO HAVE A ROAD LAID OUT FOR YOU THAN TO MAKE IT UP AS YOU GO ALONG, DON'T YOU THINK?
TO KNOW THAT OUR CHOICES HAVE ALREADY BEEN CHOSEN FOR US.
THAT'S AN... INTERESTING THOUGHT.
BENEFITS OF A CLASSICAL EDUCATION.
I COME UP WITH LITTLE NUGGETS OF WISDOM LIKE THAT ALL THE TIME THESE DAYS. IT'S A CRAZY OLD MAN THING.
I SWEAR, I SOUND MORE LIKE YODA EVERY YEAR.
YODA. WAS HE A PHILOSOPHER OR SOMETHING?
PRETTY MUCH.

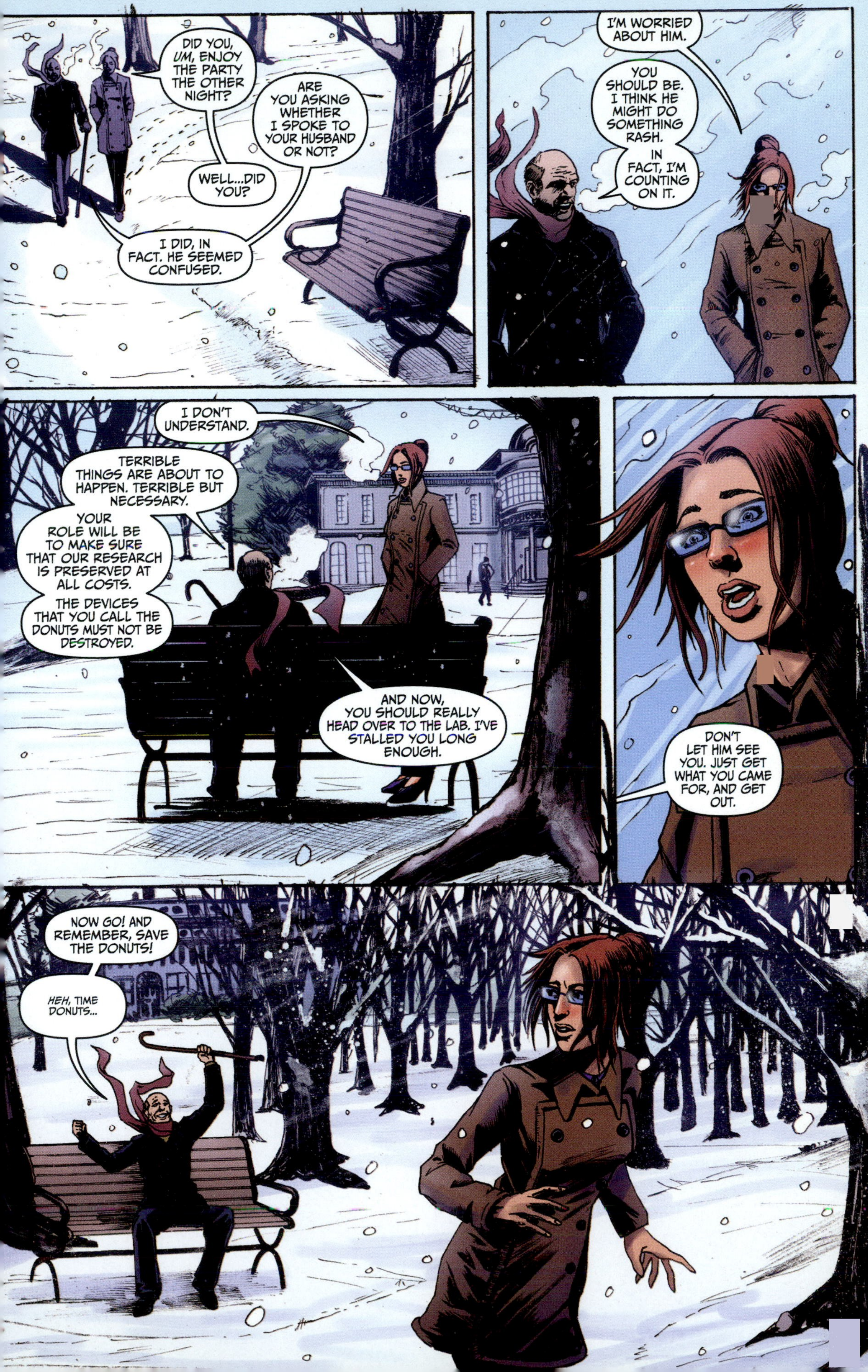
DID YOU, *UM*, ENJOY THE PARTY THE OTHER NIGHT?
ARE YOU ASKING WHETHER I SPOKE TO YOUR HUSBAND OR NOT?
WELL...DID YOU?
I DID, IN FACT. HE SEEMED CONFUSED.
I'M WORRIED ABOUT HIM.
YOU SHOULD BE. I THINK HE MIGHT DO SOMETHING RASH.
IN FACT, I'M COUNTING ON IT.
I DON'T UNDERSTAND.
TERRIBLE THINGS ARE ABOUT TO HAPPEN. TERRIBLE BUT NECESSARY.
YOUR ROLE WILL BE TO MAKE SURE THAT OUR RESEARCH IS PRESERVED AT ALL COSTS.
THE DEVICES THAT YOU CALL THE DONUTS MUST NOT BE DESTROYED.
AND NOW, YOU SHOULD REALLY HEAD OVER TO THE LAB. I'VE STALLED YOU LONG ENOUGH.
DON'T LET HIM SEE YOU. JUST GET WHAT YOU CAME FOR, AND GET OUT.
NOW GO! AND REMEMBER, SAVE THE DONUTS!
HEH, TIME DONUTS...

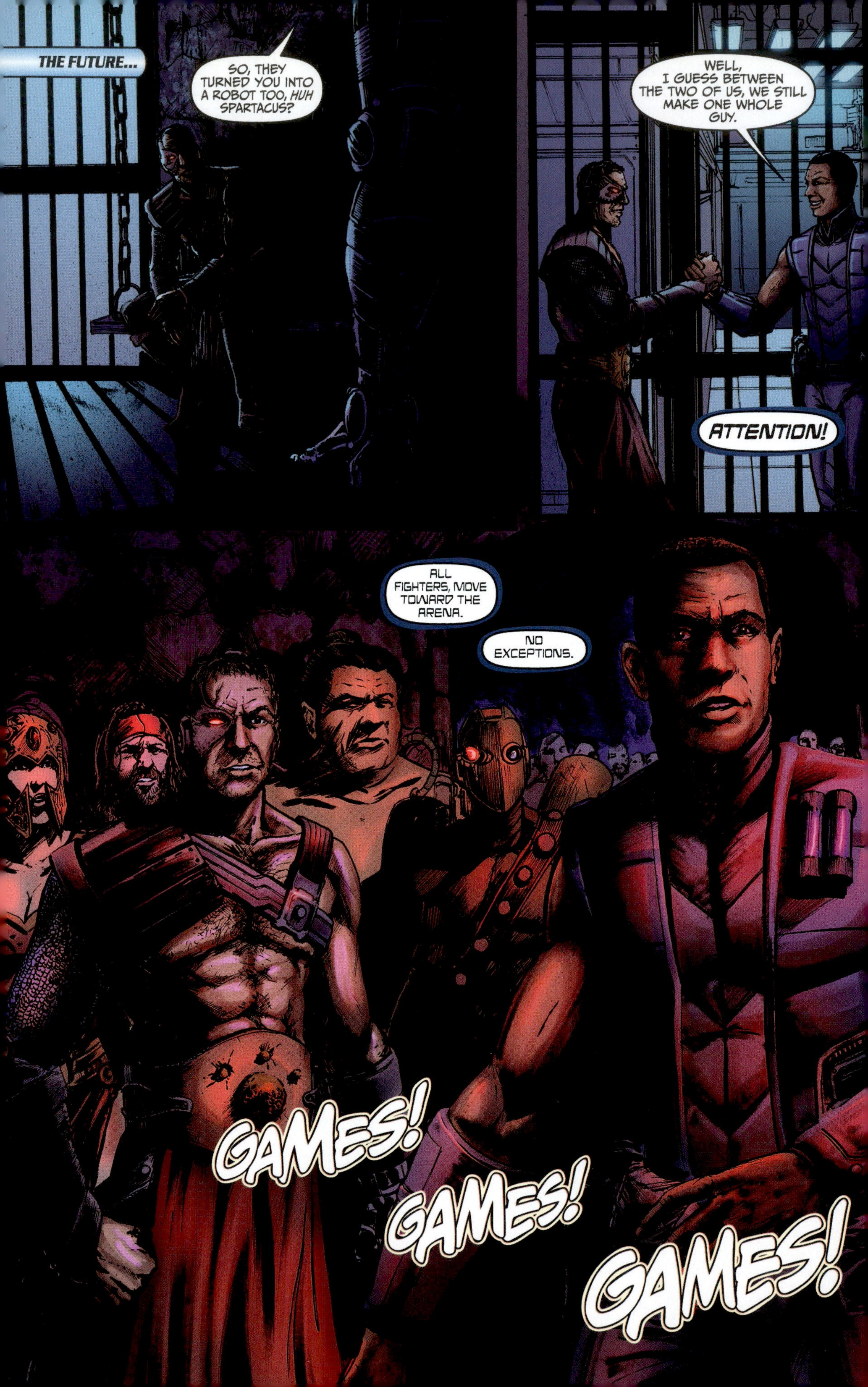
THE FUTURE...
SO, THEY TURNED YOU INTO A ROBOT TOO, HUH SPARTACUS?
WELL, I GUESS BETWEEN THE TWO OF US, WE STILL MAKE ONE WHOLE GUY.
ATTENTION!
ALL FIGHTERS, MOVE TOWARD THE ARENA.
NO EXCEPTIONS.
GAMES!
GAMES!
GAMES!

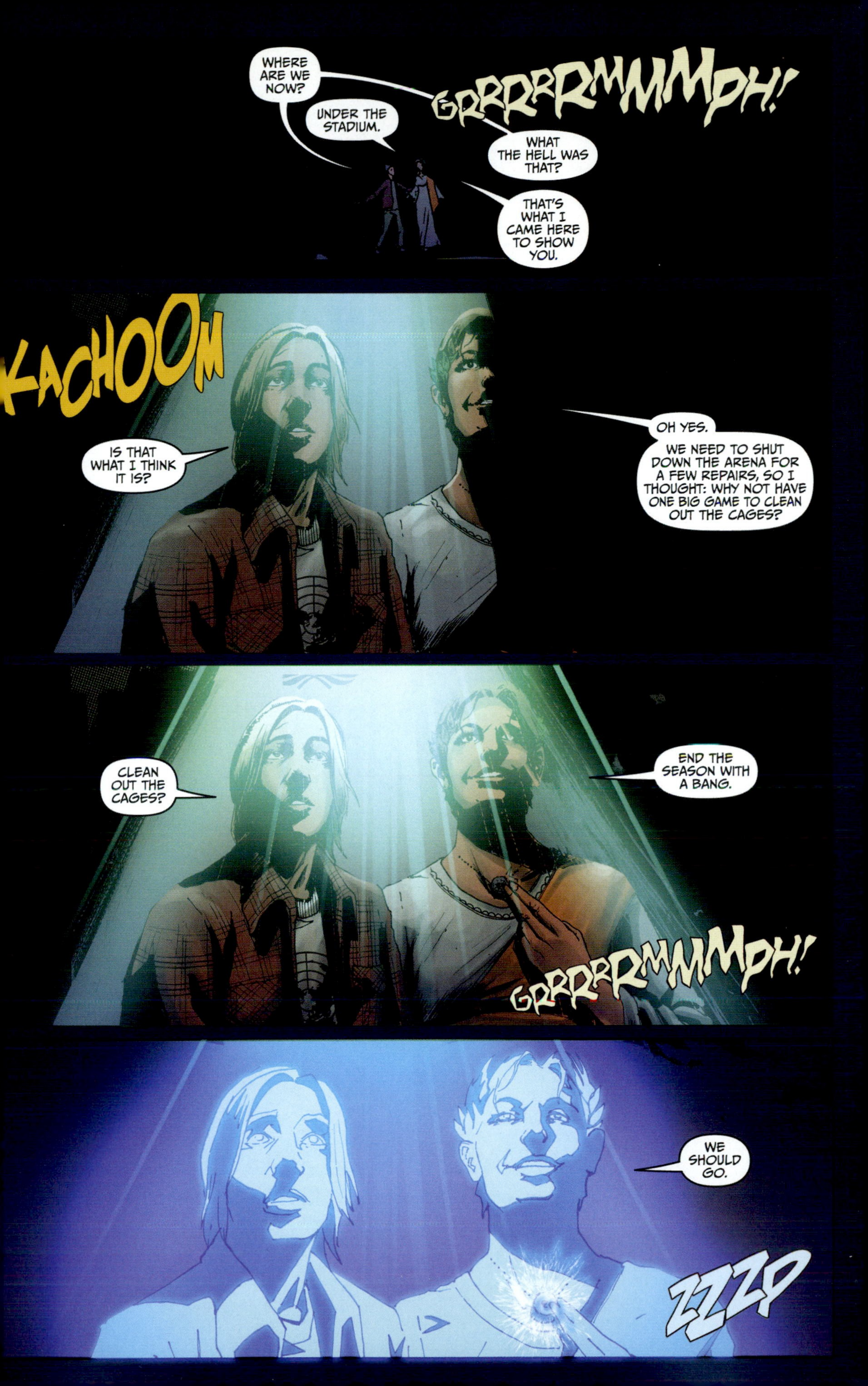
WHERE ARE WE NOW?
GRRRRRMMMMPH!
UNDER THE STADIUM.
WHAT THE HELL WAS THAT?
THAT'S WHAT I CAME HERE TO SHOW YOU.
KACHOOM
IS THAT WHAT I THINK IT IS?
OH YES.
WE NEED TO SHUT DOWN THE ARENA FOR A FEW REPAIRS, SO I THOUGHT: WHY NOT HAVE ONE BIG GAME TO CLEAN OUT THE CAGES?
CLEAN OUT THE CAGES?
END THE SEASON WITH A BANG.
GRRRRRMMMMPH!
WE SHOULD GO.
ZZZP

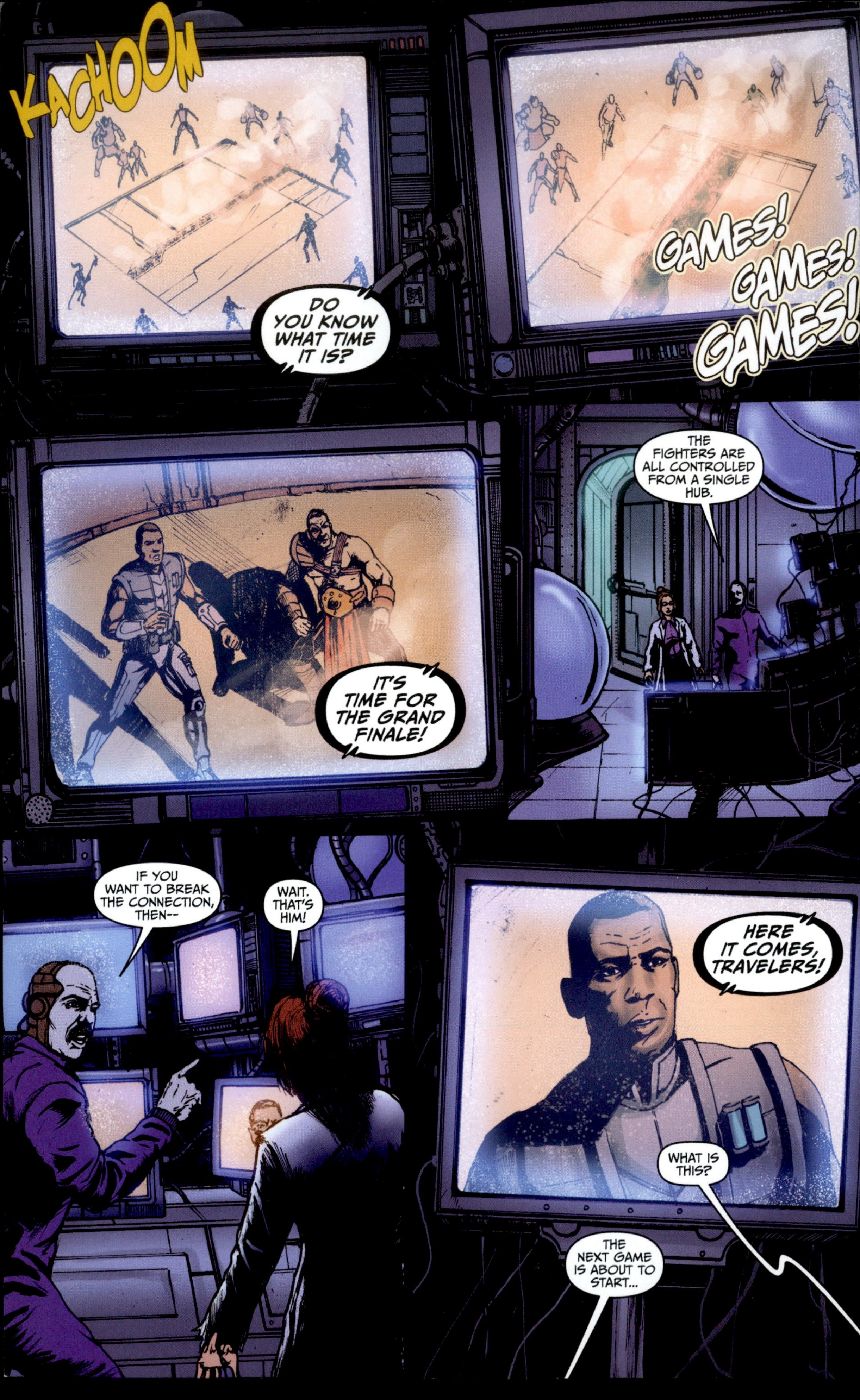
KACHOOM
DO YOU KNOW WHAT TIME IT IS?
GAMES! GAMES! GAMES!
IT'S TIME FOR THE GRAND FINALE!
THE FIGHTERS ARE ALL CONTROLLED FROM A SINGLE HUB.
IF YOU WANT TO BREAK THE CONNECTION, THEN--
WAIT. THAT'S HIM!
HERE IT COMES, TRAVELERS!
WHAT IS THIS?
THE NEXT GAME IS ABOUT TO START...

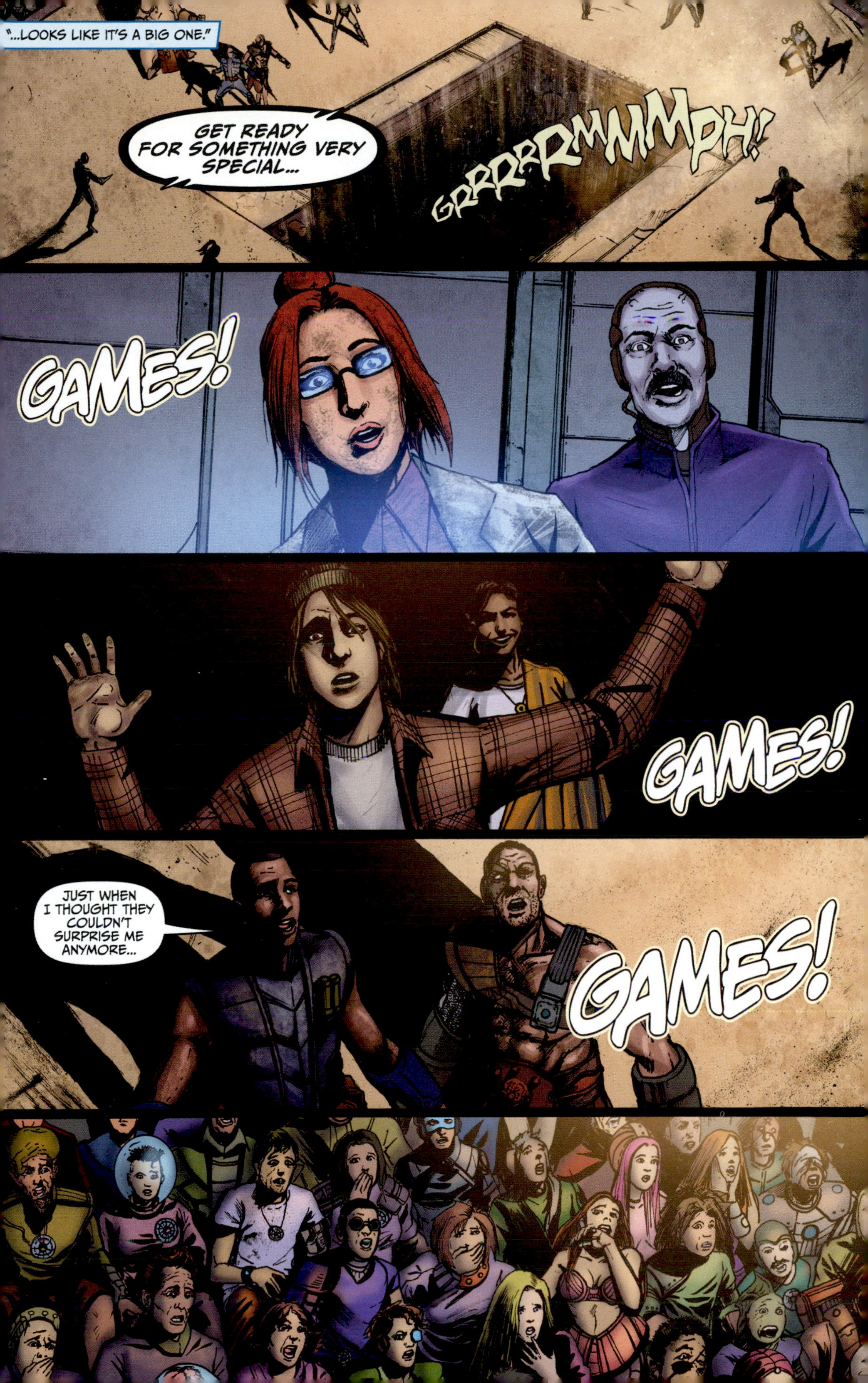
"...LOOKS LIKE IT'S A BIG ONE."
GET READY FOR SOMETHING VERY SPECIAL...
GRRRRRMMMMPH!
GAMES!
GAMES!
JUST WHEN I THOUGHT THEY COULDN'T SURPRISE ME ANYMORE...
GAMES!

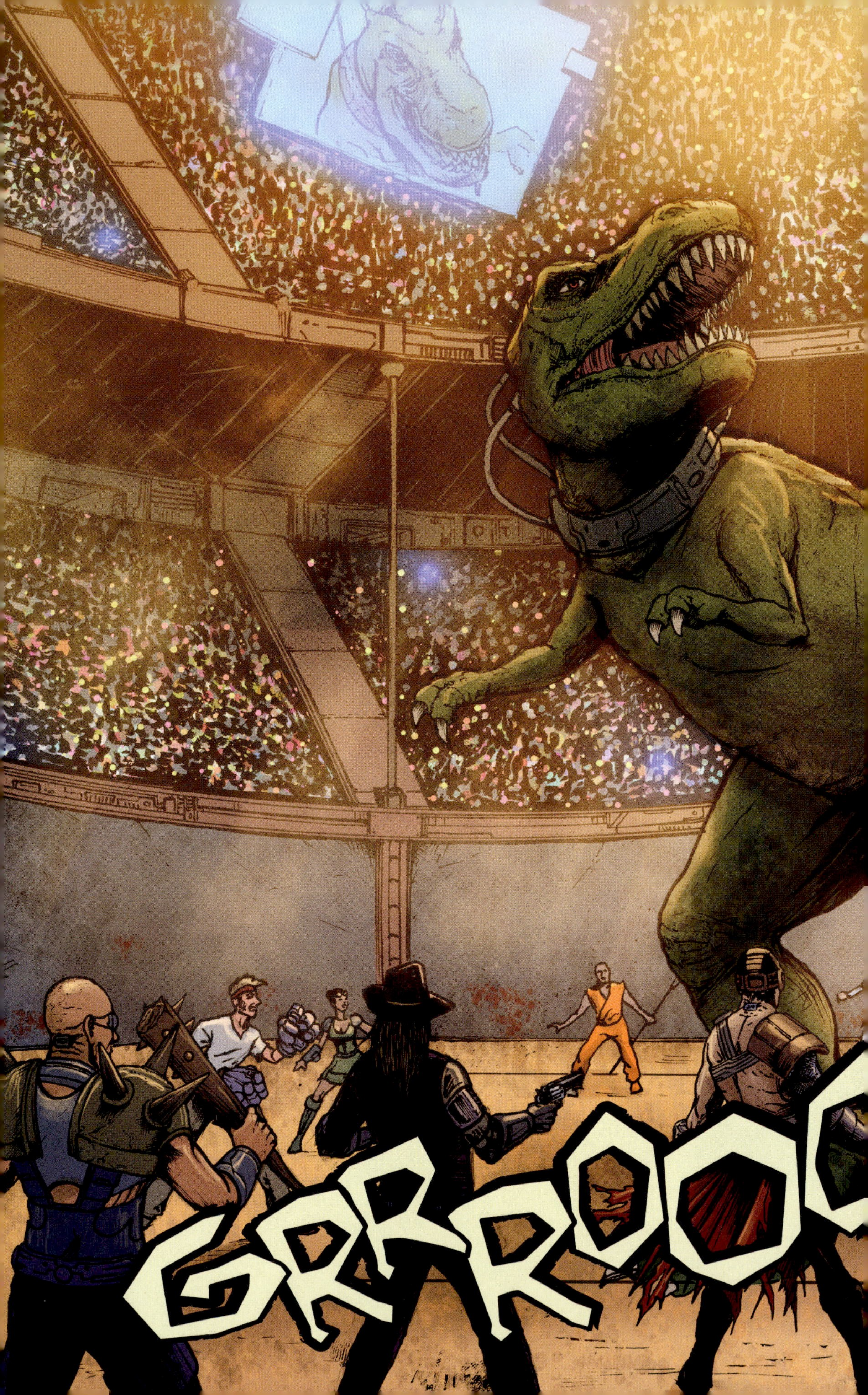
GRRROO

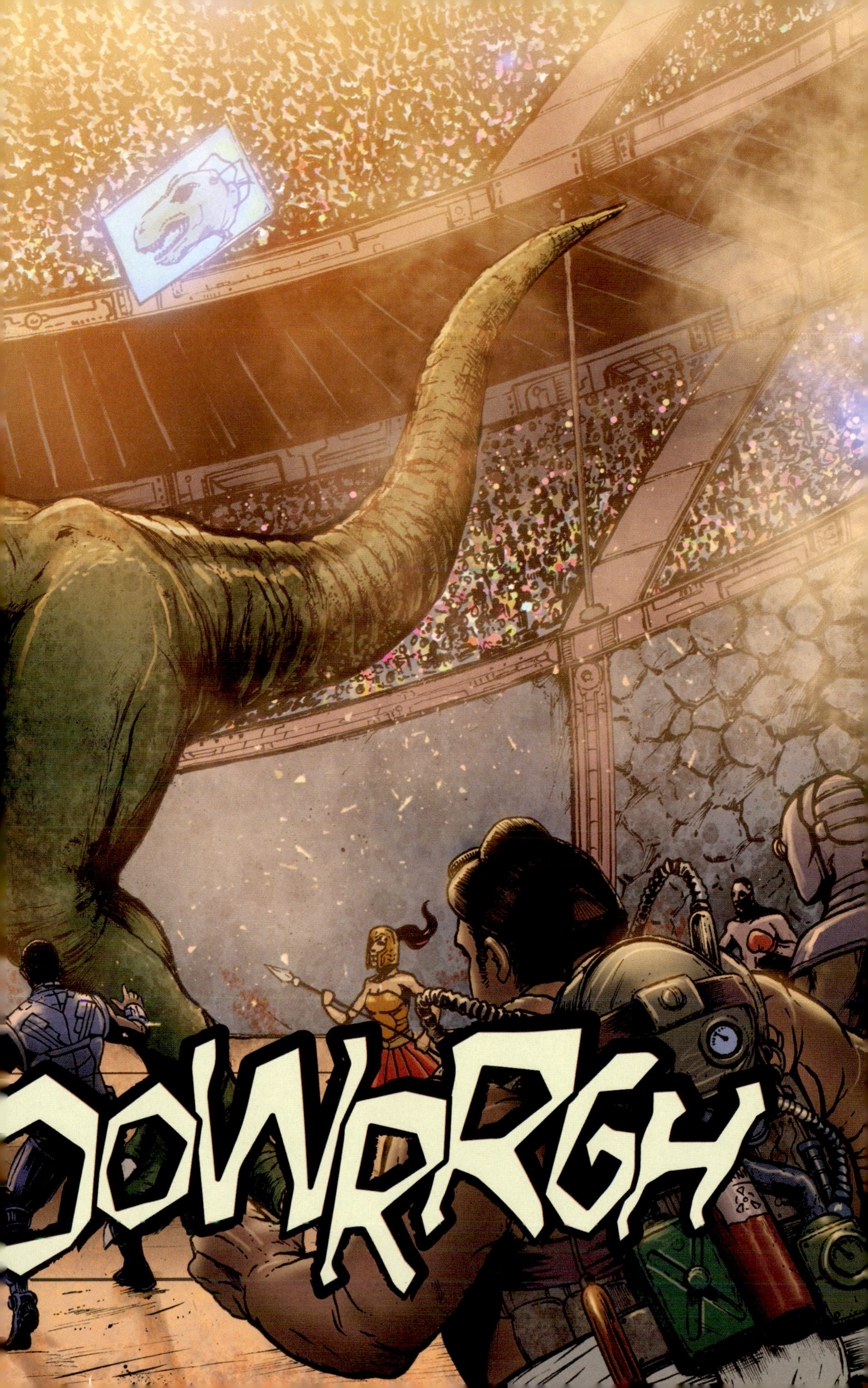
OOWRRGH

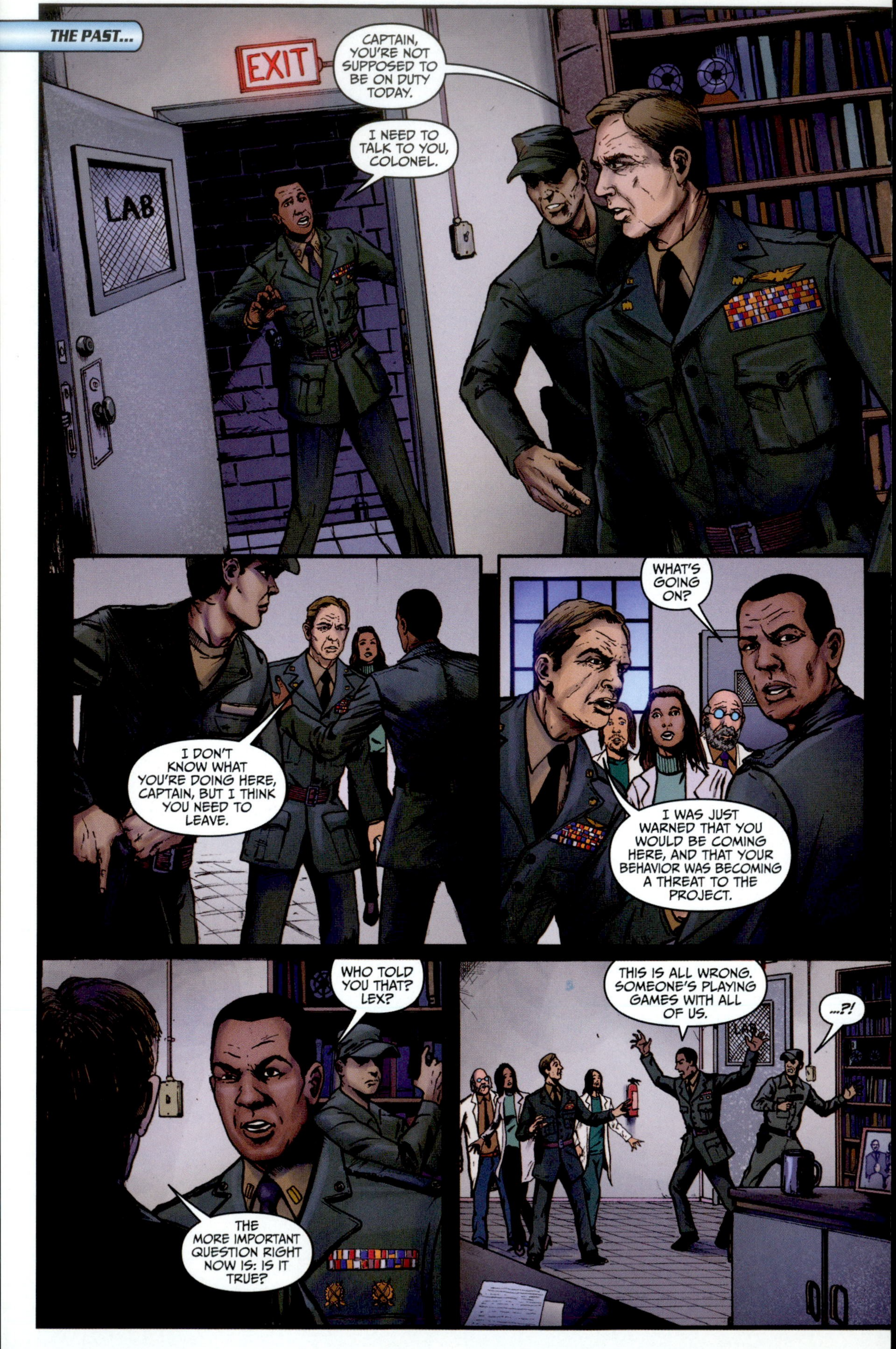
THE PAST...
EXIT
CAPTAIN, YOU'RE NOT SUPPOSED TO BE ON DUTY TODAY.
I NEED TO TALK TO YOU, COLONEL.
LAB
I DON'T KNOW WHAT YOU'RE DOING HERE, CAPTAIN, BUT I THINK YOU NEED TO LEAVE.
WHAT'S GOING ON?
I WAS JUST WARNED THAT YOU WOULD BE COMING HERE, AND THAT YOUR BEHAVIOR WAS BECOMING A THREAT TO THE PROJECT.
WHO TOLD YOU THAT? LEX?
THE MORE IMPORTANT QUESTION RIGHT NOW IS: IS IT TRUE?
THIS IS ALL WRONG. SOMEONE'S PLAYING GAMES WITH ALL OF US.
...?!

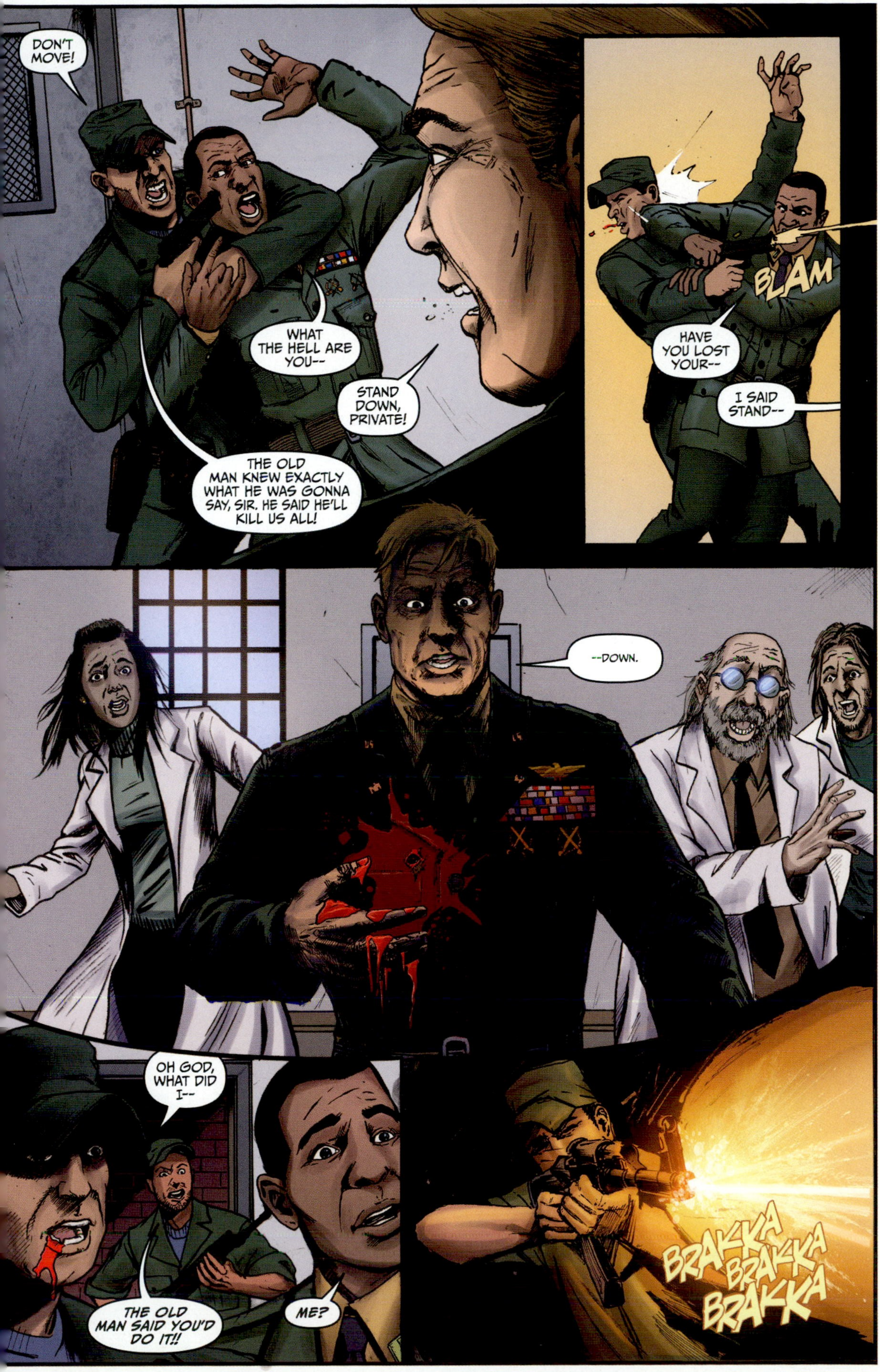
DON'T MOVE!
WHAT THE HELL ARE YOU--
STAND DOWN, PRIVATE!
THE OLD MAN KNEW EXACTLY WHAT HE WAS GONNA SAY, SIR. HE SAID HE'LL KILL US ALL!
BLAM
HAVE YOU LOST YOUR--
I SAID STAND--
--DOWN.
OH GOD, WHAT DID I--
THE OLD MAN SAID YOU'D DO IT!!
ME?
BRAKKA BRAKKA BRAKKA

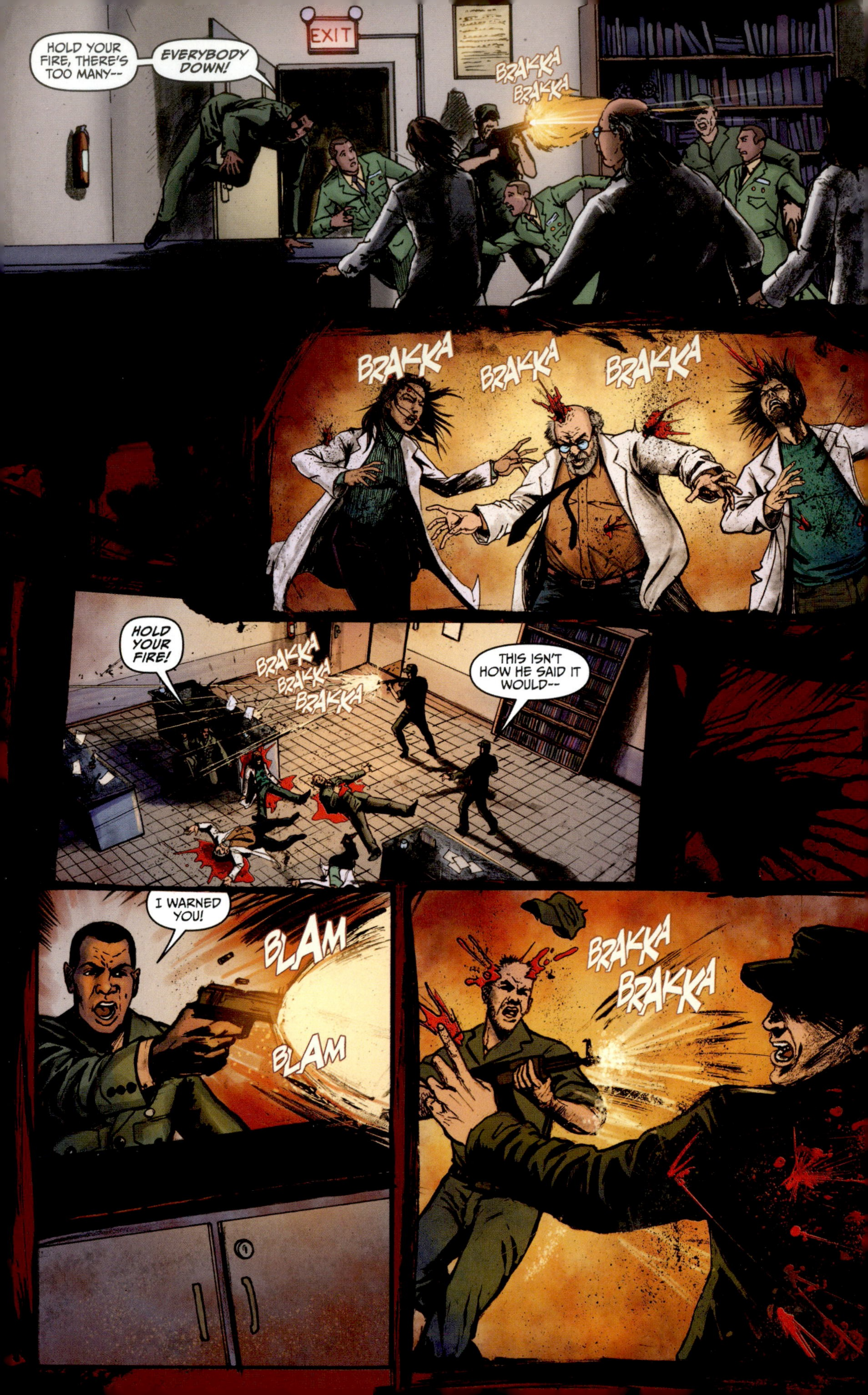
HOLD YOUR FIRE, THERE'S TOO MANY--
EVERYBODY DOWN!
EXIT
BRAKKA BRAKKA
BRAKKA
BRAKKA
BRAKKA
HOLD YOUR FIRE!
BRAKKA BRAKKA BRAKKA
THIS ISN'T HOW HE SAID IT WOULD--
I WARNED YOU!
BLAM
BLAM
BRAKKA BRAKKA

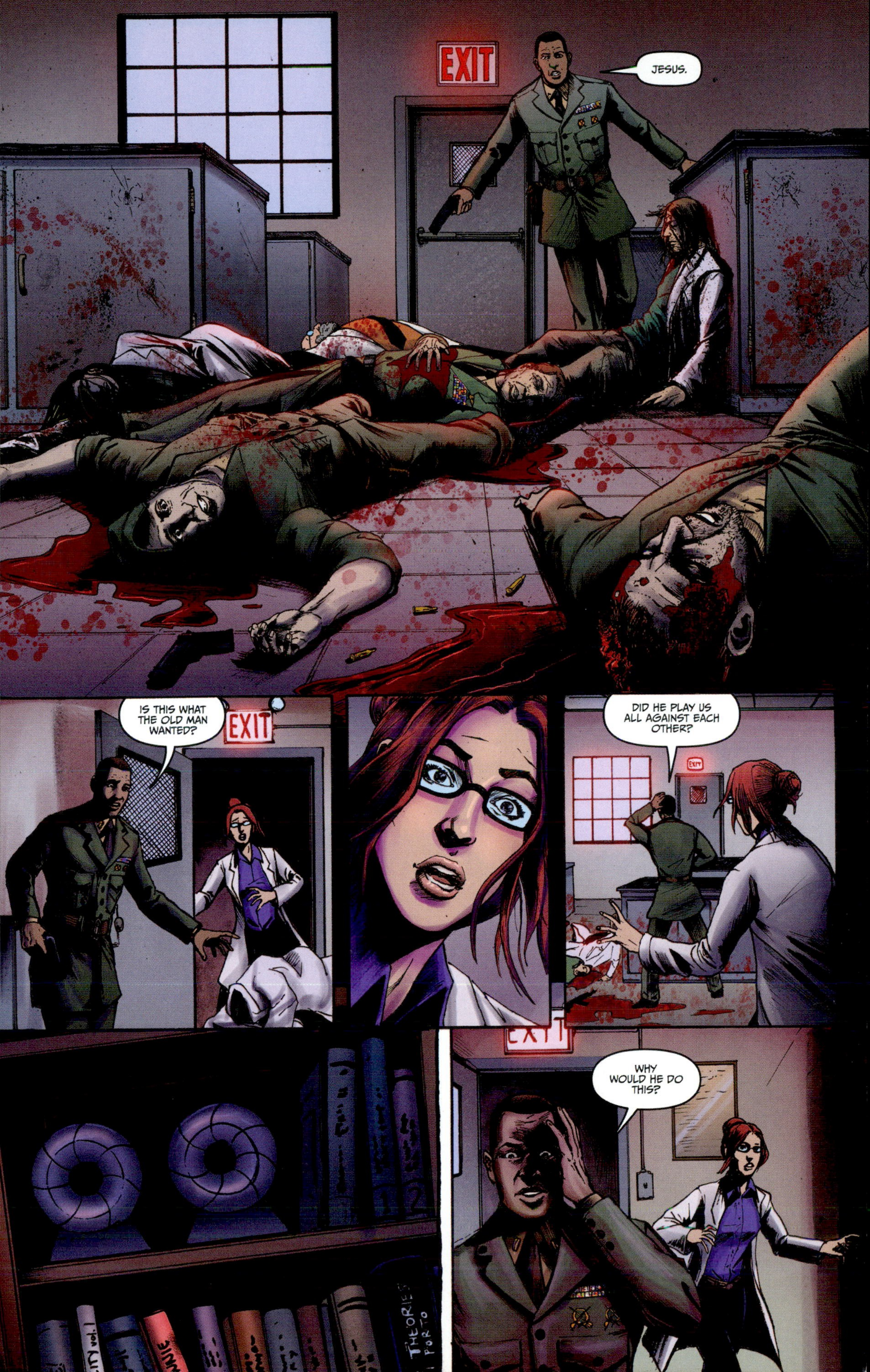
EXIT
JESUS.
IS THIS WHAT THE OLD MAN WANTED?
EXIT
DID HE PLAY US ALL AGAINST EACH OTHER?
WHY WOULD HE DO THIS?
THEORIES

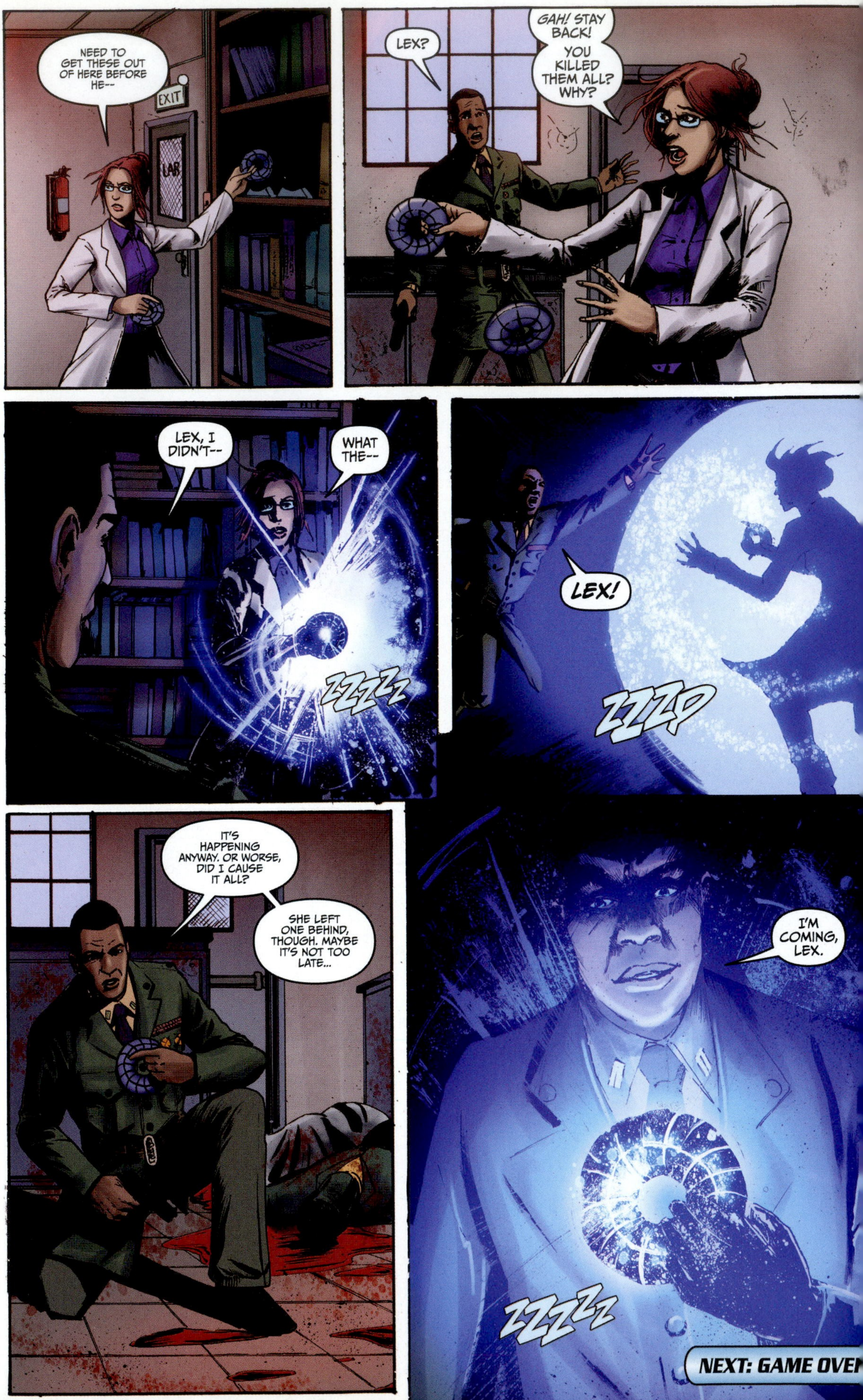

NEED TO GET THESE OUT OF HERE BEFORE HE--
EXIT
LAB
LEX?
GAH! STAY BACK!
YOU KILLED THEM ALL? WHY?
LEX, I DIDN'T--
WHAT THE--
ZZZZZ
LEX!
ZZZP
IT'S HAPPENING ANYWAY. OR WORSE, DID I CAUSE IT ALL?
SHE LEFT ONE BEHIND, THOUGH. MAYBE IT'S NOT TOO LATE...
I'M COMING, LEX.
ZZZZZ
NEXT: GAME OVE

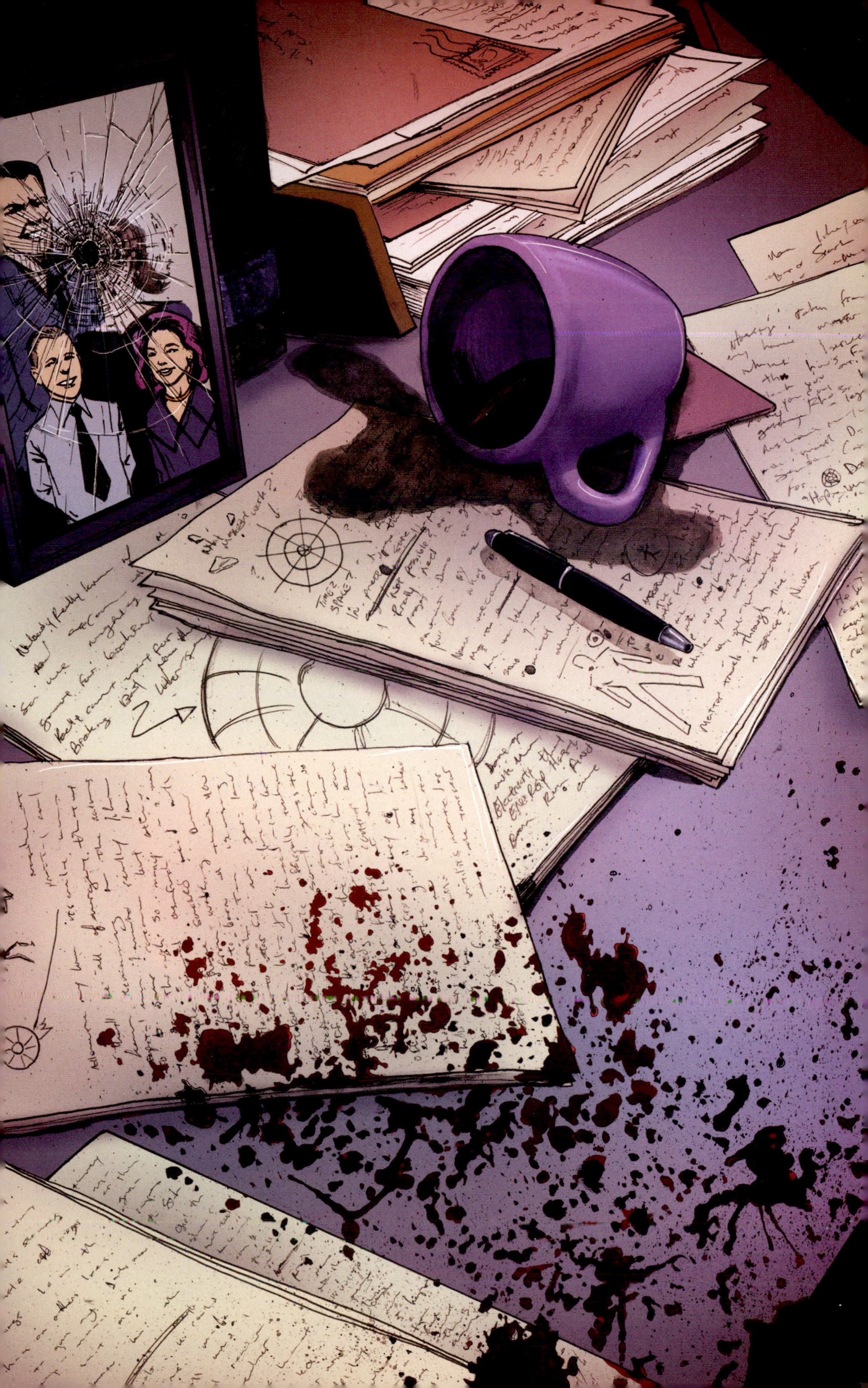

WILL ROBSON

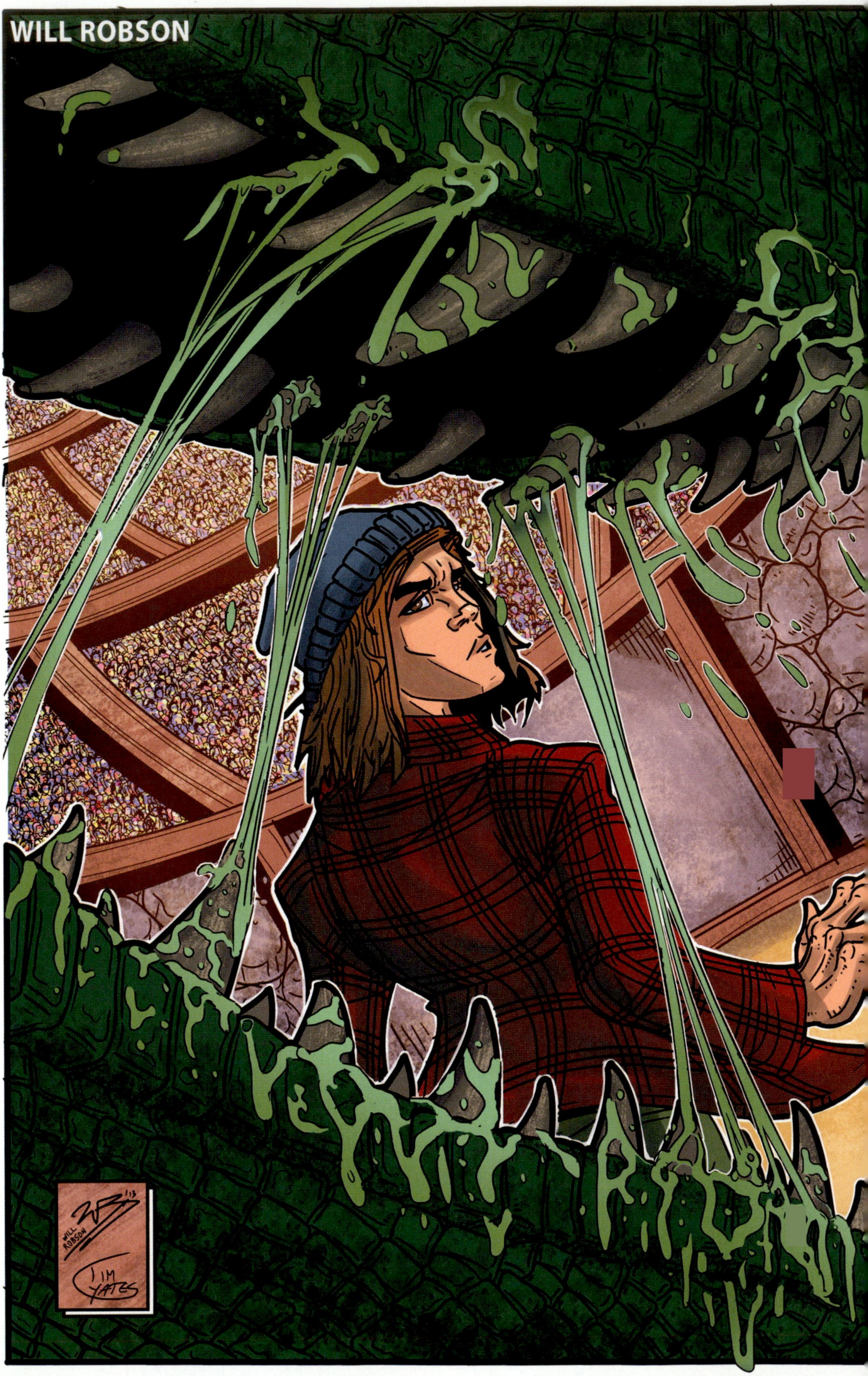
WILL ROBSON
TIM YATES

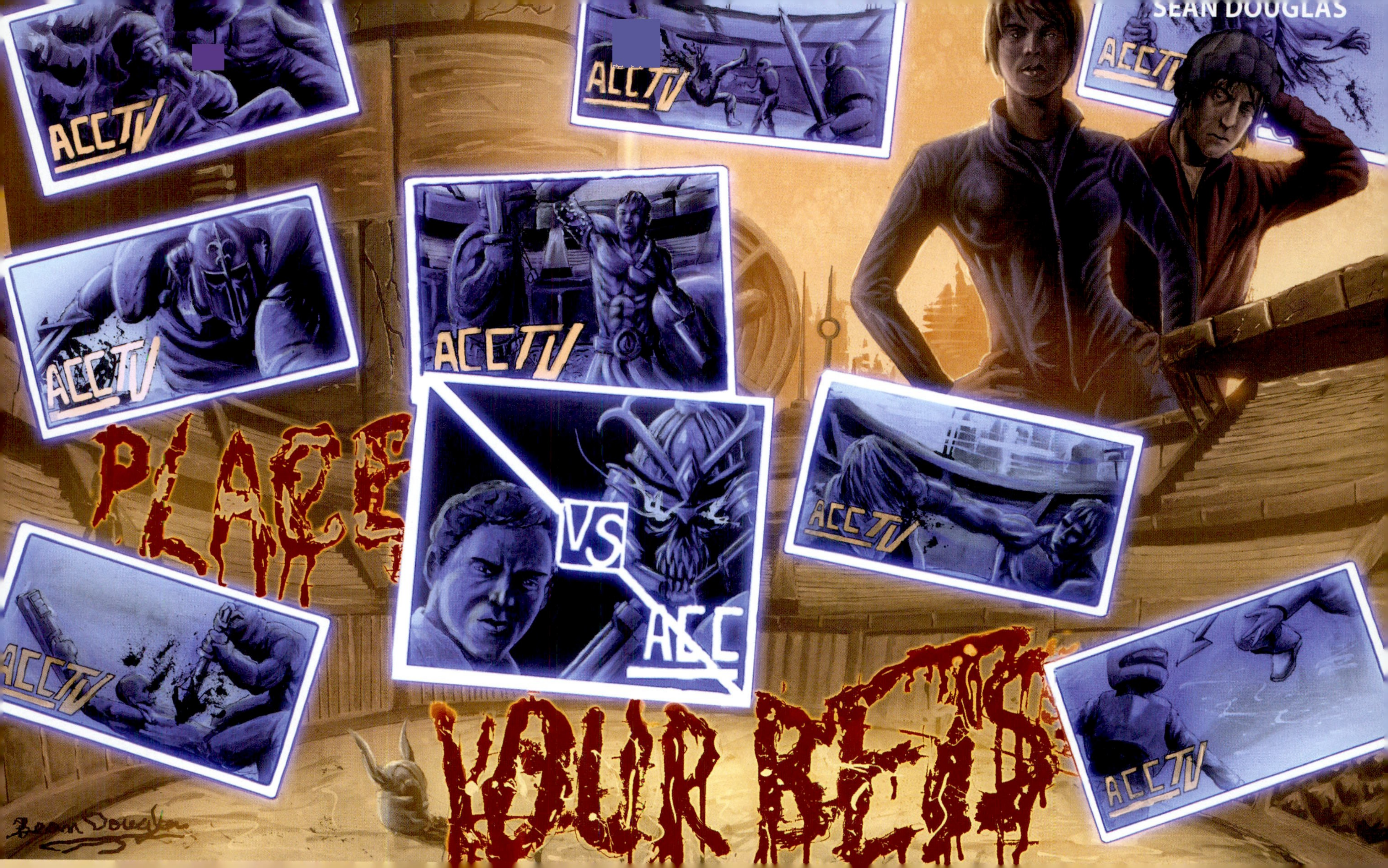
SEAN DOUGLAS
PLACE YOUR BETS
ACCTV
VS
ACC

6 TIMELESS

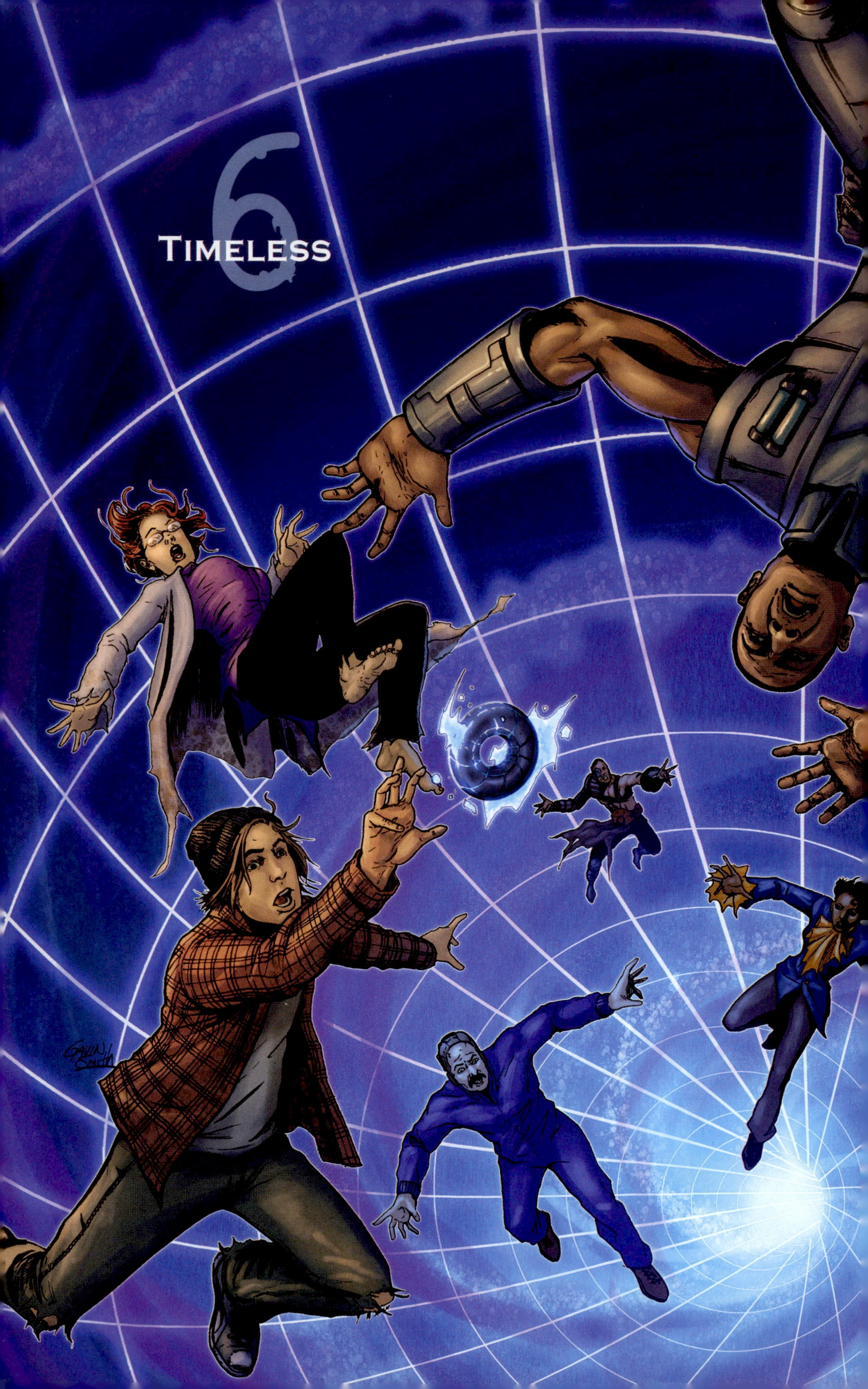

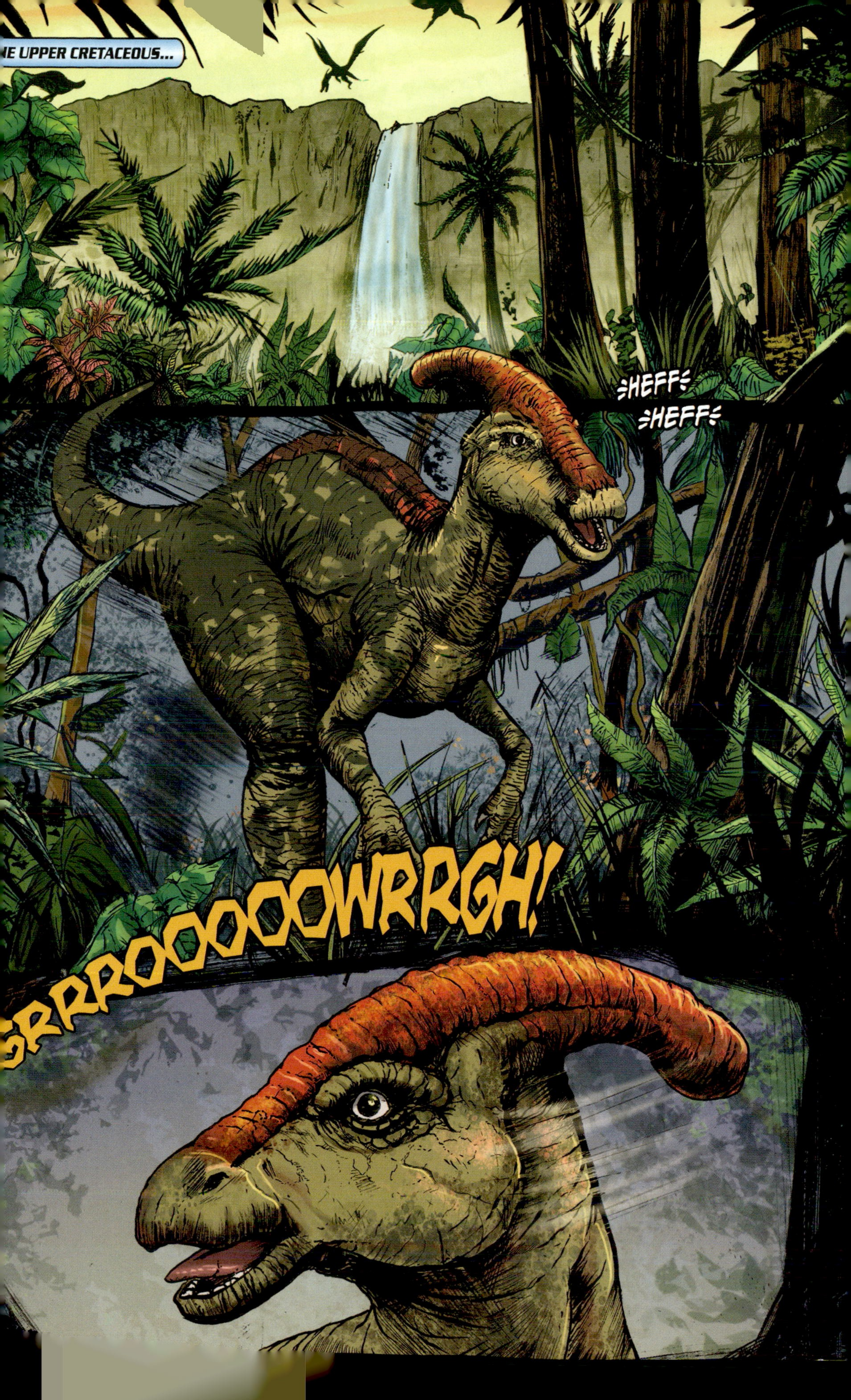
...E UPPER CRETACEOUS...
HEFF
HEFF
GRRROOOOOOWRRGH!

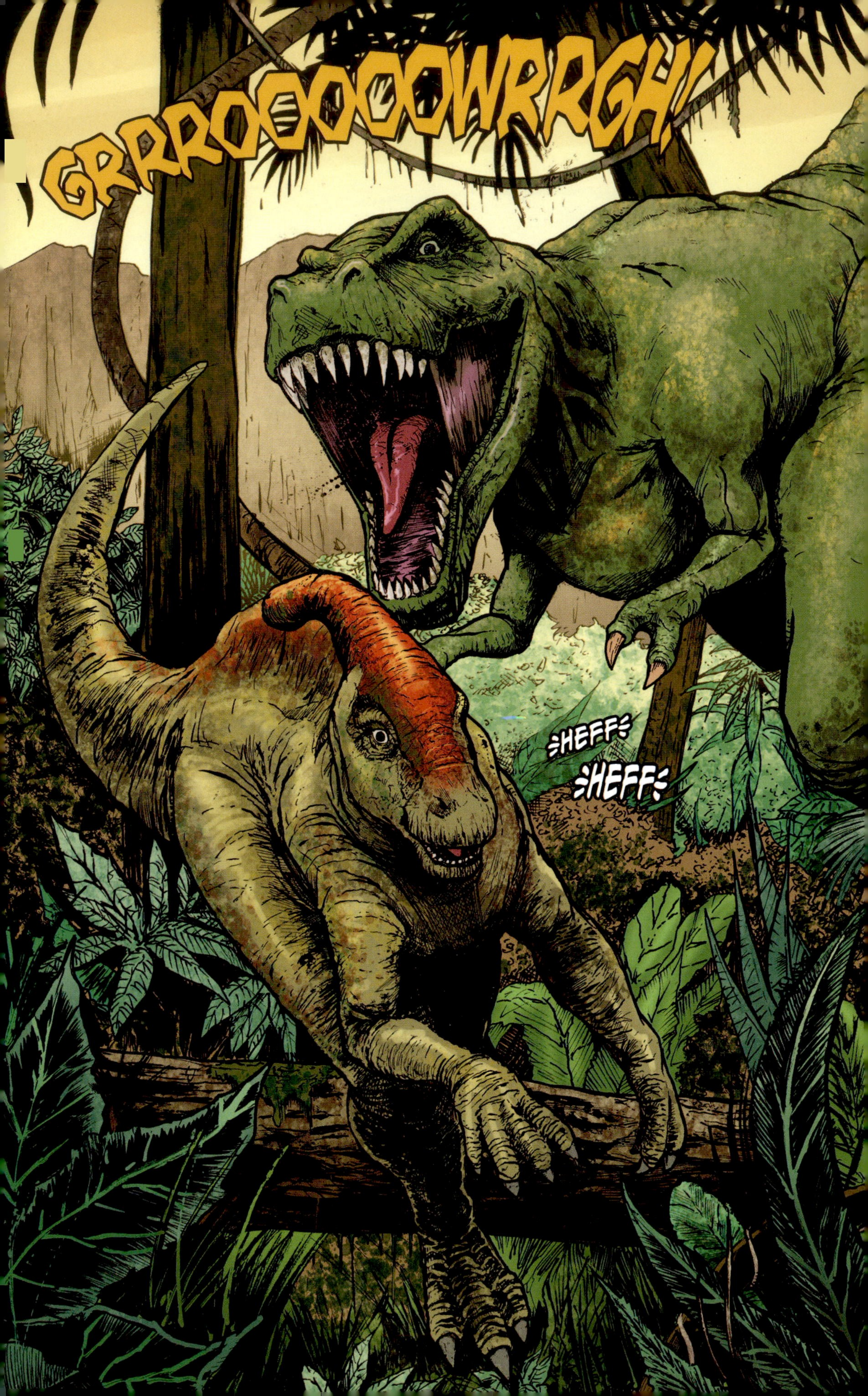
GRRROOOOOOWRRGH!
HEFF
HEFF

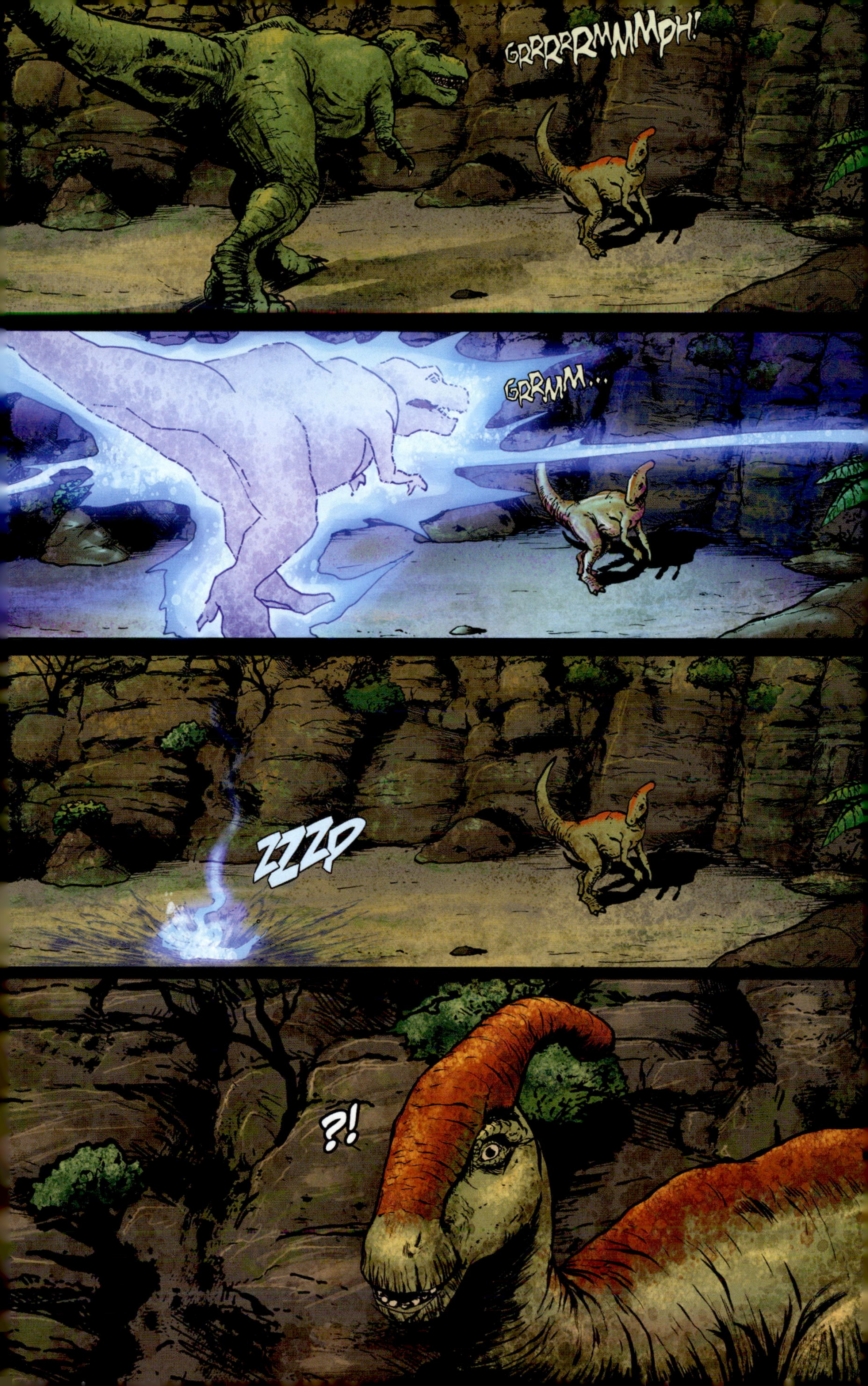
GRRRRRMMMPH!
GRRMM...
ZZZP
?!

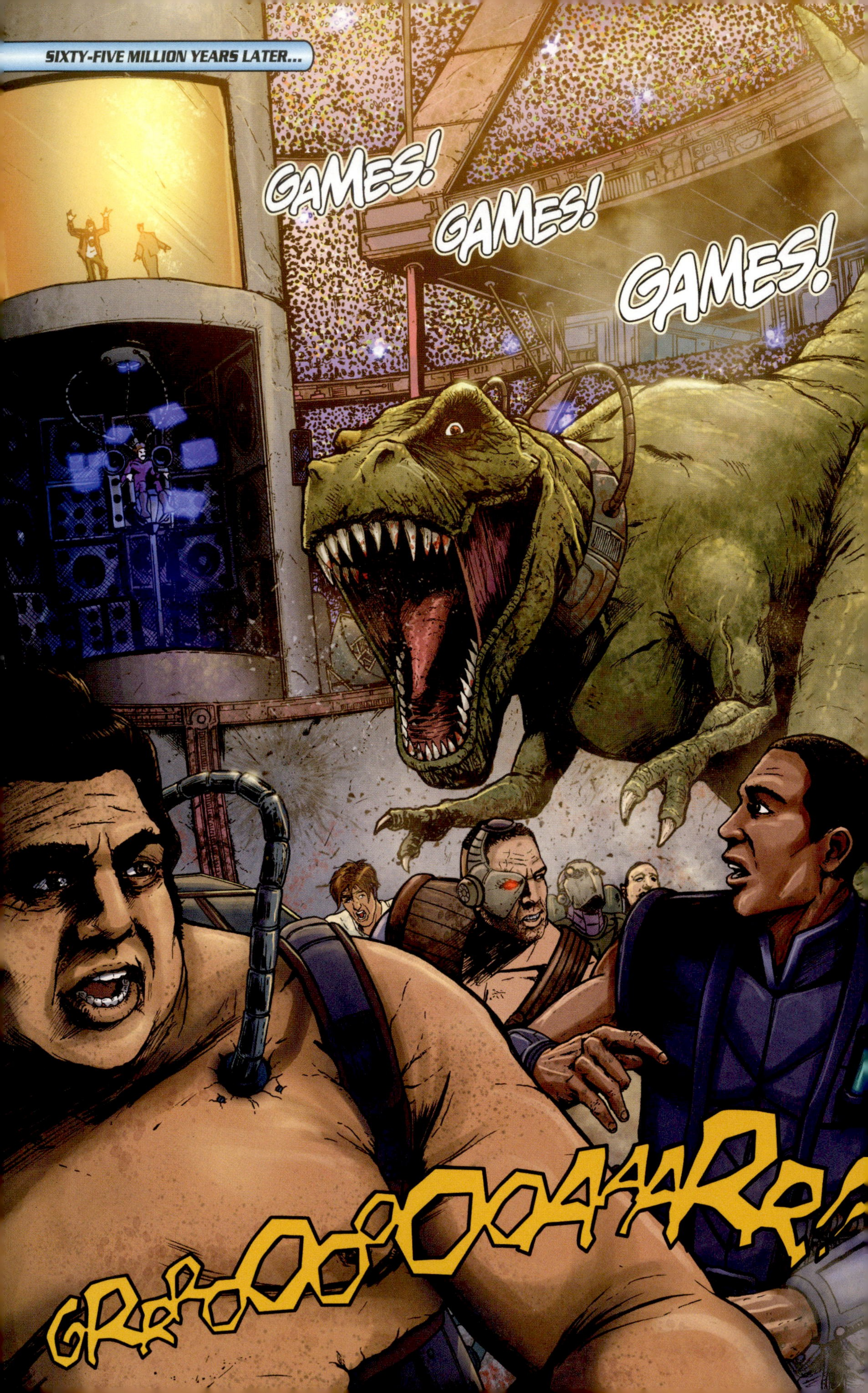
SIXTY-FIVE MILLION YEARS LATER...
GAMES!
GAMES!
GAMES!
GRRROOOOOOOOAAAARR

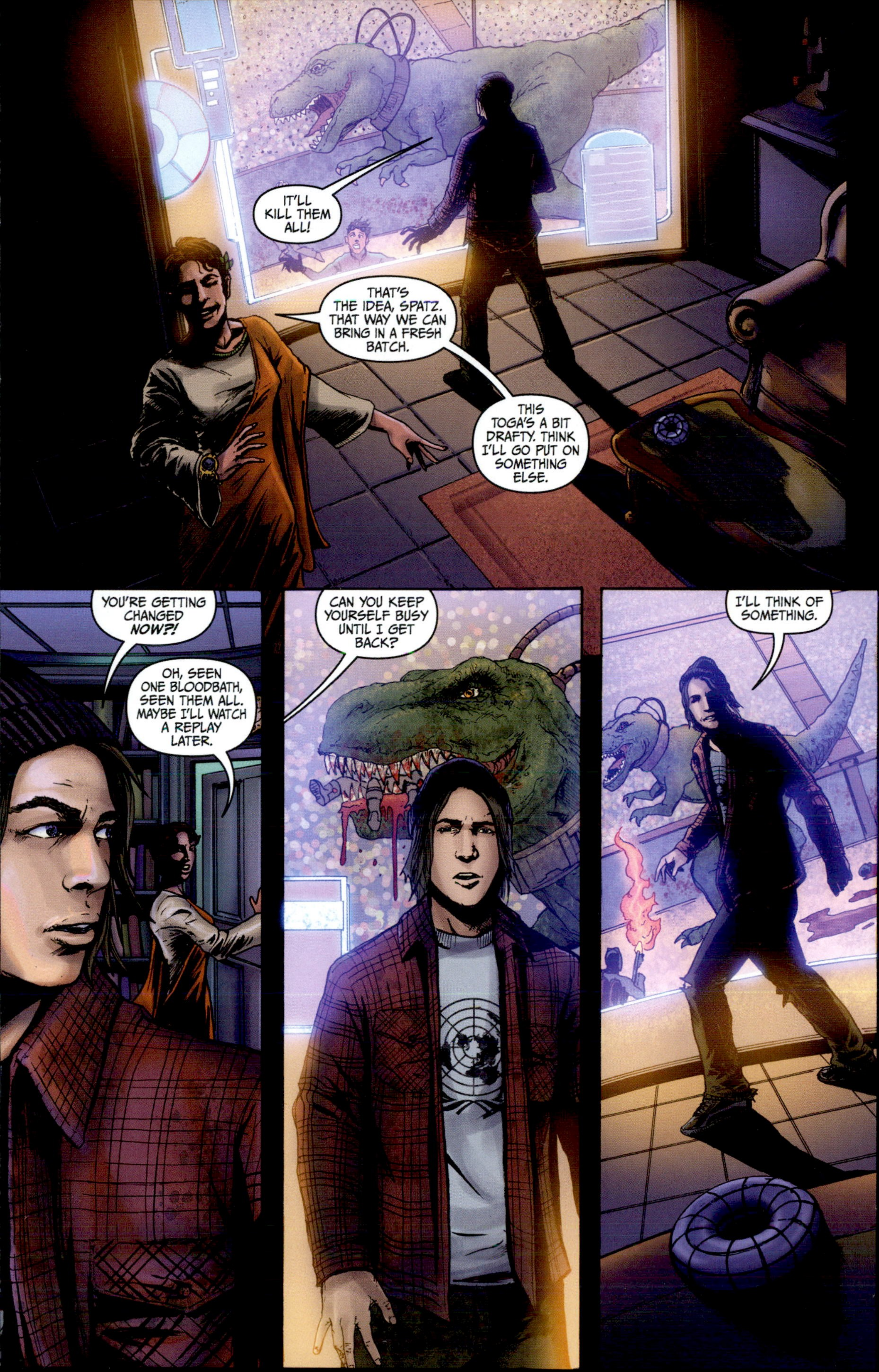
IT'LL KILL THEM ALL!
THAT'S THE IDEA, SPATZ. THAT WAY WE CAN BRING IN A FRESH BATCH.
THIS TOGA'S A BIT DRAFTY. THINK I'LL GO PUT ON SOMETHING ELSE.
YOU'RE GETTING CHANGED *NOW?!*
OH, SEEN ONE BLOODBATH, SEEN THEM ALL. MAYBE I'LL WATCH A REPLAY LATER.
CAN YOU KEEP YOURSELF BUSY UNTIL I GET BACK?
I'LL THINK OF SOMETHING.

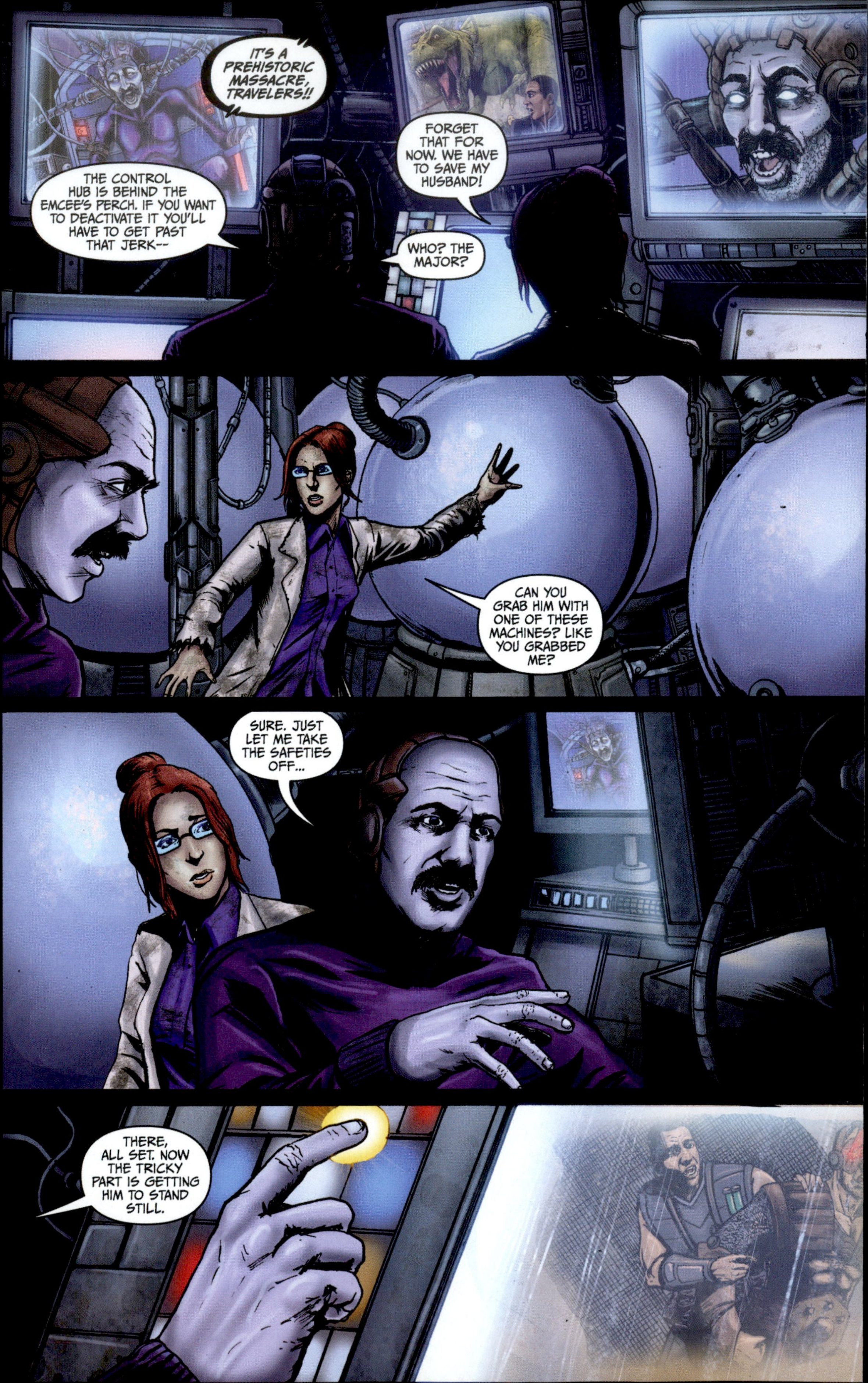

IT'S A PREHISTORIC MASSACRE, TRAVELERS!!
THE CONTROL HUB IS BEHIND THE EMCEE'S PERCH. IF YOU WANT TO DEACTIVATE IT YOU'LL HAVE TO GET PAST THAT JERK--
FORGET THAT FOR NOW. WE HAVE TO SAVE MY HUSBAND!
WHO? THE MAJOR?
CAN YOU GRAB HIM WITH ONE OF THESE MACHINES? LIKE YOU GRABBED ME?
SURE. JUST LET ME TAKE THE SAFETIES OFF...
THERE, ALL SET. NOW THE TRICKY PART IS GETTING HIM TO STAND STILL.

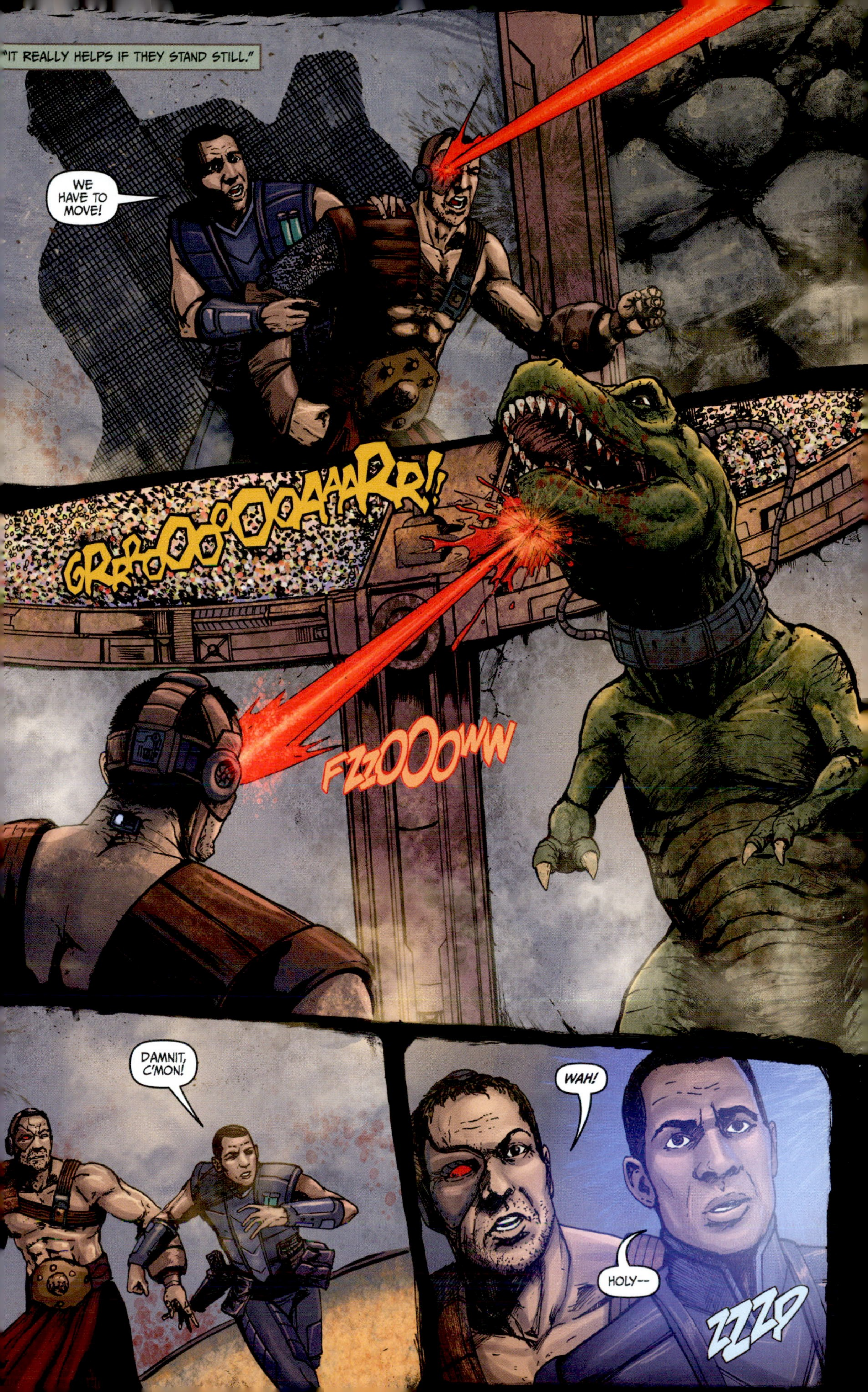
"IT REALLY HELPS IF THEY STAND STILL."
WE HAVE TO MOVE!
GRROOOOOOAAARR!!
FZZOOOWW
DAMNIT, C'MON!
WAH!
HOLY--
ZZZP

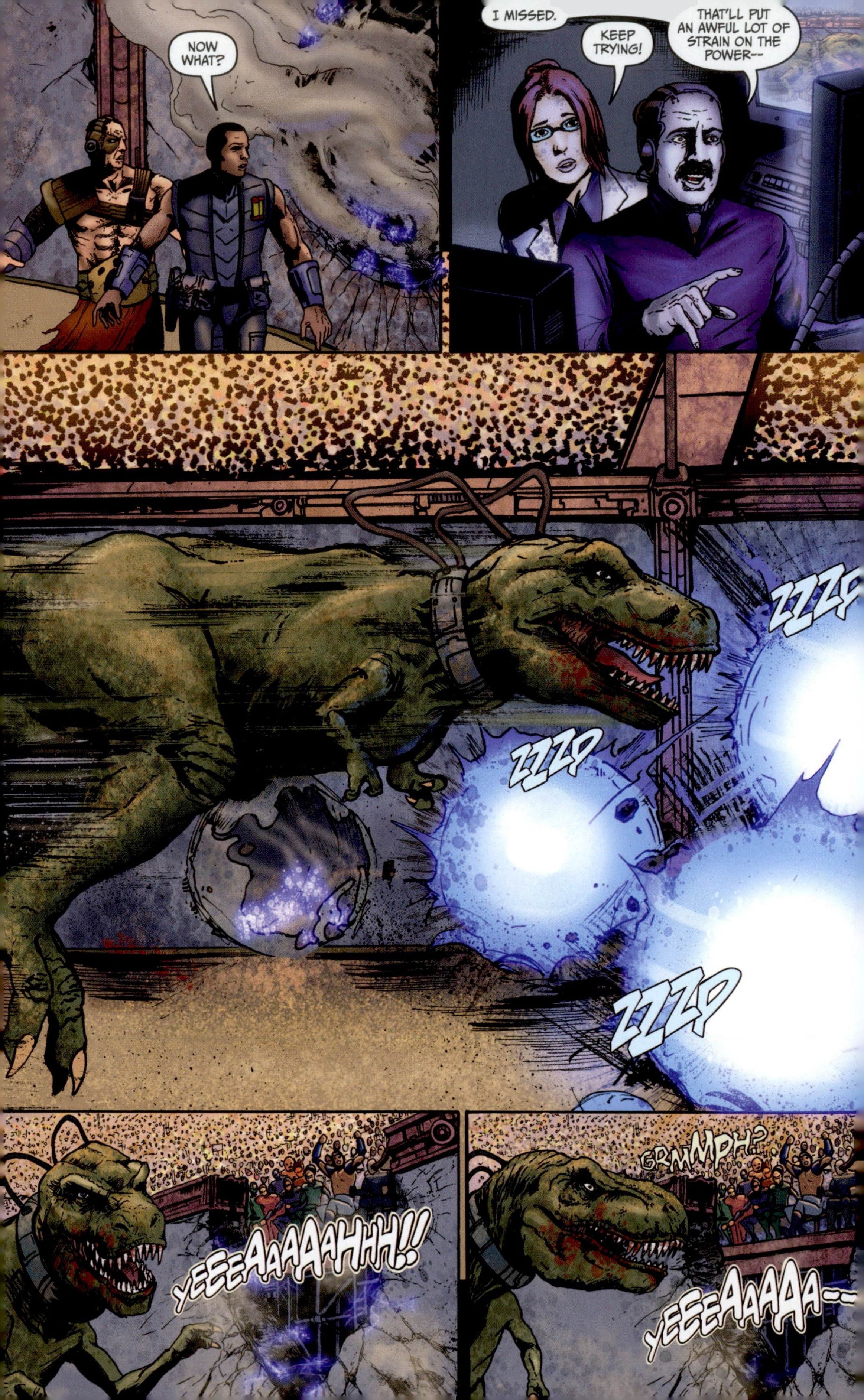
NOW WHAT?
I MISSED.
KEEP TRYING!
THAT'LL PUT AN AWFUL LOT OF STRAIN ON THE POWER--
ZZZP
ZZZP
ZZZP
YEEEAAAAAHHH!!
GRMMPH?
YEEEAAAAA--

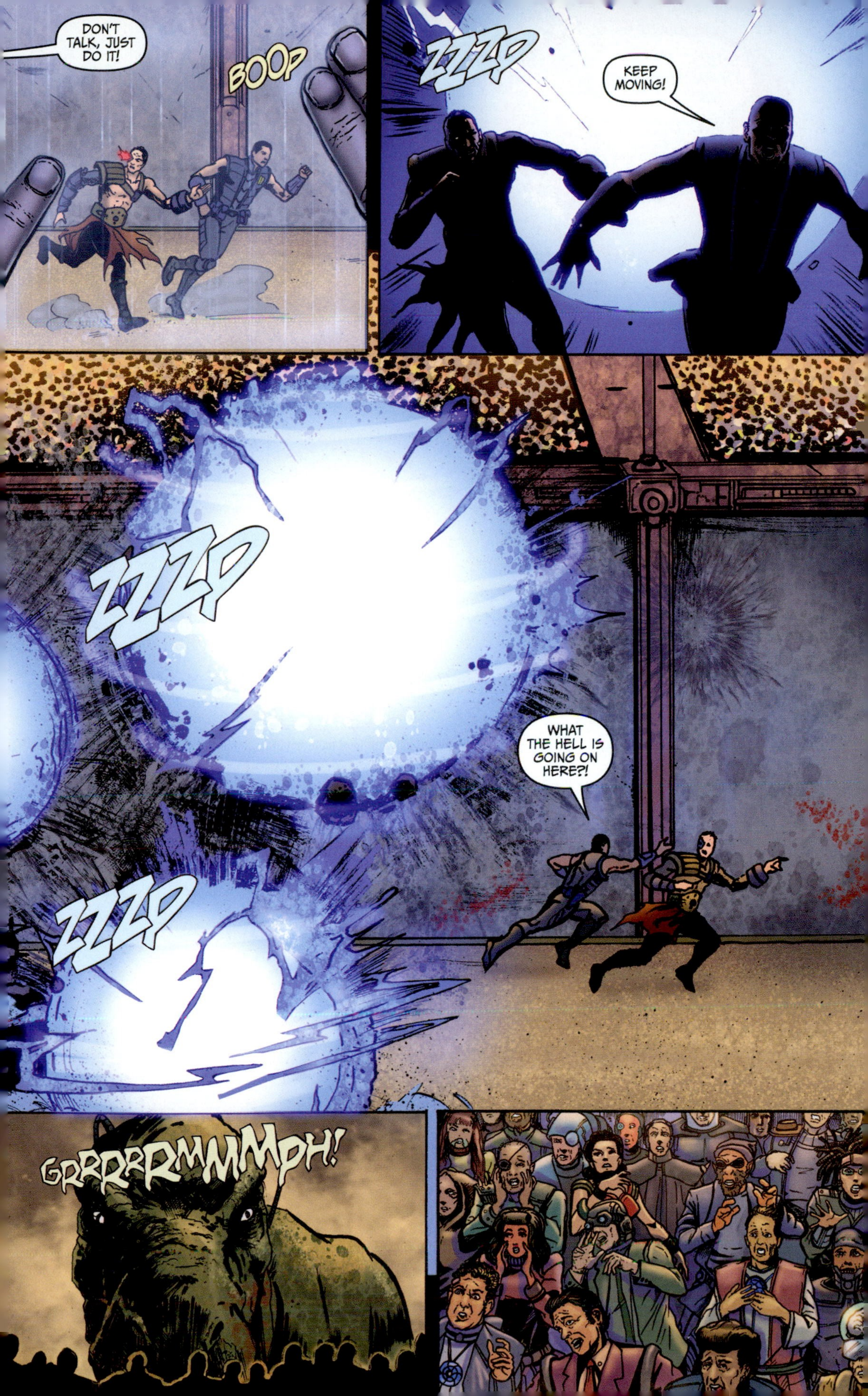
DON'T TALK, JUST DO IT!
BOOP
ZZZP
KEEP MOVING!
ZZZP
WHAT THE HELL IS GOING ON HERE?!
ZZZP
GRRRRRMMMMPH!

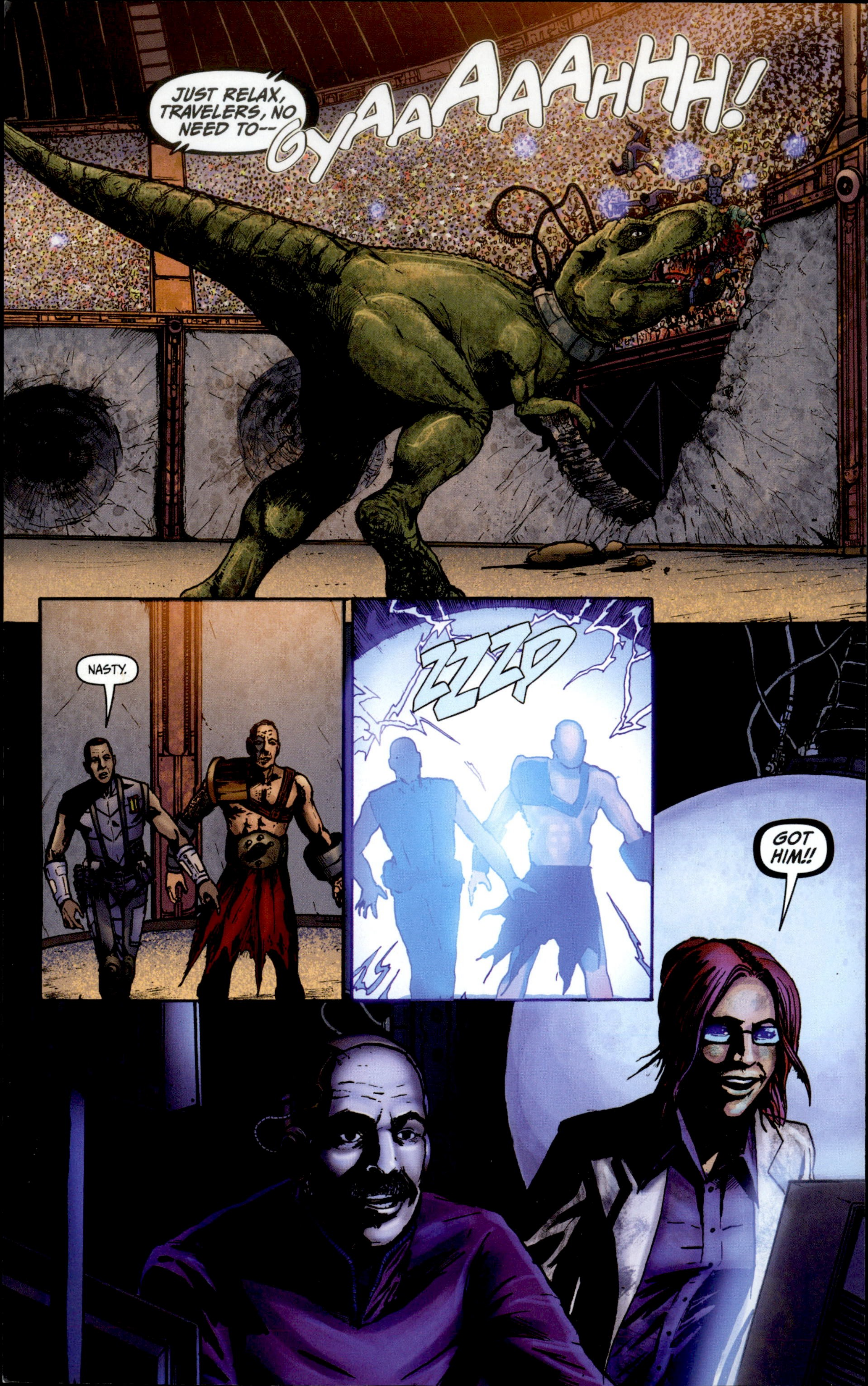
JUST RELAX, TRAVELERS, NO NEED TO--
GYAAAAAAHHH!
NASTY.
ZZZD
GOT HIM!!

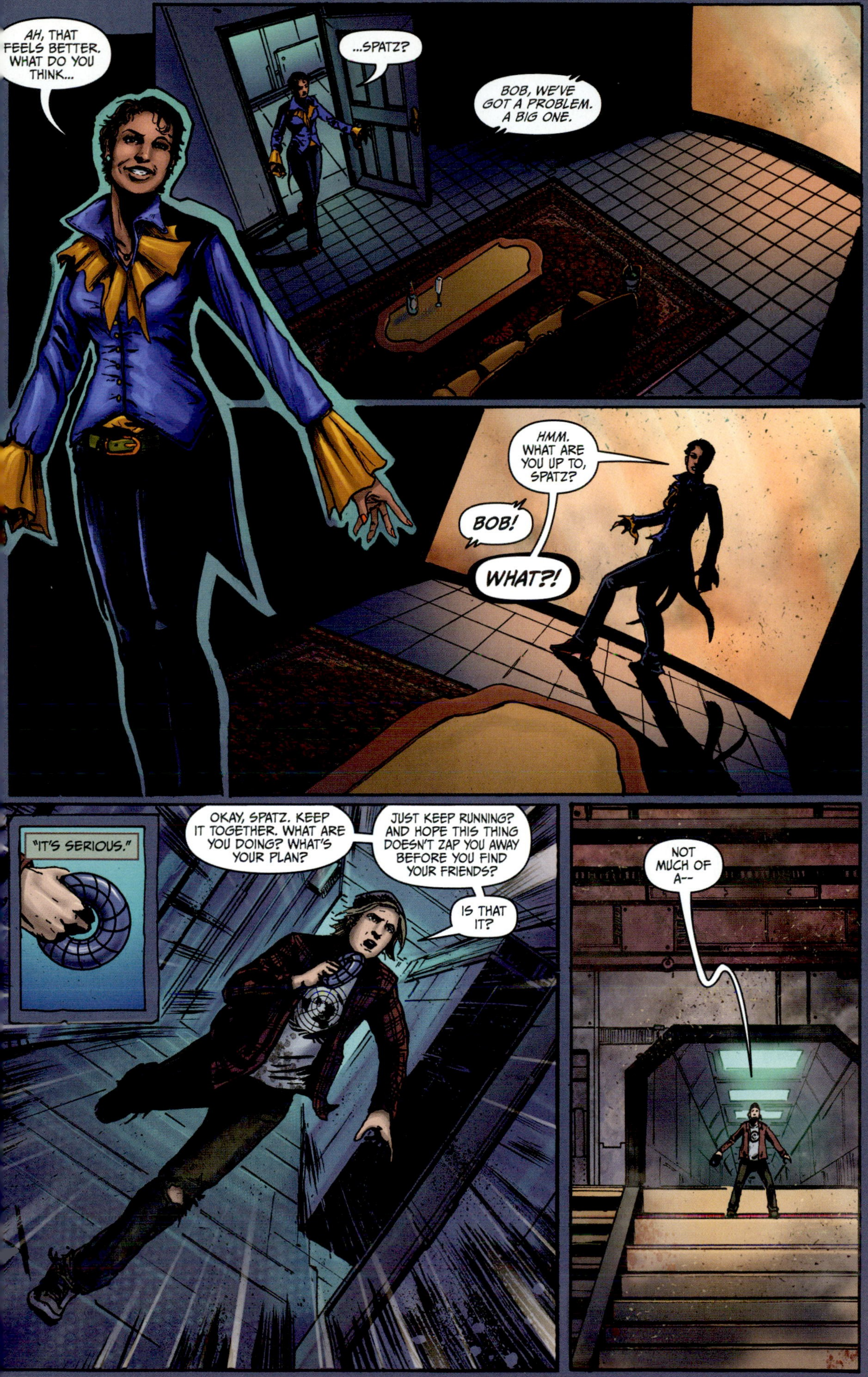
AH, THAT FEELS BETTER. WHAT DO YOU THINK...
...SPATZ?
BOB, WE'VE GOT A PROBLEM. A BIG ONE.
HMM. WHAT ARE YOU UP TO, SPATZ?
BOB!
WHAT?!
"IT'S SERIOUS."
OKAY, SPATZ. KEEP IT TOGETHER. WHAT ARE YOU DOING? WHAT'S YOUR PLAN?
JUST KEEP RUNNING? AND HOPE THIS THING DOESN'T ZAP YOU AWAY BEFORE YOU FIND YOUR FRIENDS?
IS THAT IT?
NOT MUCH OF A--

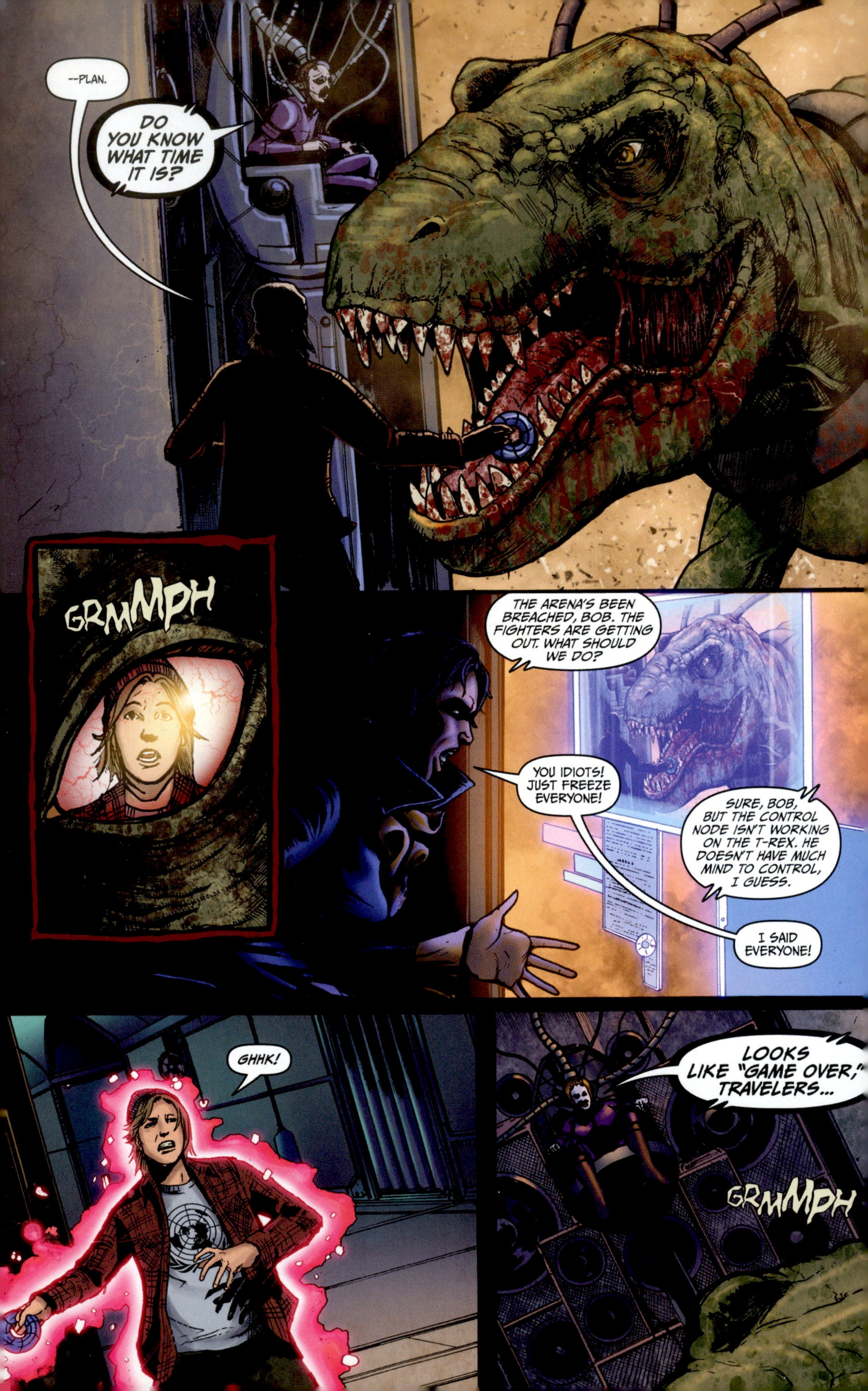
--PLAN.
DO YOU KNOW WHAT TIME IT IS?
GRMMPH
THE ARENA'S BEEN BREACHED, BOB. THE FIGHTERS ARE GETTING OUT. WHAT SHOULD WE DO?
YOU IDIOTS! JUST FREEZE EVERYONE!
SURE, BOB, BUT THE CONTROL NODE ISN'T WORKING ON THE T-REX. HE DOESN'T HAVE MUCH MIND TO CONTROL, I GUESS.
I SAID EVERYONE!
GHHK!
LOOKS LIKE "GAME OVER," TRAVELERS...
GRMMPH

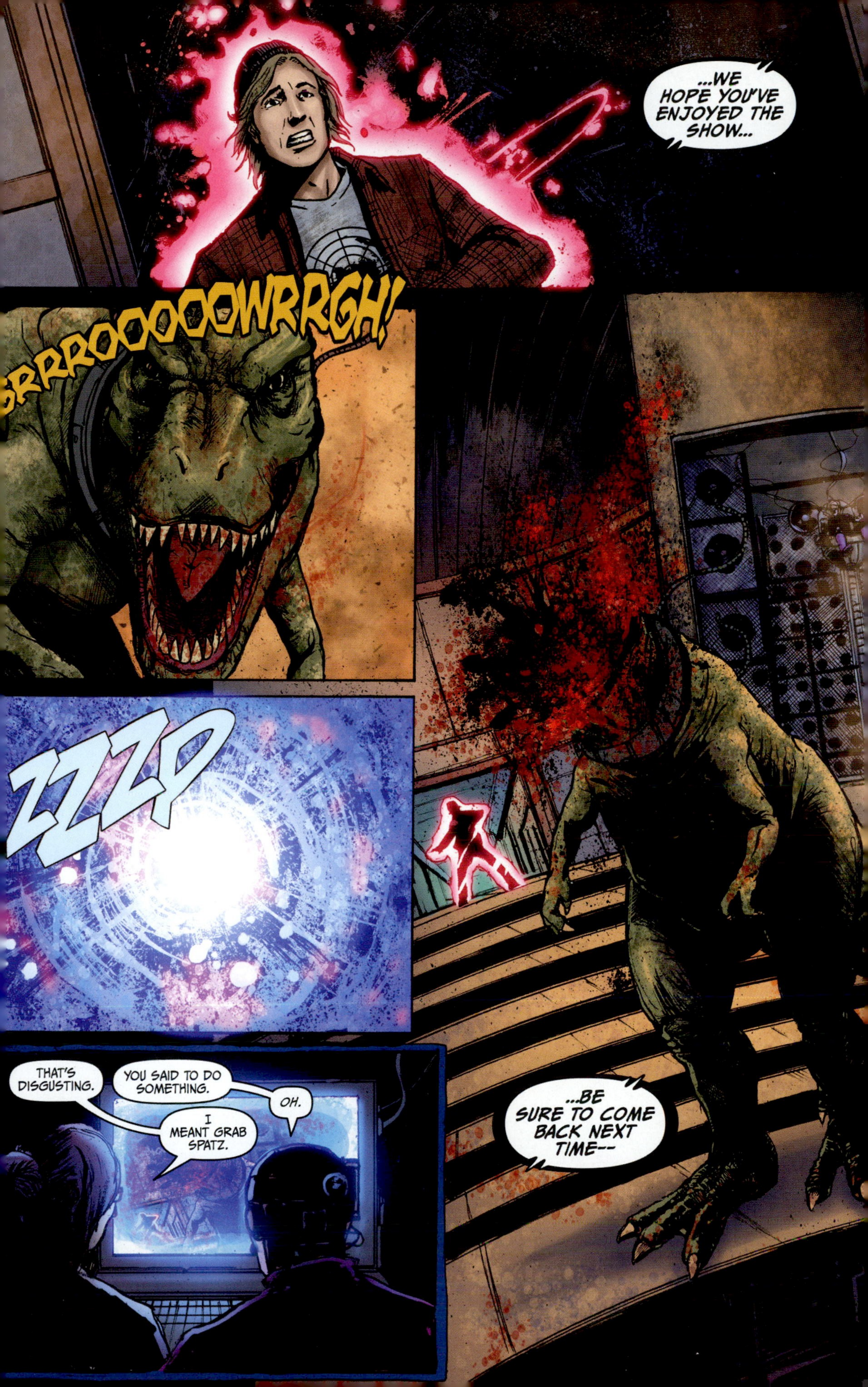
...WE HOPE YOU'VE ENJOYED THE SHOW...
GRRROOOOOOWRRGH!
ZZZP
...BE SURE TO COME BACK NEXT TIME--
THAT'S DISGUSTING.
YOU SAID TO DO SOMETHING.
I MEANT GRAB SPATZ.
OH.

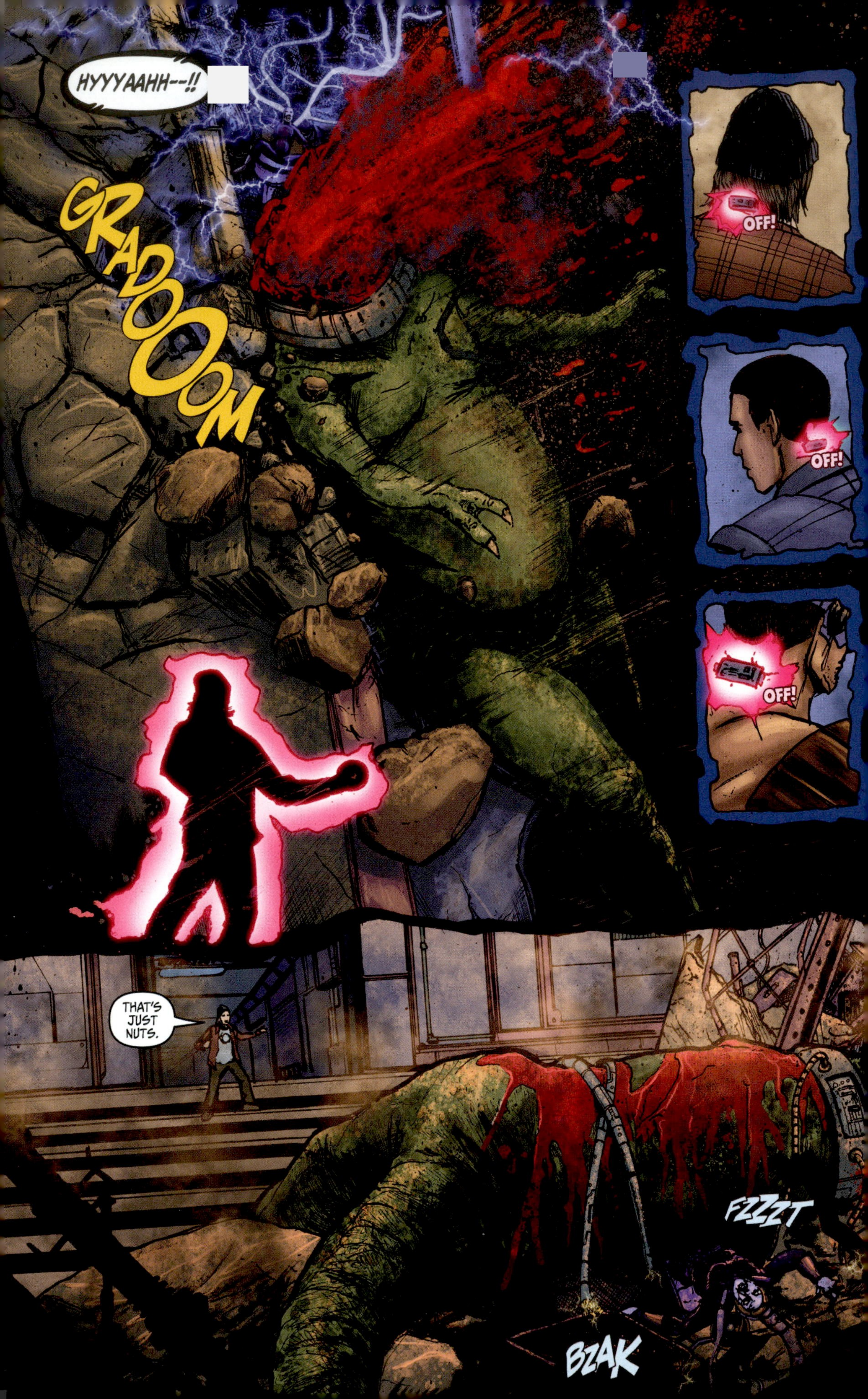
HYYYAAHH--!!
GRADOOOOM
OFF!
OFF!
OFF!
THAT'S JUST NUTS.
FZZZT
BZAK

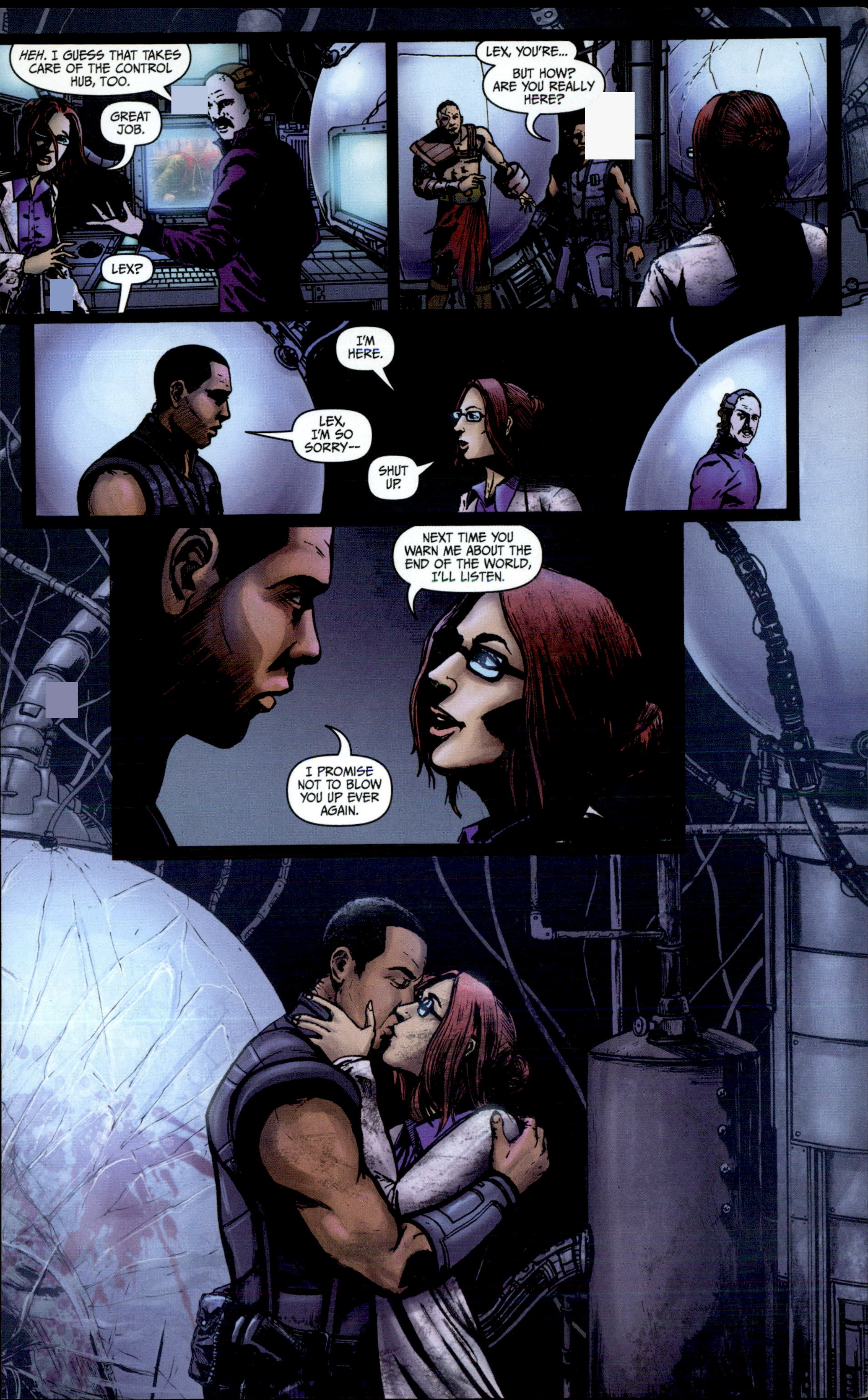
HEH. I GUESS THAT TAKES CARE OF THE CONTROL HUB, TOO.
GREAT JOB.
LEX?
LEX, YOU'RE...
BUT HOW? ARE YOU REALLY HERE?
I'M HERE.
LEX, I'M SO SORRY--
SHUT UP.
NEXT TIME YOU WARN ME ABOUT THE END OF THE WORLD, I'LL LISTEN.
I PROMISE NOT TO BLOW YOU UP EVER AGAIN.

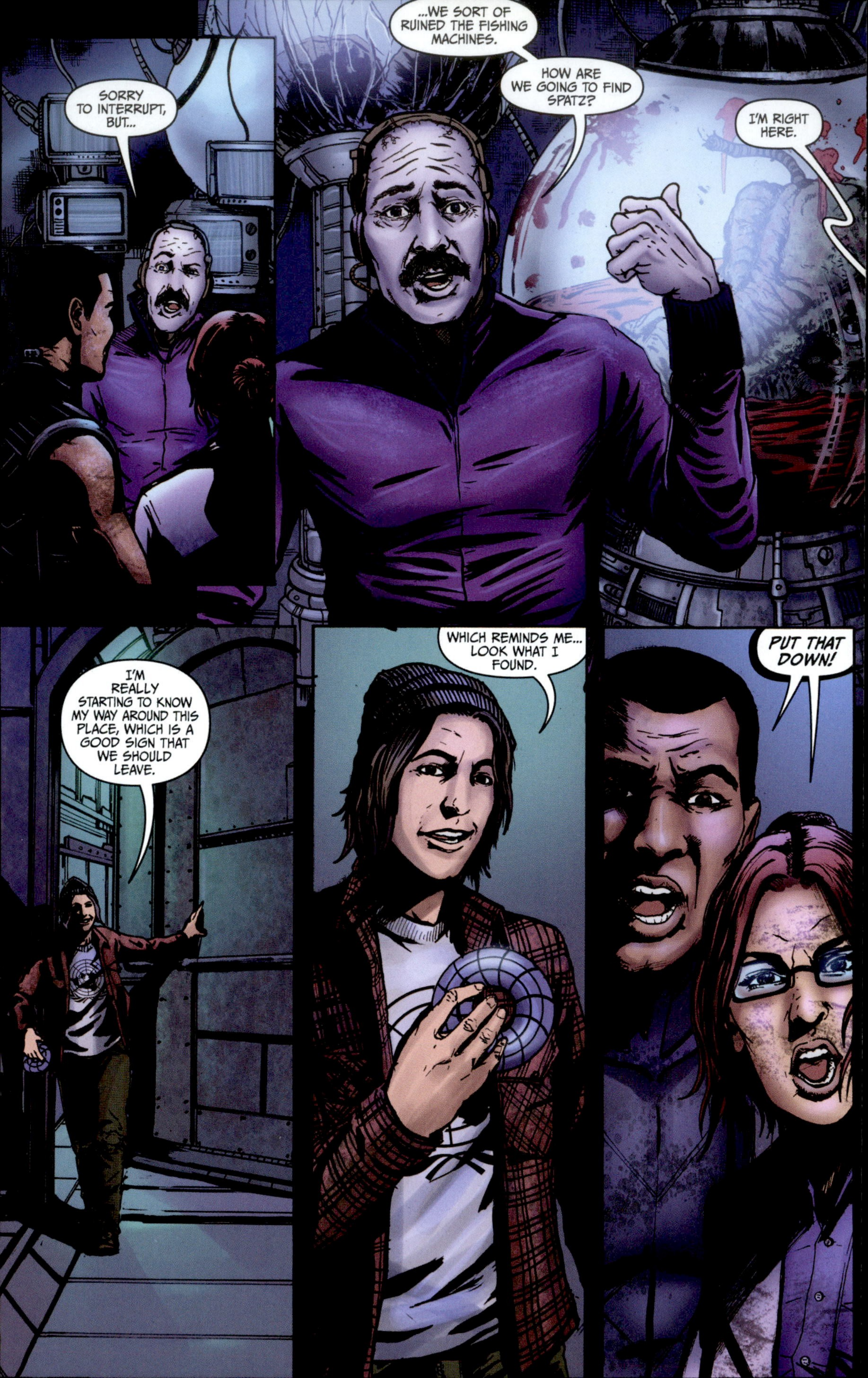
SORRY TO INTERRUPT, BUT...
...WE SORT OF RUINED THE FISHING MACHINES.
HOW ARE WE GOING TO FIND SPATZ?
I'M RIGHT HERE.
I'M REALLY STARTING TO KNOW MY WAY AROUND THIS PLACE, WHICH IS A GOOD SIGN THAT WE SHOULD LEAVE.
WHICH REMINDS ME... LOOK WHAT I FOUND.
PUT THAT DOWN!

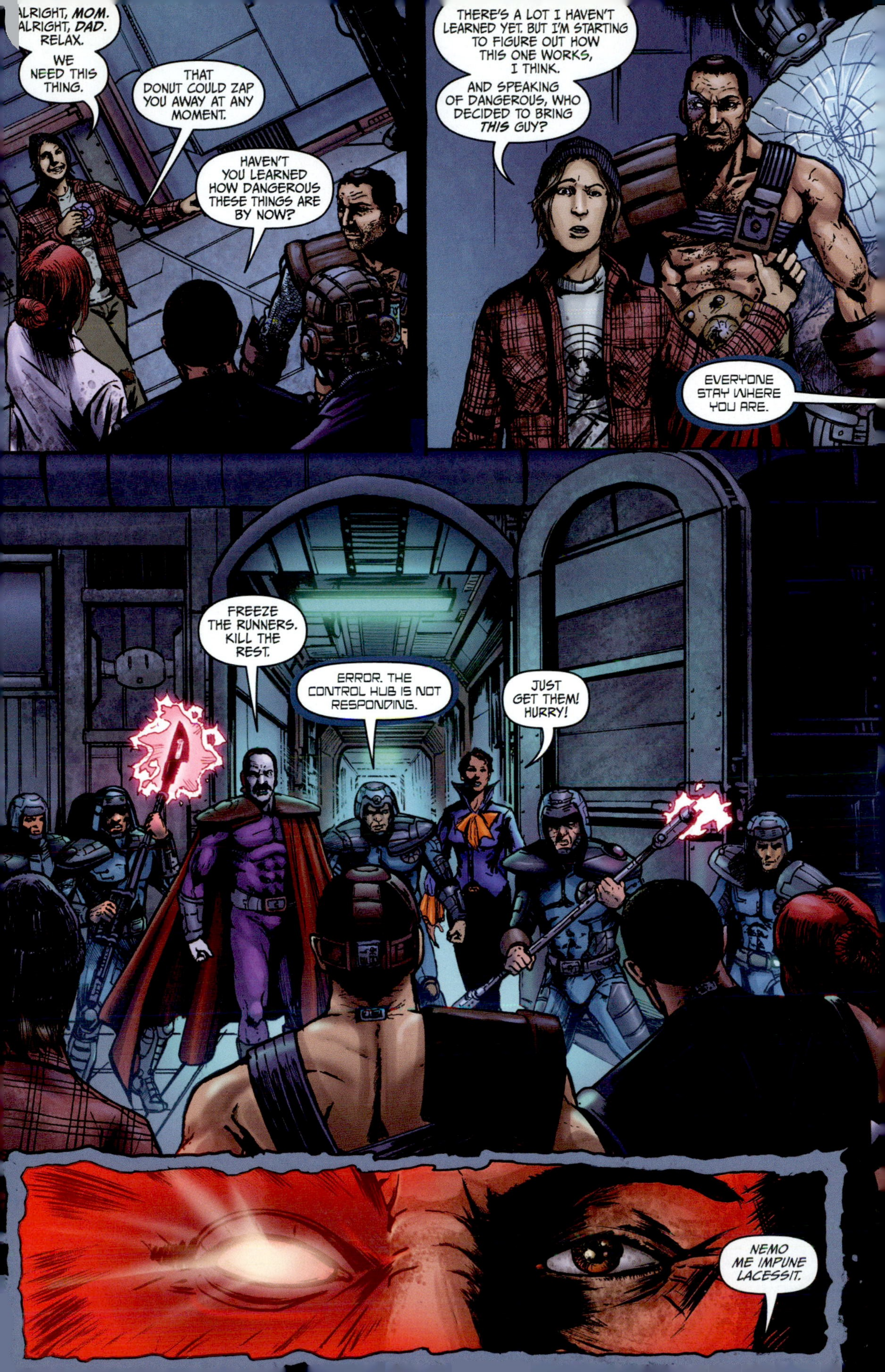
ALRIGHT, MOM. ALRIGHT, DAD. RELAX.
WE NEED THIS THING.
THAT DONUT COULD ZAP YOU AWAY AT ANY MOMENT.
HAVEN'T YOU LEARNED HOW DANGEROUS THESE THINGS ARE BY NOW?
THERE'S A LOT I HAVEN'T LEARNED YET. BUT I'M STARTING TO FIGURE OUT HOW THIS ONE WORKS, I THINK.
AND SPEAKING OF DANGEROUS, WHO DECIDED TO BRING THIS GUY?
EVERYONE STAY WHERE YOU ARE.
FREEZE THE RUNNERS. KILL THE REST.
ERROR. THE CONTROL HUB IS NOT RESPONDING.
JUST GET THEM! HURRY!
NEMO ME IMPUNE LACESSIT.

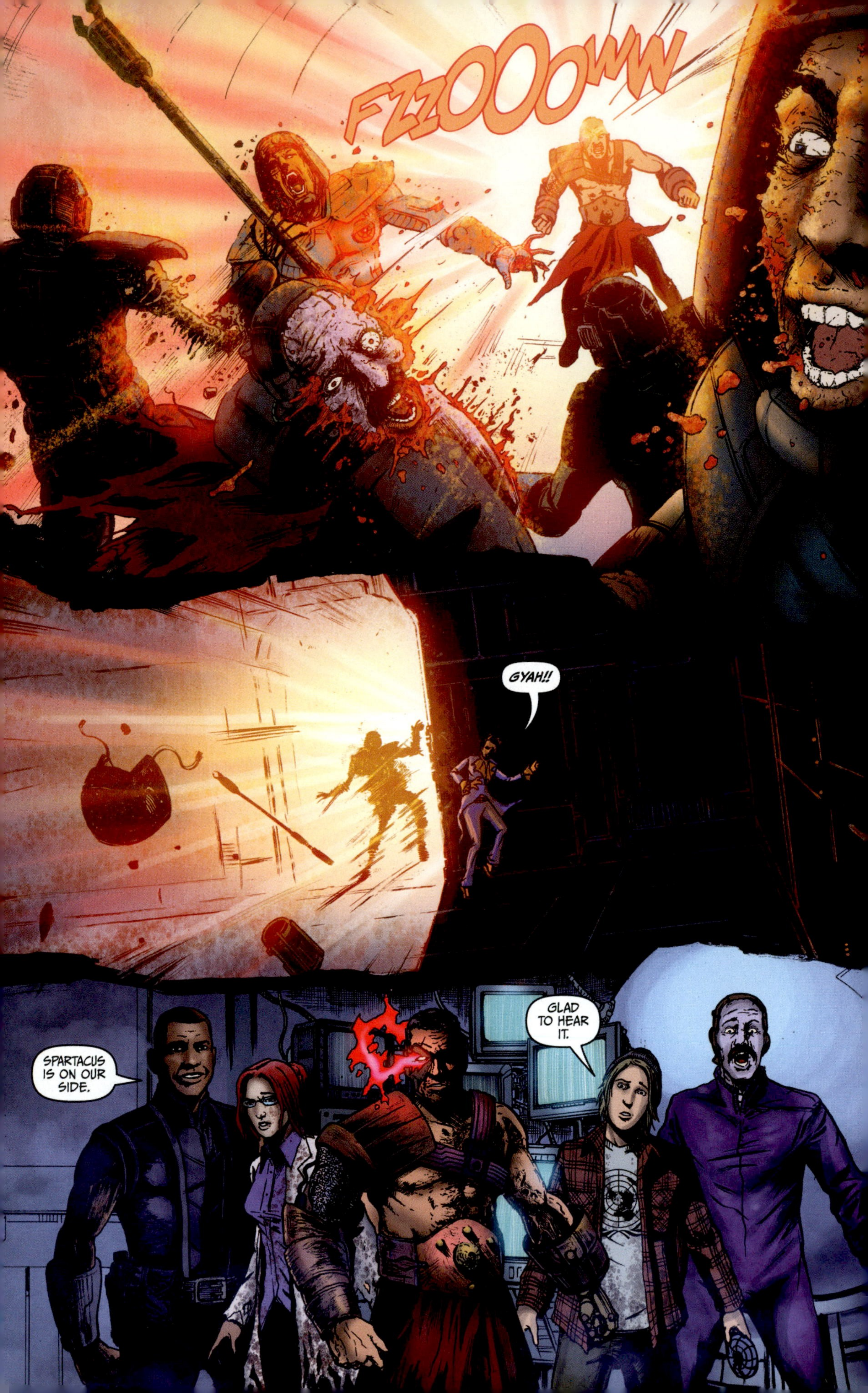
FZZOOOOWW
GYAH!!
SPARTACUS IS ON OUR SIDE.
GLAD TO HEAR IT.

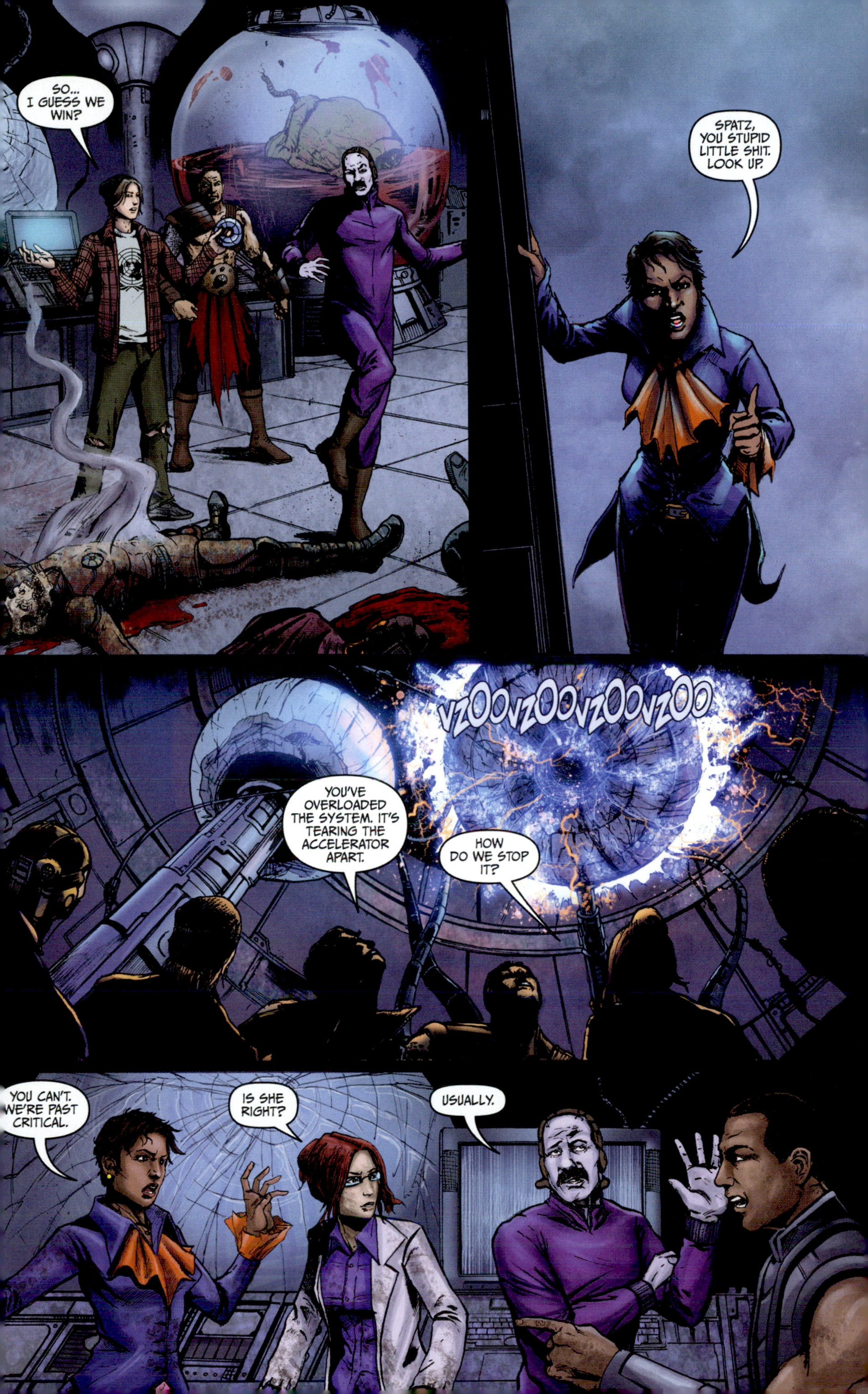
SO... I GUESS WE WIN?
SPATZ, YOU STUPID LITTLE SHIT. LOOK UP.
VZOOVZOOVZOOVZOO
YOU'VE OVERLOADED THE SYSTEM. IT'S TEARING THE ACCELERATOR APART.
HOW DO WE STOP IT?
YOU CAN'T. WE'RE PAST CRITICAL.
IS SHE RIGHT?
USUALLY.

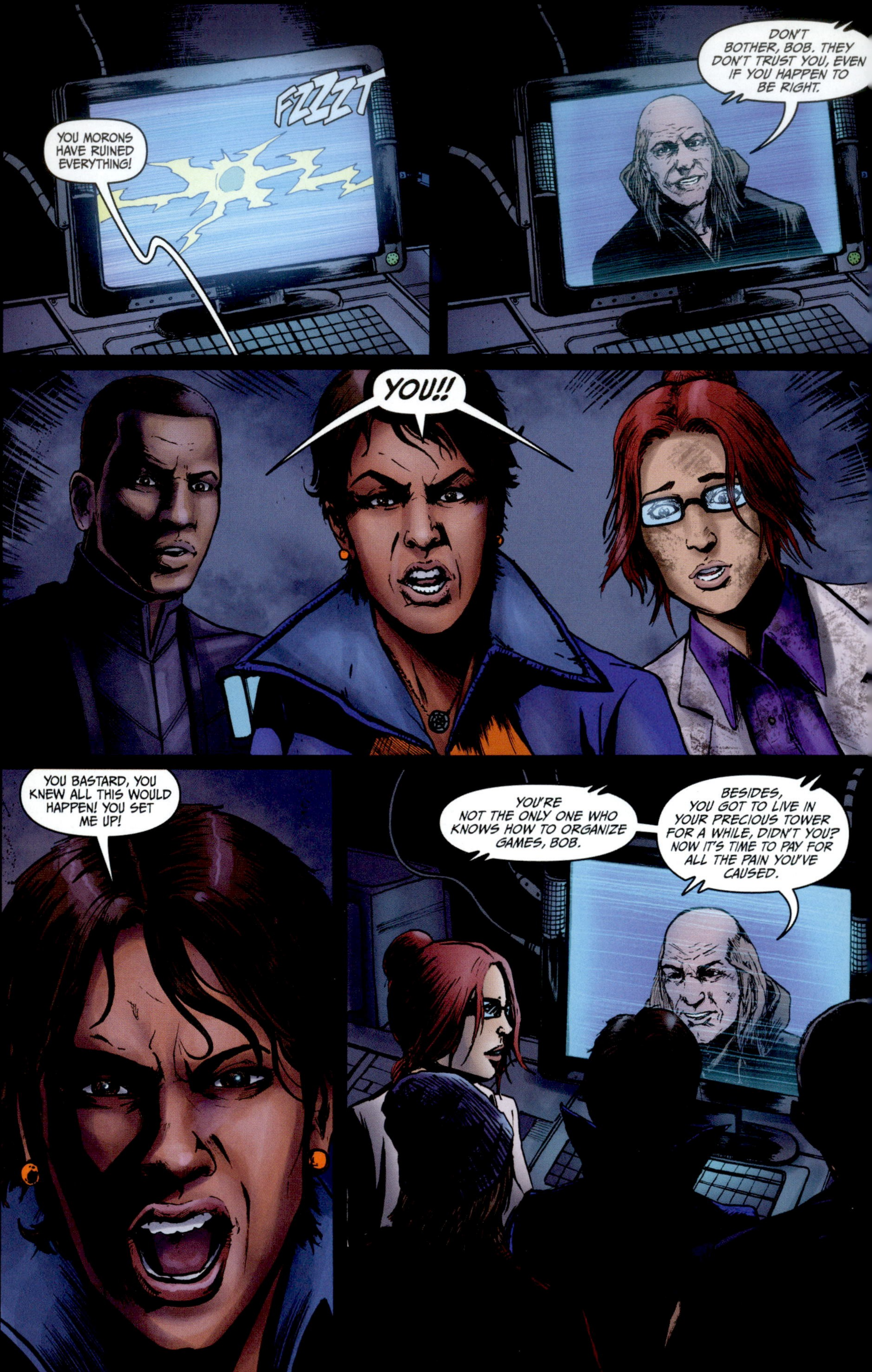
FZZZT
YOU MORONS HAVE RUINED EVERYTHING!
DON'T BOTHER, BOB. THEY DON'T TRUST YOU, EVEN IF YOU HAPPEN TO BE RIGHT.
YOU!!
YOU BASTARD, YOU KNEW ALL THIS WOULD HAPPEN! YOU SET ME UP!
YOU'RE NOT THE ONLY ONE WHO KNOWS HOW TO ORGANIZE GAMES, BOB.
BESIDES, YOU GOT TO LIVE IN YOUR PRECIOUS TOWER FOR A WHILE, DIDN'T YOU? NOW IT'S TIME TO PAY FOR ALL THE PAIN YOU'VE CAUSED.

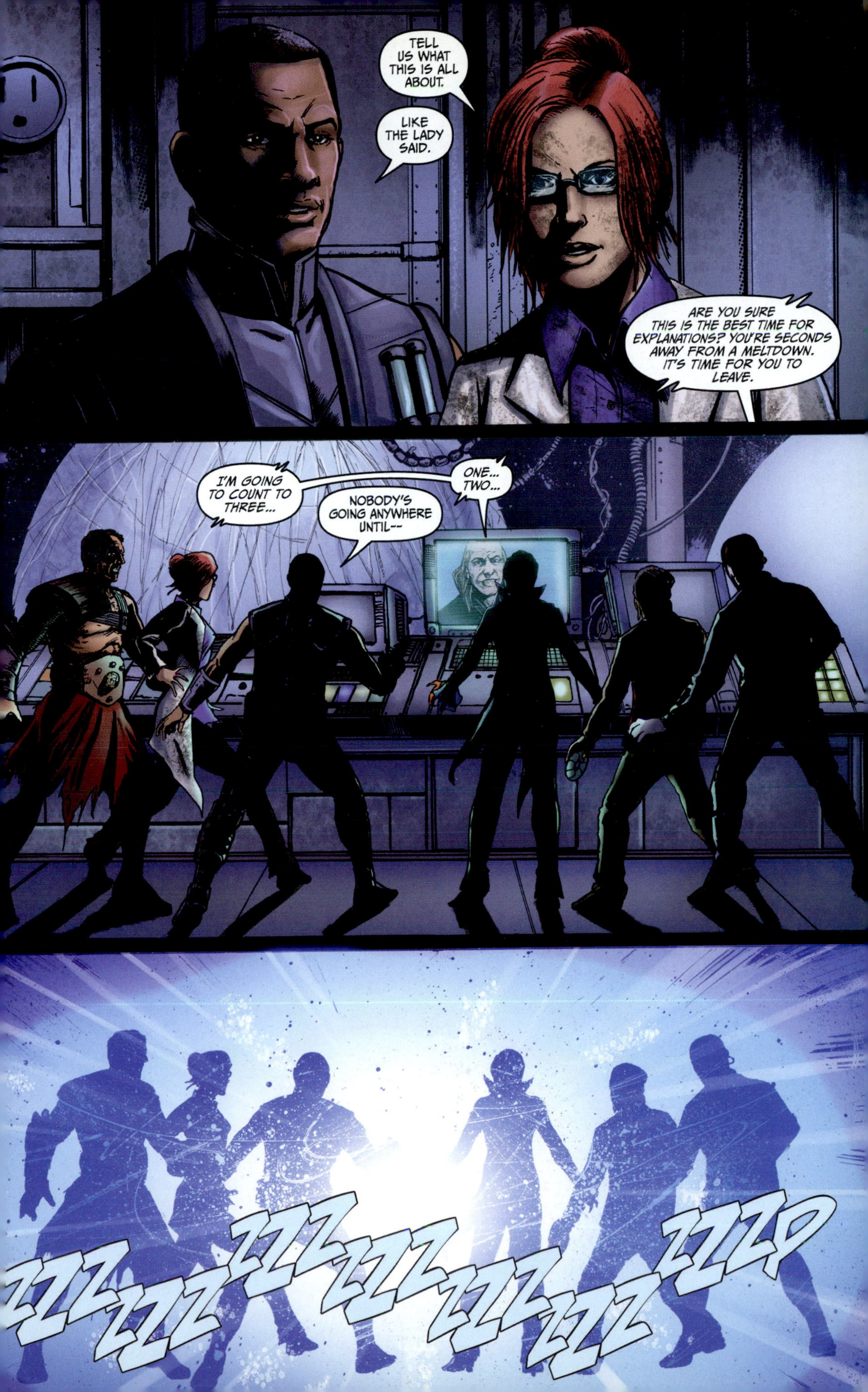
TELL US WHAT THIS IS ALL ABOUT.
LIKE THE LADY SAID.
ARE YOU SURE THIS IS THE BEST TIME FOR EXPLANATIONS? YOU'RE SECONDS AWAY FROM A MELTDOWN. IT'S TIME FOR YOU TO LEAVE.
I'M GOING TO COUNT TO THREE...
NOBODY'S GOING ANYWHERE UNTIL--
ONE... TWO...
ZZZZZZZZZZZZZZZZZZZZZZZZZZZZZZZZZZZZZZZZZZZ

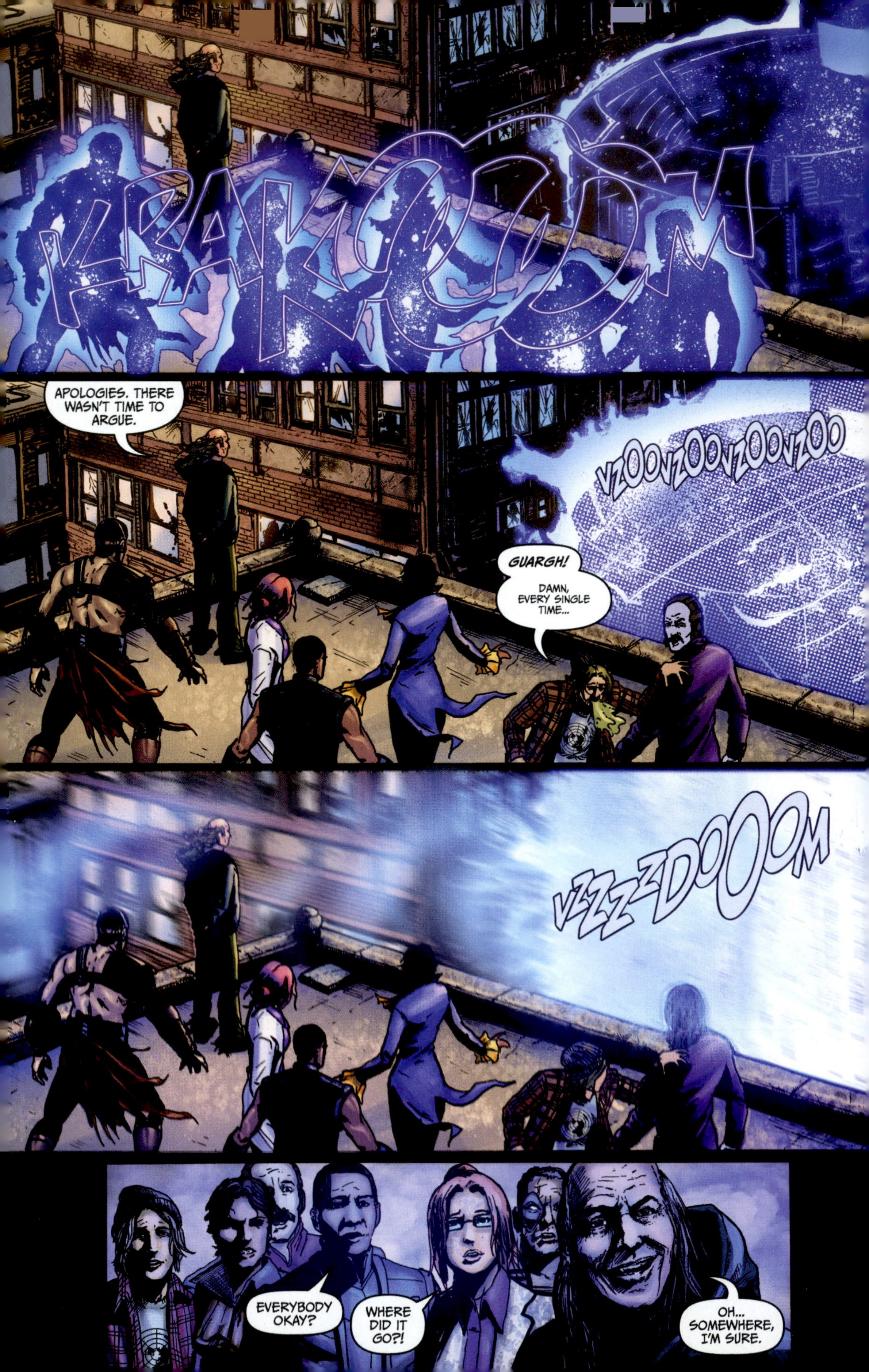
KRAKOOM
APOLOGIES. THERE WASN'T TIME TO ARGUE.
VZOONZOONZOONZOO
GUARGH!
DAMN, EVERY SINGLE TIME...
VZZZZDOOOOM
EVERYBODY OKAY?
WHERE DID IT GO?!
OH... SOMEWHERE, I'M SURE.

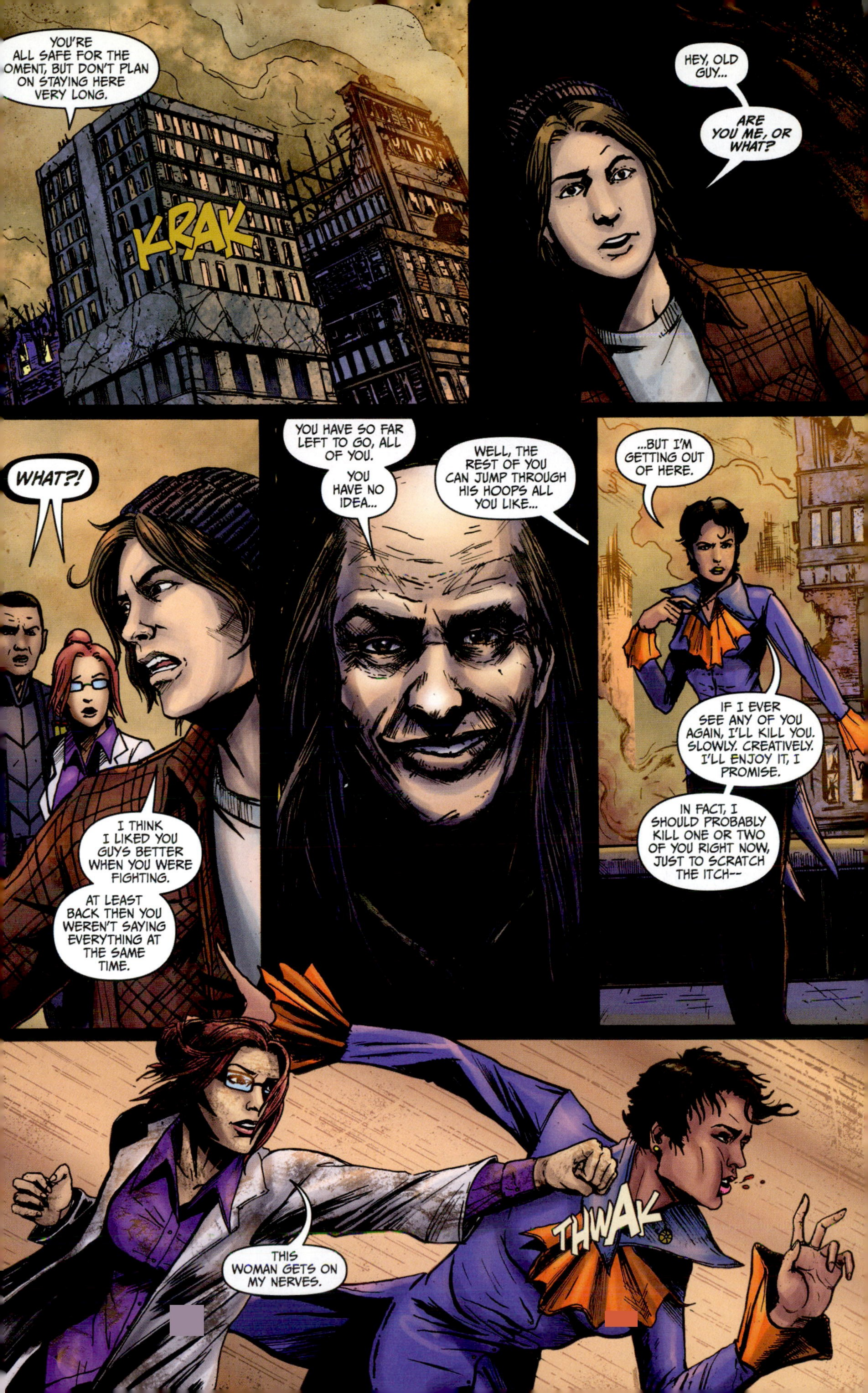
YOU'RE ALL SAFE FOR THE OMENT, BUT DON'T PLAN ON STAYING HERE VERY LONG.
KRAK
HEY, OLD GUY...
ARE YOU ME, OR WHAT?
WHAT?!
I THINK I LIKED YOU GUYS BETTER WHEN YOU WERE FIGHTING.
AT LEAST BACK THEN YOU WEREN'T SAYING EVERYTHING AT THE SAME TIME.
YOU HAVE SO FAR LEFT TO GO, ALL OF YOU.
YOU HAVE NO IDEA...
WELL, THE REST OF YOU CAN JUMP THROUGH HIS HOOPS ALL YOU LIKE...
...BUT I'M GETTING OUT OF HERE.
IF I EVER SEE ANY OF YOU AGAIN, I'LL KILL YOU. SLOWLY. CREATIVELY. I'LL ENJOY IT, I PROMISE.
IN FACT, I SHOULD PROBABLY KILL ONE OR TWO OF YOU RIGHT NOW, JUST TO SCRATCH THE ITCH--
THIS WOMAN GETS ON MY NERVES.
THWAK

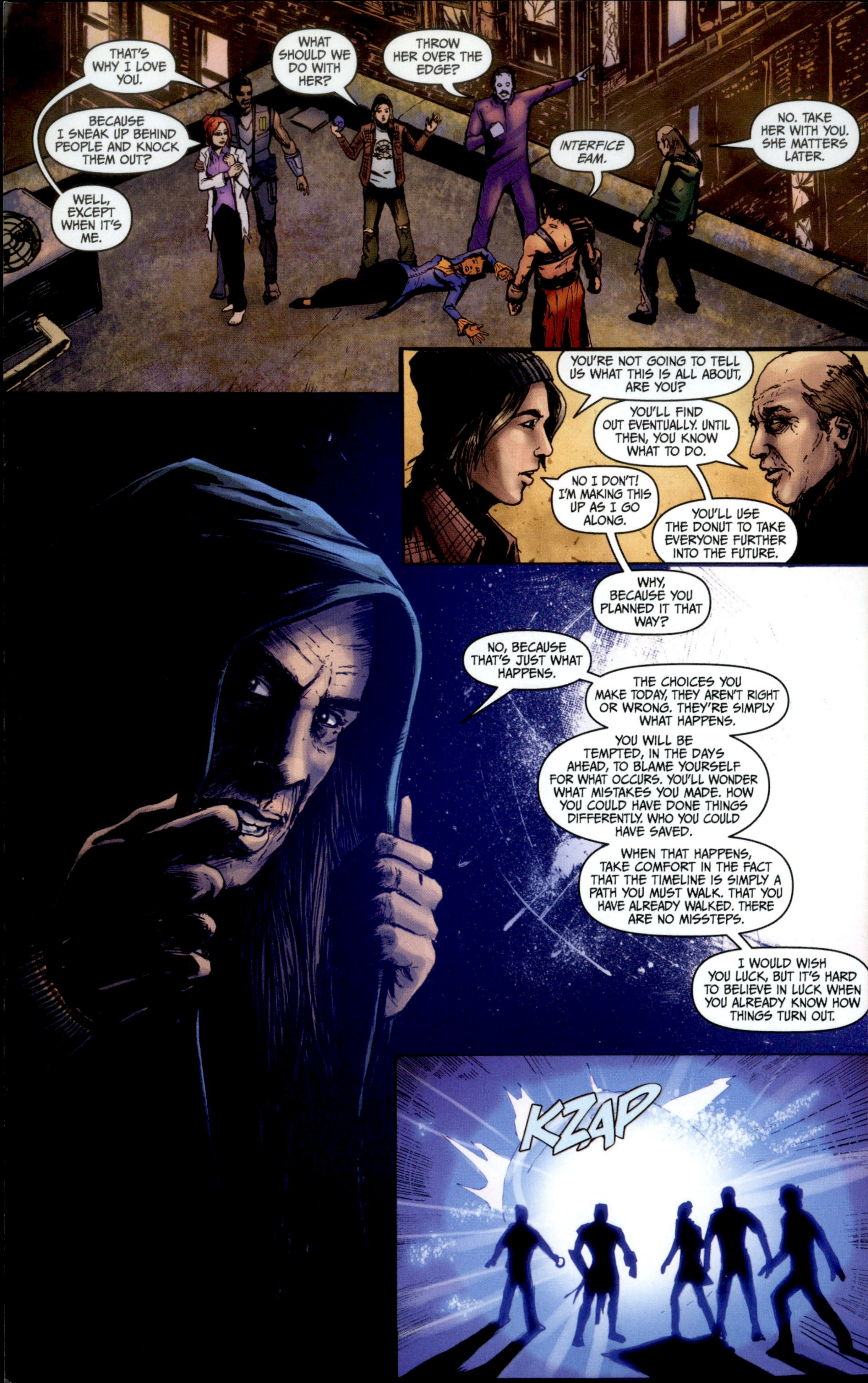
THAT'S WHY I LOVE YOU.
BECAUSE I SNEAK UP BEHIND PEOPLE AND KNOCK THEM OUT?
WELL, EXCEPT WHEN IT'S ME.
WHAT SHOULD WE DO WITH HER?
THROW HER OVER THE EDGE?
INTERFICE EAM.
NO. TAKE HER WITH YOU. SHE MATTERS LATER.
YOU'RE NOT GOING TO TELL US WHAT THIS IS ALL ABOUT, ARE YOU?
YOU'LL FIND OUT EVENTUALLY. UNTIL THEN, YOU KNOW WHAT TO DO.
NO I DON'T! I'M MAKING THIS UP AS I GO ALONG.
YOU'LL USE THE DONUT TO TAKE EVERYONE FURTHER INTO THE FUTURE.
WHY, BECAUSE YOU PLANNED IT THAT WAY?
NO, BECAUSE THAT'S JUST WHAT HAPPENS.
THE CHOICES YOU MAKE TODAY, THEY AREN'T RIGHT OR WRONG. THEY'RE SIMPLY WHAT HAPPENS.
YOU WILL BE TEMPTED, IN THE DAYS AHEAD, TO BLAME YOURSELF FOR WHAT OCCURS. YOU'LL WONDER WHAT MISTAKES YOU MADE. HOW YOU COULD HAVE DONE THINGS DIFFERENTLY. WHO YOU COULD HAVE SAVED.
WHEN THAT HAPPENS, TAKE COMFORT IN THE FACT THAT THE TIMELINE IS SIMPLY A PATH YOU MUST WALK. THAT YOU HAVE ALREADY WALKED. THERE ARE NO MISSTEPS.
I WOULD WISH YOU LUCK, BUT IT'S HARD TO BELIEVE IN LUCK WHEN YOU ALREADY KNOW HOW THINGS TURN OUT.
KZAP

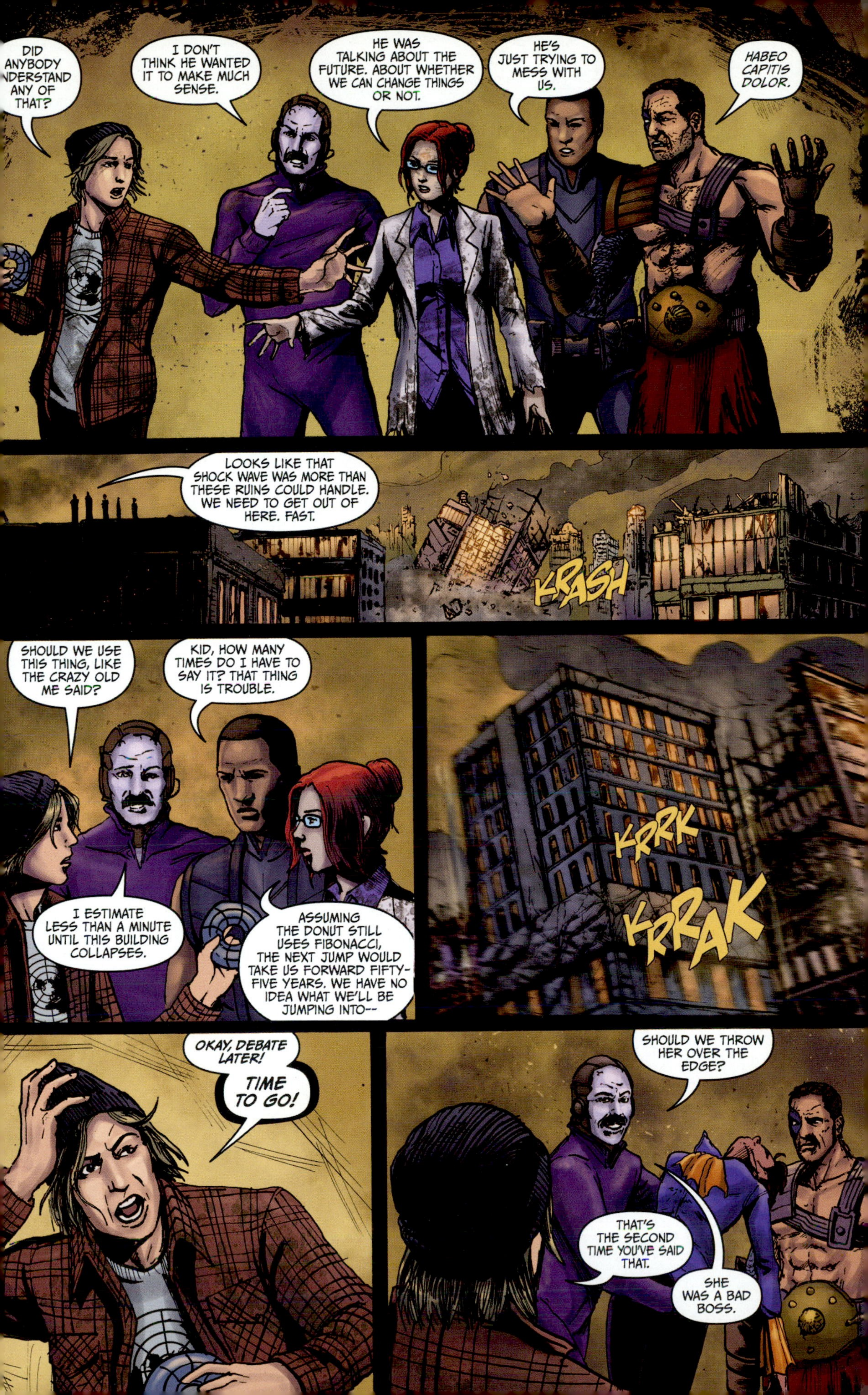
DID ANYBODY NDERSTAND ANY OF THAT?
I DON'T THINK HE WANTED IT TO MAKE MUCH SENSE.
HE WAS TALKING ABOUT THE FUTURE. ABOUT WHETHER WE CAN CHANGE THINGS OR NOT.
HE'S JUST TRYING TO MESS WITH US.
HABEO CAPITIS DOLOR.
LOOKS LIKE THAT SHOCK WAVE WAS MORE THAN THESE RUINS COULD HANDLE. WE NEED TO GET OUT OF HERE. FAST.
KRASH
SHOULD WE USE THIS THING, LIKE THE CRAZY OLD ME SAID?
KID, HOW MANY TIMES DO I HAVE TO SAY IT? THAT THING IS TROUBLE.
I ESTIMATE LESS THAN A MINUTE UNTIL THIS BUILDING COLLAPSES.
ASSUMING THE DONUT STILL USES FIBONACCI, THE NEXT JUMP WOULD TAKE US FORWARD FIFTY-FIVE YEARS. WE HAVE NO IDEA WHAT WE'LL BE JUMPING INTO--
KRRK
KRRAK
OKAY, DEBATE LATER!
TIME TO GO!
SHOULD WE THROW HER OVER THE EDGE?
THAT'S THE SECOND TIME YOU'VE SAID THAT.
SHE WAS A BAD BOSS.

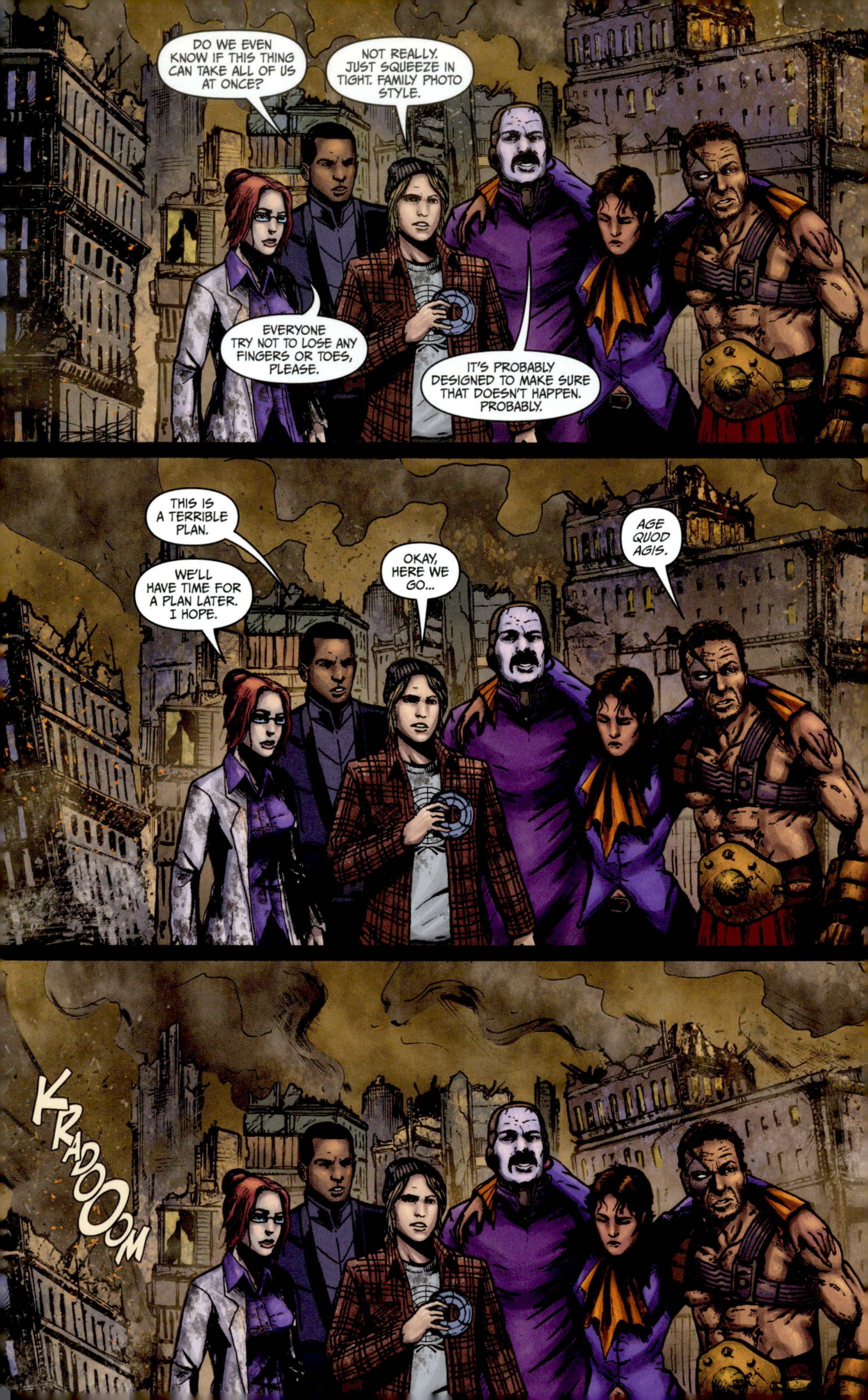
DO WE EVEN KNOW IF THIS THING CAN TAKE ALL OF US AT ONCE?
NOT REALLY. JUST SQUEEZE IN TIGHT. FAMILY PHOTO STYLE.
EVERYONE TRY NOT TO LOSE ANY FINGERS OR TOES, PLEASE.
IT'S PROBABLY DESIGNED TO MAKE SURE THAT DOESN'T HAPPEN. PROBABLY.
THIS IS A TERRIBLE PLAN.
WE'LL HAVE TIME FOR A PLAN LATER. I HOPE.
OKAY, HERE WE GO...
AGE QUOD AGIS.
KRADOOOM

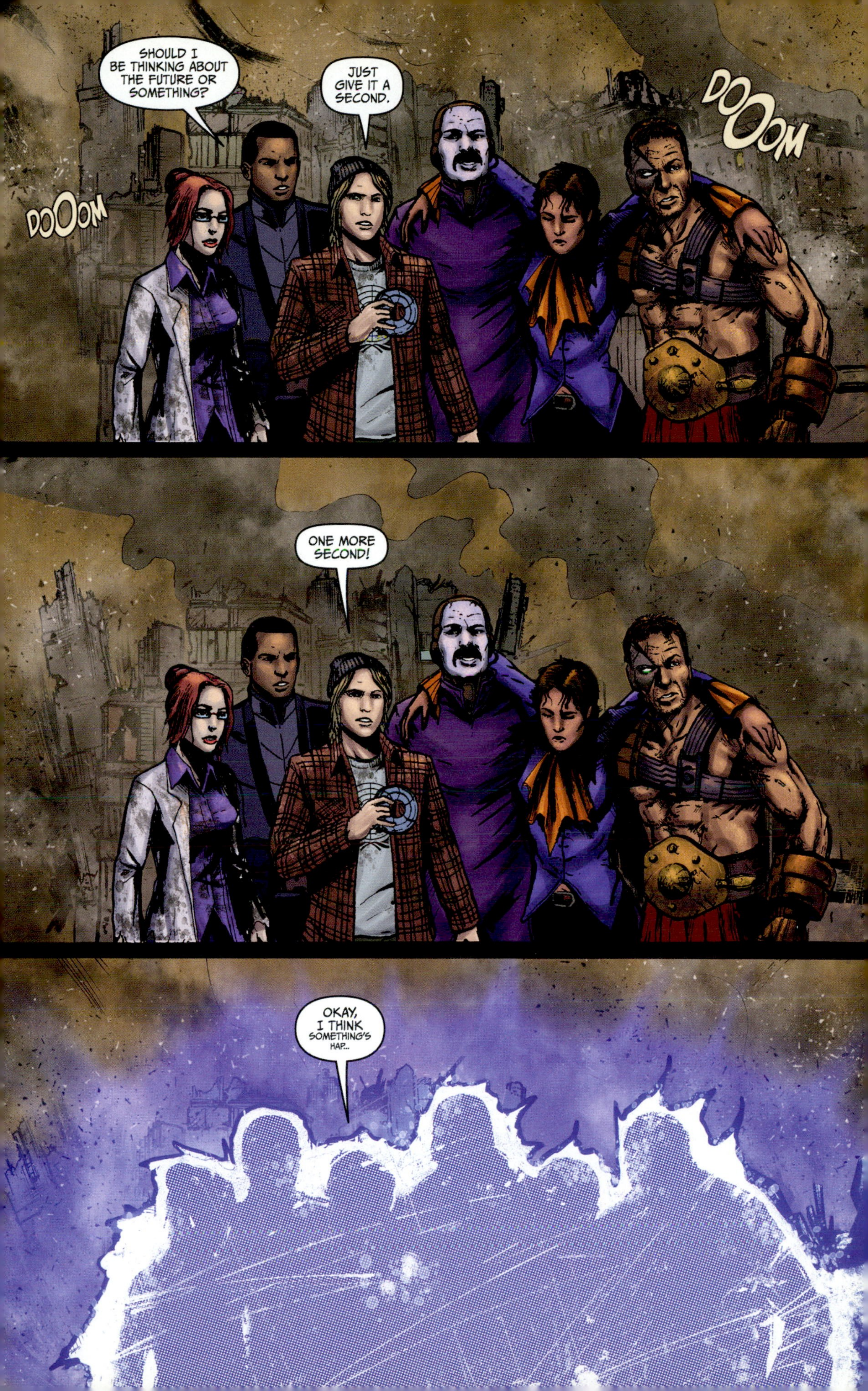
SHOULD I BE THINKING ABOUT THE FUTURE OR SOMETHING?
JUST GIVE IT A SECOND.
DOOOM
DOOOM
ONE MORE SECOND!
OKAY, I THINK SOMETHING'S HAP...

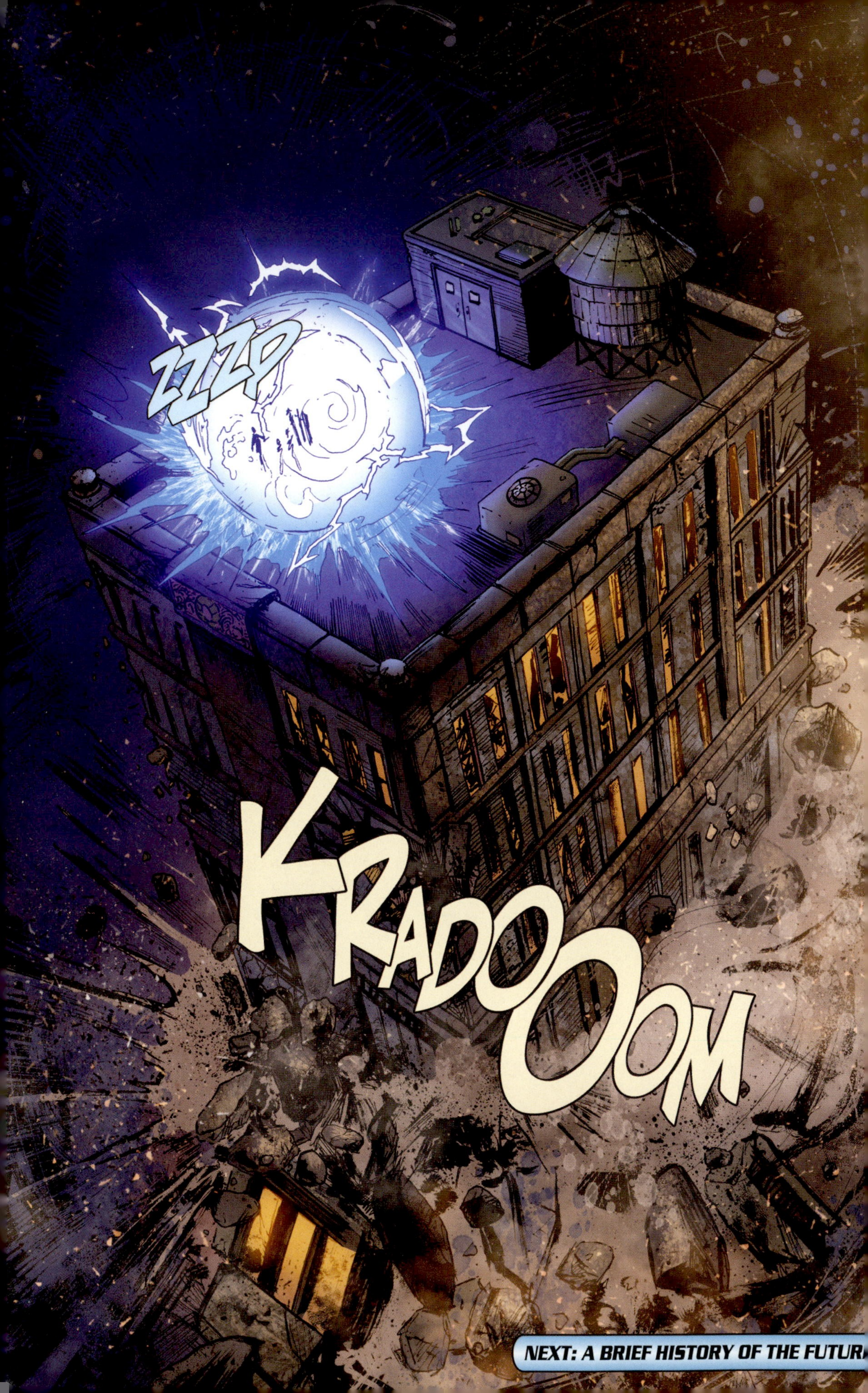
ZZZP
KRADOOOM
NEXT: A BRIEF HISTORY OF THE FUTUR

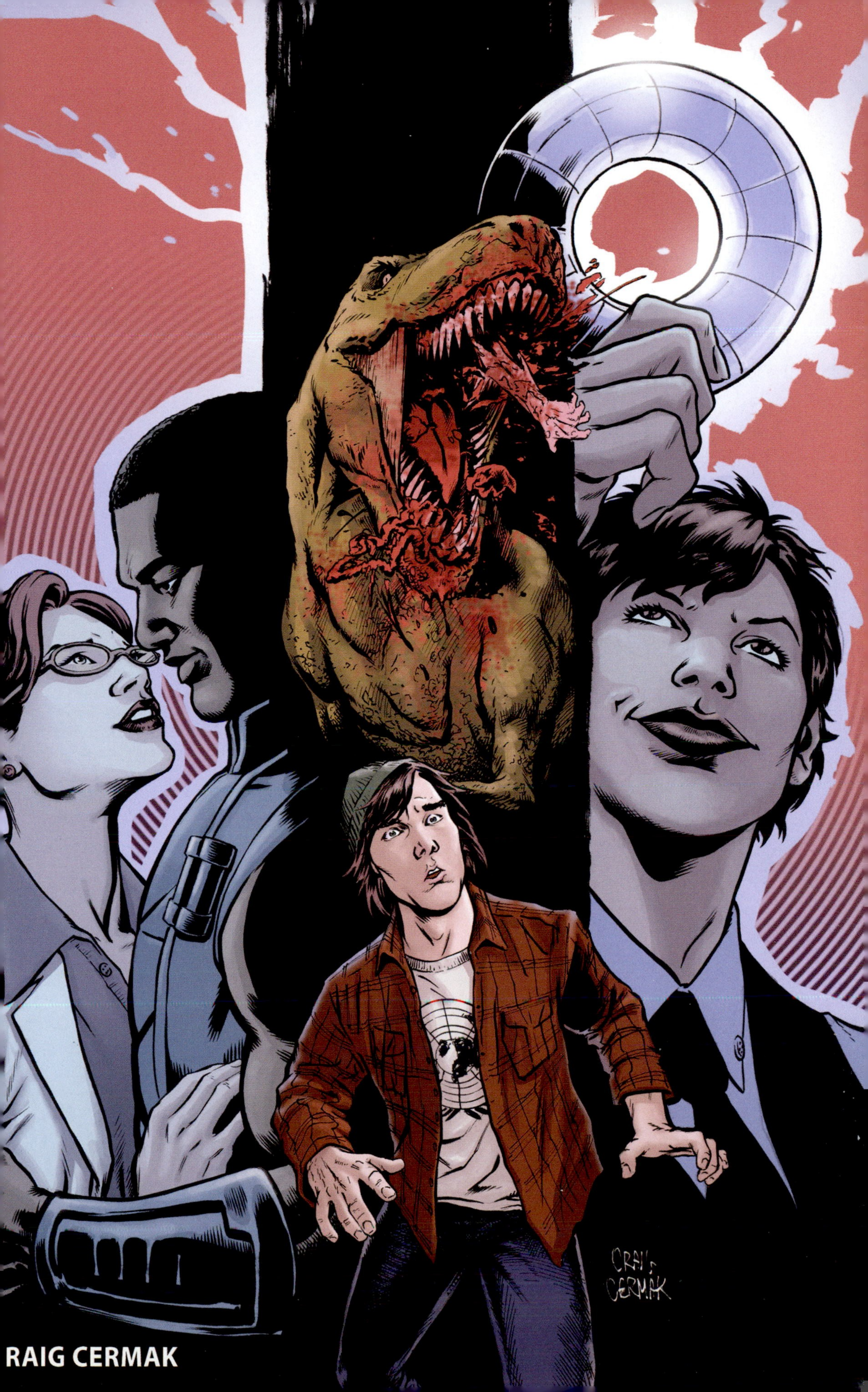
RAIG CERMAK

MARK MORALES

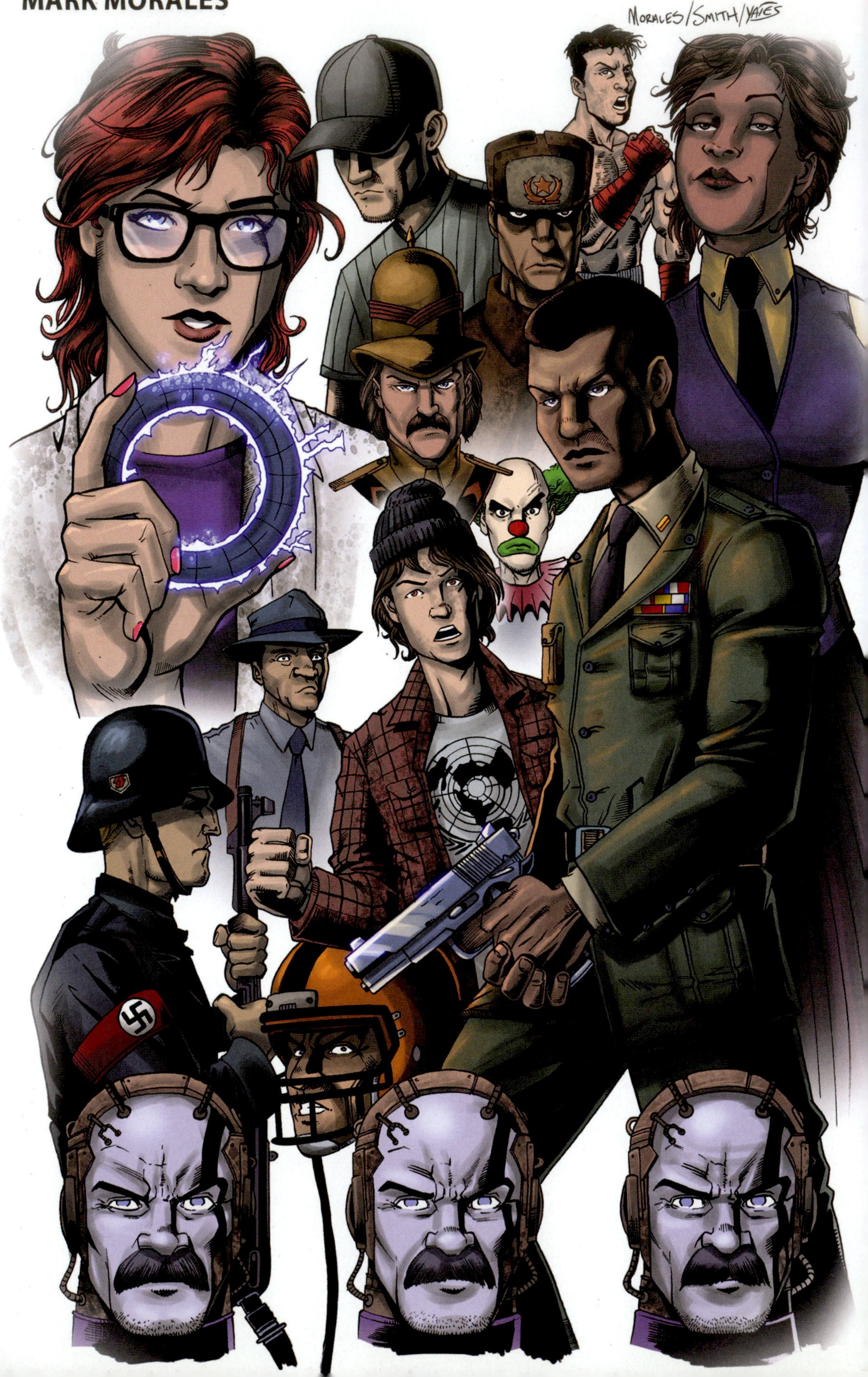
MORALES/SMITH/YATES

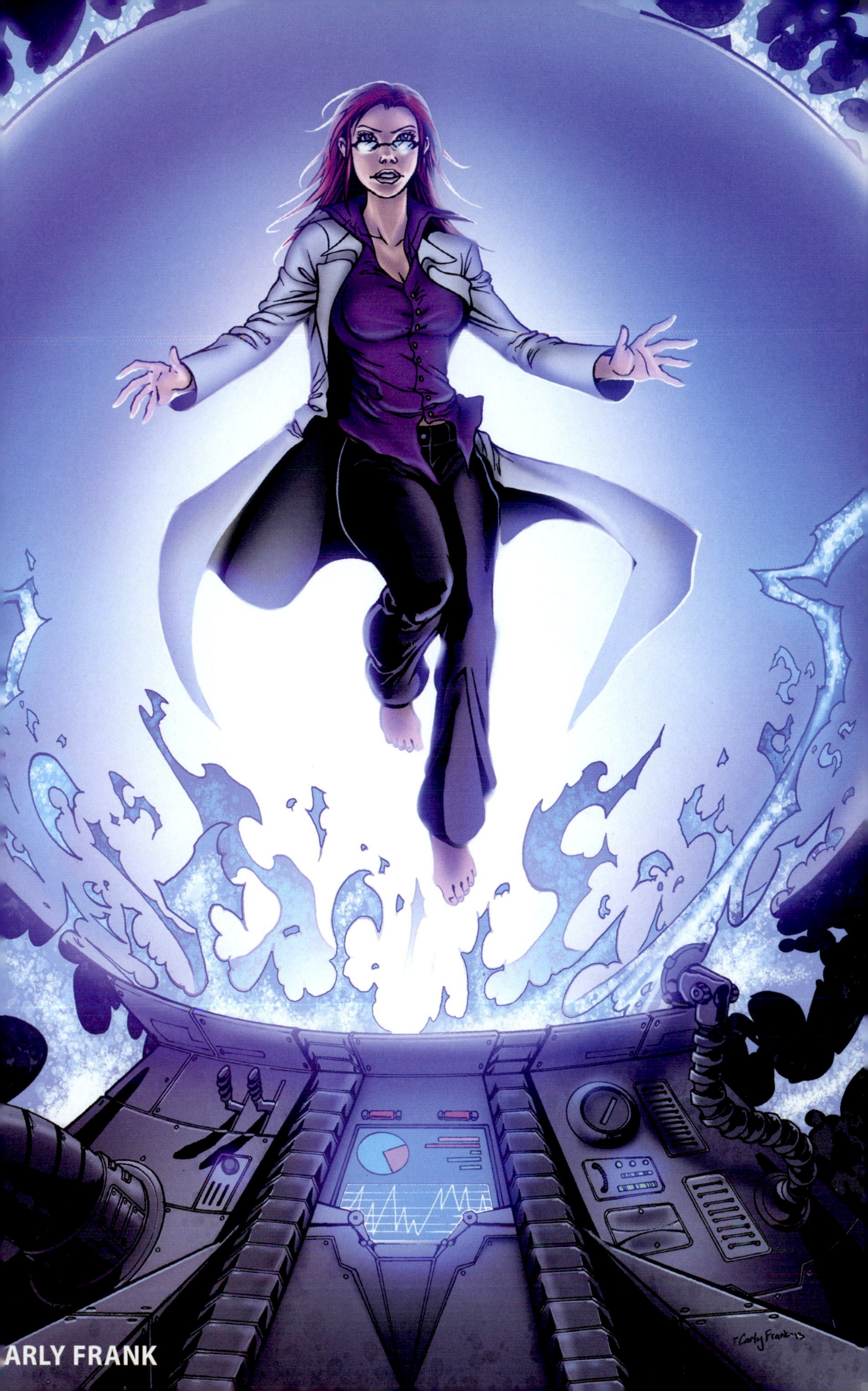

ARLY FRANK

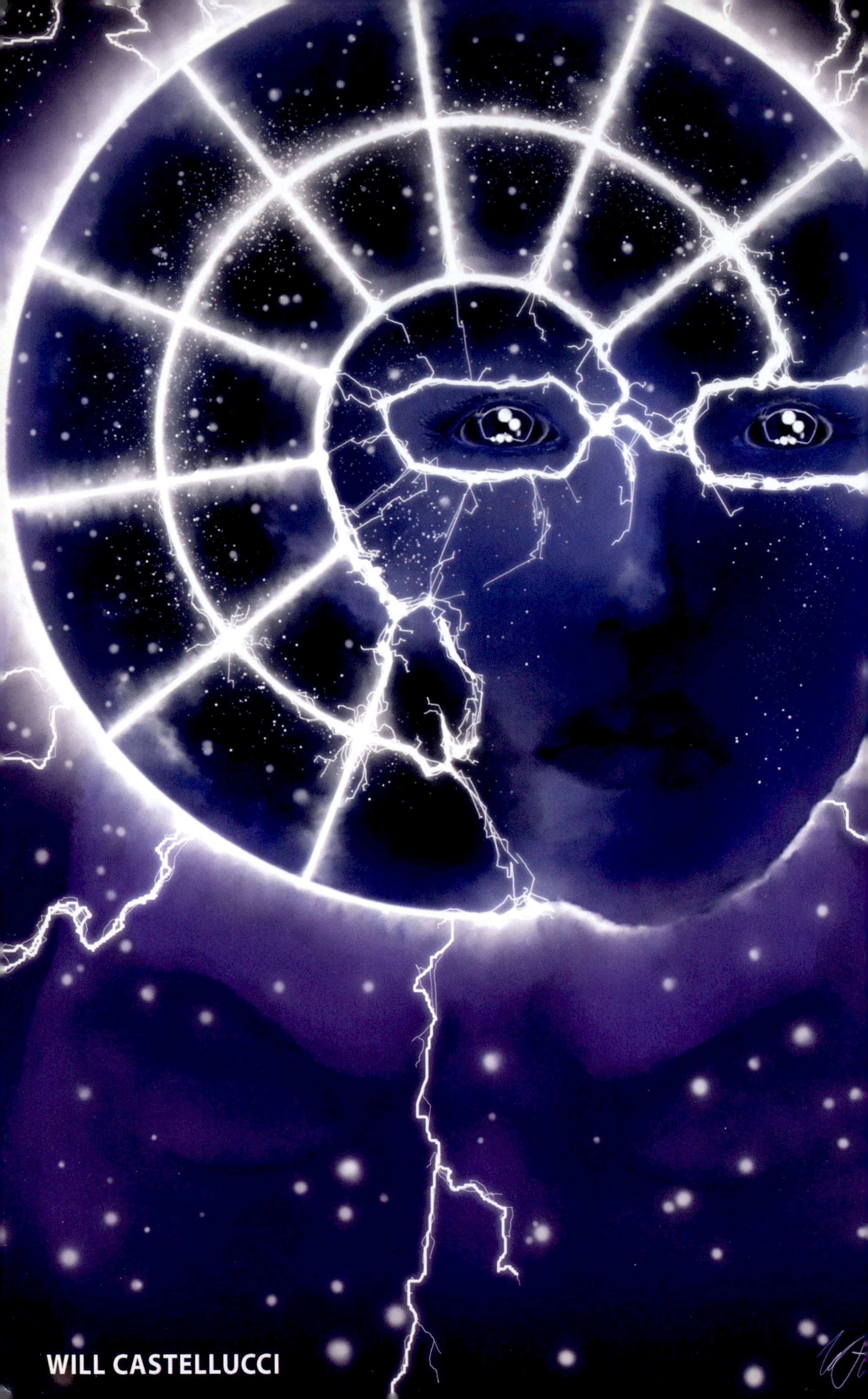
WILL CASTELLUCCI

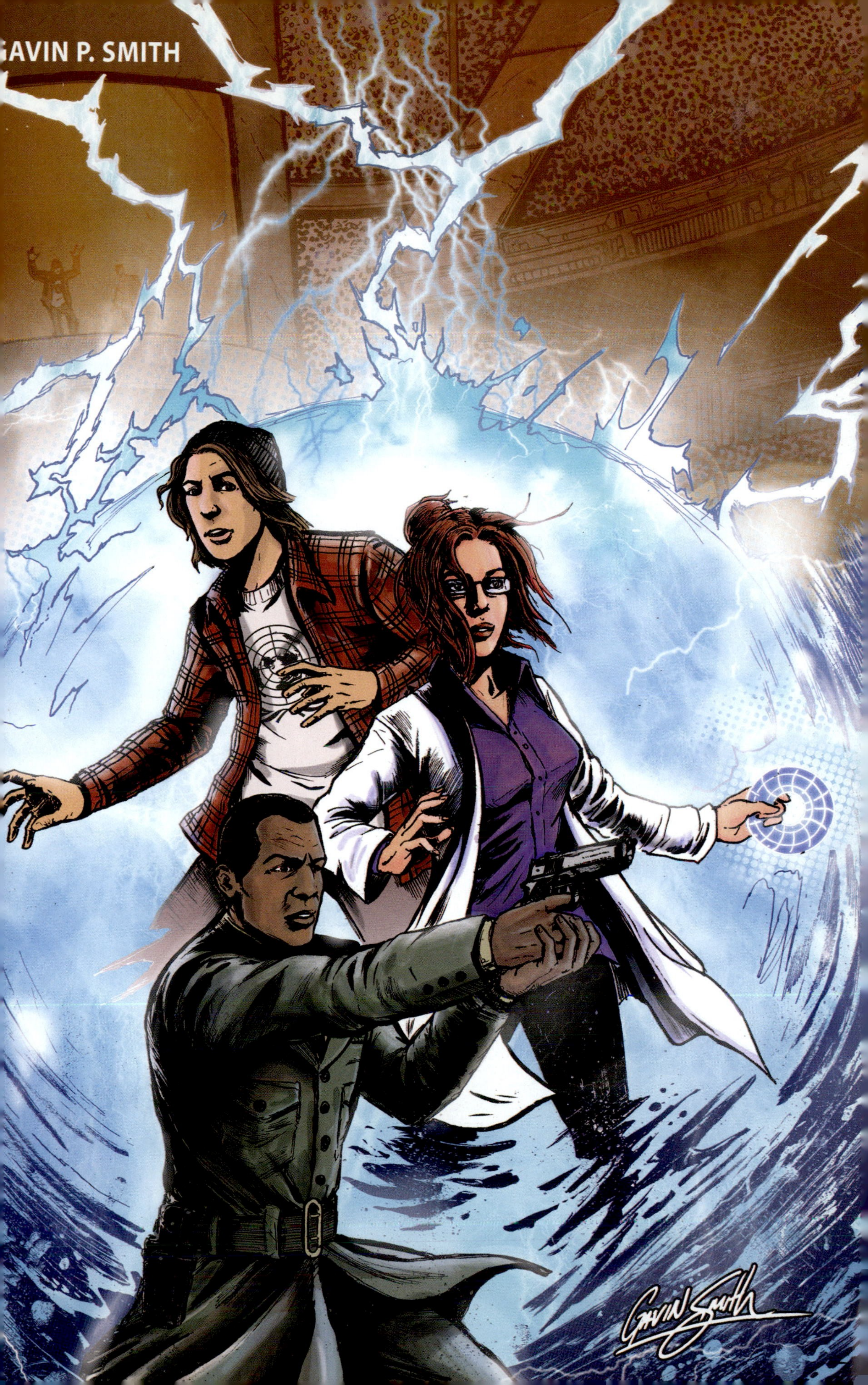
AVIN P. SMITH
Gavin Smith

Jeremy Schneider has been capturing images on film and video as a director of photography for almost two decades. His diverse credit list includes sports, documentaries, corporate infomercials, music videos and high-profile network and cable series like "Survivor," "The Apprentice" and "Project Runway." As a publisher of "The Accelerators" and "Anne Bonnie," Jeremy exists in a state of constant awe at the artistic and storytelling talent at work on these comics, and is glad that these guys are on his side.

Michael Misconi has been wor   he entertainment industry for over 11 years from television shows and commercials to narrative and documentary films. Michael considers himself a sci-fi addict, so serving as a publisher on "The Accelerators" fulfill one of his lifelong dreams to produce a compelling science-fiction story ... and, yo know, actually have people read it.

Adam Miller has been a film and video editor for the better part of two decades. No matter what medium he works in, he has always been a visual storyteller. In 2012, with the creation of Blue Juice Comics, his passion shifted toward publishing, where he now works in layout and design. Whether he's working on comics, quoting movies or spending time with his family, he always lives by his motto, "Lorem ipsum."

Tim Yates was trained in comic art at The Kubert School, and has been working on comics professionally since he graduated in 2011. Tim began his professional caree as a colorist, working for various compani on dozens of titles. Tim is the colorist on "The Accelerators," and creator/writer/art on Blue Juice's other comics s   " Bonnie." Tim has a life-size re pirate ship the Crimson Dawn in his backya and a working prototype of the time-trav donut from "The Accelerators." One of th above sentences is a lie. Though Tim wish they were all true.

Gavin Smith is a freelance artist who lives in Indianapolis, Indiana. He is the artist on the comic books "The Accelerators" and "Charge," and also produced art for a Motion Comic for AT&T. In 2012 he created and self-published his own comic book, "Human City," after graduating from The Kubert School in 2011. He is currently trying to balance drawing, sleeping and talking in the third person.

Thomas Mumme has been making movie and TV shows since the 20th century and j recently jumped into publishing and editi books and comics with "The Accelerators, "Anne Bonnie" and "Dudley and the Toy Keeper's Chest." Two years ago he had n idea how to make or publish a comic, an now he is responsible for this thing that you're holding in your hands.

R.F.I. Porto is a screenwriter and creator living and working in Brooklyn, NY. His love of comics began late, and under questionable circumstances: After stealing a volume of "The Sandman" from a college bookstore, Porto was so impressed that he brought it back and paid for it. He sometimes wonders who steals the stuff he writes.

Walt Flanagan is a modern-day Renaissance Man. Along with being the store manager of Jay and Silent Bob's Secret Stash in Red Bank, NJ, he is also a comic book artist, podcaster, actor, songwriter and reality TV personality. Walt is co-host of the highly rated "Tell 'Em Steve-Dave!" podcast with longtime friends Bryan Johnson and Brian Quinn, and is also the lead in AMC's "Comic Book Men." Flanagan has provided the art for the comic books "Karney," "War of the Undead" and "Cryptozoic Man," as well as the Kevin Smith Batman books "Cacophony" and "The Widening Gyre" for DC Comics.

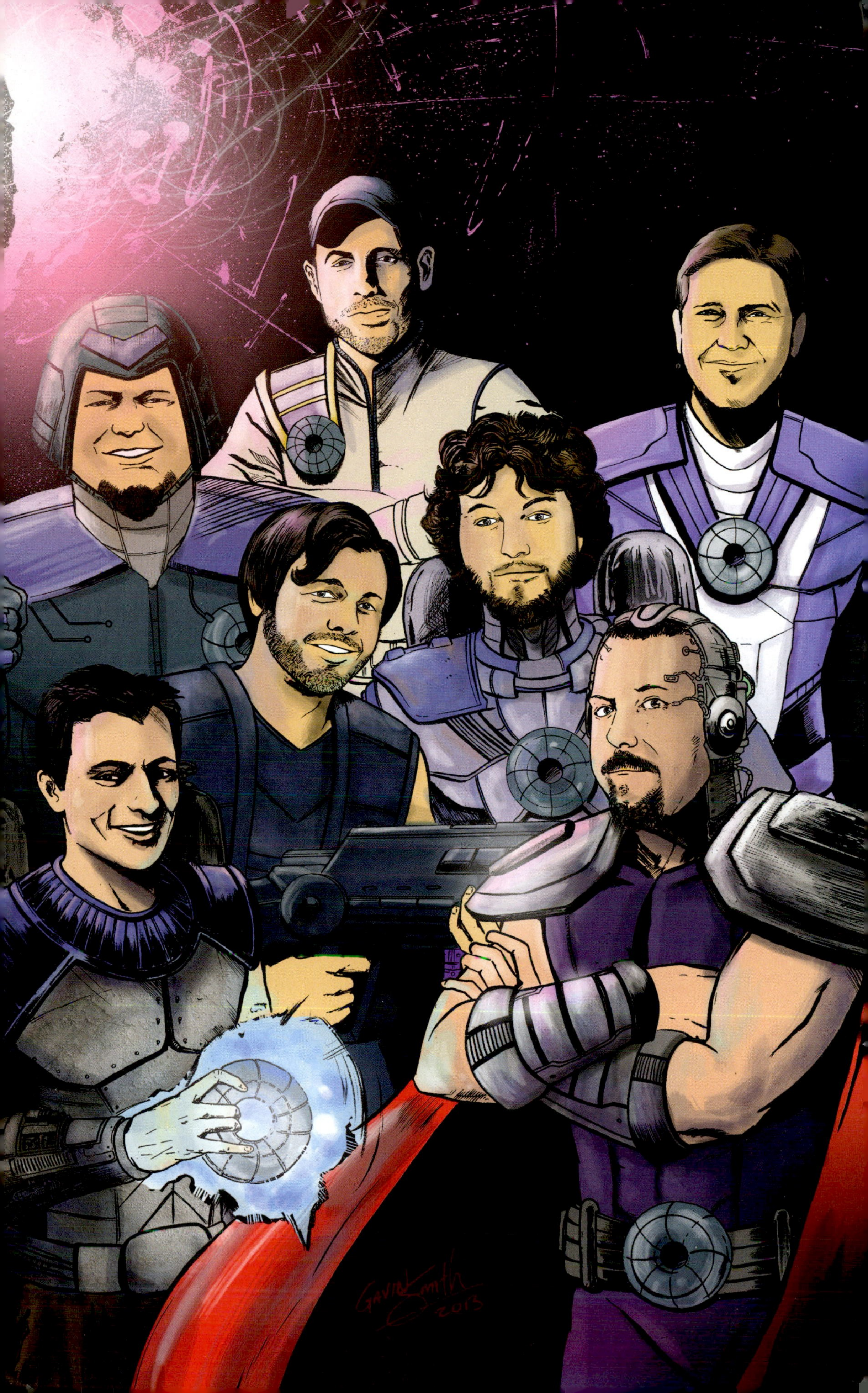
Gavin Smith 2013

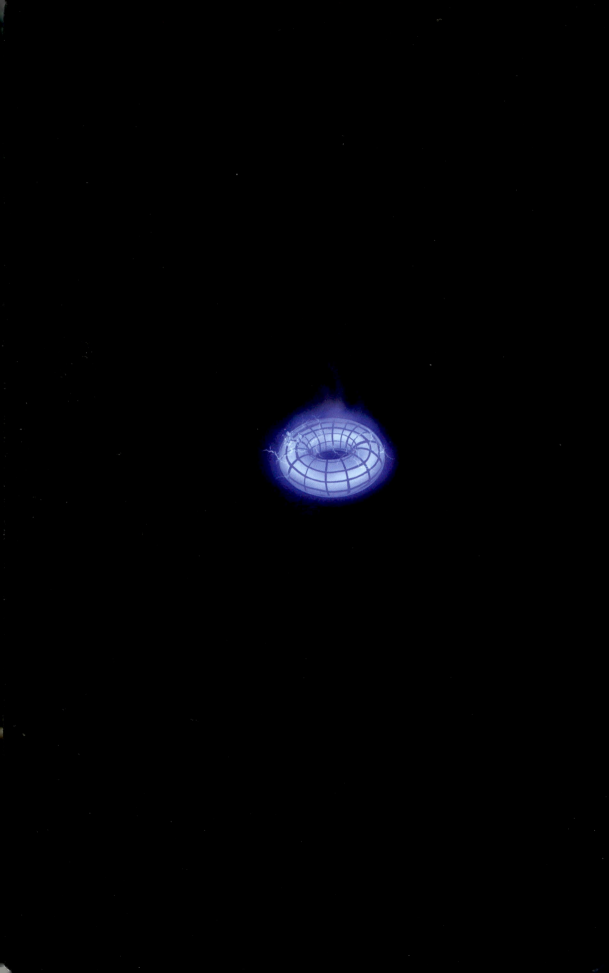